Twentieth-Century

M000266494

Twentieth-Century French Philosophy

Key Themes and Thinkers

Alan D. Schrift

Blackwell
Publishing

© 2006 by Alan D. Schrift

BLACKWELL PUBLISHING
350 Main Street, Malden, MA 02148-5020, USA
9600 Garsington Road, Oxford OX4 2DQ, UK
550 Swanston Street, Carlton, Victoria 3053, Australia

The right of Alan D. Schrift to be identified as the Author of this Work has been
asserted in accordance with the UK Copyright, Designs, and Patents Act 1988.

First published 2006 by Blackwell Publishing Ltd

2   2006

Library of Congress Cataloging-in-Publication Data

Scrift, Alan D., 1955–
Twentieth-Century French philosophy: key themes and thinkers / Alan D. Schrift.
p.   cm.
Includes bibliographical references and index.
ISBN-13: 978-1-4051-3217-6 (hardcover: alk. paper)
ISBN-10: 1-4051-3217-5 (hardcover: alk. paper)
ISBN-13: 978-1-4051-3218-3 (pbk. : alk. paper)
ISBN-10: 1-4051-3218-3 (pbk. : alk. paper)
1. Philosophy, French—20th century. I. Title.

B2421.S365 2005
194—dc22
2005004141

A catalogue record for this title is available from the British Library.

Set in 11/13pt Ehrhardt
by SPI Publisher Services, Pondicherry, India

The publisher's policy is to use permanent paper from mills that operate a
sustainable forestry policy, and which has been manufactured from pulp
processed using acid-free and elementary chlorine-free practices. Furthermore,
the publisher ensures that the text paper and cover board used have met
acceptable environmental accreditation standards.

For further information on
Blackwell Publishing, visit our website:
www.blackwellpublishing.com

To Pascale, my partner in all things French

Contents

But from the end of the eighteenth and beginning of the nineteenth centuries onward – the Napoleonic university was established at precisely this time – we see the emergence of something like a sort of great uniform apparatus of knowledge, with its different stages, its different extensions, its different levels, and its pseudopodia. The university's primary function is one of selection, not so much of people (which is, after all, basically not very important) as of knowledges. It can play this selective role because it has a sort of *de facto* – and *de jure* – monopoly, which means that any knowledge that is not born or shaped within this sort of institutional field – whose limits are in fact relatively fluid but which consists, roughly speaking, of the university and official research bodies – that anything exists outside it, any knowledge that exists in the wild, any knowledge that is born elsewhere, is automatically, and from the outset, if not actually excluded, disqualified *a priori*. That the amateur scholar ceased to exist in the eighteenth and nineteenth centuries is a well-known fact. So the university has a selective role: it selects knowledges. Its role is to teach, which means respecting the barriers that exist between the different floors of the university apparatus. Its role is to homogenize knowledges by establishing a sort of scientific community with a recognized status; its role is to organize a consensus. Its role is, finally, to use, either directly or indirectly, State apparatuses to centralize knowledge. We can now understand why something resembling a university, with its ill-defined extension and frontiers, should have emerged at the beginning of the nineteenth century, or in other words at the very time when this disciplinarization of knowledges, this organization of knowledges into disciplines, was going on.

Michel Foucault, Society Must Be Defended

Preface

Just what is "the Sorbonne"? Is it a building? An institution? Does it operate under the auspices of the French government or does it function as an independent agency? And the École Normale Supérieure? Is that like a high school? Or a university? Or an institute of advanced study? As I began to work on an introduction to twentieth-century French philosophy, I came to realize that not only I, but also many people who considered themselves relatively well informed about recent French philosophy, did not really know the answers to many questions like these. More importantly, as my research evolved, I came to recognize that the answers to questions concerning the various academic institutions in France told a great deal about the history of philosophy in France in the twentieth century. For example, the supposed faddishness that is often noted as characteristic of French philosophy is not, I came to recognize, so much the consequence of "intellectual fashion" or personal choices as it is the result of the highly centralized and regulated system of academic instruction and professional certification that has marked the intellectual formation of virtually every significant French philosopher. To give an example, consider the following: in the four decades preceding 1960, almost no books on Nietzsche were published by philosophers in France. During the 1960s, beginning with Gilles Deleuze's *Nietzsche et la philosophie* in 1962, books, essays, and journal issues devoted to Nietzsche's work appear frequently. While many have wondered what sparked the Nietzsche explosion in France in the 1960s, and a "natural" hypothesis would be to assume that this interest arose in response to the publication in Germany of Heidegger's two-volume *Nietzsche* in 1961, a knowledge of French academic practices suggests another explanation: Nietzsche's *On the Genealogy of Morals* appears on the reading list of the *agrégation de philosophie* – the annual examination that must be passed by anyone hoping for an academic career in philosophy – in 1958, the first time his work appears on that examination's reading list in over thirty years. His works reappear on the reading lists for several of the following years, which means that many philosophy instructors whose teaching prepares students for this examination, as well as all students finishing their higher education during these years, would be spending considerable time reading Nietzsche's work. That so much published scholarship would follow from so many students and teachers reading Nietzsche's works in preparation for this examination is not at all surprising, and examples like this one, I would argue, explain a great deal about so-called French scholarly fads. (The *agrégation de philosophie* is discussed in some detail in appendix 1.)

One of the primary goals of this text is to provide some of the institutional and academic background that helps to explain how philosophy in France has developed during the twentieth century. It is my conviction that the relative lack of awareness among English-language students and scholars of the French academic system and the role it has played in the intellectual formation of French philosophers has resulted in a lack of attention to many significant factors that have influenced the historical unfolding of philosophy in France. This lack of attention is most apparent in the cases of post-1960 "poststructuralist" French thinkers and it manifests itself in a number of ways. First, there is the general sense that while many of these thinkers respond to some extent to their structuralist predecessors, they are inspired more directly by German philosophers: Husserl, Heidegger, Nietzsche, and Hegel, in particular. By chronicling the entire century and recalling some of the lively philosophical debates in the century's first six decades, I hope to correct the conjoined misconceptions that "French Philosophy" began with existentialism and functions in large part in response to the German master thinkers.

A second, related point, concerns a "cult of genius" that has surrounded many of the leading French philosophers of the century, a cult that some of these thinkers have themselves cultivated, with the result that the interlocutors with whom they were engaged and the teachers from whom they learned are often completely eclipsed from view. The fault is not always with the French, however, as their eager English-speaking audience is all too happy to ignore the hints that they themselves sometimes give. So, to take a well-documented example, in Michel Foucault's inaugural address upon taking his position at the Collège de France, he credited Georges Dumézil, Georges Canguilhem, and Jean Hyppolite for the roles they played in his intellectual evolution. Yet how many scholars who have published on Foucault, and students who have studied his work, would have to confess to not having read a word written by any of these three? There has been, throughout the twentieth century, a number of great "teachers" whose influence on French philosophy has been enormous – teachers like Alain, Wahl, Kojève, Bachelard, Canguilhem, Hyppolite, or Jankélévitch – and by highlighting the roles they have played, I think a better sense of the evolution of French thought can be garnered.

A third and final point is also worth mentioning. The enormous popularity of the major figures in contemporary French philosophy – Derrida, Foucault, Deleuze, Lyotard, Kristeva, Irigaray, Lacan, et al. – has not only led to many very influential figures from earlier in the century being largely if not totally forgotten, but has also eclipsed the significant work of a range of other contemporary philosophers. These two eclipses have different causes and reflect different phenomena. The latter – those important figures in France who have not yet been or are only just being "discovered" by an English-speaking audience – include figures like Jacques Bouveresse, Gilles-Gaston Granger, Jules Vuillemin, Clément Rosset, and Alain Badiou, who for differing reasons have just never caught on sufficiently to justify the expense of translating and publishing their work. (That this is changing in the case of Badiou's work is worth noting.) But it is the former – the "forgetting" of earlier influential figures – that is, I think, more intellectually interesting, as it has a great deal to do with the abrupt and rather odd dismissal of all things existentialist that followed the rise of structuralism.

To be sure, much of this had to do with a typically Oedipal French intellectual gesture, namely, the exiling of Jean-Paul Sartre from theoretical relevance. One could certainly argue that no intellectual force exercised so dominant an influence on French thought this century as did Sartre, which makes his disappearance all the more suspect. But not only has Sartre been overlooked. In addition, almost everything that had any connection with him – and this was quite a lot – has also been ignored for quite a while. I mean here not only Sartre's major "existential" interlocutors Maurice Merleau-Ponty and Simone de Beauvoir, but also the religious critics to whom he was responding such as the Personalist Edouard Mounier or the Catholic Gabriel Marcel, and the various Marxist controversies that he was a party to during the 1940s and 1950s. And then there was his influence on and support for the challenges to colonialism raised by, among others, Frantz Fanon, Aimé Césaire, and Albert Memmi. Things are changing recently for the better in this regard, and there is now, to be sure, some renewed interest in the work of Merleau-Ponty, Beauvoir, and the so-called "black existentialists." There is even renewed interest in Sartre's political as well as existentialist philosophical writings in circles other than those focused on teaching undergraduate existentialism classes, where Sartre's popularity has never waned. But there are still important figures and developments, particularly in the first decades of the twentieth century, and in the years between World War II and the rise of structuralism, that need to be recalled if the French twentieth century is to be told philosophically. That is what this text seeks to do.

In part one, I offer a narrative account of developments in French philosophy through the twentieth century. My focus in this narrative is two-fold: first, I want to recall the evolution of French thought from its spiritualist and positivist roots in the nineteenth century through several major developments: the introduction of phenomenology, both Hegelian and Husserlian; the two responses to phenomenology: existentialism's "philosophy of the subject" and what the French call *épistémologie*'s "philosophy of the concept"; the emergence of the human sciences and structuralism's challenge to philosophy; and the various ways that philosophical thinking reemerged after structuralism. Throughout this narrative, I will emphasize two features that are often overlooked as one tells the "official story" of how French philosophy moves from Bergson to existentialism to structuralism to postmodernism: the role played by French academic institutions and practices on the specific philosophical developments that emerge, and France's indigenous philosophical tradition's contribution to what is too quickly seen as appropriations of the thought of a succession of German philosophers.

In part two, I provide biographical notes for a significant number of the philosophers who have, in my opinion, played important roles in the history of philosophy in France throughout the twentieth century. These notes are not, however, what one typically finds in a biography. Rather than rehearse the personal details of these thinkers' lives, I focus instead on the central factors in their intellectual formation: where and when they were born, where they went to *lycée*, where they prepared for the competitive entrance examination to the École Normale Supérieure, who they studied with, who they went to school with, on what they wrote their various theses and under whose direction, where they taught, etc. Attending to these details reveals how "small" the French philosophical world is in terms of the available routes one could follow on the way to a successful academic career, and shows the enormous influence played by some philosophers who, while largely unknown outside the French academy, occupied positions of institutional power that determined what several generations of students would learn.

In the first appendix, I discuss the major academic institutions that have marked the education and careers of all philosophers in France. While some of these institutions will be familiar – the Sorbonne or the École Normale Supérieure, the Collège de France or the École Pratique des Hautes Études – the ways in which they each place certain limitations on their students and faculties may not be well known. Nor will their respective relations with each other be likely to be familiar to many readers. In some cases, these relations and limitations are important, and their changes over the century might make one's position at one or another of these institutions quite different, depending on when one taught or studied there. Other institutions, like the *agrégation de philosophie*, or the prestige and influence of certain Parisian *lycées*, may not be known at all to many readers. For this reason, although it appears as an appendix, many readers might profit from reading this section before parts one and two, as some familiarity with French academic culture will help make sense of certain details in the historical narrative and the biographical notes.

In the second appendix, I have tried to produce the most comprehensive bibliography available of French philosophy in English translation. For authors who have had only a few works published in English translation, their texts appear as part of their biographical notes. But for authors whose works have been widely translated into English, I list all of their translated books plus the titles and bibliographical information of their initial French publication.

Surveying the entirety of the developments in the twentieth century in French philosophy would be a task for an encyclopedia rather than a short introduction. I have tried, however, to highlight those developments that are either most philosophically significant or most important in terms of the roles played by certain academic institutions on the intellectual formations of French philosophers. This has led my account to pay what some will no doubt regard as insufficient attention to the influence of the ideas of Marx and Freud on developments in philosophy. The reason for this is that my narrative chooses to focus on *academic* philosophy: while Marx and Freud are very much a part of the twentieth-century intellectual world out of which almost all the philosophers I discuss have arisen, they were not allowed into the philosophical curriculum of the university (or even the *classe de philosophie*) prior to the late 1960s, and even then, they are only barely present. From this perspective, then, I draw a distinction between, for example, what Althusser might be "teaching" his students – Spinoza, Rousseau, Machiavelli – and what he's working on with his colleagues – how to read *Capital*. Emphasizing the world of academic philosophy has also led to a selectivity that might appear somewhat arbitrary, especially as concerns those figures whose biographical notes I have included. In making the decisions as to who to include, I have tried to include not only all the major philosophers whose work has been well received by the English-speaking philosophical audience, but also those philosophers whose work, and teaching, has been influential on the development of generations of French philosophy students, including some students who subsequently became important philosophers in their own right. Such a list could have extended indefinitely, and while some well-known figures in philosophy and related fields have been omitted (Jean Baudrillard, Michel de Certeau, Vincent Descombes, Dominique Janicaud, Philippe Lacoue-Labarthe, Edgar Morin, Alexis Philonenko, and Jacques Rancière, among many others), I have tried to at least mention them in connecting them either to developments or to philosophical colleagues whose philosophical interests they shared. Hopefully, the story these biographies of intellectual formation tell, along with the historical narrative that precedes them and the notes on French academic institutions that follow them, is a good one, which is to say, an honest story, informative and insightful, sometimes predictable and other times surprising. Not the whole story, by any means; but a story worth telling.

Over the years that I have been working on this project, I have profited from conversations with and suggestions from many people who share with me an interest in French philosophy, including Keith Ansell-Pearson, Debra Bergoffen, Robert Bernasconi, Arnold Davidson, Duane Davis, Penelope Deutscher, Thomas Flynn, Robert Gooding-Williams, Leonard Lawlor, Todd May, William L. McBride, Philippe Moisan, Michael Naas, Diane Perpich, François Raffoul, Kas Saghafi, Margaret Simons, Daniel Smith, Charles Stivale, and Allan Stoekl. I would also like to thank Alain Badiou, Étienne Balibar, Michèle Le Doeuff, Jean-Luc Marion, and Jean-Luc Nancy for responding to my inquiries concerning specific details related to their professional careers.

My editor at Blackwell Publishing, Jeffrey Dean, has been an enthusiastic supporter of this project as it has evolved and his comments and suggestions are gratefully acknowledged here, as is the work of the production staff at Blackwell Publishing.

My research on this project has been assisted, over the years, by several undergraduate students with whom I've worked at Grinnell College. First and foremost are Susanna Drake, Jennifer Johnson, Melissa Yates, and Erinn Gilson, who did extensive work on the bibliography as well as reading sections of the manuscript. Sarah Hansen, Sara Eilert, Jeffrey Bergman, and Adrienne Celt also read parts of the manuscript and I have profited from their suggestions as well as from the proofreading of Ariel Wolter, Adam Schwartz, and Chris Forster-Smith. Angela Winburn and Helyn Wohlwend both helped in the preparation of the manuscript and their skill, attention to detail, patience, and willingness to do whatever needed to be done are greatly appreciated. I have also benefited from the financial support of the Trustees of Grinnell College and the Grinnell College Committee for the Support of Faculty Scholarship, under the direction of Dean James Swartz, and from the National Endowment of the Humanities, whose Summer Stipend in 2001 allowed me to begin my historical research at the Archives Nationale in Paris.

Alan D. Schrift

Chronology

- Events of philosophical or academic significance
- **Other significant historical events**

1200   • Official recognition of the University of Paris by King Philippe-Auguste

1257   • Robert de Sorbon founds "La Communauté des Pauvres Maîtres Étudiants en Théologie," later known as the Sorbonne

1530   • Creation of the "Collège Royal," renamed the Collège de France in 1870

1542   • First philosopher, Francesco Vimercati (Franciscus Vicomercatus, 1512?–71?), named to the faculty of the Collège Royal/Collège de France

1551   • Henri II expands the curriculum of the Collège Royal/Collège de France with the addition of a second chair in Greek and Latin philosophy, given to critic of Aristotle Petrus Ramus (Pierre de la Ramée, 1515–72)

1635   • Creation of the *Académie Française*

1766   • Establishment of the *agrégation* to certify *lycée* instructors

1789   • **French Revolution and establishment of the First Republic**

1793   • Closure of the Sorbonne

1794   • Creation of the École Normale Supérieure

1795   • Creation of the Institut de France as a union of five learned academies: the *Académie Française, Académie des Inscriptions et Belles-Lettres, Académie des Sciences, Académie des Beaux-Arts*, and the newly created *Académie des Sciences morales et politiques*

1803   • Abolition of the *Académie des Sciences morales et politiques*

1804   • **Napoleon Bonaparte proclaims the First Empire**

1806   • Reinstatement of the Sorbonne by Napoleon as a secular university

1809   • Introduction of philosophy into the *lycée* curriculum following its suppression during the Revolution

1821   • Creation of three distinct *agrégation* examinations in Sciences, Letters, and Grammar

1824   • Death of François Maine de Biran

1825   • Creation of a fourth, discipline-specific *agrégation de philosophie*
1830   • First year that instruction and examination of philosophy in *lycées* takes place in French rather than Latin
1830–42 • Auguste Comte publishes *Cours de philosophie positive* in six volumes
1832   • Reinstatement of the *Académie des Sciences morales et politiques*
1848   • **Beginning of the Second Republic**
1852   • Suppression of the *agrégation de philosophie* and the *lycée classe de philosophie*
        • **Napoleon III declares the Second Empire**
1853   • **Georges Eugène Haussmann begins reconfiguration of the streets of Paris**
1857   • Death of Auguste Comte
1858   • Birth of Émile Durkheim
1859   • Birth of Henri Bergson
1863   • Reestablishment under the direction of Minister of Public Instruction Victor Duruy of the *agrégation de philosophie* along with the *classe de philosophie* as the terminal year at *lycée*
1868   • Creation of the École Pratique des Hautes Études (EPHE)
        • Opening of the Bibliothèque Nationale
        • Birth of Émile Chartier ("Alain")
1869   • Birth of Léon Brunschvicg
1870–1 • **Franco–Prussian War**
1871   • Jules Lachelier publishes *Du fondement de l'induction*
        • **Establishment of the Third Republic**
        • **Paris Commune**
1873   • **End of German Occupation following France's defeat in the Franco–Prussian War**
1874   • Émile Boutroux publishes *La Contingence des lois de la nature*
        • **First Impressionist Exhibition staged by the Société anonyme des peintres, sculpteurs et graveurs (Pissarro, Monet, Sisley, Degas, Renoir, Cézanne, Guillaumin, and Berthe Morisot)**
1880   • Creation of the École Normale Supérieure for Girls at Fontenay
1881   • Creation of the École Normale Supérieure for Girls at Sèvres
1882   • Creation of the École Normale Supérieure-St. Cloud
        • Jules Ferry, as Minister of Public Instruction, makes primary education free, secular, and compulsory
1884   • Birth of Gaston Bachelard
1885   • The Sorbonne's Faculty of Theology is officially disbanded
1886   • Creation of the Fifth Section of the EPHE for the scientific study of religion

1888   • Birth of Jean Wahl
1889   • Bergson publishes *Essai sur les données immédiates de la conscience*
       • Birth of Gabriel Marcel
1892   • Establishment of the Fondation Thiers
1893   • Xavier Léon and Élie Halévy co-found the *Revue de métaphysique et de morale*
1894   • **Captain Alfred Dreyfus (1859–1935), a Jewish French army officer, is arrested and charged with spying for Germany**
1897   • Birth of Georges Bataille
1898   • **Opening of the Paris Metro**
       • **Émile Zola publishes "J'accuse," an open letter to the President of France, Félix Faure, calling for the reversal of Alfred Dreyfus's conviction for treason**
1900   • Election of Bergson to the Chair in Greek and Latin Philosophy at the Collège de France
       • Death of Félix Ravaisson
1901   • Creation of the Caisse des Recherches Scientifiques
       • Creation of the Société Française de Philosophie
       • Birth of Jacques Lacan
1902   • Émile Durkheim joins the Faculty of Philosophy at the Sorbonne
1903   • Elimination of requirement that the *thèse complémentaire* be written in Latin
       • École Normale Supérieure officially attached to the University of Paris
       • Birth of Jean Cavaillès
       • Death of Charles Renouvier
1904   • Bergson moves to the Chair in Modern Philosophy at the Collège de France
1905   • Birth of Jean-Paul Sartre and Raymond Aron
       • **Law of Separation of Church and State**
1906   • Birth of Emmanuel Levinas
       • **Dreyfus Affair ends when the French Court of Appeals exonerates Alfred Dreyfus of all charges**
1907   • Bergson publishes *L'Evolution créatrice*
       • **Pablo Picasso completes *Les Demoiselles d'Avignon***
       • Birth of Jean Hyppolite
1908   • Birth of Simone de Beauvoir, Claude Lévi-Strauss, and Maurice Merleau-Ponty
1909   • Brunschvicg begins his thirty-year career at the Sorbonne
       • Alain begins teaching the *première supérieure* ("*khâgne*") at Lycée Henri-IV, and continues until 1933

1910   • Initiation of the "Décades de Pontigny," organized by Paul
          Desjardins
        • First female student enrolls in the Sciences Section of the École
          Normale Supérieure-Rue d'Ulm
1911   • Victor Delbos publishes first French journal article on Husserl:
          "Husserl: Sa critique du psychologisme et sa conception d'une
          Logique pure" in *Revue de métaphysique et de morale*
1912   • Death of Henri Poincaré
1913   • Birth of Paul Ricoeur
        • **Marcel Proust (1871–1922) publishes *Swann's Way*, the first
          volume of *Remembrance of Things Past***
1914   • **Germany declares war on France**
1915   • Publication of Ferdinand de Saussure's *Cours de linguistique
          générale*
        • Birth of Roland Barthes
1917   • Death of Durkheim
1918   • Birth of Louis Althusser
        • Death of Lachelier
1919   • Alexandre Koyré emigrates to Paris
        • **World War I ends. Treaty of Versailles returns the
          province of Alsace and part of the province of Lorraine, both
          previously seized by Germany**
1921   • Death of Boutroux
1922   • Bataille begins twenty-year career at the Bibliothèque Nationale
1924   • Max Scheler invited to participate in gathering at Pontigny
        • Sartre, Aron, Paul Nizan, Georges Canguilhem, and Daniel
          Lagache enter the École Normale Supérieure
        • **André Breton publishes *Le Manifeste du surréalisme***
        • Birth of Jean-François Lyotard
1925   • Birth of Gilles Deleuze
        • **First Surrealist Exhibition at the Galerie Pierre, Paris**
1926   • Jean Hering publishes first French text to address Husserl's
          phenomenology: *Phénoménologie et philosophie religieuse*
        • Birth of Michel Foucault
1927   • Bergson awarded the Nobel Prize for Literature
        • Marcel publishes *Journal métaphysique*
        • Heidegger publishes *Sein und Zeit*
        • First three female students enroll in the Letters Section of the
          École Normale Supérieure-Rue d'Ulm
1928   • First work of German phenomenology appears in French trans-
          lation: Scheler's *Nature et formes de la sympathie. Contribution à
          l'étude des lois de la vie émotionnelle*

1929
- Husserl lectures at the Sorbonne
- Wahl publishes *La Malheur de la conscience dans la philosophie de Hegel*

1930
- Levinas publishes *La Théorie de l'intuition dans la phénoménologie de Husserl*
- Birth of Pierre Bourdieu, Jacques Derrida, Félix Guattari, Luce Irigaray, and Michel Serres

1931
- Levinas becomes a naturalized French citizen
- Levinas and Gabrielle Peiffer publish French translation of Husserl's *Cartesian Meditations*
- Heidegger's first works appear in French translation: "Was ist Metaphysik?" ("Qu'est-ce que la métaphysique?") in *Bifur*, and "Vom Wesen des Grundes" ("De la nature de la cause") in *Recherches philosophiques*

1932
- Étienne Gilson elected to the Chair in the History of Philosophy in the Middle Ages at the Collège de France
- Bergson publishes *Les Deux sources de la morale et de la religion*
- Emmanuel Mounier founds the journal *Esprit*

1933–9
- Alexandre Kojève lectures on Hegel at the École Pratique des Hautes Études

1935
- Marcel publishes *Être et avoir*

1936
- Sartre publishes "La Transcendance de l'ego" in *Recherches philosophiques*

1937
- Birth of Alain Badiou and Hélène Cixous

1938
- Establishment of Husserl Archives in Louvain, Belgium
- Sartre publishes *La Nausée*
- Death of Husserl

1939
- Reorganization and establishment of the Centre National de la Recherche Scientifique
- **France declares war on Nazi Germany**

1939–41
- Hyppolite publishes his translation into French of Hegel's *Phenomenology of Spirit*

1940
- *Statut des Juifs* (October 3) prohibits Jews from holding any public office, including any teaching position
- **German Army occupies Paris (June 14)**
- **Armistice signed (June 22) with Germany dividing France into Occupied and Unoccupied Zones, the latter under the administration of the French government at Vichy led by Marshal Henri Philippe Pétain**

1941
- Death of Bergson

1942
- Merleau-Ponty publishes *La Structure du comportement*
- Albert Camus publishes *L'Étranger* and *Le Mythe de Sisyphe: Essai sur l'absurde*

	• Lévi-Strauss meets Roman Jakobson at the École Libre des Hautes Études in New York
1943	• Sartre publishes *L'Être et le néant*
1944	• Cavaillès executed by the Nazis
	• **Paris liberated by US Army (August 25)**
1945	• Merleau-Ponty publishes *Phénoménologie de la perception*
1946	• Hyppolite publishes *Genèse et structure de la "Phénoménologie de l'esprit" de Hegel*
	• Sartre publishes *L'Existentialisme est un humanisme*
	• **Establishment of the Fourth Republic**
	• **Beginning of the French Indochina War**
	• Heidegger writes *Ueber den Humanismus* ("Letter on Humanism") in response to questions posed by Jean Beaufret
	• Sartre, Beauvoir, and Merleau-Ponty begin as founding editors of *Les Temps modernes*
	• Bataille founds the journal *Critique*
1947	• Creation of the Sixth Section of the EPHE organized around the social or human sciences
	• Beauvoir publishes *Pour une morale de l'ambiguïté*
1948	• Althusser appointed *agrégé-répétiteur* ("caïman") at the École Normale Supérieure, a position he holds until 1980
1949	• Beauvoir publishes *Le Deuxième sexe*
	• Lévi-Strauss publishes *Les Structures élémentaires de la parenté*
	• Cornelius Castoriadis and Claude Lefort found the revolutionary group and journal *Socialisme ou Barbarie*
1950	• Creation of the *Certificat d'Aptitude au Professorat de l'Enseignement Secondaire* (CAPES) as an alternative certification to the *agrégation*
	• Ricoeur publishes his translation into French of Husserl's *Ideas I*
1951	• Martial Guéroult elected to the Chair in the History and Technology of Philosophical Systems at the Collège de France
	• Death of Alain
1952	• Merleau-Ponty elected to the Chair in Philosophy at the Collège de France
	• First Colloquium at Cerisy-la-Salle
1953	• Lacan, together with Daniel Lagache and Françoise Dolto, founds the Société française de psychanalyse
	• Lacan begins his public seminars
1954	• **Following the fall of Dien Bien Phu (May 7), France pledges to withdraw from Indochina (July 20)**
	• **Beginning of the Algerian revolt against French rule**

1955
- Georges Canguilhem replaces Bachelard as Director of the Institut d'Histoire des Sciences et des Techniques and Chair in the History and Philosophy of Science at the Sorbonne, positions he holds until 1971
- Cerisy Colloquium *Qu'est-ce que la philosophie: Autour de Martin Heidegger*, organized by Jean Beaufret

1956
- **French colonies of Morocco and Tunisia gain independence**

1957
- Camus receives the Nobel Prize for Literature
- **Rome Treaty signed by France, Germany, Belgium, Italy, the Netherlands, and Luxembourg, establishes the European Economic Community**

1958
- The Sorbonne's "Faculté des lettres" officially renamed the "Faculté des lettres et sciences humaines"
- **Charles de Gaulle elected president after a new constitution establishes the Fifth Republic**
- Creation of the *Doctorat de troisième cycle* for letters and human sciences
- Creation of *licence* and *Doctorat de troisième cycle* in sociology
- Lévi-Strauss publishes *Anthropologie structurale*

1958–60
- **The first feature films by directors associated with the French "New Wave" cinema, including, in 1959, *Les Quatre Cent Coups/ The 400 Blows* by François Truffaut (1932–84) and *A bout de souffle/ Breathless* by Jean-Luc Godard (1930–)**

1959
- Lévi-Strauss elected to the Chair in Social Anthropology at the Collège de France

1960
- Sartre publishes *Critique de la raison dialectique*
- First issue of the journal *Tel Quel* is published
- Death of Camus

1961
- Foucault publishes *Histoire de la folie à l'âge classique*
- Frantz Fanon publishes *Les Damnés de la terre*, with a preface by Sartre
- Death of Merleau-Ponty

1962
- Jules Vuillemin elected to Chair in the Philosophy of Consciousness at the Collége de France
- **France grants independence to Algeria**
- Deleuze publishes *Nietzsche et la philosophie*

1963
- Hyppolite elected to the Chair in the History of Philosophical Thought at the Collège de France
- Public debate over Racine between Barthes and Raymond Picard, editor of the Pléiade edition of Racine's works and Professor of Literature at the Sorbonne

1964   • Creation of the University of Nanterre (later Paris X)
        • Lacan founds L'École Freudienne de Paris
        • Barthes publishes *Eléments de sémiologie*
1965   • Althusser publishes *Pour Marx*
1966   • Foucault publishes *Les Mots et les choses: Une archéologie des
          sciences humaines*
        • Lacan publishes *Écrits*
1967   • Ricouer leaves the Sorbonne to join the Department of Philosophy
          at the University of Nanterre, where he is appointed Dean of the
          Faculty of Letters in 1969
        • Derrida publishes *De la grammatologie*, *La Voix et le phénomène*,
          and *L'Écriture et la différence*
1968   • Creation of the University of Vincennes (later Paris VIII).
          Foucault is put in charge of organizing the Department of
          Philosophy and offers positions to, among others, Alain Badiou,
          Étienne Balibar, François Châtelet, Daniel Defert, Gilles
          Deleuze, Judith Miller, Jacques Rancière, René Schérer, and
          Michel Serres
        • Deleuze publishes *Différence et répétition*
        • **"Events of May '68," including closure of the University of
          Nanterre (May 2), police invasion of the Sorbonne (May 3),
          student demonstrations and strikes, and workers' occupation
          of factories and general strike**
1970   • Foucault elected to the Chair of the History of Systems of
          Thought at the Collège de France
        • Hélène Cixous, Gérard Genette, and Tzvetan Todorov found
          the literary journal *Poétique*
1971   • Reorganization of the University of Paris
1972   • Colloquium on Nietzsche at Cerisy
1973   • Julia Kristeva publishes *La Révolution du langage poétique*
        • Lacan publishes the first volume of his *Séminaire*
1974   • Luce Irigaray publishes *Speculum de l'autre femme*
        • Creation of the first doctoral program in women's studies
          in Europe, the *Centre de recherches en études féminines*, at the
          University of Paris VIII-Vincennes, directed by Hélène Cixous
1975   • The Sixth Section of the EPHE is renamed the École des
          Hautes Études in Sciences Sociales
        • Foundation of GREPH, the *Groupe de Recherches sur
          l'Enseignement Philosophique*
        • Foucault publishes *Surveiller et punir: Naissance de la prison*
1976   • Foucault publishes *Histoire de la sexualité. 1. La Volonté de
          savoir*

1977   •   Barthes elected to the Chair of Literary Semiology at the Collège de France

         •   **The Centre Georges Pompidou, designed by architects Renzo Piano (1937–) and Richard Rogers (1933–), opens in Paris**

1978   •   Vladimir Jankélévitch retires after 26 years as holder of the Chair in Moral Philosophy at the Sorbonne

1980   •   Lacan officially dissolves the École Freudienne de Paris

         •   Deaths of Sartre and Barthes

1981   •   Bourdieu elected to the Chair in Sociology at the Collège de France

         •   Marguerite Yourcenar (1903–87) is the first woman elected to the *Académie Française*

         •   Death of Lacan

1982   •   Foundation of the Collège International de Philosophie by François Châtelet, Jacques Derrida, Jean-Pierre Faye, and Dominique Lecourt

1983   •   Death of Aron

1984   •   *Doctorat de troisième cycle* becomes the only doctoral degree granted

         •   Creation of the *Habilitation à diriger des recherches*

         •   Death of Foucault

1985   •   Merger of the École Normale Supérieure-rue d'Ulm and École Normale Supérieure for Girls at Sèvres

         •   Merger of the École Normale Supérieure-St. Cloud and the École Normale Supérieure for Girls at Fontenay

         •   First complete translation into French of Heidegger's *Sein und Zeit*

1986   •   Gilles-Gaston Granger elected to Chair in Comparative Epistemology at the Collège de France

         •   Death of Beauvoir

1987   •   Canguilhem becomes the first philosopher to be awarded the Centre National de la Recherche Scientifique's highest distinction, the *Médaille d'or*

1988   •   Establishment of the Archives Husserl de Paris at the École Normale Supérieure, directed by Jean-François Courtine

1990   •   Serres elected to the Académie Française

         •   Death of Althusser

1992   •   Death of Guattari

1994   •   Jacques Bouveresse elected to the Chair of Philosophy of Language and Consciousness at the Collège de France

         •   Publication of Foucault's *Dits et écrits* in four volumes

1995   •   Death of Deleuze

1998   •   Death of Lyotard

1999   •   Badiou leaves Vincennes to become Professor and Head of the
            Philosophy Department at the École Normale Supérieure
        •   Creation of two new Chairs at the Collège de France, in Phil-
            osophy of the Biological and Medical Sciences and Philosophy
            and History of Scientific Concepts (filled in 2001 by Anne
            Fagot-Largeault and Ian Hacking, respectively)

Part I

Is there such a thing as "French philosophy"? At the start of the twentieth century, there was little doubt how that question should be answered. Victor Delbos, a scholar of Spinoza, Kant, and post-Kantian philosophy, and the author of the first French publication on Husserl, gave a course on this theme at the Sorbonne in 1915–16. Published posthumously in 1919, Delbos's course set out to demonstrate that there was indeed a national identity to philosophy in France – independent of German and English influences – that must be preserved and defended.[1] This identity, he claimed, which began with Descartes and could be traced through Pascal, Malebranche, Voltaire, the Encyclopedists (Diderot, D'Alembert), Rousseau, the Ideologues (Destutt de Tracy, Condorcet), Maine de Biran, Comte, into the present, distinguished itself in particular from German philosophy by means of its commitment both to clarity and to the cultivation of the human spirit.[2] Eleven years later, in his preface to the first French text to examine twentieth-century German philosophy – Georges Gurvitch's *Les Tendances actuelles de la philosophie allemande* (1930: "Present Tendencies in German Philosophy") – Léon Brunschvicg, the dominant academic philosopher of the day, also affirmed the idea of a specific national identity to philosophy. While no less committed than Delbos to the idea of a philosophy's national identity, Brunschvicg took a more

---

[1] See Maurice Blondel's preface to Victor Delbos, *La Philosophie française* (Paris: Librairie Plon, 1919), p. i. In his first French publication on Husserl, "Husserl: Sa critique du psychologisme et sa conception d'une logique pure," *Revue de métaphysique et de morale, XIXe année*, no. 5 (September–October 1911): 685–98, Delbos discussed the first volume of Husserl's *Logical Investigations* without addressing directly Husserl's phenomenology.

[2] There is little question that Delbos's motivations for writing this text must be seen in part as a patriotic response to Germany's aggression in World War I. Delbos died in 1916, shortly before completing the course.

dialogic view of the relations between French and German philosophy. French philosophy, he wrote, could be traced to Descartes and the Cartesian commitment to the unity of reason, while German philosophy had its origins in Kant's bifurcation of reason between the analytical and the dialectical.[3] Rather than preserving and defending the French philosophical tradition against foreign interventions, Brunschvicg argued that a dialogue between the French and German philosophical traditions was essential for each tradition's self-elaboration.

By the end of the century, however, a different argument was being offered for the identity of French philosophy. Pierre Macherey,[4] for example, writes that although there are no unifying features in terms of which one could identify a uniquely "French" philosophy, it still makes sense to speak about French philosophy in terms of two institutional forms: the French language and the French tradition of public instruction.[5] Both emerged in their modern forms following the French Revolution, and both continue to this day to mark the practical activity of philosophizing in France.

The perspective of the following pages inclines more toward Macherey's view than those of Delbos and Brunschvicg. To speak of "French philosophy" is not to speak of a unified tradition that shares certain philosophical assumptions. It is, rather, to speak of a historical unfolding of philosophical discourse that took place in the French language in the twentieth century and that was marked by certain events and developments, both historical and intellectual. In what is presented below, there is no assumption of a single set of shared properties, shared philosophical commitments, or shared goals. There is only the empirical fact that the figures discussed below, whether or not born in France or native French speakers, did their philosophical work in the French language and were engaged with and informed by the institutional practices of the French academic world.

It might seem strange, some thirty-plus years after the announcement of the end of grand narratives, to set out to tell the story of the history of

---

[3]   See Léon Brunschvicg, "Préface," in Georges Gurvitch, *Les Tendances actuelles de la philosophie allemande* (Paris: Librairie Vrin, 1930), p. 6.

[4]   See Pierre Macherey, "Y a-t-il une philosophie française?" in *Histoires de dinosaure: Faire de la philosophie 1965–1997* (Paris: Presses universitaires de France, 1999), pp. 313–22.

[5]   See appendix 1 for supplementary information about the French academic system and explanations of some of the components of that system not likely to be familiar to most readers.

philosophy in France in the twentieth century. But that is what this volume seeks to do. It will not, however, presume to be offering the one and only history of twentieth-century French philosophy. Rather, it will accept the point made by Jean-François Lyotard that no single grand narrative can be told that will be sufficient to explain an entire epoch.[6] But it will also work from the assumption that by relating several of the little narratives (*petits récits*) concerning the debates between vitalism and neo-Kantianism, the introduction of phenomenology, the First and Second World Wars, the rise and fall of existentialism, the debates concerning Marxism and the role of the Soviet Union, the Algerian war, the challenge to philosophy from the human sciences, May '68, the emergence of feminism, etc., a useful picture of the evolution of philosophy in France during the twentieth century can emerge. Such a picture will, it is hoped, challenge certain assumptions about who were the major influences on the developments in French philosophy over the past century, as it will challenge the tendency of each subsequent generation to downplay its own origins out of the seminar rooms and lecture halls in which the preceding generations taught them.

[6] See Jean-François Lyotard's "Introduction" to *The Postmodern Condition: A Report on Knowledge*, trans. Geoff Bennington and Brian Massumi (Minneapolis: University of Minnesota Press, 1984), pp. xxiii–xxv; see also p. 60.

1

The Early Decades

The names of the philosophers whose work was, at the beginning of the twentieth century, most influential and widely read in France are today all but unknown to English-speaking philosophers. Even among the figures who dominated French philosophy in the first three decades of the twentieth century, only Henri Bergson's name and work are likely to be familiar to many. In addition to Bergson, four figures stand out in the opening years of the century: Félix Ravaisson (1813–1900), Charles Renouvier (1815–1903), Émile Boutroux (1845–1921), and Jules Lachelier (1832–1918).

Ravaisson and Renouvier were students together at the École Normale Supérieure, and both drew upon the work of François Maine de Biran (1766–1824) and the French spiritualist tradition.[1] Ravaisson returned to teach at the École Normale, where his students included Lachelier, Boutroux, and Bergson. During his long career, Ravaisson occupied several important administrative posts, including *Inspecteur Général* for Higher Education in Letters (1852–88) and President of the *jury d'agrégation*. He wrote an important two-volume work on Aristotle's metaphysics (*Essai sur la métaphysique d'Aristote* [1837–46;

---

[1] Although he published little during his lifetime, Maine de Biran has had a significant influence on French philosophy. Focusing on psychological introspection as the foundation for a "science of man," Maine de Biran responded to Descartes's emphasis on man as a "thinking thing" by suggesting instead that the self is primarily a willing agent. To the Cartesian formula "I think, therefore I am" (*Cogito, ergo sum*), Maine de Biran proposed to substitute *Volo, ergo sum* ("I will, therefore I am"), arguing that human beings are most truly themselves in their willed actions and not just their thinking. His works were first published in a four-volume edition by Victor Cousin in 1841, with more complete editions edited subsequently by Pierre Tisserand (*Oeuvres de Maine de Biran*, 14 vols. [Paris: Félix Alcan and Presses universitaires de France, 1920–49]) and François Azouvi (*Oeuvres de Maine de Biran*, 20 vols. [Paris: Vrin, 1984–2001]).

"Essay on Aristotle's Metaphysics"]), a work on habit that suggests a philosophy of nature in which habit is understood as spirit made nature (*De l'habitude* [1938; "On Habit"]), and an influential work, at the request of the Minister of Public Instruction, on the history of nineteenth-century French philosophy (*La Philosophie en France au XIXe siècle* [1868; "Philosophy in France in the Nineteenth Century"]). Bringing together the psychological insights of Maine de Biran and a philosophy of nature drawn from Schelling's metaphysics, Ravaisson's writings had a profound influence on both Catholic philosophy and the development of personalism in France.

Charles Renouvier was a critic of Hegelianism and one of the central figures in the development of French neo-Kantianism. Emphasizing the relativity of phenomenalism (i.e., the view that our knowledge of the phenomenal world is a function of how things appear to us rather than how they are in themselves), and criticizing the existence of essences (noumena) that cannot be represented, Renouvier was the founder of French neo-critical idealism, a position he called *Criticisme*. Late in his life, he moved toward a more Leibnizian metaphysical position, and Renouvier's emphasis on liberty and reflective consciousness as the defining characteristics of human beings as persons led him to formulate several of the premises of personalism. Among Renouvier's most influential works are his four-volume *Essais de critique générale* (1854–64; "Essays of General Critique"), *Le Personnalisme* (1903; "Personalism"), and the posthumously published *Critique de la doctrine de Kant* (1906; "Critique of Kant's Philosophy").

Émile Boutroux was a specialist in Leibniz and seventeenth-century German philosophy. In addition to German idealism, he also drew on resources in French spiritualism and the natural sciences as he sought to reconcile the tensions between metaphysics and science. Boutroux anticipated and influenced the work of both Henri Bergson and Gaston Bachelard. Like Ravaisson and Lachelier, Boutroux taught at the École Normale Supérieure, but unlike them, he did not remain there, moving instead to the prestigious Chair in the History of Modern Philosophy at the Sorbonne, a position he held from 1888 to 1902. Through his teaching positions and his important works on the relations between science and philosophy, Boutroux was one of the dominant figures in French academic philosophy in the first two decades of the twentieth century. Among his important works, several were translated into English, including his best-known work, *La Contingence des lois de la nature* (1874; English translation: *The Contingency of the Laws of Nature*

[1916]), and *De l'idée de loi naturelle dans la science et la philosophie contemporaines* (1895; English translation: *Natural Law in Science and Philosophy* [1914]).

Perhaps the most influential of these four philosophers was Jules Lachelier, who taught at the École Normale Supérieure from 1864 to 1875. Critical of both Comtean positivism and empiricism, Lachelier sought to ground his idealist philosophy in a theory of induction that could resist the challenges of skepticism. His work had a profound impact on the intellectual development of many French thinkers, including Léon Brunschvicg, Jean Jaurès, Maurice Blondel, and Henri Bergson, whose 1889 doctoral thesis *Essai sur les données immédiates de la conscience* (*Time and Free Will: An Essay on the Immediate Data of Consciousness*) was dedicated to Lachelier. Although he did not publish much, Lachelier's years at the École Normale and, like Ravaisson, his many years as *Inspecteur Général* (1879–1900) and President of the *jury d'agrégation* (1900–10), made him the most important and influential philosophical figure in France for almost forty years. In addition, his major work, *Du fondement de l'induction* (*On the Foundation of Induction*), published in 1871, and an important essay, "Psychologie et métaphysique," first published in 1885, were frequently found on the list of required readings for *diplômes* in the 1920s and 1930s and were well known to virtually all students of philosophy in France prior to World War I.[2]

French surveys of late nineteenth- and early twentieth-century philosophy typically organize their topic around three basic philosophical positions: positivism, idealism, and, situated between these two extremes, various versions of positions they call spiritualism.[3] This division does not so neatly fit the figures discussed above, however, for while Ravaisson and Renouvier link their work to the spiritualist tradition, Renouvier is also strongly inclined toward Kantian idealism. And while Boutroux and Lachelier both draw upon German idealist thinking, Boutroux's sympathies with Leibniz and criticisms of Kant make him much more receptive to certain positivist themes than one would expect of an idealist thinker. Nevertheless, during the early decades of the twentieth century, philosophers in France do largely identify themselves with

---

[2] Both of these works appear in English translation in *The Philosophy of Jules Lachelier*, ed. and trans. Edward G. Ballard (The Hague: Martinus Nijhoff, 1960).

[3] Typical, in this regard, is the interesting survey by Jean Guitton, *Regards sur la pensée française 1870–1940: Leçons de captivité* (Paris: Beauchesne, 1968).

these three traditions as they respond to each other and to recent developments in both mathematics and science.[4]

Positivism

Outside France, Auguste Comte is perhaps the best-known French philosopher of the nineteenth century. Comte's positivism blends an empiricist commitment to the idea that knowledge is based on sensuously experienced facts (*posita*) with the French enlightenment faith in reason and progress. The foundation of Comte's philosophy is what he called "The Law of Three Stages," which he claimed explained the evolution of thought. The history of the sciences, according to Comte, shows that thought necessarily evolves through three stages. The most primitive stage is the theological stage of fictitious thinking, which views all things as animated by a will and in which facts are explained in terms of actions in accordance with a will. The second stage is the metaphysical stage of abstract thinking, in which abstract concepts replace personal wills as the principles of explanation. In metaphysical thinking, concepts like force, substance, or spirit, rather than supernatural direction, form the basis of the explanatory account, and the goal of metaphysical explanation is to refer everything to one Nature or Absolute (e.g., Spinoza or Hegel). According to Comte, metaphysics is a transitional stage between theology and the third stage of scientific or positive thinking, which gives up the search for absolute knowledge (in the form of a first cause or final will) and seeks instead to work through observation and experimentation. What results in this third stage is a criticism of metaphysical speculation for having replaced the more primitive theological principle of explanation in terms of a personal will with explanations in terms of abstract concepts. Metaphysics must, Comte concludes, give way to scientific, "positive" explanation that establishes "a connection between single phenomena and some general

---

[4] We cannot here discuss the impact of developments in mathematics (Dedekind, Cantor) or science (Planck, Einstein) on developments in French philosophy in the early years of the twentieth century. For a discussion of this impact on early twentieth century philosophy in general, the reader is encouraged to examine the introduction and first chapter of Christian Delacampagne, *A History of Philosophy in the Twentieth Century*, trans. M. B. DeBevoise (Baltimore: Johns Hopkins University Press, 1999).

facts [or laws], the number of which continually diminishes with the progress of the science."[5]

In the early twentieth century, Comte's positive philosophy was often found on the reading list for the *agrégation*[6] and was a frequent topic of students' theses. More significant for developments in French philosophy in the early twentieth century was the fact that the dominant figure carrying forward the positivist tradition in the later years of the nineteenth century, Émile Durkheim (1858–1917), joined the philosophy faculty at the Sorbonne in 1902. The founder of the "French school" of sociology, Durkheim had studied philosophy with Émile Boutroux at the École Normale Supérieure and passed the *agrégation* in philosophy in 1882. He joined the faculty of the Sorbonne as the replacement for Ferdinand Buisson (1841–1932) as "Chair in the Science of Education" in 1906, eventually renaming this the "Chair in the Science of Education and Sociology" in 1913.

Through his administrative assignments and interest in educational reform, Durkheim came to occupy a position of great influence at the Sorbonne. His lecture-courses on education were the only compulsory courses at the Sorbonne, being required for all students who sought

---

[5] Auguste Comte, *The Positive Philosophy of Auguste Comte*, Vol. 1, trans. Harriet Martineau (London: George Bell and Sons, 1896), p. 2.

[6] Comte's works appeared on the reading list for the *concours* in 1901, 1902, 1904, 1908, 1909, and 1910 (indicating the influence of Durkheim), and four more times between 1919 and 1928. Although absent for most of the 1930s and 1940s, his works returned to the reading list in 1949 and stayed through most of the 1950s, appearing in 1950, 1951, and 1955–8 (indicating the influence of Canguilhem, who served as *Inspecteur Général de philosophie* from 1948 to 1955). Overall, Comte appears on the reading list 20 times between 1900 and 1959, far more often than any other nineteenth-century philosophers except Schopenhauer, who appears 30 times, and John Stuart Mill, who appears 18 times. It should be noted, however, that almost all of Schopenhauer's and Mill's appearances come after 1910, the year that certain candidates could be excused from the Greek option, substituting for an explication of a Greek text either an explication of an English or a German text (typically, the *concours* offered two choices from each language). Only six of Schopenhauer's appearances on the reading list come outside of this German option (for the written examination in 1905, 1943, and 1944, and for the oral expositions in 1914, 1915 [although the *agrégation* was canceled in 1914 and 1915], and 1933), and in the majority of his appearances – including every year from 1946 to 1959 – it is the third book of *Die Welt als Wille und Vorstellung* that is offered as one of the two German text options. This information is taken from the annual postings of the Programme du Concours de l'Agrégation de Philosophie that appear in the *Revue Universitaire*.

teaching credentials in philosophy, history, literature, or language.[7] Durkheim's mix of positivism (drawn from Comte, but cleansed of its dogmatic and political-theological leanings) and rationalism (drawn from Renouvier and his idea that morality can be studied scientifically), conjoined with an attentiveness to empirical detail, was a major presence at the Sorbonne in the early decades of the twentieth century, and this led to an intense rivalry among those who followed Durkheim's courses at the Sorbonne and those following Bergson's lectures at the Collège de France. Durkheim's subsequent influence on the academic field of sociology has been profound, and his emphasis on philosophical and moral reflection conjoined with empirical study began a tradition within French philosophy that would draw several philosophy *agrégés* away from philosophy, including among the more well-known examples, his nephew, Marcel Mauss (1872–1950), and, in later years, Raymond Aron, Claude Lévi-Strauss, Henri Lefebvre, and Pierre Bourdieu. While his influence at the time of his death on the social sciences was far greater than it was on philosophy, Durkheim's emphasis on empirical study also led to a tradition that encouraged those pursuing their philosophical reflections on the natural and social sciences to do so with a solid grounding in those sciences, and the proximity of scientific research and French philosophy in general can be traced to Durkheim's own fusion of these two modes of inquiry that, in other intellectual cultures, often proceed along entirely distinct paths.

Idealism

Along with Durkheim, the other dominant figure at the Sorbonne in the early decades of the twentieth century was Léon Brunschvicg (1869–1944). Brunschvicg was without question the leading figure in French idealism and the most important representative of twentieth-century French neo-Kantianism. Together with his friends Xavier Léon and Élie Halévy, Brunschvicg co-founded the *Revue de métaphysique et de morale* in 1893, and in 1901 he was instrumental in the founding of the Société Française de Philosophie. Brunschvicg came to the Sorbonne in 1909 and taught there for 30 years. During these years, he produced his major works, including three large historical studies that

---

[7]   See Steven Lukes, *Émile Durkheim: His Life and Works* (London: Penguin, 1973), p. 372.

chronicle the increasing sophistication with which the mind comes to understand itself and its constitution of experience in the realms of mathematics, causality, and morality and religion: *Les Étapes de la philosophie mathématique* (1912; "Stages in the Philosophy of Mathematics"), *L'Expérience humaine et la causalité physique* (1920; "Human Experience and Physical Causality"), and *Le Progrès de la conscience dans la philosophie occidentale* (1927; "The Development of Consciousness/Conscience[8] in Western Philosophy").

Brunschvicg's idealism draws its inspiration from Kant's, but it is informed as well by a Hegelian attention to historical development and a Comtean respect for the givenness of the external world and the ultimate unity of knowledge. Like all idealists, Brunschvicg accepts that we can have no knowledge of a thing as it is in itself, independent of our consciousness of it. But contrary to subjective idealists like Berkeley, Brunschvicg does not deny the existence of a world external to our consciousness; he argues instead that the relation between subject and object is itself a relation that emerges within and is known to consciousness. And unlike the transcendental idealism of Kant, Brunschvicg does not understand the objects of knowledge to be constituted on the basis of *a priori* and unchanging categories; instead, the objects of our knowledge unfold historically as the mind reflects on its own activity. In his three historical studies, he thus followed the development of knowledge in mathematics, nature, and morality as the progressive process of new discoveries of reality that follow from the increasingly sophisticated self-reflective activity of consciousness.

Like Durkheim, Brunschvicg's courses at the Sorbonne were extremely popular: for example, in the 1919–20 academic year, every student at the École Normale Supérieure who registered to take the *agrégation* lists taking Brunschvicg's course on "La conscience."[9] While many of the more famous students who took his classes, including Gaston Bachelard, Simone de Beauvoir, Emmanuel Levinas, Claude Lévi-Strauss, Maurice Merleau-Ponty, Paul Ricoeur, and Jean-Paul Sartre, chose not to follow him toward idealism, one can in most cases see their

---

[8] It is important to keep in mind that the French word *conscience* means both 'consciousness' and 'conscience.' In Brunschvicg's text, he clearly intends both meanings. That the French *conscience* can mean both 'consciousness' and 'conscience' has been responsible for more than a few misunderstandings and mistranslations of French philosophical thought by English readers.

[9] These records can be found at the Centre d'Accueil et de Recherche des Archives Nationales (CARAN), Paris, carton AJ/61/192.

work evolving in critical response to Brunschvicg's. For those many students who followed his courses on Plato, Descartes, Spinoza, and Kant, his lectures, in the words of Jean-Toussaint Desanti, accustomed them "to see something like an internal logic according to which these names represented the high-points in Reason's Odyssey, necessary reference points along the unfolding of philosophy as manifested in history."[10] Through his books, his institutional positions with the Société Française de Philosophie and the *jury d'agrégation*, and his 30 years of teaching at the Sorbonne, Brunschvicg's influence on French academic philosophy in the first four decades of the twentieth century was second to none.

Spiritualism

The third position, and the one that can be seen to have had the greatest impact on subsequent French philosophy in the first half of the twentieth century, is spiritualism. Spiritualism does not so much define a philosophical position as name a tradition in French thought that has its origins in the ideas of Maine de Biran and that emphasizes, in contrast to nineteenth-century materialism, the importance of the will. As a consequence, spiritualism was the most multiform and diverse of the early philosophical movements in France, taking both religious and non-religious forms, and within each of these forms, significant differences can be found among the leading representatives. In terms of both immediate influence and enduring philosophical impact, the most prominent of the spiritualists was Henri Bergson (1859–1941). Indeed, Bergson was the most dominant figure in French philosophy for much of his lifetime, in part because of his position for many years as a holder of a Chair in Philosophy at the Collège de France, and in part because the accessibility of his writing gave him a large audience outside the academic community. While his turn toward evolution and away from Kant alienated him from the academic centers of power at the Sorbonne (with Brunschvicg and Durkheim) and the École Normale Supérieure (with Boutroux), his exploration of evolutionary theory in terms of the spiritual force he called *élan vital* captured the imagination

---

10   Jean-Toussaint Desanti, "A Path in Philosophy," trans. Kathleen McLaughlin, in *Philosophy in France Today*, ed. Alan Montefiore (Cambridge: Cambridge University Press, 1983), p. 54. This interesting collection includes 11 essays from important French philosophers who were asked to reflect on their own work and several of the essays address the authors' intellectual formations.

of French writers and society at large, and had a great influence on other, more religious spiritualist philosophers.

While Bergson's philosophy most directly responds to both the positivists' rejection of metaphysics and the idealists' hyper-intellectualism and discounting of the epistemological importance of the body, it also offers a broader challenge to the dominant tradition in the history of metaphysics that has privileged being over becoming and understood time in the Aristotelian sense of an endless series of discrete and singular moments.[11] According to Bergson, to analyze time as a series of distinct moments ultimately conceives time according to the model of space, and this had led metaphysicians to understand ultimate reality in terms of that which does not change (e.g., Plato's Forms). Instead, Bergson claims that we must understand time as we experience it, as *durée* or duration, which does not proceed from moment to moment but moves instead as a continuous stream of becoming (as both Bergson and William James recognized, the similarity between Bergson's idea of duration and James's "stream of consciousness" is clear). Duration, Bergson writes, is experienced as "a qualitative multiplicity, with no likeness to number; an organic evolution which is yet not an increasing quantity; a pure heterogeneity within which there are no distinct qualities. In a word, the moments of inner duration are not external to one another."[12]

What links these inner moments of duration is what Bergson called *élan vital* (vital impulse), the driving force that underlies all life (echoes of Spinoza's *conatus* should be heard here). The center of Bergson's vitalism, *élan vital* was his way to account for the evolutionary process of becoming while avoiding what he saw to be two unsatisfactory explanations of evolutionary change: mechanism and finalism. Where the mechanistic interpretation of evolution saw the process as one of pure chance which, according to Bergson, could not account for the apparently purposive increase in organic complexity, the finalist interpretation saw the evolutionary process as overly determined and unable to account for the randomness and contingency that was for him so clearly a part of natural history. Bergson's alternative was to see evolution as a *creative* process, one that was inherently capable of producing something new, unlike either mechanism or finalism, which saw

---

[11] Bergson's views are, in this regard, much closer to Heidegger's than Heidegger's few brief and dismissive comments on Bergson in *Being and Time* would indicate.

[12] Henri Bergson, *Time and Free Will: An Essay on the Immediate Data of Consciousness*, trans. F. L. Pogson (New York: Macmillan, 1910), p. 226.

the future as, respectively, either causally or teleologically determined. The key to understanding evolution as creative was to understand the life force or *élan vital* as "virtually multiple [*virtuellement multiple*],"[13] as making possible any of several actual futures. As Gilles Deleuze has noted, when Bergson talks about *élan vital*, "it is always a case of a virtuality in the process of becoming actualized, a simplicity in the process of differentiating, a totality in the process of dividing up."[14] And insofar as what is virtual holds many possible future actuals, contrary to the deterministic consequences of either mechanistic or finalist accounts of evolution, Bergson's account of evolution allows for the creation of the new and the different.

Among the more religious spiritualist philosophers, Bergson's impact can be seen on both Thomists and non-Thomists alike. In fact, of the more important spiritualist philosophers in the first decades of the twentieth century, it is only Maurice Blondel on whom Bergson's philosophy had little influence. Blondel studied with Boutroux at the École Normale and, like many *normaliens*, he was greatly influenced by Boutroux's emphasis on freedom and by his lack of sympathy for Bergson's thought. Of the spiritualist philosophers, Blondel was perhaps the dominant thinker working outside the Thomist tradition and his most important work, *Action*, first published in 1893, was one of the most widely read and influential texts of these early decades. For all the other significant Christian spiritualists, however, Bergson was a powerful influence, whether directly through his lectures, which were heard by Jacques Maritain, Pierre Teilhard de Chardin, and Gabriel Marcel, or indirectly, as in the case of Emmanuel Mounier, whose mentors (Maritain, Charles Péguy [1873–1914], and Jacques Chevalier [1882–1962]) were themselves deeply influenced by Bergson.

Whether framed in terms of Sorbonne rationalism vs. anti-university spiritualism, or neo-Kantianism vs. vitalism, the rivalry between Brunschvicg and Bergson dominated French philosophy in the early decades of the twentieth century.[15] Yet as we will see, their influence began to diminish in the 1920s and dropped off considerably in the years

---

[13] See Henri Bergson, *L'Evolution créatrice* (Paris: Félix Alcan, 1914), p. 280.

[14] Gilles Deleuze, *Bergsonism*, trans. Hugh Tomlinson and Barbara Habberjam (New York: Zone Books, 1988), p. 94.

[15] Although the rivalry between their respective followers was often harsh, the relations between Bergson and Brunschvicg themselves were quite cordial. Vladimir Jankélévitch discusses Brunschvicg's respect for Bergson's work and sympathy for Bergson's physical ailments and the harsh treatment he received by academic

approaching World War II. There are several reasons for this which have little to do with their respective philosophical positions. Bergson suffered from a debilitating form of arthritis and, although he remained officially a member of the Collège de France until 1921, his poor health prevented him from teaching after 1914. More importantly, Bergson's health made it difficult for him to work, with the result that, following the appearance of *Creative Evolution* in 1907, 25 years would pass until his next, and final, important work, *Two Sources of Morality and Religion*, would appear in 1932. While some, like Sartre, admitted to being inspired to begin the serious study of philosophy by Bergson,[16] the more typical response of the advanced students at the École Normale Supérieure is expressed by Merleau-Ponty, who in 1959 reflected back on how little attention was paid by his contemporaries to Bergson. Although students at the Sorbonne and École Normale were more hostile to Bergson and more sympathetic to Brunschvicg, Merleau-Ponty confesses that "if we had been more careful readers of Bergson, and if more thought had been given to him, we would have been drawn to a much more concrete philosophy, a philosophy much less reflexive than Brunschvicg's."[17]

---

philosophers in a 1969 essay, "Léon Brunschvicg," reprinted in *Sources* (Paris: Éditions du Seuil, 1984), pp. 133–41, esp. 133–5.

[16] Sartre recounts the impact of reading Bergson, specifically his *Essai sur les données immédiates de la conscience* (*Time and Free Will: An Essay on the Immediate Data of Consciousness*), on his turn from literature to philosophy at the École Normale Supérieure in the 1976 film *Sartre*, transcribed and published as *Sartre By Himself*, trans. Richard Seaver (New York: Urizen Books, 1978), p. 27. While Sartre is critical of Bergson's work when he does address it in, for example, *The Psychology of Imagination* and *Being and Nothingness*, there can be little doubt that Bergson's persona, as a writer for an audience outside the academy and winner of the Nobel Prize for Literature, made a lasting impression on the young Sartre.

[17] Maurice Merleau-Ponty, "The Philosophy of Existence," trans. Allen S. Weiss in *Texts and Dialogues*, ed. Hugh J. Silverman and James Barry, Jr. (Atlantic Highlands, NJ: Humanities Press International, 1992), p. 132. In another 1959 essay, "Bergson in the Making," Merleau-Ponty admits to how badly Bergson was read at the time, and how much more there is to his philosophy than what was "identified with the vague cause of spiritualism" (Maurice Merleau-Ponty, "Bergson in the Making," trans. Richard McCleary, in *Signs* [Evanston, IL: Northwestern University Press, 1964], p. 182). Subsequent readers of French philosophy would have to wait for Gilles Deleuze to bring out what Merleau-Ponty refers to in this essay as the "audacious" Bergson. See, for example, Deleuze's *Bergsonism*, as well as his two volumes on cinema.

Brunschvicg, for his part, remained institutionally powerful for many years in his positions as Sorbonne professor, frequent member of the *jury d'agrégation*, and jury president from 1936 to 1938. His support for women who wanted to study philosophy at the Sorbonne also was significant.[18] But confronting the events of World War I led students away from idealism, and the events leading up to World War II, and France's eventual occupation by Germany, made things difficult for Jews in France. It is worth noting that three of the dominant figures in French philosophy in these early decades—Durkheim, Brunschvicg, and Bergson—were all Jews whose careers and lives were directly affected by anti-Semitism. Both Durkheim and Brunschvicg were active Dreyfusards who took part in the campaign to exonerate Alfred Dreyfus, a Jewish officer falsely accused of spying for the Germans, and both were attacked by the social and political conservatives who saw the Sorbonne falling victim to Germanic philosophizing and Jewish cultural influences. In 1940, Brunschvicg was forced to flee Paris for the free zone in the south, leaving his library behind, and eventually settling in Aix-en-Provence. Because of the advancing German forces, he was forced to move several more times before his death in January, 1944. Bergson, although born to Jewish parents, late in his life became spiritually committed to Catholicism and would most likely have converted; he refused to do so, however, at a time when French Jews were most seriously threatened. Having been made an "Honorary Aryan" by the Vichy government in recognition of his contributions to French intellectual culture, Bergson to his credit refused to renounce his Jewish background or accept any special treatment, which likely contributed to his death in early January, 1941.

Beyond these historical factors, there were also, to be sure, philosophical factors that led the generation of students of the late 1920s and 1930s to make a general turn away from the spiritual and ideal and toward the concrete. For either a theist like Marcel or Merleau-Ponty, or an atheistic thinker like Sartre or Beauvoir, the otherworldly character of idealism or spiritualism did not satisfy their desire to understand the concrete data of human experience, whether it be the wholesale carnage of World War I or the more mundane details of

---

[18] Brunschvicg's wife, Cécile Brunschvicg (1877–1946), was one of the leading feminists of her day, and she credits her husband with being a strong advocate of women's suffrage. See Deidre Bair, *Simone de Beauvoir: A Biography* (New York: Summit Books, 1990), p. 654n32.

a human life. For some, this turn was both explicitly politicized and directed toward the academic philosophical institutions. Paul Nizan, a Marxist who was a close friend of Sartre and a fellow *normalien*, made the dissatisfaction with the Sorbonne mandarins the explicit theme of his 1930 text *Les Chiens de garde* (*The Watchdogs*). While indicting many of the leading philosophers of the day (Bergson, Lalande,[19] Parodi,[20] Bouglé),[21] it is Léon Brunschvicg in particular who bears the brunt of Nizan's attack on the bourgeois tendencies of academic philosophy, whose supreme function, he writes,

> is to obscure the miseries of contemporary reality: the spiritual destitu-
> tion of vast numbers of men, the fundamental dichotomy in their
> consciousness, and the increasingly intolerable disparity between what
> they could achieve and what little they have actually accomplished... It
> serves to divert the exploited from the contemplation of their own
> degradation and debasement – an activity that might prove dangerous
> to the exploiters... In a word, the purpose of this philosophy is to
> explain, to fortify, and to propagate the half-truths manufactured by
> the bourgeoisie and so useful in consolidating its power.[22]

The turn away from idealism and spiritualism was taken up explicitly by Jean Wahl in his 1932 work *Vers le concret* ("Toward the Concrete").

[19] André Lalande (1867–1963) was co-founder in 1901 of the Société Française de Philosophie. He held a Chair in Philosophy at the Sorbonne from 1904 to 1936, and served as President of the *jury d'agrégation* from 1920 to 1927 and 1931 to 1934. Lalande's most influential work, and his preoccupation from 1902, was his project of editing a collection of detailed definitions of philosophical terms, the *Vocabulaire technique et critique de la philosophie*. Between 1902 and 1923, the Société Française de Philosophie devoted 21 of its bi-monthly meetings to working through the vocabulary alphabetically, publishing subsequently its presentations and dis-cussions in its bulletin. The first complete edition of the *Vocabulaire* was published in 1926, and currently it is in its eighteenth edition, the first nine editions having been overseen by Lalande.

[20] Dominique Parodi (1870–1955) served off and on as *Inspecteur Général* of Public Instruction from 1919 to 1934 and was editor of the *Revue de métaphysique et de morale* from 1935 to 1955.

[21] Célestin Bouglé (1870–1940) was a sociologist associated with Durkheim, who taught at the Sorbonne in the Department of Philosophy from 1908 to 1940, with a Chair as Professor of Social Economy from 1919 to 1940. He also served as Adjunct Director (1927–35), and then Director (1935–40), of the École Normale Supérieure.

[22] Paul Nizan, *The Watchdogs: Philosophers and the Established Order*, trans. Paul Fittingoff (New York: Monthly Review Press, 1971), pp. 91–2.

Wahl argued in successive chapters on William James, Alfred North Whitehead, and Gabriel Marcel, that we see in their works a dialectic between thought and its object that refuses to lose touch with the real. The principal enemy for James, Whitehead, and Marcel is "mental aridity [*sécheresse mentale*]," and because they each retain an attention to the body and to lived experience, their dialectics, unlike Hegel's, remain oriented toward the concrete.[23] We see a similar motivation driving Alexandre Kojève's historical and materialist reading of Hegel's master–slave dialectic as he argues that "History is the history of the working Slave" who will become free by transcending himself through labor: "The future and History hence belong not to the warlike Master, who either dies or preserves himself indefinitely in identity to himself, but to the working Slave. The Slave, in transforming the given World by his work, transcends the given and what is given by that given in himself."[24] And, perhaps most significantly, this is a fundamental motivation for those who, like Sartre and Merleau-Ponty, were turning to Husserl and Heidegger, whose method of phenomenological description and account of Being-*in*-the world were just what they needed to turn away from Brunschvicg and Bergson and turn, in the words of Jean Wahl's text, *vers le concret.*[25]

23   Jean Wahl, *Vers le concret* (Paris: Vrin, 1932), p. 13. Although this text is comprised of three studies of James, Whitehead, and Marcel, the footnotes in the preface make clear that Wahl's orientation toward the concrete is guided by his reading of Heidegger's *Being and Time.*

24   Alexandre Kojève, *Introduction to the Reading of Hegel*, ed. Raymond Queneau, trans. James H. Nichols, Jr. (New York: Basic Books, 1969), pp. 20, 23.

25   In *Search for a Method*, Sartre mentions Wahl's text as enjoying a "great success" among his generation. See Jean-Paul Sartre, *Search for a Method*, trans. Hazel Barnes (New York: Alfred A. Knopf, 1963), p. 19. Dominique Janicaud makes a similar observation about Sartre's attraction to phenomenology. Commenting on Sartre's "brief, but dazzling [1939] manifesto for the new 'phenomenological ontology' [entitled] 'Intentionality: A Fundamental Idea of Husserl's Phenomenology,' " (Jean-Paul Sartre, *Situations I* [Paris: Éditions Gallimard, 1947], pp. 31–5; English translation by Joseph P. Fell, *Journal of the British Society for Phenomenology*, vol. 1, no. 2 [May 1970]: 4–5), Janicaud writes: "Against André Lalande, Léon Brunschvicg, and Émile Meyerson, who analyzed and celebrated the mind's power of assimilation and unification, Sartre lays claim to 'something solid,' without however wanting to return to either a gross sensualism, an objectivism, or a more subtle type of realism à la Henri Bergson." See Dominique Janicaud, *The Theological Turn of French Phenomenology*, trans. Bernard G. Prusack, in Janicaud et al., *Phenomenology and the "Theological Turn": The French Debate* (New York: Fordham University Press, 2000), p. 18.

2

Phenomenology on the Way to Existentialism

The third and fourth decades of the twentieth century see a significant change in philosophical sensibilities in France. On the one hand, we find the emergence of both Thomist and non-Thomist philosophy as cultural forces working primarily outside the academic centers. Neither Thomists like Jacques Maritain or Pierre Teilhard de Chardin, nor non-Thomists like Gabriel Marcel or Emmanuel Mounier, taught at the Sorbonne or École Normale Supérieure. But they published widely in books and journals, and their interest in questions concerning human existence both attracted a wide audience and would play a significant role in the development of existentialism. Maritain, for example, called his brand of Thomism "Existentialist Intellectualism."[1] Gabriel Marcel, for his part, can be credited with publishing the twentieth century's first work of existential philosophy, *Metaphysical Journal*,[2] in 1927, the same year that Martin Heidegger published *Being and Time*.[3] And Marcel's major philosophical work, *Being and Having*, which explores such existential themes as being-in-the-world, facticity, embodiment, and freedom, was published in 1935, eight years before Jean-Paul Sartre's *Being and Nothingness*. Another proto-existentialist thinker, Emmanuel Mounier, brought together Catholic spiritualism with socialist materialism. Through his journal *Esprit*, founded in 1932, Mounier became one of the leading spokespersons for personalism, a philosophical position which attracted, among others, a young Maurice Merleau-Ponty

---

[1] See Jacques Maritain, *Existence and the Existent*, trans. Lewis Galantiere and Gerald B. Phelan (New York: Pantheon Books, 1948), p. 47. Maritain's text opens with the claim that this short work will be "an essay on the existentialism of St. Thomas Aquinas" (p. 1).

[2] Gabriel Marcel, *Journal métaphysique* (Paris: Éditions Gallimard, 1927); *Metaphysical Journal*, trans. Bernard Wall (Chicago: Regnery, 1952).

[3] Although the styles of these two texts are very different, they examine many of the same themes.

and Paul Ricoeur, and which Ricoeur described as "a pedagogy concerning communal life linked to an awakening of the person."[4]

In addition to the influence of Christian philosophy outside the academy, within the academic centers of power and influence these decades saw young philosophy students turn away from the four B's – Bergson, Blondel, Boutroux, and Brunschvicg – and discover German philosophy's three H's: Hegel, Husserl, and Heidegger. This turn from France to Germany was also a turn from spiritualism to phenomenology, from idealism to existentialism, and from the influence of Thomas Aquinas to the influence of Marx. Events in European history also play a role here, as the introduction of German philosophy was facilitated by the immigration to France of several eastern European philosophers: Russian Alexandre Koyré emigrated to Paris in 1919 and was the first person to introduce Husserlian phenomenology to the French; fellow Russian Alexandre Kojève emigrated to Paris in 1927 and his lectures on Hegel at the École Pratique des Hautes Études from 1933 to 1939 played a major role in the French Hegel revival; and Lithuanian Emmanuel Levinas, who came first to France in 1923 to study at the University of Strasbourg and became a naturalized French citizen in 1931, the year after he published the first French book on Husserl,[5] and the year before he published one of the first articles in French on Heidegger.[6]

It is difficult to establish a precise chronology during these transitional years, but several influential events can be noted which mark the transformation of French philosophy away from the spiritualist or idealist metaphysics of Bergson and Brunschvicg and toward the more rigorous rationalism of phenomenology. First and foremost is the

[4] Paul Ricoeur, "Emmanuel Mounier: A Personalist Philosopher," in *History and Truth*, trans. Charles A. Kelbley (Evanston, IL: Northwestern University Press, 1965), p. 136.

[5] As Levinas notes in the preface to *Théorie de l'intuition dans la phénoménologie de Husserl* (Paris: Félix Alcan, 1930) (English translation: *The Theory of Intuition in Husserl's Phenomenology*, trans. André Orianne [Evanston, IL: Northwestern University Press, 1973]), his was not the first French text to address Husserl's phenomenology. That distinction goes to Jean Hering's *Phénoménologie et philosophie religieuse* (Paris: Félix Alcan, 1926). Levinas's text was, however, the first book published in French devoted *exclusively* to Husserl's thought.

[6] Emmanuel Levinas, "Martin Heidegger et l'ontologie," *Revue philosophique de la France et de l'étranger* CXIII, no. 5/6 (1932): 395–431; English translation: "Martin Heidegger and Ontology," trans. Committee of Public Safety, *Diacritics* 26, no. 1 (Spring 1996): 11–32.

introduction of phenomenology itself, first in the presence of Max
Scheler (1874–1928) and Husserlian phenomenology and then in the
renaissance of Hegel studies in France. Scheler, who in the early 1920s
was regarded in Germany as second only to Husserl in importance
within the phenomenological movement, was the first of the leading
phenomenologists to be invited to visit France, in 1924[7] and again in
1926, and his 1923 text *Wesen und Formen der Sympathie* (*The Nature of
Sympathy*) was the first work of phenomenology to appear in French
translation, published by Payot in 1928.[8] In 1927–8, Georges Gurvitch,
then a Professor at the Russian University in Prague, offered an open
course at the Sorbonne on "The School of Phenomenological Philosophy in Germany," and in his influential book on present tendencies in
German philosophy, Scheler's work receives the lengthiest treatment.[9]
And as already mentioned, major roles in bringing Husserl's work to the
attention of the French were played by two émigrés, Alexandre Koyré
and Emmanuel Levinas. Levinas in particular, in addition to publishing
the first French book devoted exclusively to Husserl, was co-translator,
with Gabrielle Peiffer, of the first edition of Husserl's work to appear in

---

[7] In 1924, Scheler was invited to the annual ten-day gathering of writers and intellectuals (the "Décades de Pontigny"), organized by Paul Desjardins (1859–1940) at
his home, the former Abbey of Pontigny. Scheler there introduced his phenomenology to the French through lectures, in German, on the contemporary significance
of St. Augustine and Meister Eckhardt. These gatherings at Pontigny, which took
place during the summers from 1910 to 1939 and were attended by, among others,
Nicolas Berdyaev, Martin Buber, André Gide, André Malraux, François Mauriac,
André Maurois, and Paul Valéry, served as the model for the gatherings organized
since 1952 by the Centre Culturel de Cerisy at the chateau at Cerisy-la-Salle
belonging to Desjardins' daughter Anne Heurgon-Desjardins (1899–1977).

[8] Max Scheler, *Nature et formes de la sympathie. Contribution à l'étude des lois de la vie
émotionnelle*, trans. M. Lefebvre (Paris: Payot, 1928). See Herbert Spiegelberg, *The
Phenomenological Movement: A Historical Introduction*, 3rd edn. (The Hague: Martinus Nijhoff, 1982), pp. 431–2.

[9] Spiegelberg goes so far as to claim that in the beginning, Scheler and Heidegger were
more important to the introduction of phenomenology in France than was Husserl
(*The Phenomenological Movement*, p. 431), and he correctly notes that Georges
Gurvitch's *Les Tendances actuelles de la philosophie allemande* devotes about 30
percent of its pages to Scheler, with chapters of 86 pages on Scheler, 56 on Husserl,
54 on Lask and Hartmann, and 28 on Heidegger. But there may be an explanation
other than that Gurvitch saw Scheler as the most significant phenomenologist, for as
Gurvitch notes in his preface, the chapters on Husserl and Lask–Hartmann had been
published previously, while the chapter on Scheler was new and was a major
motivation for his bringing out this particular volume.

French, the 1931 *Méditations cartésiennes*.[10] This text, which differs from the German *Cartesianische Meditationen*,[11] was in fact a revised version of Husserl's "Introduction to Transcendental Phenomenology," two lectures – the so-called "Paris Lectures"[12] – that Husserl delivered in Paris at the Sorbonne on February 23 and 25, 1929 in response to an invitation by the Institut d'Études germaniques and the Société Française de Philosophie.

Husserl's own presentation at the Sorbonne did not overwhelm his audience, and the reviews of his *Méditations cartésiennes* in the two leading philosophical journals were unfavorable.[13] But the reception of his work in the early 1930s by the younger generation was much more enthusiastic. In the first volume of her autobiography, Simone de

10   Edmund Husserl, *Méditations cartésiennes. Introduction à la phénoménologie*, trans. Gabrielle Peiffer and Emmanuel Levinas (Paris: Armand Colin, 1931). These "Cartesian Meditations" differ significantly from the further revised German text, which was published following Husserl's death in 1950 as the first volume of Husserl's collected works: *Husserliana 1. Cartesianische Meditationen und Pariser Vorträge*, ed. Stephen Strasser (The Hague: Martinus Nijhoff, 1950/1973). Husserl was apparently not satisfied with the original French translation, which was strongly criticized by his former student Roman Ingarden (Ingarden's criticisms are published in *Husserliana I*, pp. 203–18), and this likely influenced his decision to rework the text before its eventual German publication as the first volume of the *Husserliana*. The *Husserliana* volume was translated into French by Marc de Launey as *Méditations cartésiennes et les conférences de Paris* in *Oeuvres complètes (Husserliana)* (Dordrecht: Kluwer, 1991; Paris: Presses universitaires de France, 1994).

11   English translation: *Cartesian Meditations: An Introduction to Phenomenology*, trans. Dorion Cairns (The Hague: Martinus Nijhoff, 1960).

12   English translation: *The Paris Lectures*, trans. Peter Koestenbaum (The Hague: Martinus Nijhoff, 1964).

13   In the *Revue de métaphysique et de morale* XXXIX, no. 1 (Jan./March 1932): 1–2, and *Revue philosophique de la France et de l'étranger* CXIV, nos. 1–2 (Jan./Feb. 1933): 133–5. Where the first review lists no author, Émile Bréhier authored the review in the *Revue philosophique*. While Bréhier questions whether, contrary to his intentions, Husserl's *cogito* looks more like Kant's than Descartes's, the earlier reviewer comments that the book is "Laborious, difficult, mercilessly abstract," and that "In reading it, one is tempted to ask sometimes whether the effort is not disproportionate to the results" (p. 2). This reviewer concludes, however, that Husserl has produced a considerable body of work and that this book, flawed as it might be, deserves a place in every serious philosophical library. For an account of Husserl's reception in France, see Gene H. Frickey, *The Origins of Phenomenology in France, 1920–1940*, Ph.D. dissertation (Indiana University, 1979). See also Spiegelberg, *The Phenomenological Movement*, pp. 431–5.

Beauvoir relates the story of how Raymond Aron returned to Paris in 1932 for a break from his studies at the French Institute in Berlin and first introduced Sartre and Beauvoir to Husserl's phenomenology at a Montparnasse café.

> We ordered the speciality of the house, apricot cocktails; Aron said, pointing to his glass: "You see my dear fellow, if you are a phenomenologist, you can talk about this cocktail and make philosophy of it!" Sartre turned pale with emotion at this. Here was just the thing he had been longing to achieve for years – to describe objects just as he saw and touched them, and extract philosophy from the process. Aron convinced him that phenomenology exactly fitted in with his special preoccupations: by-passing the antithesis of idealism and realism, affirming simultaneously both the supremacy of reason and the reality of the visible world as it appears to our senses.[14]

Later that evening, Sartre stopped at a bookshop on Boulevard Saint-Michel and purchased Emmanuel Levinas's new book on Husserl,[15] which Beauvoir tells us he was so eager to begin that "he leafed through the volume as he walked along, without even having cut the pages."[16]

The introduction of Husserlian phenomenology was followed in short order by a renewal of interest in Hegel's philosophy, in particular, Hegel's *Phenomenology of Spirit*. Jean Wahl's *La Malheur de la conscience dans la philosophie de Hegel* ("The Unhappy Consciousness in Hegel's Philosophy"), published in 1929, marks the beginning of the Hegel renaissance in France as it offers a reading of Hegel that is more "existential" and less focused on "System." Shortly thereafter, first Koyré and then Alexandre Kojève lectured on Hegel at the École Pratique des Haute Études, and Kojève's seminar in particular, which ran from 1933 to 1939, attracted an audience that included several individuals who would be dominant figures on the French intellectual scene for much of the twentieth century, including among others Raymond Aron, Georges Bataille, André Breton, Aron Gurwitsch, Jacques Lacan, and Maurice Merleau-Ponty. The third major figure in the French Hegel renaissance, Jean Hyppolite, published his French translation of Hegel's *Phenomenology of Spirit* in two parts between 1939

---

[14]   Simone de Beauvoir, *The Prime of Life*, trans. Peter Green (New York: World Publishing, 1962), p. 112.

[15]   Although Beauvoir does not mention the title of Levinas's book, it could only have been *Théorie de l'intuition dans la phénoménologie de Husserl*.

[16]   Beauvoir, *The Prime of Life*, p. 112.

and 1941, following this with his monumental commentary on the *Phenomenology* in 1946, which to this day remains perhaps the dominant interpretation of Hegel in French philosophy.[17]

It is easy to see why Kojève's reading of Hegel would have attracted the young Parisian philosophers. Where the British Hegelians emphasized Hegel's absolute idealism, Kojève highlighted Hegel's *existential* and *political* import as the precursor to Marx. We noted earlier Kojève's materialist reading of Hegel's master–slave dialectic in which the slave becomes free by transcending himself through work. Kojève also emphasizes the inevitable failure of the master to retain mastery insofar as it is the master's "tragic situation" to depend for self-certainty on being "recognized by someone whom he does not recognize." Insofar as the master "can be satisfied only by recognition from one whom he recognizes as worthy of recognizing him," the master finds himself in what Kojève calls the "existential impasse" of depending on an evaluation from one whose judgment he does not value.[18] What Hegel's dialectic tells us, Kojève concludes, is that the future belongs to the slave, that is, the proletarian, who can emancipate himself through his labor.

It was not just the political message of Kojève's reading that drew the younger generation to Hegel, as we can see by comparing his existential–ontological account of self-consciousness with Jean-Paul Sartre's existential ontology. While Sartre is often included among those who attended Kojève's Hegel seminars, the detailed records of registered students kept by the École Pratique des Haute Études do not mention him. That said, it is clear that Sartre was familiar with Kojève's reading of Hegel, and Kojève's influence on several formulations found in *Being and Nothingness* is readily apparent. To cite only one far from insignificant example, consider the following: Sartre defines the being of human being *qua* being-for-itself as "being what it is not and not being what it is [*étant ce qu'il n'est pas et n'étant pas ce qu'il ist*],"[19] while

---

[17] For an account of the importance of Hyppolite's work written at this time, see Georges Canguilhem, "Hegel en France," first published in *Revue d'histoire et de philosophie religieuses* XXVIII–XXIX (1948–9): 282–97, and reprinted in *Magazine littéraire*, no. 293 (Nov. 1991): 26–9.

[18] Alexandre Kojève, *Introduction to the Reading of Hegel*, ed. Raymond Queneau, trans. James H. Nichols, Jr. (New York: Basic Books, 1969), p. 19.

[19] Jean-Paul Sartre, *Being and Nothingness*, trans. Hazel E. Barnes (New York: Philosophical Library, 1956), p. lxvii; *L'Être et le néant* (Paris: Éditions Gallimard, 1943), p. 33.

elsewhere he defines human reality as "a being which is what it is not and which is not what it is [*un être qui est ce qu'il n'est pas et qui n'est pas ce qu'il est*]."[20] Kojève, on the other hand, offers the following dialectical account of the I of self-consciousness: "not to be what it is (as static and given being, as natural being, as 'innate character') and to be (that is, to become) what it is not [*ne pas être ce qu'il est (en tant qu'être statique et donné, en tant qu'être naturel, en tant que 'caractère inné') et être (c'est-à-dire devenir) ce qu'il n'est pas*]." He follows this account with the following gloss: "Thus, this I will be its own product: it will be (in the future) what it has become by negation (in the present) of what it was (in the past), this negation being accomplished with a view to what it will become [*Ce Moi sera ainsi son propre oeuvre: il sera (dans l'avenir) ce qu'il est devenu par la négation (dans le présent) de ce qu'il a été (dans le passé), cette négation étant effectuée en vu de ce qu'il deviendra*]."[21]

The rapid transformation of Hegel's place on the French philosophical scene was truly remarkable. In 1930, Koyré could report to the first philosophical congress on Hegel in The Hague that, unlike the situations in Germany, England, and Italy, a tradition of Hegel studies had never developed in France and there was little to report in terms of French Hegel scholarship. For all practical purposes, Koyré reported, there were no Hegelian studies in France.[22] But 16 years later, following Kojève's lectures, the appearance of *Being and Nothingness*, and the recent appearance of Hyppolite's translation of Hegel's *Phenomenology of Spirit* and his commentary on Hegel, the situation had been so transformed that Merleau-Ponty could comment, in the essay "Hegel's Existentialism," that "All the great philosophical ideas of the past century – the philosophies of Marx and Nietzsche, phenomenology, German existentialism, and psychoanalysis – had their beginnings in Hegel; it was he who started the attempt to explore the irrational and integrate it into an expanded reason which remains

20   Sartre, *Being and Nothingness*, p. 58; *L'Être et le néant*, p. 97.
21   Kojève, *Introduction to the Reading of Hegel*, p. 5; *Introduction à la lecture de Hegel: Leçons sur la "Phénoménologie de l'Esprit" professées de 1933 à 1939 à l'École des Hautes Études*, ed. Raymond Queneau (Paris: Éditions Gallimard, 1947), pp. 12–13.
22   See Alexandre Koyré, "Rapport sur l'état des études hégéliennes en France," in *Études d'histoire de la pensée philosophique* (Paris: Éditions Gallimard, 1971), pp. 225–49. The substance of Koyré's report is a discussion of some of the reasons why French philosophy, which had welcomed Kant, Fichte, and Schelling, had been so unreceptive to Hegel up to that point.

the task of our century."[23] That Hegel's fortunes in France would be viewed less enthusiastically a few decades later must also be noted, as we can document by the following comment, 25 years after Merleau-Ponty's pronouncement, from Foucault's 1970 inaugural address at the Collège de France, that "our age, whether through logic or epistemology, whether through Marx or through Nietzsche, is attempting to flee Hegel." Foucault's point, however, is not as clear as this remark might indicate, for he continues: "But truly to escape Hegel involves an exact appreciation of the price we have to pay to detach ourselves from him. It assumes that we are aware of the extent to which Hegel, insidiously perhaps, is close to us; it implies a knowledge, in that which permits us to think against Hegel, of that which remains Hegelian. We have to determine the extent to which our anti–Hegelianism is possibly one of his tricks directed against us, at the end of which he stands, motionless, waiting for us."[24]

Heidegger, the third of the German influences, was also introduced into France in the early 1930s. Although *Being and Time* would not be translated into French until 1985, translations of Heidegger's essays "What is Metaphysics?" and "On the Essence of Reasons" both appeared in French journals in 1931.[25] In the 1930s and 1940s, however, it is often difficult to distinguish Heidegger's influence from Husserl's, as most of those who read their works (Levinas, Wahl, Sartre, Merleau-Ponty, Ricoeur) tended to interpret each through the other. Although it may be apocryphal, Herbert Spiegelberg relates the following anecdote that speaks to this point: "When asked soon after the War about his early acquaintance with Sartre, Heidegger did not first remember him by name; then he identified him as 'the Frenchman who had always

23 Maurice Merleau-Ponty, "Hegel's Existentialism," in *Sense and Non-Sense*, trans. Hubert L. Dreyfus and Patricia Allen Dreyfus (Evanston, IL: Northwestern University Press, 1964), p. 63. Merleau-Ponty's essay appeared originally in *Les Temps modernes*, vol. 1, no. 7 (April 1946): 1311–19. Two years later Georges Canguilhem opens his essay "Hegel en France" with a similar remark: "Contemporary philosophical thought is dominated by Hegelianism" (p. 282).

24 Michel Foucault, "The Discourse on Language," trans. Rupert Swyer in *The Archaeology of Knowledge*, trans. A. M. Sheridan Smith (New York: Pantheon Books, 1972), p. 235. Insofar as Foucault's Chair had been held previously by Jean Hyppolite, one must wonder how much of this comment is a genuine homage to Hegel and how much of it is an homage to his former teacher and friend Hyppolite.

25 "Was ist Metaphysik?" appears as "Qu'est-ce que la métaphysique?" trans. M. Corbin-Petithenry in *Bifur* (June 1931): 1–27, and "Vom Wesen des Grundes" appears as "De la nature de la cause," trans. A. Bessey in *Recherches philosophiques* (1931–2): 83–124; both were published originally in German in 1929.

confused him with Husserl'."[26] It is clear, however, that as the young philosophers of the 1930s were looking elsewhere than idealism and spiritualism in their desire to make philosophy more concrete, they felt great sympathy toward Heidegger's ontological description of Being-in-the-world and Husserl's phenomenological method for describing that world. As Merleau-Ponty put it in the preface to the *Phenomenology of Perception*, the experience of reading Husserl or Heidegger was not so much an experience "of encountering a new philosophy as of recognizing what [we] had been waiting for."[27]

What Merleau-Ponty might have meant by this is easy to imagine. We've seen what they objected to in Bergson's spiritualist vitalism and Brunschvicg's idealist rationalism. At the outset of *The German Ideology*, Marx and Engels ridiculed their idealist philosophical peers, ending the preface with the following comment:

> Once upon a time a valiant fellow had the idea that men were drowned in water only because they were possessed with the idea of gravity. If they were to knock this notion out of their heads, say by stating it to be a superstition, a religious concept, they would be sublimely proof against any danger from water. His whole life long he fought against the illusion of gravity, of whose harmful results all statistics brought him new and manifold evidence. This honest fellow was the type of the new revolutionary philosophers in Germany.[28]

Paul Nizan opened his attack on the philosophical establishment of his day with a similar sentiment:

> How much longer will the young people who are starting their careers in Philosophy and the amateurs who are now turning to Philosophy be content to work in the dark, unable to answer any questions concerning the import and the scope of the investigations they are pursuing?[29]

[26]   Herbert Spiegelberg, *The Phenomenological Movement: A Historical Introduction* (The Hague: Martinus Nijhoff, 1960), Vol. 2, p. 463n2. Interestingly, this comment does not appear in the third revised edition of Spiegelberg's text, published in 1982.

[27]   Maurice Merleau-Ponty, *Phenomenology of Perception*, trans. Colin Smith (London: Routledge and Kegan Paul, 1962), p. viii.

[28]   Karl Marx and Friedrich Engels, *The German Ideology* (New York: International Publishers, 1970), p. 37.

[29]   Paul Nizan, *The Watchdogs: Philosophers and the Established Order*, trans. Paul Fittingoff (New York: Monthly Review Press, 1971), p. 5.

Not all of Nizan's contemporaries put their objections to the philosophical positions of the older generation in the explicitly political framework that Nizan worked from, but many shared the view that French philosophy had lost touch with the real world and they desired, as the title of Jean Wahl's book made clear, a philosophical approach that would allow them to move toward the concrete. This approach they found in Husserl's method of phenomenological description and Heidegger's account of phenomenological ontology.

While both spiritualism and idealism came with all sorts of metaphysical commitments, phenomenology was, first and foremost, a method and not a theory or doctrine with positive content. For Husserl, the goal of phenomenology was to attain absolutely valid knowledge of things through a method of rigorous and presuppositionless description, and the philosopher was to be a "perpetual beginner" who would take nothing for granted. Instead, armed with the methodological tools of the phenomenological *epoche* – the bracketing or suspension of preconceptions – and the phenomenological reduction, which would allow a "pure description" of the contents of our experience without any interpretive contribution from us, the phenomenologist would, contrary to the idealist or spiritualist, be a *radical empiricist* who, in the words of Husserl's motto, could get "*zu den Sachen selbst*" or "to the things themselves." The way to get to this pure description is the task of the phenomenological method.

The starting point of philosophical reflection, according to Husserl, is what he called the world of the natural attitude or natural standpoint, by which he meant our unsophisticated, unreflective consciousness of the world-as-experienced. Philosophy begins by going beyond the world of the natural standpoint, by establishing a psychical distance between self and world by means of what Husserl called the phenomenological *epoche* or bracketing of the natural standpoint in the sense of placing it within brackets and suspending all our prior assumptions about it. The goal of the *epoche* is thus to bracket all presuppositions about the world – all theoretical assumptions, all scientific, religious, philosophical constructions and interpretations – in order to reveal the underlying structures of the world and thus to get to the things themselves. The *epoche* facilitates the phenomenological reduction, which Husserl considered his most important discovery, by allowing us to "reduce" (*reducere*: to lead back to the source or origin) what we bring to experience and allow the objects of experience to present themselves to us as they are, thereby reducing the cultural world to the world of our immediate experience – the *Lebenswelt* – the world as lived.

While Husserl himself talked about several different kinds of reductions – the phenomenological reduction from objective realities to pure objects of experience; the transcendental reduction from the empirical ego to the transcendental ego; and the eidetic reduction from fact to *eidos* or essence (the necessary structure that makes a thing what it is) – what the French took from Husserlian phenomenology was first and foremost a methodology that grounded philosophical reflection in the immediate world of lived experience (*vécu*).[30]

Beyond this methodological rigor that would do "philosophy as rigorous science,"[31] phenomenology also provided a theory of consciousness that, unlike the idealist account, could remain connected to the world. Following his teacher, Franz Brentano (1838–1917), Husserl argued that consciousness is intentional, which is to say that consciousness is always consciousness-of-something. Where Descartes began with the dyadic structure of the *ego cogito* or "I think," phenomenology starts with a triadic structure *ego cogito cogitatum* or "I think object-thought." In other words, consciousness is always accompanied by an intentional object of consciousness: when we love, we always love *something*; when we fear, we are always afraid *of something*. Consciousness is essentially directed toward what it is not – its object. Which is to say that, contrary to the Cartesian model that was seen to underlie both spiritualism and idealism, phenomenology claimed that every act of consciousness (*cogito* or *noesis*) was conjoined to an object of consciousness (*cogitatum* or *noema*).

By shifting the focus from the relation between the *ego* and the *cogito* to the relation between the act of consciousness and its object, intentionality was seen as a way to escape the subject–object dualism that produced the idealist problem of needing to prove the existence of the world outside consciousness. Instead, the phenomenological account saw *noesis* and *noema* (*cogito* and *cogitatum*) as correlative, thereby shifting attention from the question of the reality of the world to questions of the world's meaning for consciousness. Where Husserl's own account, especially as presented in his lectures in Paris and in the *Méditations cartésiennes*, might have remained too ego-centered and subject to a

30   See Jean André Wahl, *Vers le concret* (Paris: Vrin, 1932), p. 18.
31   This was the title of a famous essay of Husserl's: "Philosophie als strenge Wissenschaft," *Logos* I (1910): 289–314.

critique of being too transcendental—as Sartre made clear in his *Transcendence of the Ego*, when he argued that Husserl's transcendental ego was both superfluous to a phenomenological description and a hindrance that would ultimately defy analysis[32]—Heidegger's account of phenomenology grounded it firmly in a hermeneutic-interpretive description of existence that made the meaning of Being and its basic ontological structures phenomenology's central concern.[33]

With Heidegger, the French found a way to use the phenomenological method to describe the concrete modes of human being. Where Husserl saw phenomenology as offering a method to describe reality free from all interpretation, Heidegger saw in phenomenology a method for doing fundamental ontology, that is, for recuperating and asking once again the question of the meaning of Being. What is to be analyzed by phenomenology, according to Heidegger, is the *meaning* of Being, which entails that it is not just facts but *meaningful* facts that are to be analyzed, and, therefore, interpretation will be a necessary component of phenomenological description insofar as interpretation (*Auslegung*) is the articulation, the laying-out (*legt aus*) of meanings already understood.

Heidegger also gave the French a way to "existentialize" phenomenology insofar as the question of the "meaning of Being" is also the question of what it means to be. Although Heidegger may have wanted this question to remain ontological, his analysis of the various ways of Being of human being – Being-in (*In-sein*), Being-with (*Mitsein*), Being-toward-death (*Sein zum Tode*), Being-in-the-world (*In-der-Welt-sein*), etc. – showed how a phenomenological analysis could be put to use describing the concrete data of human experience: Being-with-others, Being-anxious, Being-guilty, Being-free, and so on. It showed as well that philosophy could no longer divorce itself from history insofar as what it means to be is "to be in time." In other words, the sort of being that a human being is is historical: historicity (*Geschichtlichkeit*) is the temporal mode of the Being of human being. As we will see, what the French ultimately do with phenomenology will depart significantly from its German roots in Husserl, Scheler, and Heidegger. But what cannot be questioned is the enthusiasm with which phenomenology was received by French philosophy students of the 1920s and 1930s, as

---

[32]   See Jean-Paul Sartre, *The Transcendence of the Ego: An Existentialist Theory of Consciousness*, trans. Forrest Williams and Robert Kirkpatrick (New York: Noonday Press, 1957), pp. 40ff.

[33]   See Martin Heidegger, *Being and Time*, section 7.

evidenced, for example, in Wahl's preface to *Vers le concret* or by Merleau-Ponty in the opening paragraph of the preface to the *Phenomenology of Perception*:

> Phenomenology is the study of essences; and according to it, all problems amount to finding definitions of essences: the essence of perception, or the essence of consciousness, for example. But phenomenology is also a philosophy which puts essences back into existence, and does not expect to arrive at an understanding of man and the world from any starting point other than that of their "facticity." It is a transcendental philosophy which places in abeyance the assertions arising out of the natural attitude, the better to understand them; but it is also a philosophy for which the world is always "already there" before reflection begins – as an inalienable presence; and all its efforts are concentrated upon re-achieving a direct and primitive contact with the world, and endowing that contact with a philosophical status.[34]

---

[34] Merleau-Ponty, *Phenomenology of Perception*, p. vii.

3

Existentialism and its Other

Thus far, we see that the story of the importation of phenomenology into France, first via Husserl, and then via Heidegger, overlooks the fact that for much of the 1920s, Scheler is at least as important a phenomenological presence in France as is Husserl. This fact gains in significance when we recall that in the 1930s, it is Gabriel Marcel who is the best-known French representative of the phenomenological approach to philosophy. Moreover, for the French themselves, the appearance of phenomenology is not necessarily identified primarily with Husserl or Heidegger; indeed, in the 1930s, it can be argued that the major phenomenological presence in France was Hegel's.

As we move into the 1940s, a new story takes shape as phenomenology gives way to existentialism, and there is no doubt that the dominant French philosophical development during the late 1930s and 1940s was the emergence of existentialism as a philosophical position. Although largely associated with Jean-Paul Sartre, as has already been mentioned, it was in fact Christian philosopher Gabriel Marcel who should be credited with writing the first work of existentialist philosophy in the twentieth century, his *Metaphysical Journal*, published in 1927. While Marcel pursued his interests in a theologically informed existentialism, Sartre's aggressively atheistic approach to existentialism, put forward in his literary works as well as the *magnum opus* of existentialist philosophy, *Being and Nothingness*, came to be most closely identified with the existentialist approach. With Maurice Merleau-Ponty and Simone de Beauvoir, Sartre founded the influential left-wing journal *Les Temps modernes* in 1946, and for many years this journal was the primary medium through which the existentialists put forward their philosophical and political views.

The range of thinkers and writers associated with existentialism makes it difficult to isolate any set collection of theses to which all would agree. As a philosophy of human existence, existentialism attempts to provide concrete descriptions of the data of human existence: freedom, anxiety, guilt, responsibility, despair, death, relations with others, etc. For the existentialists, philosophy should concern itself with the human subject in its entirety, not just, as with Descartes, the subject as a thinking thing or, as with Kant, the subject as a rational moral agent. The result is that one finds the existential thinkers highlighting different components of what it means to be human: for Marcel, the dominant themes are embodiment and freedom; for Sartre, freedom, facticity, and being-with-others; for Merleau-Ponty, embodiment, temporality, and perception; for Beauvoir, gendered embodiment, freedom, and ethics; for Camus, despair, alienation, and solidarity.

What unites the existentialists is a denial of any given human nature. Instead, human beings exist first, and then define themselves in terms of action. This is what Sartre means when he says that the starting point that unites all existentialists is that "existence precedes essence,"[1] and Beauvoir has the same idea in mind when she claims, "One is not born, but rather becomes, a woman."[2] Focusing for the moment on Sartre's ontological account in *Being and Nothingness*, he distinguishes between two modes of being: being-in-itself (*être-en-soi*) and being-for-itself (*être-pour-soi*). Being-in-itself – the being of objects, of things – is definable in terms of the properties it has. In other words, being-in-itself is what it is, it has a predefined essence. Being-for-itself – the being of human being, of consciousness, of subjects – is not definable in this way. A human being is not sad, or happy, or aggressive in the same way that a table is 3 feet high, sturdy, brown, etc. Rather, a human being makes itself sad or happy through its free choices. Where being-in-itself is what it is, being-for-itself is a being which is what it is not and which is not what it is; it is a lack of being, a project of acquiring being.

---

[1]   Jean-Paul Sartre, *Existentialism and Human Emotions*, trans. Bernard Frechtman (New York: Philosophical Library, 1957), p. 13. This text is the translation of Sartre's lecture, given in Paris on October 29, 1945, in which he defended existentialism against both religious (Catholic) and political (communist) critics. Sartre's text was first published as *L'Existentialisme est un humanisme* (Paris: Les Éditions Nagel, 1946).

[2]   Simone de Beauvoir, *The Second Sex*, trans. H. M. Parshley (New York: Alfred E. Knopf, 1952), p. 301. This is the opening sentence of Book Two of the English translation of *The Second Sex*. The passage continues: "No biological, psychological, or economic fate determines the figure that the human female presents in society; it is civilization as a whole that produces this creature, intermediate between male and eunuch, which is described as feminine."

Sartre clarifies the relationship of being-for-itself and being-in-itself as they relate to human existence in his analysis of freedom and facticity, situation and project. Freedom refers to the fact that nothing is given to human beings, that a human's being is a lack of being with no given essence. Instead, human beings must make themselves through their choices and actions, through their projects, their freely chosen plans of action. What this means is that human being is future-directed: we hurl ourselves into our future in making the free choices we do. Freedom, then, is the choice of my self as a way of being; freedom is not a property of the for-itself, nor does freedom pre-exist its choice. For the existentialists, the question is not: is there freedom of the will? The will just *is* free.

Freedom does not exist in a vacuum, however; freedom exists as engaged in a resisting world confronted by facticity, which is to say that freedom and choice always exist in a situation. In fact, part of the facticity of freedom is that freedom is not able to not be free, or, as Sartre puts it, "man is condemned to be free."[3] More generally, facticity names what is given to freedom, what we are thrown into, the "facts" of the situation: one's birth, one's physical appearance, one's past, one's location, place, environment, other people, etc. Although given, the facticity of the in-itself is never given as brute facts; it is always engaged as resisting or cooperating only in light of the projecting of freedom. For the existentialist, facticity only acquires value and meaning through incorporation into a project, through being engaged in a free project of the for-itself. This is what defines the existential situation: the for-itself is nothing other than its situation and being-in-situation defines human reality (*réalité humaine*)[4] in terms of its being-there (facticity) and being-beyond (transcendence). The situation is neither objective

---

[3] Sartre, *Existentialism and Human Emotions*, p. 23. See also Jean-Paul Sartre, *Being and Nothingness*, trans. Hazel E. Barnes (New York: Philosophical Library, 1956), pp. 509, 553.

[4] *Réalité humaine* was the unfortunate French phrase chosen by Heidegger's first French translator, Henry Corbin, to translate Heidegger's "Dasein." Corbin (1903–78), a philosopher and Germanist who became a leading French scholar of Islam, was a student of Étienne Gilson. He translated several selections from Heidegger, including extracts from *Sein und Zeit* in which the translation of "Dasein" as *réalité humaine* first appears, in *Qu'est-ce que la métaphysique?* (Paris: Éditions Gallimard, 1938). Sartre alludes to this translation in his 1945 lecture *L'Existentialisme est un humanisme*: " . . . *cet être c'est l'homme ou, comme dit Heidegger, la réalité humaine*" (p. 21). Many, including Heidegger himself, have noted the unfortunate subjectivist connotation of this translation which was partly responsible for the French existentializing of Heidegger's primarily ontological analysis in *Being and Time*.

(pure given) nor subjective (pure constitution); it is constituted neither by freedom nor the given: it emerges through the illumination of the given by freedom which gives to it its valence as opportunity or impediment. The situation is thus the reciprocal interpenetration of freedom and facticity: the world in which a free for-itself finds itself confronted by the facticity of the in-itself (one's birth, past, place, environment, death, others) which demands to be incorporated or appropriated into one's project. This, ultimately, is the existential paradox of freedom: freedom and situation are reciprocally constituted, there is freedom only in a situation and there is a situation only through freedom. For the existentialist, we have no excuse for our situation, because all factors in it are freely chosen and have only the meaning that we freely choose to give them. As Sartre melodramatically concludes, "Everything that happens to me is *mine*."[5]

The standard English-language history of French philosophy sees the years between the appearance of *Being and Nothingness* in 1943 and the emergence of structuralism in the late 1950s to be years totally dominated by Sartrean existentialism. According to this history, Sartre is the master thinker, Simone de Beauvoir is his muse, Maurice Merleau-Ponty his right-hand man, and Albert Camus existentialism's prodigal son. While many have already debunked this hagiographical version of the reign of existentialism, there remains a sense that although this story is somewhat of a caricature, it bears, like most caricatures, a strong resemblance to the truth. But while this may resemble the truth insofar as we consider existentialism as a cultural presence in France, if we restrict our focus to the philosophical world, it is seriously mistaken. That is to say, while there is little question that Sartre was the dominant intellectual in France during these years, and *Les Temps modernes* the dominant cultural journal, it is not at all clear that Sartre was the dominant *philosophical* presence. Sartre was indeed a dominant cultural presence who had a profound influence on the reading public through his essays and plays as well as his imprimatur. For example, Sartre not only influenced the postcolonial critiques of Frantz Fanon, Albert Memmi, Aimé Césaire, and others; he also used his influence, by writing prefaces, to help these writers to find an audience. In addition to writing prefaces for Fanon's 1961 *The Wretched of the Earth*,[6] and

---

[5] Sartre, *Being and Nothingness*, p. 554.
[6] Trans. Constance Farrington (New York: Grove Press, 1968).

Memmi's 1957 *The Colonizer and the Colonized*,[7] Sartre also served on
the initial editorial board of the important journal *Présence Africaine*,
founded in 1947, and wrote a preface, "Orphée noir," to Léopold Sédar
Senghor's important 1948 literary collection *Anthologie de la nouvelle
poésie nègre et malgache de langue française.*[8] But insofar as Sartre
remained almost entirely outside the academic, and in particular, the
university world, several others had as much if not more impact on
developments in the evolution of French philosophy. First among
these is Merleau-Ponty, whose teaching at the École Normale Supérieure, the Sorbonne, and the Collège de France had a profound influence on many of the dominant philosophers in the second half of the
twentieth century.

We will return in a moment to the role played by Merleau-Ponty, but
first we must acknowledge that there is in fact an entire tradition in
French philosophy that developed alongside the emergence of existentialism and that, while largely unrecognized in the English-speaking
philosophical world and not well known outside French academic
circles, has been widely recognized in France as playing a major role
in the ultimate unseating of existentialism as a dominant philosophical
position in the second half of the century. In his 1978 "Introduction" to
the English translation of Georges Canguilhem's *The Normal and the
Pathological*, Michel Foucault tells a story of the rise of "contemporary
philosophy in France" that is worth recalling here in some detail.
According to Foucault's story, there are in fact two modalities of
philosophizing that emerge from the introduction of Husserlian
phenomenology in France in the late 1920s. On the one hand, there is
the "philosophy of experience, of sense and of subject" that he identifies
with Sartre and Merleau-Ponty. But in addition to this philosophy of
the subject which emphasizes reflexivity and consciousness, there was,
according to Foucault, another Husserlian trajectory, one associated
with formalism, intuitionism, and the theory of science. This second
modality of French philosophizing produced "a philosophy of knowledge, of rationality and of concept" that Foucault associates with the

---

[7] Trans. Howard Greenfeld (New York: Orion Press, 1965).

[8] Léopold Sédar Senghor, ed., *Anthologie de la nouvelle poésie nègre et malgache de
langue française* (Paris: Presses universitaires de France, 1948). Sartre's "Orphée
noir" was republished in *Situations III* (Paris: Éditions Gallimard, 1949), pp. 229–
86. It appears in English translation by John MacCombie, revised by Robert
Bernasconi, as "Black Orpheus" in *Race*, ed. Robert Bernasconi (Oxford: Blackwell,
2001), pp. 115–42.

work of Gaston Bachelard, Jean Cavaillès, and Georges Canguilhem.[9] In "La Vie: L'Expérience et la science," which was a revision of this essay for a special issue of the *Revue de métaphysique et de morale* devoted to Canguilhem, and the final essay that Foucault prepared for publication, he added Alexandre Koyré's name to Bachelard, Cavaillès, and Canguilhem as representatives of the philosophy of the concept. More importantly, however, he now traced this cleavage in French philosophy back to the nineteenth century, suggesting that we see the same two strands in the distinctions between "Bergson and Poincaré, Lachelier and Couturat, Maine de Biran and Comte."[10]

What the French refer to as *épistémologie* is largely associated with this second modality, and the importance of this tradition can be seen through the rise of structuralism and what followed structuralism in France.[11] And as Foucault correctly notes, this tradition first appeared in France at the same time as did existentialism. Like existential phenomenology, this epistemological tradition arose in response to the spiritualist tendencies of French philosophy in the late nineteenth and early twentieth centuries. But unlike existentialism, the orientation of this epistemological tradition pointed less toward the problems of classical metaphysics and more toward the physical and natural sciences. Bachelard submitted his *thèse d'Etat, Essai sur la connaissance approchée*

[9] Michel Foucault, "Introduction" to Georges Canguilhem, *The Normal and the Pathological*, trans. Carolyn R. Fawcett in collaboration with Robert S. Cohen (New York: Zone Books, 1991), pp. 8–9; *Dits et écrits III* (Paris: Éditions Gallimard, 1994), p. 430.

[10] Michel Foucault, "La Vie: L'Expérience et la science," *Revue de métaphysique et de morale*, no. 1 (Jan./March 1985): 3–14. This essay is reprinted in *Dits et écrits IV* (Paris: Éditions Gallimard, 1994), and the citation appears on p. 764. Although Foucault's distinction here is surely important, the two traditions need not have developed so distinctly. Not only do we find Merleau-Ponty turning toward structuralist ideas in his final years, a turning that might have brought these two traditions together, were it not for Merleau-Ponty's untimely death in 1961. But there was another untimely death that might have produced an altogether different relationship between the two traditions, namely the death of Jean Cavaillès. One of the founders of the French Resistance, Cavaillès was captured by the Germans and executed in 1944, at the age of 41.

[11] While it would be impossible to prove, one might wonder whether, outside France, the existential–phenomenological tradition's initial dismissal of structuralism and hostility toward poststructuralists like Foucault, Deleuze, or Derrida is related to its almost total lack of awareness of the role played by this "epistemological" tradition in the education of all students of philosophy at the Sorbonne or École Normale Supérieure from the mid-1940s onward.

("Essay on Approximate Knowledge") in 1927, while Canguilhem was a
normalien with Sartre and submitted his first thesis, on Comte, in 1926
and his second thesis, *Essai sur quelques problèmes concernant le normal et
le pathologique* ("Essay on Some Problems Concerning the Normal and
the Pathological"), in 1943, the same year Sartre published *Being and
Nothingness*. Where Sartre and Marcel chose to work outside the dominant French educational institutions, Bachelard and Canguilhem were
major figures within these institutions, occupying in succession the
position of Director of the Institut d'Histoire des Sciences et des
Techniques and Chair in the History and Philosophy of Science at the
Sorbonne from 1940 to 1971.

Jean Cavaillès, for his part, at the age of 28 came to occupy the
influential position of *agrégé-répétiteur* ("*caïman*") at the École Normale
Supérieure. More so than either Bachelard or Canguilhem, Cavaillès
was deeply interested in phenomenology, as his interest in mathematics
led him to Husserl, and in particular, Husserl's *Formal and Transcendental Logic* and *Logical Investigations*. That a philosopher interested in
science, mathematics, and logic would be drawn to Husserl should not
be surprising when we consider, for example, remarks like the following, from Husserl's chapter on "The Idea of Pure Logic": "Our treatment has shown that questions as to the ideal conditions of the
possibility of *knowledge* in general, and of theoretical knowledge in
particular, ultimately leads us back to certain *laws*, whose roots are to
be found purely in the content of knowledge, or of the categorial
concepts that it falls under, and which are so abstract that they contain
no reference to knowledge as an act of a knowing subject."[12] While not
denying that phenomenology offered a philosophy of consciousness,
insofar as each act of consciousness appeared conjoined to an object of
consciousness, Cavaillès concluded that phenomenology provided not
only "a philosophy of consciousness but [also] a philosophy of the
concept which can provide a theory of science."[13] Cavaillès had a
profound influence on many of the students with whom he worked in
his four years as *caïman* and, had he lived longer and had the influence
on subsequent generations of *normaliens* that others in his position

---

[12]   Edmund Husserl, *Logical Investigations*, Vol. 1, trans. J. N. Findlay (New York:
       Humanities Press, 1970), p. 234.
[13]   Jean Cavaillès, "On Logic and the Theory of Science," trans. Theodore J. Kisiel in
       Phenomenology and the Natural Sciences, ed. Joseph Kockelmans and Theodore
       J. Kisiel (Evanston, IL: Northwestern University Press, 1970), p. 409.

exercised – for example Althusser, who served as *caïman* from 1948 to 1980 – one must wonder whether someone like Foucault, who clearly situates himself in the tradition of the "philosophy of the concept," would have come to be as hostile to phenomenology as he was.[14]

Foucault's distinction between a philosophy of the subject and a philosophy of the concept, between a tradition that attends to reflexivity and one that focuses on epistemology, is important for several reasons. First, it accurately reflects the fact that existentialism was not the only French philosophy in the years between Sartre's and Marcel's early works and the 1960s. Second, it acknowledges that there were, in fact, two distinct receptions of Husserlian phenomenology in France: one that attended to the Husserl of *Ideas I* and gave rise to existential phenomenology (Sartre, Merleau-Ponty) and phenomenological hermeneutics (Ricoeur), and another that attended to the Husserl of *Formal and Transcendental Logic* and *Logical Investigations* and gave rise to phenomenological reflections on science and mathematics that are much more sympathetic to the concerns of analytic philosophy than to Heidegger (Cavaillès, as well as his students Jean-Toussaint Desanti, Jules Vuillemin, Gilles-Gaston Granger). Third and finally, Foucault's distinction acknowledges that there was already an indigenous philosophical tradition in France to which the supporters of structuralism could appeal as they sought to challenge the hegemony of existentialism and the philosophy of the subject.

---

[14] See, here, Foucault's comment in the foreword to the English edition of *The Order of Things* (New York: Random House, 1970), p. xiv, where he both denies that he adheres to the methods of structuralism, and specifies phenomenology—insofar as it "gives absolute priority to the observing subject" and leads to a transcendental consciousness—as the one (and only?) philosophical position toward which he has no sympathy. Elsewhere, however, Foucault acknowledges that this "philosophy of the concept" which gave rise to analyses of the history of the sciences, "is no doubt rooted in phenomenology" and that "the historical problem of the historicity of the sciences has some relations and analogies, echoes up to a certain point, with this problem of the constitution of meaning" that is central to phenomenology as well as structuralism. (Michel Foucault, "What is Critique?" Lecture given at the Sorbonne to the Société française de Philosophie on May 27, 1978, trans. Kevin Paul Geiman in *What is Enlightenment? Eighteenth-Century Answers and Twentieth-Century Questions*, ed. James Schmidt [Berkeley: University of California Press, 1996], p. 390.)

4

Structuralism and the
Challenge to Philosophy

The year 1960 is often viewed as the year that existentialism as a living philosophy in France ended: Albert Camus, who was still largely associated with the existentialist movement, died in a car accident on January 4; Merleau-Ponty published *Signs*, a collection which opened with essays on Saussure, linguistics, sociology, and Lévi-Strauss; and Sartre, who remained the dominant presence in existentialist philosophy, published *The Critique of Dialectical Reason*, which he himself described as a "structural, historical anthropology."[1] But focusing on the events of 1960 would be deceptive, because the intervention of structuralism was, by 1960, already well under way, as was the diminishing of the influence of philosophy in general. That is to say, by 1960, structuralism had already emerged as a dominant intellectual paradigm, and the institutional importance of the Department of Philosophy at the Sorbonne was already being challenged by the more interdisciplinary departments at the École Normale Supérieure and the centers of research in the human sciences at the École Pratique des Hautes Études, as well as the Sorbonne's own newly formed Department of Sociology, led by Raymond Aron.[2]

The emergence of structuralism as a dominant intellectual force can be tied to many factors, not the least of which being a number of political and historical events – the end of World War II and the beginnings of the

---

[1] Jean-Paul Sartre, *Search for a Method*, trans. Hazel E. Barnes (New York: Knopf, 1963), p. xxxiv. It is worth noting, however, that Sartre refrains from using the adjective *structurale*, which one finds in Lévi-Strauss's *Anthropologie structurale*, using instead what one might regard as a Heideggerian ontic term, *structurelle*. Peter Caws suggests that this might indicate Sartre's emphasizing the structuring activity rather than the structured system. See his *Sartre* (London: Routledge and Kegan Paul, 1979), p. 143.

[2] Aron was appointed to a Professor's Chair in Sociology in 1957, and by 1960 had already become an influential presence on the Sorbonne faculty whose courses drew students away from philosophy and toward the human sciences.

Cold War, the Soviet invasion of Hungary, colonial unrest in Vietnam and Algeria – that left many politically active students dissatisfied with the relatively ahistorical and otherworldly reflections of the Sorbonne philosophers. Some, following a path taken earlier by Lévi-Strauss, left philosophy altogether. Others, intrigued by the seminars and figure of Jacques Lacan, thought a psychoanalytic understanding of language and the unconscious could make better sense of events than traditional philosophical reflection.

That students of philosophy would turn to the human sciences is not so strange when one recalls the proximity of philosophy and the human sciences in the French educational system. Until 1965, a student of philosophy was required to undertake advanced work and be certified[3] in one of the sciences, whether hard (physics, mathematics, chemistry, biology) or soft (psychology, ethnology, prehistory)[4] in order to qualify to take the *agrégation de philosophie* and receive a teaching credential in philosophy.[5] In addition, because the field of sociology was not a subject recognized for advanced degrees in France, many of the great French sociologists and anthropologists, including Émile Durkheim, Lucien Lévy-Bruhl, Claude Lévi-Strauss, Raymond Aron, Henri Lefebvre, and Pierre Bourdieu, had their educational training and advanced degrees in philosophy and, for those working at universities, taught within departments of philosophy. But once both a *licence* and *Doctorat de troisième cycle* (undergraduate and doctoral degrees) were approved in

---

[3] To be certified, one had to take a series of courses, upon completion of which one took an examination that, if passed, resulted in the awarding of a *Certificat*.

[4] Prehistory is defined in André Lalande's *Vocabulaire technique et critique de la philosophie* (Paris: Presses universitaires de France, 1928) as: "Part of history that is too ancient to be known by written documents or traditions, and that can only be induced from existing material traces, or reconstructed by reasoning from *a priori* considerations" (18th ed., p. 814).

[5] The requirement that one be certified in a science prior to registering to take the *agrégation* was mandated in the Decree of June 18, 1904, upon the initiative of Léon Brunschvicg. See René Boirel, *Brunschvicg, sa vie, son oeuvre* (Paris: Presses universitaires de France, 1964), p. 19. This requirement was set aside by the Decree of May 26, 1964. Michel Serres discusses the significance of being certified in a science with Bruno Latour in *Conversations on Science, Culture, and Time*, trans. Roxanne Lapidus (Ann Arbor: University of Michigan Press, 1995), p. 35. The fact that significant work in a science was required for an academic career in philosophy explains, in part, why Merleau-Ponty and Foucault wrote their first works in conjunction with research in psychiatry and psychiatric hospitals, and why a number of the important French philosophers, including among others Jean Cavaillès, Gilles Deleuze, Michel Serres, and Alain Badiou, are familiar with and make use of advanced concepts in mathematics.

sociology in April 1958, largely on the initiative of Raymond Aron, it became possible for students interested in the theoretical study of society to completely avoid doing advanced work in departments of philosophy. In fact, according to Pierre Bourdieu and Jean-Claude Passeron, ten years after the creation of the *licence* in sociology, there were "in Paris as many students registered for this new degree . . . as there [were] candidates for the Degree in Philosophy."[6]

In addition to these institutional features that facilitated the emergence of structuralism in France, there was also an important philosophical development at work, one that had its analogue in the previous emergence of existentialism. For, as the transformation from spiritualism to existentialism was motivated by the discovery of three German philosophers – Hegel, Husserl, and Heidegger – a philosophical opening for structuralism was cleared by the rediscovery of three other German thinkers, those named by Paul Ricoeur in 1965 the "masters of suspicion" – Marx, Nietzsche, and Freud.[7] While these thinkers are more commonly associated with French philosophy *after* structuralism, it was really the structuralists' desire to locate the underlying structures of kinship, society, or the unconscious that led them to read Marx, Nietzsche, and Freud as kindred spirits who sought to decipher the superstructural world in terms of underlying infrastructural relations of economic forces and class struggle, relations of normative forces and wills to power, and relations of psychic forces and unconscious libidinal desires, respectively.[8]

The emergence of structuralism is often discussed in terms of the appearance of several master thinkers – Claude Lévi-Strauss, Jacques

---

6   Pierre Bourdieu and Jean-Claude Passeron, "Sociology and Philosophy in France Since 1945: Death and Resurrection of a Philosophy without a Subject," *Social Research* 34, no. 1 (Spring 1967): 193.

7   See Paul Ricoeur, *Freud and Philosophy: An Essay on Interpretation*, trans. Denis Savage (New Haven, CT: Yale University Press, 1970), p. 32. For the first time in almost thirty years, Nietzsche begins to appear on the *Programme* for the *agrégation de philosophie* in the late fifties (1958) and sixties. Charles Soulié suggests that his appearance might "constitute a concession of the *jury d'agrégation* to modernity" insofar as Nietzsche was the "most canonical" of the three "masters of suspicion." (Charles Soulié, "Anatomie du goût philosophique," *Actes de la recherche en sciences sociales*, no. 109 [October 1995]: 12.)

8   For a good account of what resources the structuralists found in Nietzsche, Freud, and Marx, see Michel Foucault, "Nietzsche, Freud, Marx," trans. Alan D. Schrift in *Transforming the Hermeneutic Context: From Nietzsche to Nancy*, ed. Alan D. Schrift and Gayle L. Ormiston (Albany: State University of New York Press, 1990), pp. 59–67.

Lacan, Roland Barthes, Louis Althusser – whose work revolutionized how one thought about the human sciences, psychoanalysis, literature, and Marx. That those thinkers who are most closely identified with the so-called "death of the subject" should have become themselves the subjects of fascination bordering on hero worship is an irony worth noting. Some of these individuals – most notably Lacan – certainly cultivated the mystique that surrounded them and used it to further their theoretical projects. But that structuralism could emerge with such apparent speed and eclipse the enormous intellectual presence of Sartrean existentialism should be explained not by the cults of personality surrounding these master thinkers, but by the institutional forces that were at work and the personal interactions that took place in the French academy during the years that Sartre, Beauvoir, and *Les Temps modernes* were so influential outside the academy.

In the history of the development of structuralism in France, a major role is played by the Russian linguist Roman Jakobson (1896–1982). One of the founders of the Moscow Circle and a leading figure of Russian formalism, Jakobson left Russia for Prague in 1920, and his turn away from formalist and toward structuralist linguistics is marked by the founding of the Linguistic Circle of Prague (the "Prague School") in 1926. In his collaborations with other linguists, most notably fellow Russian émigré Nikolai Troubetzkoy (1890–1938), he was largely responsible for the development of phonology. It was in Prague that Jakobson first learned of the Swiss linguist, and creator of many of the basic concepts of structuralism, Ferdinand de Saussure and his *Course in General Linguistics*. In fact, while Saussure's *Course* makes frequent reference to a science that will study language as a "system," it was in Jakobson's presentation in Prague at the First International Congress of Slavists in October 1929 that the word "structuralism" first appears:

> Were we to comprise the leading ideas of present-day science in its most various manifestations, we could hardly find a more appropriate designation than *structuralism*. Any set of phenomena examined by contemporary science is treated not as a mechanical agglomeration but as a structural whole, and the basic task is to reveal the inner, whether static or developmental, laws of this system.[9]

---

[9] Originally published in the Czech weekly ČIN on October 31, 1929, Jakobson cites this remark at the start of his essay "Retrospect" in Roman Jakobson, *Selected Writings, Vol. II* (The Hague: Mouton, 1971), p. 711. Bertil Malmberg goes so far

In 1941, Jakobson emigrated to the United States, where he taught first in New York at the École Libre des Hautes Études. Jakobson's linguistic interests extended to ethnography and folklore and, in 1942, the dean of this French university-in-exile, fellow Russian émigré Alexandre Koyré, introduced Jakobson to another exile, Claude Lévi-Strauss. The two became friends, and from Jakobson Lévi-Strauss learned the basic principles of Saussurean linguistics. More importantly, their encounters in New York led Lévi-Strauss to recognize that the Saussurean analysis of sign systems could be extended beyond linguistic sign systems. With this realization, structuralism as a general method of analysis began.

Jakobson played an equally important role in the intellectual development of Jacques Lacan, to whom he was introduced by Lévi-Strauss in 1950 and with whom he became good friends. Like Lévi-Strauss, Lacan first learned of Saussurean linguistics from Jakobson and, again like Lévi-Strauss, he quickly realized that the structuralist methods of linguistic analysis could be extended to psychoanalysis and the sign systems of the unconscious. Where Lévi-Strauss had argued, in *Structural Anthropology*, that "the kinship system is a language,"[10] Lacan, for his part, would claim that, for example, psychoanalytic interpretation is based "on the fact that the unconscious is structured in the most radical way like a language, that a material operates in it according to certain laws, which are the same laws as those discovered in the study of actual languages, languages that are or were actually spoken,"[11] and that "what the psychoanalytic experience discovers in the unconscious is the whole structure of language."[12]

---

as to refer to Jakobson's propositions presented in The Hague at the First International Congress of Linguists, April 10–15, 1928, as the "official birthdate of European structuralism" ("Linguistique européene et linguistique américaine à la lumière du débat actuel," *Moderna språk* 67, [1973]: 366). Jakobson's remarks were in fact written in October 1927 and approved and co-signed by S. Karcevskij (1884–1955) and N. Troubetzkoy.

[10]   Claude Lévi-Strauss, *Structural Anthropology*, trans. Claire Jacobson and Brooke Grundrest Schoepf (New York: Basic Books, 1963), p. 47.

[11]   Jacques Lacan, "The Direction of the Treatment and the Principles of its Power," in *Écrits: A Selection*, trans. Alan Sheridan (New York: W. W. Norton, 1977), p. 234.

[12]   Lacan, "The Agency of the Letter in the Unconscious or Reason since Freud," in *Écrits*, p. 147.

Among the institutional forces that facilitated the rise of structuralism, and a factor that has not been sufficiently recognized, is the important academic position during the 1950s occupied by someone whose name is more commonly associated with the existentialists than the structuralists. I refer here to none other than Maurice Merleau-Ponty, who played a major role in the success of structuralism.[13] In his teaching at the Sorbonne, Merleau-Ponty encouraged his philosophy students to explore psychoanalysis, child psychology, and linguistics, and he was one of the first to indicate the importance of the work of Ferdinand de Saussure. In his 1951 lecture "On the Phenomenology of Language," presented at the First International Phenomenology Colloquium in Brussels, he credits Saussure for noting that the elements in a language do not individually signify anything and should not be considered as vehicles for the transmission of meaning; rather "each of them signifies only its difference in respect to the others... and as this is true of them all, there are only differences of signification in a language."[14] In his inaugural lecture at the Collège de France in 1952, he noted that the theory of signs that was developed in modern linguistics perhaps offers a conception of historical meaning that gets "beyond the opposition of *things* versus *consciousness*" and that Saussure "could have sketched a new philosophy of history."[15]

In addition to introducing the thought of Saussure into the academy, Merleau-Ponty was also a strong supporter of the work and career of Claude Lévi-Strauss. Shortly after his own election in 1952 to the Collège de France, he played a major role in Lévi-Strauss's election to the Chair in Social Anthropology, and his subsequent essay, "From Mauss to Claude Lévi-Strauss," strongly defended Lévi-Strauss's

[13]   Though not himself a structuralist, Pierre Bourdieu speaks to Merleau-Ponty's drawing students away from existentialism: "I never really got into the existentialist mood. Merleau-Ponty was something different, at least in my view. He was interested in the human sciences and in biology, and he gave you an idea of what thinking about immediate present-day concerns can be like when it doesn't fall into the sectarian over-simplifications of political discussion ... He seemed to represent one potential way out of the philosophical babble found in academic institutions." (Pierre Bourdieu, "Fieldwork in Philosophy," in *In Other Words: Essays Towards a Reflexive Sociology*, trans. Matthew Adamson [Stanford, CA: Stanford University Press, 1990], p. 5.)

[14]   Maurice Merleau-Ponty, "On the Phenomenology of Language," in *Signs*, trans. Richard C. McCleary (Evanston, IL: Northwestern University Press, 1964), p. 88.

[15]   Maurice Merleau-Ponty, *In Praise of Philosophy*, trans. John Wild and James M. Edie (Evanston, IL: Northwestern University Press, 1963), pp. 54–5.

reading of Mauss and his approach to anthropology while making clear Merleau-Ponty's own appreciation of what structuralism had to offer philosophy:

> This notion of structure, whose present good fortune in all domains responds to an intellectual need, establishes a whole system of thought. For the philosopher, the presence of structure outside us in natural and social systems and within us as symbolic function points to a way beyond the subject–object correlation which has dominated philosophy from Descartes to Hegel. By showing us that man is eccentric to himself and that the social finds its center only in man, structure particularly enables us to understand how we are in a sort of circuit with the socio-historical world.[16]

While Merleau-Ponty saw structuralism and phenomenology as compatible,[17] with the former providing an objective analysis of underlying social structures that would complement the latter's description of lived experience,[18] the structuralists themselves were much less convinced of the need for or value of phenomenology as they engaged in their various structuralist inquiries. In part, this was due to their association of phenomenology with a philosophy of the subject, a philosophy that their theoretical anti-humanism had to oppose. But in part, this was also a consequence of their polemic against the figure of Sartre, a figure associated with both existentialism and phenomenology and one who each of the four dominant structuralist thinkers chose to establish as the "other" (sometimes an other who looks more like a

---

[16] Maurice Merleau-Ponty, "From Mauss to Claude Lévi-Strauss," in *Signs*, trans. Richard C. McCleary (Evanston, IL: Northwestern University Press, 1964), p. 123.

[17] Although it surely did not have consequences quite as significant as Merleau-Ponty's actions in terms of the turn from existentialism to structuralism, one might also note Simone de Beauvoir's favorable 1949 review of Lévi-Strauss's *The Elementary Structures of Kinship* in *Les Temps modernes*. Following a relatively straightforward recounting of Lévi-Strauss's theses concerning the incest prohibition, Beauvoir concludes by noting the fundamental concordance between some of Lévi-Strauss's descriptions and the theses of existentialism concerning facticity and being-with-others. She situates Lévi-Strauss's thought in the "grand humanist current that considers human existence as furnishing within itself its own justification," and concludes her review by advising her readers that "one must read [this book]." (Simone de Beauvoir, *"Les Structures élémentaires de la parénte* par Claude Lévi-Strauss," *Les Temps modernes* [November 1949]: 943–9, esp. 949.) Unfortunately for the future of existentialism, many took her advice.

[18] See Merleau-Ponty, "From Mauss to Claude Lévi-Strauss," p. 119.

caricature of Sartre) against whom their theoretical projects were the required alternative. We thus find Lévi-Strauss, most notably in the closing chapter of *The Savage Mind*—published in 1962 and dedicated "To the memory of Maurice Merleau-Ponty"—setting Sartre up as the definitive representative of humanism against whom he puts forward the rhetoric of the "death of the subject," writing that "I believe the ultimate goal of the human sciences to be not to constitute, but to dissolve man."[19] Lévi-Strauss's entire closing chapter, "History and Dialectic," is a response to Sartre's *Critique of Dialectical Reason*, and his rhetoric of the "dissolution of man" must be read in the context of this Sartrean text.

It is important to note that Lévi-Strauss's polemical response was not unprovoked, as Sartre concluded *Search for a Method*—the prefatory essay to the *Critique*—with a direct attack on Marxist anthropology for having expelled man from Marxist knowledge: "The foundation of Marxism, as a historical, structural anthropology, is man himself inasmuch as human existence and the comprehension of the human are inseparable . . . In other words, the foundation of anthropology is man himself, not as the object of practical Knowledge, but as a practical organism producing Knowledge as a moment of its *praxis*."[20] Throughout *Search for a Method*, Sartre returns to this rhetoric, arguing that "contemporary Marxism . . . has entirely lost the meaning of what it is to be a man . . . Our intention is not . . . to reject Marxism in the name of a third path or of an idealist humanism, but to reconquer man within Marxism," and again that "What contemporary Marxists have forgotten is that man, alienated, mystified, reified, etc., still remains a man. When Marx speaks of reification, he does not mean to show that we are transformed into things but that we are men condemned to live humanly the condition of material things."[21]

For Lévi-Strauss, on the other hand, Sartre is guilty of overstating the domain of dialectical reason and excluding any role for "analytical reason." Only by supplementing dialectical reason with analytical reason, he argues, can one illuminate the conceptual schemes that mediate between *praxis* and practices, and it is precisely the task of the anthropologist to bring to light these conceptual schemes. Lévi-Strauss argues

[19]   Claude Lévi-Strauss, *The Savage Mind* (Chicago: University of Chicago Press, 1966), p. 247.
[20]   Sartre, *Search for a Method*, pp. 176, 179.
[21]   Sartre, *Search for a Method*, pp. 82–3, p. 104n.

that, like Marx before him, Sartre privileges history as the science of *praxis* from which human practices follow directly, and he concludes that it is because Sartre sees an unmediated link between *praxis* and practices that Sartre could propose a method – the "progressive–regressive method" – according to which one could understand a human being in terms of "the circularity of the material conditions and the mutual conditioning of the human relations established on that basis."[22] While not dismissing history, Lévi-Strauss claims that it is ultimately ethnology, through a theory of superstructures, that will disclose the conceptual schemes as "empirical and intelligible entities" that mediate between human *praxis* and social practices.[23] And, insofar as "he who begins by steeping himself in the allegedly self-evident truths of introspection never emerges from them," Sartre remains, like Descartes before him, "the prisoner of his *Cogito*." Where Descartes's *Cogito* was psychological and individual, "by sociologizing the *Cogito*, Sartre merely exchanges one prison for another. Each subject's group and period now take the place of timeless consciousness."[24] And, as a consequence, Lévi-Strauss concludes that far from getting to the right meaning in history, "in Sartre's system, history plays exactly the part of a myth."[25]

The polemic against Sartre is by no means limited to Lévi-Strauss, though the other structuralist figures do not usually confront him so directly, as we can see with Louis Althusser implicating Sartre as the champion of the humanistic approach to Marx, against whom he directs his project of reading Marx as a scientist of social forces:

> Strictly in respect to theory . . . one can and must speak openly of *Marx's theoretical anti-humanism*, and see in the *theoretical anti-humanism* the absolute (negative) precondition of the (positive) knowledge of the human world itself, and of its practical transformation. It is impossible to *know* anything about men except on the absolute precondition that the philosophical (theoretical) myth of man is reduced to ashes. So any thought that appeals to Marx for any kind of restoration of a theoretical anthropology or humanism is no more than ashes, theoretically.[26]

---

22 Sartre, *Search for a Method*, p. 75.
23 Lévi-Strauss, *The Savage Mind*, p. 130.
24 Lévi-Strauss, *The Savage Mind*, p. 249.
25 Lévi-Strauss, *The Savage Mind*, p. 254.
26 Louis Althusser, *For Marx*, trans. Ben Brewster (New York: Pantheon, 1969), pp. 229–30. Sartre is also an implied target in Althusser's essay "Marxism is not a Historicism," in Louis Althusser and Étienne Balibar, *Reading Capital*, trans. Ben Brewster (London: New Left Books, 1970), pp. 119–44. Althusser is not always so

Similarly, there can be little doubt that Roland Barthes's *Writing Degree Zero* is a manifesto for structuralist literary theory in opposition to Sartre's own *What is Literature?* Although Barthes's text was published in 1953 and Sartre's in 1948, most of Sartre's text in fact appeared in 1947 in the pages of *Les Temps modernes*, while sections of Barthes's work also appeared in 1947 in the newspaper *Combat*, edited at the time by Albert Camus. Lest there be doubt that Barthes is responding to Sartre, consider that although the opening sections of each book are titled, in English translation, "What is Writing?", this masks a significant distinction insofar as it translates Sartre's "*Qu'est-ce qu'écrire?*" while Barthes writes "*Qu'est-ce que l'écriture?*"[27] Translating these two questions as "What is Writing?" thus obscures the fact that whereas Sartre's focus is on the activity (the verb *écrire*) of a subject ("What is [it] to write?"), Barthes instead draws attention to the object produced (the noun *écriture*) as a structure ("What is writing?").

Lacan's relation to Sartre is more complicated in that both draw heavily from Kojève's interpretation of Hegel and, in particular, from the analysis of desire, which Lacan and Sartre both establish as a defining characteristic of human being. As a consequence, while often making reference to Sartre, and especially to images from his fiction and his examples in *Being and Nothingness*, Lacan rarely challenges his positions directly.[28] This is not surprising inasmuch as Sartre and Lacan both understand desire as lack. Lacan designates the function of desire "as *manque-à-être*, a 'want-to-be,' " and he defines psychoanalysis itself as being "engaged in the central lack in which the subject experiences himself [*sic*] as desire."[29] Sartre, on the other hand, identifies freedom, consciousness, and being-for-itself with desire as lack:

---

indirect, as we see for example in his "Reply to John Lewis," where he expresses doubt concerning whether we are likely to find anything that will help us to understand history in the pages of *Critique of Dialectical Reason*. See Louis Althusser, *Essays in Self-Criticism*, trans. Grahame Lock (London: New Left Books, 1976), pp. 59–61.

27   Susan Sontag discusses Barthes's text as a rejoinder to Sartre's in her preface to the English translation of *Writing Degree Zero*, trans. Annette Lavers and Colin Smith (New York: Hill and Wang, 1968), pp. x–xvi.

28   One important exception is his discussion of the gaze in *The Four Fundamental Concepts of Psycho-Analysis*, ed. Jacques-Alain Miller, trans. Alan Sheridan (New York: W. W. Norton, 1978), pp. 82–5, where he credits Sartre for a brilliant description of the gaze in *Being and Nothingness* while totally rejecting Sartre's phenomenological analysis of the gaze.

29   Lacan, *The Four Fundamental Concepts of Psycho-Analysis*, pp. 29, 265.

The for-itself is defined ontologically as the *lack of being*, and possibility belongs to the for-itself as that which it lacks . . . The for-itself chooses because it is lack; freedom is really synonymous with lack. Freedom is the concrete mode of being of the lack of being . . . Fundamentally man is *the desire to be*, and the existence of this desire is not to be established by an empirical induction; it is the result of an *a priori* description of the being of the for-itself, since desire is a lack and since the for-itself is the being which is to itself its own lack of being.[30]

But while their accounts of desire may be similar, Lacan nevertheless holds little sympathy for many central claims of Sartrean existentialism insofar as his entire approach to psychoanalysis depends on Sartre's being mistaken in his argument that the intentionality of consciousness – "consciousness is always consciousness-of-something" means there is nothing in consciousness that is not an object of consciousness – renders the unconscious a fiction. And while Sartre is not named in Lacan's famous essay on "The Mirror Stage," delivered in 1949, there can be little doubt that his audience understood Sartre to be implicated when he announced his opposition to "any philosophy directly issuing from the *Cogito*," or when he claimed that

existentialism must be judged by the explanations it gives of the sub-jective impasses that have indeed resulted from it; a freedom that is never more authentic than when it is within the walls of a prison; a demand for commitment, expressing the impotence of a pure consciousness to master any situation; a voyeuristic–sadistic idealization of the sexual relation; a personality that realizes itself only in suicide; a consciousness of the other that can be satisfied only by Hegelian murder.[31]

Structuralism was of course more than just a negative response to Sartre, phenomenology, and the philosophy of the subject. Drawing upon the four binary oppositions central to Saussurean linguistics –

[30] Sartre, Jean-Paul, *Being and Nothingness*, trans. Hazel E. Barnes (New York: Philosophical Library, 1956), p. 565. For further discussion on Sartre, Lacan, and the philosophical tradition of viewing desire as lack, see my "Spinoza, Nietzsche, Deleuze: An Other Discourse of Desire," in *Philosophy and Desire*, ed. Hugh A. Silverman (New York: Routledge, 2000), pp. 173–85.

[31] Jacques Lacan, "The Mirror Stage as Formative of the Function of the I as Revealed in Psychoanalytic Experience," in *Ecrits*, pp. 1, 6. One should compare these remarks with some of Merleau-Ponty's comments in the closing chapter on "Freedom" in *Phenomenology of Perception*, where he makes a similar criticism of Sartre.

signifier (*signifiant*) and *signified* (*signifié*), *langue* and *parole*, *synchronic* and *diachronic*, *infrastructure* and *superstructure* – and privileging in their analyses the former term in each binary pair, the structuralists were able to develop anthropological, literary, psychoanalytic, and Marxist theories that diminished the role of the individual subject or agent while highlighting the underlying relations that govern social and psychic practices. Saussure defined the linguistic sign as the unity of a sound-image (signifier) and a concept (signified). The signifier is that aspect of a sign that can become perceptible, the psychological imprint of the word-sound or the impression it makes on our senses, while the signified is a set of psychological associations, the mental picture or description associated with a signifier. In general, then, the signifier is the material (auditory or visual) component of a sign, while the signified is the mental concept associated with that sign. By *langue*, Saussure meant the set of interpersonal rules and norms which speakers of that language must obey if they are to communicate; *langue* is, then, the theoretical system or structure of a language like English, French, or Italian. *Parole*, on the other hand, is the actual manifestations of the system in speech and writing, the speech act, language as used. The distinction between *langue* and *parole* is the distinction between structure and event, between a collective product passively assimilated by the individual and the individual act. By synchronic, Saussure named the structural properties of a system at a particular historical moment, while the diachronic referred to the historical dimension of a language, the historical evolution of its elements through various stages. Finally, infrastructure refers to the set of underlying relations that explain the superstructure or surface structure that is open to observation and description. For Saussure, *langue* functions as the infrastructure to *parole* as superstructure while, oversimplifying greatly, on Althusser's reading of Marx, the relations of means and modes of material production are the infrastructure, while ideology (family, religion, law, social organizations, etc.) is the resultant superstructure. Or on Lacan's reconstruction of Freud, the dynamic of id, ego, superego plays itself out at the infrastructural level, while the observable superstructural effects are displayed through neurotic behavior.

It is important to recognize that what unites the structuralists is less a shared set of philosophical theses than a shared set of methodological assumptions and a willingness to work with the concepts of Saussurean linguistics. Lévi-Strauss makes this point explicitly in an essay published in 1945 in *Word: Journal of the Linguistic Circle of New York*, which began with the admission that "Linguistics occupies a special place among the social sciences, to whose ranks it unquestionably belongs."[32] He goes on to predict that "structural linguistics will certainly play the same renovating role with respect to the social sciences that nuclear physics, for example, has played for the physical sciences" and, asking himself in what forms this revolutionary transformation will appear, suggests that this question was already answered by N. Troubetzkoy, "the illustrious founder of structural linguistics,"[33] in the following "programmatic statement" that Lévi-Strauss paraphrases:

> He reduced the structural method to four basic operations. First, structural linguistics shifts from the study of *conscious* linguistic phenomena to study of their *unconscious* infrastructure; second, it does not treat *terms* as independent entities, taking instead as its basis of analysis the *relations* between terms; third, it introduces the concept of *system* – "Modern phonemics does not merely proclaim that phonemes are always part of a system; it *shows* concrete phonemic systems and elucidates their structure" – finally, structural linguistics aims at discovering *general laws*, either by induction "or . . . by logical deduction, which would give them an absolute character."[34]

Lévi-Strauss's structural analysis of myths, for example, suggests we interpret myths as *parole* or speech acts that are expressions of and variations on a few basic structural relations that form a culture's *langue*, the set of interpersonal rules and norms that operate unconsciously and that actors in a culture must obey if they are to function. So, in *The Raw and the Cooked*,[35] Lévi-Strauss analyzes 187 separate myths, showing them all to be variations, transformations, reversals, inversions, etc., of a deep structural opposition between the raw and the cooked, which is itself, at the superstructural level of myth, the expression of the underlying infrastructural opposition of nature and culture.

[32]   Claude Lévi-Strauss, "Structural Analysis in Linguistics and in Anthropology," reprinted as the second chapter of *Structural Anthropology*. The quote appears on p. 31.

[33]   We should note that only a few pages earlier in *Structural Anthropology*, Lévi-Strauss refers to the publication of Saussure's *Course in General Linguistics* as marking "the advent of structural linguistics" (p. 20).

[34]   Lévi-Strauss, *Structural Anthropology*, p. 33. The two quotes are from N. Troubetzkoy, "La Phonologie actuelle," in Henri Delacroix et al., *Psychologie du langage* (Paris: Félix Alcan, 1933), p. 243.

[35]   Claude Lévi-Strauss, *The Raw and the Cooked*, trans. John and Doreen Weightman (New York: Harper and Row, 1969).

This methodological privileging of structure – the underlying rules or "general laws" – over event – the act of articulating the myth – leads structuralism to place emphasis on synchronic relations rather than diachronic developments. The structuralists are thus concerned with studying particular systems or structures under somewhat artificial and ahistorical conditions in hope of explaining their present functioning. This is apparent in Lévi-Strauss's reading of Marcel Mauss, which argues that Mauss attends to a more superficial diachronic analysis of "total social facts," thereby missing the opportunity to reveal what is in fact a complicated synchronic structure of giving–receiving–reciprocating.[36] We see it as well in Althusser's concentration on the various ideological state apparatuses at work at a given time in a society rather than the historical evolution of these various cultural formations,[37] and in Barthes's emphasis on writing (*écriture*) as a function that exceeds the author's desire to express or communicate (which Barthes associates with "style").[38]

---

[36] See Claude Lévi-Strauss, *Introduction to the Work of Marcel Mauss*, trans. Felicity Baker (London: Routledge and Kegan Paul, 1987), pp. 45–8.

[37] See, for example, Louis Althusser, "Ideology and Ideological State Apparatuses," in *Lenin and Philosophy and Other Essays*, trans. Ben Brewster (London: New Left Books, 1971), pp. 127–86.

[38] For Barthes's clearest contrast between writing and style, see the introduction and part one of *Writing Degree Zero*.

5

After Structuralism

The period that follows the dominance of the structuralist paradigm, which has rather unhappily been baptized "poststructuralism" in American critical theory, extends roughly from 1966 through the end of the twentieth century. Under this totalizing appellation are brought together a number of theorists and theoretical positions that, in France, are often positioned quite far apart.[1] To mention only the two most commonplace examples of grouping together theorists whose positions are quite distinct, the poststructuralist trio of "French feminists" – Julia Kristeva, Luce Irigaray, and Hélène Cixous – are often brought together in English, and especially American discussions, while their own interpersonal relations in France are quite strained; they do not participate in the same discursive communities, their works are rarely treated together, and they are not in any way representative of the women's movement in France. Similarly, the labels "poststructuralist," "deconstructionist," and "postmodernist" are often used interchangeably to group together Jacques Derrida, Michel Foucault, Gilles Deleuze, and Jean-François Lyotard, while in the French context, only Derrida would be associated with deconstruction, and only Lyotard with postmodernism.[2] More importantly, each of these thinkers is considered to have a distinct project that results only very rarely in any two of them

---

[1] It is not only the English-language philosophical community that has made this move, however. For a German version, see Manfred Frank, *What is Neo-Structuralism?* trans. Sabine Wilke and Richard Gray (Minneapolis: University of Minnesota Press, 1989), which discusses Jacques Derrida, Michel Foucault, Jacques Lacan, Gilles Deleuze, and others, and often blurs the line between structuralism and poststructuralism.

[2] Foucault addresses the point explicitly on a number of occasions. See, for example, his 1983 interview with Gérard Raulet, where he confesses to not really understanding what is named by "postmodernism," and failing to understand what common problem is thought to be addressed by those thinkers grouped together as

being treated together by writers *sympathetic* to their work.[3] In fact, more to the point, one might on occasion find Deleuze and Foucault discussed together, or Derrida and Lyotard, but one almost never finds discussions in French philosophical venues of Foucault *and* Derrida, or Deleuze *and* Derrida.[4]

While the American reception has tended to overlook the important differences between these thinkers,[5] there are nevertheless certain themes and trends that do emerge in various ways in the work of many of the French philosophers and theorists who follow structuralism. In some cases, these should be seen as correctives to the excesses of structuralism, in other cases as various ways in which thinkers coming into prominence in the late 1960s and early 1970s were to give expression to the Nietzschean-Freudian-Marxian spirit of the times, and in still other cases as a way of retrieving themes from some of the French traditions that had fallen out of favor during the scientistic orientation of the 1950s and early 1960s (the return of certain ethical, spiritual, and religious themes, along with some positions associated with phenomenology and existentialism). What cannot be denied, and should not be underestimated, is that the hegemony of structuralist social scientific

---

"postmodernists" (Michel Foucault, "Critical Theory/Intellectual History," trans. Jeremy Harding in *Politics, Philosophy, Culture: Interviews and Other Writings, 1977–1984*, ed. Lawrence D. Kritzman [New York: Routledge, 1988], p. 34). In another late interview, Foucault makes clear that it is a mistake to confuse his method of analysis with deconstruction; see "Polemics, Politics, and Problematizations: An Interview," trans. Lydia Davis in *The Foucault Reader*, ed. Paul Rabinow (New York: Pantheon Books, 1984), p. 389.

3   It should be noted that this observation applies *only* to sympathetic treatments of these thinkers' works. Their *un*sympathetic critics, on the other hand, often group them together, as one sees, for example, in Luc Ferry and Alain Renaut, *French Philosophy of the Sixties: An Essay on Antihumanism*, trans. Mary Schnackenberg Cattani (Amherst: University of Massachusetts Press, 1990). The problems with this text have been well documented; see, for example, Dominique Lecourt's criticisms in *The Mediocracy: French Philosophy since the Mid-1970s*, trans. Gregory Elliott (London: Verso, 2001).

4   This becomes especially clear when one looks at the work of the various thinkers – former students or fellow travelers – associated with these "master thinkers." Consider, for example, how little acknowledgment of the work of Foucault or Deleuze one finds in thinkers associated with Derrida like Jean-Luc Nancy or Philippe Lacoue-Labarthe.

5   As it has tended to ignore other developments in French philosophy unrelated to these thinkers, about which more will be said in the conclusion to part I.

thinking in the late 1950s and early 1960s was followed by the reemergence of the value of specifically *philosophical* thinking. Where the structuralist theorists had turned away from philosophy, theorists following structuralism readily identify themselves as philosophers.[6] But unlike most philosophical thinkers in France who precede the rise of the structuralist social sciences, French philosophers after structuralism engage in philosophical reflection and analysis while taking account of the institutional forces that inform philosophical thinking itself. Situating these philosophical thinkers *after* structuralism, four themes in particular need to be highlighted: (1) the return to thinking *historically*; (2) the return of thinking about the *subject*; (3) the emphasis on *difference*; and (4) the return to thinking *philosophically* about ethics and religion.

The Return to Thinking Historically

There are many ways in which the philosophical thinking in France that came after structuralism can be viewed as a corrective to the overemphasis on synchrony that one finds in structuralist writing. There is no single reason behind this, nor a single form in which French philosophy after structuralism seeks to think time, temporality, or history. But where the structuralists sought to understand the extratemporal functioning of systems (whether social, psychic, economic, or literary), thinkers like Foucault, Derrida, Deleuze, or Lyotard attend to the historical unfolding of the phenomena they choose to examine. In part, the attention to time, temporality, and history can be viewed as a consequence of the intellectual resources to which these thinkers appeal, resources that were not necessarily central to the work of their structuralist predecessors. Foucault, for example, draws upon the study of the history of science and scientific change in the work of Canguilhem and Bachelard,[7] while

---

[6] Foucault is, of course, something of an exception here, as he often refused to identify himself as a philosopher. So is Pierre Bourdieu, whose work is often associated with "poststructuralism" but whose disciplinary positioning as a sociologist is often explicitly anti-philosophical.

[7] In this and the remarks to follow, the reader should take my observations to be painting a picture, with very broad strokes, of French philosophy after structuralism. That is to say, my remarks here do not intend to be either definitive or exclusive, by which I mean, for example, that noting Foucault's appeal to Bachelard is not meant to imply that a structuralist like Althusser could not also appeal to Bachelard, which he clearly did with his notion of "epistemological break."

Deleuze returns to Bergson's theories of time and *durée* (duration). For Derrida, it is primarily Heidegger's focus on Being and the history of philosophy as a history of the forgetting of the ontological difference (the difference between Being and beings) that leads him to think in terms of the *history* of metaphysics as a history of logocentrism and onto-theology. For many of these thinkers, the move in Heidegger's thought from the thinking of Being (*Sein*) to the thinking of *Ereignis* – the event of appropriation – can be seen to inspire, whether directly or indirectly, their respective attempts to develop a philosophy of the event, just as the attention to Nietzsche in the late 1960s and 1970s, and in particular to his notion of the eternal recurrence, led many to rethink traditional notions of temporality and history.

It is easy to see that a concern with history and the event characterizes many of the thinkers who follow structuralism. To begin with one of the most obvious examples, we find Foucault's entire philosophical *oeuvre* deeply inflected with an attention to history. The guiding thesis of his early work was that there exists, at any give time, an order of things that makes the social functioning of the time possible. This order operates within the fundamental codes of a culture: those governing its language, its schemes of perception, its techniques, exchanges, values, etc. Unlike Kant's transcendental project—one with which the work of Lévi-Strauss is quite compatible, as Paul Ricoeur noted when he referred to Lévi-Strauss's anthropological theory as "a Kantianism without a transcendental subject"[8]—for Foucault this order is a *historical a priori*: neither transcendental nor universal, the order Foucault describes is a *historically* specific constellation that exists prior to experience. But it is at the same time prior to *reason* insofar as the standards of rationality at work at any particular historical moment are themselves determined on its basis. This order also establishes the basis on which knowledge and theory become possible, as Foucault argued in *The Order of Things* and, based on this order, certain ideas appear, certain perceptions, values, and distinctions become possible.

For many, this idea of a *historical a priori* is simply a contradiction in terms. For Foucault, however, experience is thoroughly historicized: one's experience is "constructed" from the *a priori* – one might even say "structural" – rules that govern experience and social practices at a

---

[8]   Paul Ricoeur, "Structure and Hermeneutics," trans. Kathleen McLaughlin, in *The Conflict of Interpretations: Essays in Hermeneutics*, ed. Don Ihde (Evanston, IL: Northwestern University Press, 1974), p. 52.

particular point in history. At other times, there were other *a priori* rules
that governed social practices, and people's experiences were, as a
consequence, constructed differently. To take an over-simplified example, when the first missionaries left Europe to colonize the New
World, their historical *a priori* determined their experience of indigenous peoples as something like a species other than themselves. They
took with them a set of social rules prior to experiencing the indigenous
peoples that led them to experience non-white humans as non-human.
Today, regardless of how prejudiced one might be in terms of devaluing
other races, it is extremely rare to find someone who will *genuinely* deny
the status as "human being" to people of other races. On Foucault's
account, the rules that "govern" how we understand and experience
race-based traits relating to a being's status as "human" have changed
over time, which is to say, the *a priori* is historical. This historical *a priori*
is ultimately what determines the "order of things," by which Foucault's
French title – *Les mots et les choses* – meant the relation between words
(conceptual understandings) and things (reality as experienced).

While Foucault eventually gave up this language, he never renounced
the importance of grounding thought historically, a fact that he obvi-
ously wanted brought to the fore insofar as he requested that his Chair
at the Collège de France, the Chair associated since its creation in 1932
with the history of philosophy, be renamed the "Chair in the History of
Systems of Thought." In a late interview, Foucault responds to a
question concerning the structure of his "genealogy project," by focusing on its historical dimension:

> Three domains of genealogy are possible. First, a historical ontology of
> ourselves in relation to truth through which we constitute ourselves as
> subjects of knowledge; second, a historical ontology of ourselves in
> relation to a field of power through which we constitute ourselves as
> subjects acting on others; third, a historical ontology in relation to ethics
> through which we constitute ourselves as moral agents.[9]

Foucault goes on to add that while all three domains "were present,
albeit in a somewhat confused fashion, in *Madness and Civilization*," in
later works, particular domains were emphasized: "The truth axis was
studied in *The Birth of the Clinic* and *The Order of Things*. The power

---

[9]   Michel Foucault, "On the Genealogy of Ethics: An Overview of Work in Progress,"
      interview conducted in April, 1983 and published in *The Foucault Reader*, p. 351.

axis was studied in *Discipline and Punish*, and the ethical axis in *The History of Sexuality*."[10] In the end, the goal of Foucault's genealogical project is to unite these three analytic dimensions (truth, power, ethics) in an attempt to produce a "critical ontology of ourselves . . . conceived as an attitude, an ethos, a philosophical life in which the critique of what we are is at one and the same time the *historical* analysis of the limits that are imposed on us and an experiment with the possibility of going beyond them."[11]

Insofar as Jacques Derrida's philosophical project began as an attempt to deconstruct logocentrism as a metaphysics of presence which invariably privileges the temporal present, reflecting on time, history, and the event has also been a recurring theme throughout Derrida's writings. We can survey this quality in a number of exemplary instances. First, in his presentation at the 1966 colloquium at Johns Hopkins University on structuralism – "The Languages of Criticism and the Sciences of Man" – which marked the beginning of the end of the reign of structuralist discourse, Derrida opened ironically with the remark that "perhaps something has occurred in the history of the concept of structure that could be called an 'event,' " noting that it was precisely the function of structuralist discourse to reduce or suspect the meaning of this "loaded word."[12] A second example: his coining of the neologism *différance* sought to situate at the foundation of deconstructive analysis an attentiveness to both meanings of the French verb *différer*: to defer in terms of delay over time and to differ in terms of spatial non-identity. Insofar as *différance* names the movement of both temporal deferring and spatial differing, it stands as the transcendental condition for the possibility of differentiation, that is, *différance* is what makes differences possible. A third example: the event of temporal deferral is essential to the differences Derrida brings out between writing and speech and marks all the deconstructive themes – signature, graft, citation, iterability, context – that he addresses in his deconstruction of the speech/writing binary in "Signature Event Context." A fourth and final example: insofar as the problematic of the gift, whether or not named as such, has been at work

---

[10] Foucault, "On the Genealogy of Ethics," p. 352.
[11] Michel Foucault, "What is Enlightenment," trans. Catherine Porter, in *The Foucault Reader*, p. 50. Emphasis added.
[12] Jacques Derrida, "Structure, Sign, and Play in the Discourse of the Human Sciences," in *Writing and Difference*, trans. Alan Bass (Chicago: University of Chicago Press, 1978), p. 278.

in his texts "more or less constantly,"[13] then so have the themes of time and the event. For, as he notes in *Given Time*, the structure of the gift, like the structure of Being and of time, is the structure of an event, an event of forgetting and deferral, an event of *différance*.[14] In fact, what the gift gives, in the end, is nothing but time – time to forget, time to return, time for a delayed reciprocation that is no longer simply a return.

Foucault and Derrida's attention to time and history is not exceptional, however, for it characterizes much of the important work done by the major figures in French philosophy after structuralism. For example, Pierre Bourdieu, critical in his early works of objectivist accounts of gift exchange, also focused his account of gifts on the theme of time, specifically the time-lag between gift and counter-gift that stands as the condition for the possibility of the gift. Because objectivist accounts like that of Lévi-Strauss failed to understand the societally motivated individual and collective misrecognition (*méconnaissance*) of the rules governing the exchange of gifts, they were led to focus their analyses almost entirely on the relation of reciprocal equivalence between gift and counter-gift. For Bourdieu, this objectivist, economistic focus on reciprocity collapses the time-lag between gift and counter-gift, and turns the gift exchange into a straightforward return to the gift's donor of what she is due from the gift's original recipient. By failing to attend to time, the objectivist account is thus unable to distinguish gift exchange from either "*swapping*, which . . . telescopes gift and counter-gift into the same instant," or "*lending*, in which the return of the loan is explicitly guaranteed by a juridical act and is thus *already accomplished* at the very moment of the drawing up of a contract capable of ensuring that the acts it prescribes are predictable and calculable."[15]

For Gilles Deleuze, on the other hand, time is a constant theme, running through his reflections on Bergsonian duration, Nietzsche's eternal return, and his theory of cinema (the second volume of which

---

[13] Jacques Derrida, *Given Time*, trans. Peggy Kamuf (Chicago: University of Chicago Press, 1992), p. ix.

[14] See Derrida, *Given Time*, pp. 17–27.

[15] Pierre Bourdieu, *Outline of a Theory of Practice*, trans. Richard Nice (New York: Cambridge University Press, 1977), p. 5. See also, for a further example of Bourdieu's arguing for a turn toward history, the chapter "The Historicity of Reason" in *Pascalian Meditations*, trans. Richard Nice (Stanford, CA: Stanford University Press, 2000), pp. 93–127, esp. pp. 106ff., where he speaks of the specific task of the social sciences to ground their thinking in "*historical reason*."

is *The Time-Image*). In fact, one could claim that in his two major texts, *Difference and Repetition* and *The Logic of Sense*, Deleuze is offering us a new way to think about time in order to think the logic of events. One could also here cite Jean-François Lyotard's *post*-modernism and the thinking of the event of the post, as well as his reflections on the *arrive-t-il?* – the is-it-happening? – of the *différend*; or Alain Badiou's call for philosophy to return to systematic thinking by recognizing the compossibility of four "generic conditions" – the matheme, the political, the poem, and love – in terms of the transformations each has undergone via four recent events: Cantor–Gödel–Cohen's account of multiplicity, the political upheavals between May '68 and the Solidarity movement in Poland, Celan's call for the poem to think its other, and Lacan's refiguring the concept of love. What all these examples make clear is that the evolution in France from structuralism to what followed is marked by a renewed concern with thinking historically.

The Return of Thinking about the Subject

Where the rhetoric of the "death of the subject" was characteristic of the structuralists, this was never really the case with most of the philosophers labeled *post*-structuralist. To be sure, thinkers like Derrida, Foucault, or Deleuze were never comfortable with the subject-centered thinking of the existentialists or phenomenologists. But they were equally uncomfortable with the straightforwardly anti-humanist rhetoric of structuralist thinkers like Althusser or Lévi-Strauss. Thus Derrida could reply, to a question that followed his presentation at Johns Hopkins concerning the "death of the subject," "The subject is absolutely indispensable. I don't destroy the subject; I situate it. I believe that at a certain level both of experience and of philosophical and scientific discourse, one cannot get along without the notion of the subject. It is a question of knowing where it comes from and how it functions."[16]

Even Foucault, who can arguably be associated with the rhetoric of the "death of the subject" in his works of the early 1960s, can at the

---

[16] Jacques Derrida, from the discussion following "Structure, Sign, and Play in the Discourse of the Human Sciences," trans. Richard Macksey in *The Structuralist Controversy*, ed. Richard Macksey and Eugenio Donato (Baltimore, MD: Johns Hopkins University Press, 1970), p. 271.

same time be shown to have been thinking about the question of the construction of the modern subject throughout his *oeuvre*. That is to say, a distinction can and should be drawn between the "end of man" and the "death of the subject." It may well be the case that Foucault's early work, most notably *The Order of Things*, engages in thinking the end of man, as we can see, for example, in the closing pages of *The Order of Things* when he draws this conclusion concerning Nietzsche:

> Rather than the death of God – or, rather, in the wake of that death and in profound correlation with it – what Nietzsche's thought heralds is the end of his murderer; it is the explosion of man's face in laughter, and the return of masks; it is the scattering of the profound stream of time by which he felt himself carried along and whose pressure he suspected in the very being of things; it is the identity of the Return of the Same with the absolute dispersion of man.[17]

But it may be a mistake to equate the referent of "man" in these early contexts with what Foucault means by "subject." There is no question that the subject named "man" in philosophical discourse, from Descartes's Archimedean *Cogito* to Kant's autonomous rational moral agent, is a concept toward which the author of *The Order of Things* has little sympathy. But even in the 1960s, in the essay "What is an Author?" which is often seen as an anti-humanist work, Foucault's desire to deflate the subject as epistemically and discursively privileged is not conjoined with an attempt to eliminate the subject entirely. Instead, Foucault seeks to analyze the subject as a variable and complex function of discourse and power, which, he writes, means to ask not "How can a free subject penetrate the substance of things and give it meaning?" but "How, under what conditions and in what forms can something like a subject appear in the order of discourse? What place can it occupy in each type of discourse, what functions can it assume, and by obeying what rules?"[18] What this means, and what has been largely misunderstood by many of Foucault's critics, is that his so-called "anti-humanism" was not a rejection of the human per se; it was instead an assault on the philosophically modern idea that sought to remove man from the natural world and place him in a position of epistemic,

---

[17] Michel Foucault, *The Order of Things: An Archeology of the Human Sciences* (New York: Vintage Books, 1970), p. 385.

[18] Michel Foucault, "What is an Author?" trans. Josué V. Harari, in *The Foucault Reader*, p. 118.

metaphysical, and moral privilege that earlier thought had set aside for God.[19]

By the end of his career, as his attention turned specifically to sexuality and the construction of the ethical subject, Foucault himself came to see that the question of the subject, or more accurately, the question of *assujettissement* or subjectivation – the transformation of human beings into subjects of knowledge, subjects of power, and sub-jects to themselves – had been "the general theme of [his] research."[20] As we saw in the remark cited above concerning his genealogy project, Foucault conceives genealogy as a historical ontology of how human beings constitute themselves as subjects of knowledge, as subjects acting on other subjects, and as moral subjects. His work is less an anti-humanism than an attempt to think humanism and the subject after the end of (modern) man.[21] Far from being a thinker of the "death of the subject," Foucault simply refuses to accept the subject as given, as the foundation for ethical or rational thinking. The subject is, for Foucault, instead something that has been historically created and Foucault's work, in its entirety, is engaged in analyzing the various ways that human beings are transformed into subjects, whether subjects of knowledge, of power, of sexuality, or of ethics.[22]

The question of the subject was also central to the work of feminist thinkers writing after structuralism, as they sought to challenge both philosophical and psychoanalytic assumptions concerning the subject as

---

[19] Which is why Foucault ends *The Order of Things* by associating the "death of God" with the "end of man," as the citation above suggests.

[20] Michel Foucault, "Why Study Power: The Question of the Subject," in Hubert L. Dreyfus and Paul Rabinow, *Michel Foucault: Beyond Structuralism and Hermeneutics* (Chicago: University of Chicago Press, 1982), p. 209. This is reflected as well in the titles Foucault gave to the last two courses he taught at the Collège de France for which he completed the required resume: "Subjectivity and Truth" (1980–1) and "The Hermeneutic of the Subject" (1981–2).

[21] Michael Hardt and Antonio Negri note this Nietzschean aspect of Foucault's thought in *Empire* (Cambridge, MA: Harvard University Press, 2000), pp. 91–2, though they link it to Spinoza and Donna Haraway rather than Nietzsche.

[22] See the start of his essay "Why Study Power," p. 208. That Foucault had Sartre's existential subject in mind when he distances himself from the question "How can a free subject penetrate the substance of things and give it meaning?" seems clear. But whether Sartre had such a fixed and ontologically rigid notion of the subject is a question worth asking. That is to say, while *Being and Nothingness* articulates a rigid ontological dualism of being-for-itself and being-in-itself, the existential subject *qua* for-itself is never fixed or given. It exists instead as a project of being that may in

sexed or gendered male or masculine. Although there are important differences between the theoretical positions of Cixous, Irigaray, and Kristeva, insofar as these "difference feminists" argue for sexual difference and the significant and important differences between male and female desire, they had to argue that there were important differences between male and female subjects. And to make this argument required that they refuse to follow the structuralist project of entirely eliminating the subject.

The difficulties in trying to affirm a "female subjectivity" in a cultural context that assumes the subject is gendered male or that seeks to eliminate subjectivity altogether is one that has engaged most feminist theorists in France. Luce Irigaray, to take one example, acknowledges that insofar as the logic of subjectivity has, as Beauvoir first showed in *The Second Sex*, relegated women to the position of object, "the issue is not one of elaborating a new theory of which women would be the *subject* . . . but of jamming the theoretical machinery itself."[23] But at the same time, she is uncomfortable with giving up the possibility of occupying the position of the subject insofar as this is a position

---

fact be much more amenable to Foucault's exploration of the "care of the self as a practice of freedom [*souci de soi comme pratique de la liberté*]" than is generally recognized. Similarly, one might ask just how Julia Kristeva's idea of the *sujet-en-procès*, the "subject-in-process/-on-trial," differs from the Sartrean idea of the self as a project of being. Although this topic cannot be explored here, I think it is important to note that Sartre's account of the subject may be far more subtle than is presumed by many French and English-speaking philosophers. I address this point in more detail in my essay "Judith Butler: *Une nouvelle existentialiste?*" *Philosophy Today* (Spring 2001): 12–23.

[23] Luce Irigaray, *The Sex Which is Not One*, trans. Catherine Porter with Carolyn Burke (Ithaca, NY: Cornell University Press, 1985), p. 78. I do not here want to imply that Irigaray sees herself following Beauvoir's project. In fact, the opposite is closer to the truth, and Irigaray has made clear in a 1995 interview how little sympathy she has for Beauvoir's egalitarian refusal to be the Other. Contra Beauvoir, Irigaray's own position requires the necessary difference between man and woman and affirms woman's position as Other so long as being Other does not entail being second or derivative. She here suggests that the title of her major theoretical work, *Speculum of the Other Woman*, should, in fact, have been translated as *Speculum*, followed by a colon, with the following subtitle: "*On the Other: Woman*," thereby marking polemically her distance from Beauvoir. See "'Je – Luce Irigaray': A Meeting with Luce Irigaray," interview conducted by Elizabeth Hirsh and Gary A. Olson, trans. Elizabeth Hirsh and Gaëtan Brulotte in *Hypatia: A Journal of Feminist Philosophy* 10, no. 2 (Spring 1995): 93–114.

that women have heretofore never been able to occupy. She thus notes that she would prefer to see the "culture of the subject... evolve in the direction of a culture of a sexed/gendered subject and not in the direction of a heedless destruction of subjectivity."[24] Moreover, she suggests that insofar as the circulation of women as objects of social–sexual exchange has been foundational to the western patriarchal social order, we should not underestimate the possibilities for radical social transformation if women were to finally emerge as "speaking subjects."

The "speaking subject" is of course also a central focus of Kristeva's work, as she defined her project of analytical semiology or semanalysis, in part, as the "insertion of subjectivity into matters of language and meaning."[25] Such a subject would not, of course, be a Cartesian or Husserlian subject who could function as a pure source of meaning. Rather, following the discoveries of Freud, Lacan, and structural linguistics (Saussure, Benveniste), the "speaking subject" will always be a "split subject"—split between conscious motivations and the unconscious, between structure and event, and between the subject of the utterance (*sujet d'énonciation*) and the subject of the statement (*sujet d'énoncé*)—who would be "posited as the place, not only of structure and its regulated transformation, but especially, of its loss, its outlay."[26] Elsewhere, in *Revolution and Poetic Language*, this subject is developed as a subject-in-process/-on-trial (*sujet-en-procès*), a dynamic subject at the intersection of the semiotic and the symbolic, making itself and being made, but a subject nonetheless.

The Emphasis on Difference

One of the essential themes of Saussurean linguistics was that "in language there are only differences *without positive terms*."[27] By this,

24 See her interview in Alice A. Jardine and Anne M. Mencke, *Shifting Scenes: Interviews on Women, Writing, and Politics in Post-68 France* (New York: Columbia University Press, 1991), p. 103.

25 Julia Kristeva, *Desire in Language: A Semiotic Approach to Literature and Art*, ed. Leon S. Roudiez, trans. Thomas Gora, Alice Jardine, and Leon S. Roudiez (New York: Columbia University Press, 1980), p. viii.

26 Kristeva, *Desire in Language*, p. 24.

27 Ferdinand de Saussure, *Course in General Linguistics*, ed. Charles Bally and Albert Sechehaye with the collaboration of Albert Riedlinger, trans. Wade Baskin (New York: Philosophical Library, 1959), p. 120.

he meant that language functions as a system of interdependent units in which the value of each constituent unit results solely from the simultaneous presence of other units and the ways in which each unit differs from the others. This attention to difference led the structuralists to emphasize in their analyses relations rather than things, to focus on the differential relations between the objects they studied rather than on the objects themselves. While the structuralists all took note of this theme, the emphasis on difference did not become truly dominant until after the hegemony of the structuralist paradigm began to wane. We have already noted that sexual difference is a theme that almost all the feminist thinkers after structuralism have addressed. Indeed, Irigaray goes so far as to suggest that, if Heidegger is right in thinking that each epoch has but a single issue to think through, then "sexual difference is... the issue of our age."[28] Hélène Cixous, on the other hand, sees the rigid conceptualization of sexual difference as what supports the identification of the male/masculine with the Same, while the female/feminine is rendered Other. For Cixous, the way out of this patriarchal system is not via the elimination of difference but through escaping the dominant logic of difference as hierarchal opposition to a new logic of difference in which "difference would be a bunch of new differences."[29]

Sexual difference is only one form in which the French attention to difference has appeared. We have already noted how Derrida has emphasized *différance* in his deconstructive project. But more generally, the attention to difference – rather than a focus on identity or the Same – is a move one finds in almost all recent French philosophers, and is particularly central to the projects of Jean-François Lyotard and Gilles Deleuze. For Deleuze, whose work often takes a form of presentation much more in the mold of traditional philosophical analysis than the other philosophers writing after structuralism, difference has been a central and constant focus of his thinking. His *Nietzsche and Philosophy* (1962), which was the first of the major French interpretations of Nietzsche to appear, appeals to the concept of difference to show how Nietzsche departs from the Hegelian tradition, to explicate Nietzsche's will to power, and to interpret Nietzsche's thought of the eternal recurrence. In place of Hegel's "speculative element of negation, op-

---

[28] Luce Irigaray, *An Ethics of Sexual Difference*, trans. Carolyn Burke and Gillian C. Gill (Ithaca, NY: Cornell University Press, 1993), p. 5.

[29] Hélène Cixous and Catherine Clément, *The Newly Born Woman*, trans. Betsy Wing (Minneapolis: University of Minnesota Press, 1986), p. 83.

position or contradiction, Nietzsche substitutes the practical element of *difference*, the object of affirmation and enjoyment."[30] Where the dialectic is engaged in the "*labor* of the negative," according to Deleuze, Nietzsche offers a theory of forces in which active force does not negate or deny the other but "affirms its own difference and enjoys this difference."[31] Nietzsche's notion of will to power is, for Deleuze, a theory of forces in which forces are distinguished in terms of both their qualitative and quantitative differences. In fact, what Nietzsche names with the "will to power" is "the genealogical element of force, both differential and genetic. *The will to power is the element from which derive both the quantitative difference of related forces and the quality that devolves into each force in this relation.*"[32] And, given the importance that difference plays in Deleuze's reading, it is not at all surprising to find him concluding that what returns eternally is not the same or the identical; rather, what returns is the repetition of difference:

> We fail to understand the eternal return if we make it a consequence or an application of identity. We fail to understand the eternal return if we do not oppose it to identity in a particular way. The eternal return is not the permanence of the same, the equilibrium state or the resting place of the identical. It is not the "same" or the "one" which comes back in the eternal return but return is itself the one which ought to belong to diversity and to that which differs.[33]

Deleuze develops these themes much further in *Difference and Repetition* as he attempts to think the concept of difference in itself. Published in 1968, Deleuze sees this work reflecting the "generalized anti-Hegelianism" of the time in which "difference and repetition have taken the place of the identical and the negative, of identity and contradiction."[34] Hegel is not the only culprit, however; rather, he is simply the culmination of a metaphysical tradition that associates difference with opposition and the negative, while privileging identity and the Same as primary. Treating difference as derivative begins with Plato, who Deleuze claims first introduced the concept of difference,

---

[30] Gilles Deleuze, *Nietzsche and Philosophy*, trans. Hugh Tomlinson (New York: Columbia University Press, 1983), p. 9.

[31] Deleuze, *Nietzsche and Philosophy*, p. 9.

[32] Deleuze, *Nietzsche and Philosophy*, p. 50.

[33] Deleuze, *Nietzsche and Philosophy*, p. 46.

[34] Gilles Deleuze, *Difference and Repetition*, trans. Paul Patton (New York: Columbia University Press, 1994), p. xix.

not in terms of the difference between the Form and its physical copies, but in terms of the tertiary relation between the copy and its simulacra.

> Indeed, it is in this sense that difference comes only in third place, behind identity and resemblance, and can be understood only in terms of the comparative play of two similitudes: the exemplary similitude of an identical original and the imitative similitude of a more or less accurate copy...More profoundly, however, the true Platonic distinction lies elsewhere: it is of another nature, not between the original and the image but between two kinds of images, of which copies are the first kind, the other being simulacra.[35]

From Plato to Hegel, the metaphysical tradition sees the different in opposition to and derivative upon the one, while Deleuze sets out to develop an ontology of difference in which "it is not difference which presupposes opposition, but opposition which presupposes difference" and treats it as the negation of identity.[36] Deleuze's project in this work is nothing short of reversing the tradition that privileges identity by showing identity to be an optical effect produced "by the more profound game of difference and repetition." While "the primacy of identity, however conceived, defines the world of representation," his goal, on the other hand, is to "think difference in itself independently of the forms of representation which reduce it to the Same, and the relation of different to different independently of those forms which make them pass through the negative."[37]

For Lyotard, whose work is more closely tied to postmodernism than the other French philosophers, what characterizes the postmodern is, as he puts it in the introduction to *The Postmodern Condition*, an "incredulity toward metanarratives."[38] Rather than naming a specific epoch, the postmodern names instead an anti-foundationalist attitude that exceeds the legitimating orthodoxy of the moment. Postmodernity, then, does not follow modernity but resides constantly at the heart of the modern, challenging those totalizing and comprehensive master narratives (like the Enlightenment narrative of the emancipation of the rational subject or the Marxist narrative of the emancipation of the working class) that

---

[35]   Deleuze, *Difference and Repetition*, p. 127.
[36]   Deleuze, *Difference and Repetition*, p. 51.
[37]   Deleuze, *Difference and Repetition*, p. xix.
[38]   Jean-François Lyotard, *The Postmodern Condition: A Report on Knowledge*, trans. Geoff Bennington and Brian Massumi (Minneapolis: University of Minnesota Press, 1984), p. xxiv.

serve to legitimate its practices. In place of these grand meta- and master narratives, Lyotard suggests we look instead to less ambitious, "little narratives" that refrain from totalizing claims in favor of recognizing the specificity and singularity of events. Refusing to sanction the move to a metanarrative in the ethical, political, aesthetic, and metaphysical domains commits one to a philosophy of difference in that it accepts that oppositions will not be resolved in some higher unity and concludes that multiple and discordant voices are not only inevitable but desirable.

Beyond his postmodernist polemic, reflecting on difference operates at the core of both Lyotard's pagan project and what he considered his most important work, *The Différend*, which is itself an attempt to account for radical and incommensurable differences in discourse, ethics, and politics. For the pagan, what is forbidden is the acceptance of a totalizing or dominating master narrative; no single language game can present itself as *the* game, the *only* game. Paganism, for Lyotard, is not the absence of prescriptives; rather, a prescriptive utterance cannot be derived from a description. Prescriptives are ungrounded, they are "left hanging" in the sense that they cannot be derived logically or necessarily from what is the case, from ontology (as Plato thought when he presumed that if one knew the good, one would do the good). The pagan prescriptive, then, is to maximize multiplicity, to multiply narratives, and to play different language games. To be pagan is to accept that one must play several games, be inventive and imaginative in the playing of these different games, and refuse to accept any move to prohibit the playing of different games.[39]

Where paganism advocated the multiplication of differences, in *The Différend* Lyotard sought to think the insurmountably different, that is, those incommensurable differences that simply do not admit of any shared standard to which one could appeal in making judgments concerning what is different. The *différend* is thus defined as "a case of conflict, between (at least) two parties, that cannot be equitably resolved for lack of a rule of judgment applicable to both arguments."[40] For Lyotard, once one has given up on master narratives, one must also give up on a master narrative of justice or the good to which all parties will

---

[39] See Jean-François Lyotard and Jean-Loup Thébaud, *Just Gaming*, trans. Wlad Godzich (Minneapolis: University of Minnesota Press, 1985), pp. 59–61.

[40] Jean-François Lyotard, *The Différend*, trans. Georges Van Den Abbeele (Minneapolis: University of Minnesota Press, 1988), p. ix.

agree. While such a master narrative is presupposed for a democratic politics based on consensus and agreement, the political question for Lyotard is ultimately the question of how to make decisions in the case of a *différend* in which, by definition, no consensus is possible. The choice, it would seem, is either violence or a new kind of political thinking that can accommodate *différends* in a shared social space where norms work to minimize evil rather than maximize good, and where evil is itself defined in terms of the continued interdiction of different possibilities.

The Return to Thinking Philosophically about Ethics and Religion

One final theme that emerges in the years after structuralism, and that marks a significant change in French philosophizing, is the return of philosophical thinking about ethics and religion. While philosophizing about politics never waned in France, ethical and religious issues were largely absent from French academic philosophy in the years dominated first by existentialism and then by structuralism. As structuralism began to lose its hegemonic position, however, one finds religion and ethics reemerging in a number of ways as questions of morality and value begin to attract philosophy students and readers away from the more austere and scientific theories of the structuralist writers.

For example, one finds two thinkers whose careers began in the 1930s and who were, generationally, the peers of Sartre, suddenly finding newfound fame and a wider audience. Emmanuel Levinas and Vladimir Jankélévitch, both Jewish émigrés from eastern Europe who lost much of their families during the Holocaust, were students in the 1920s and published their first works in the early 1930s. Where Levinas worked for most of his career outside the university system, Jankélévitch spent much of his career at its center, holding a Chair in Moral Philosophy at the Sorbonne from 1952 to 1978. But for much of this time, Jankélévitch was the only professor of ethics at the Sorbonne, and ethics in general was less fashionable than either the history of philosophy or the more hard-nosed epistemology of scientifically minded philosophers like Georges Canguilhem. The year 1958 is typical: among the 20 chairs in philosophy at the Sorbonne, in addition to Jankélévitch's Chair in Moral Philosophy, there was one chair in aesthetics, four in general philosophy (held by Jean Wahl, Jean Hyppolite, Jean Guitton, and Paul Ricoeur), four in the history of philosophy, two in logic and philosophy of science, two in sociology (Raymond Aron and Georges Gurvitch), five in psychology (including chairs held by Daniel Lagache and Jean Piaget), and one in pedagogy.[41] In Levinas's case, we see a similar situation in that throughout most of his career, his ethical and religious works were far less popular among philosophy students and philosophers than were his phenomenological works. In the 1970s and after, however, Levinas's ethical works found new favor and a wider audience, as did Jankélévitch's, whose 1949 *Traité des vertus* was reissued in 1984–6.[42]

While Levinas and Jankélévitch's work never strays too far from the ethical, the same cannot be said of Michel Foucault. Rather, it is only in his final years that Foucault's work makes a distinctive turn toward the ethical. We have already seen how this turn emerged in Foucault's reflections on the subject. In the second and third volumes of *The History of Sexuality*, we see that his thinking has moved considerably from the focus on power that dominated *Discipline and Punish* and the first volume of *The History of Sexuality*. Now, Foucault's interest in sex is framed in terms of "the kind of relationship you ought to have with yourself, *rapport à soi*, which [he calls] ethics, and which determines how the individual is supposed to constitute himself as a moral subject of his own actions."[43] In volumes two and three of *The History of Sexuality* and several important interviews that he gave in 1983–4, Foucault talks about this relationship to self that constituted ethics in terms of four major aspects: the "ethical substance," "the mode of subjectivation [*mode d'assujettissement*]," "the forms of ethical work one performs on oneself," and "the telos of the ethical subject."[44] By "ethical substance," Foucault refers to that part of the individual which he or she constitutes as the prime material of his or her moral conduct. For the Greeks, according to Foucault, this was the acts linked

---

[41]   This information comes from *Index Generalis: France 1958: Enseignement supérieure. Recherche scientifique* (Paris: C. Klincksieck, 1959).

[42]   First published in 1949 as an 847-page volume by Éditions Bordas, *Traité des vertus* was first reissued in three volumes by Bordas: Vol. 1: *Le Sérieux de l'intention* (1968), Vol. 2: *Les Vertus et l'amour* (1970), and Vol. 3: *L'Innocence et la méchanceté* (1972). These three volumes were subsequently reissued in inexpensive paperback editions by Éditions Gallimard, Vol. 1 in 1984, Vols. 2 and 3 in 1986.

[43]   Michel Foucault, "On the Genealogy of Ethics," p. 352.

[44]   These and the formulations that follow are taken from Foucault's introduction to *The Use of Pleasure*, trans. Robert Hurley (New York: Random House, 1985), pp. 26–8, and "On the Genealogy of Ethics," pp. 352–5.

to pleasure and desire, while for Christianity, it was the flesh. Modes of subjectivation are the ways in which "the individual establishes his relation to the rule and recognized himself as obliged to put it into practice," the ways, in other words, "in which people are invited or incited to recognize their moral obligations." The forms of ethical work are the ways in which "we change ourselves in order to become ethical subjects," the self-forming activities and ascetic practices through which we transform ourselves into moral agents who comply with ethical rules. And the telos of the ethical subject is not just the immediate end to which our actions are directed, but "the kind of being to which we aspire when we behave" morally. These four aspects of ethics are part of the care of the self which Foucault comes to understand ultimately as a practice of freedom: "Freedom is the ontological condition of ethics... what is ethics, if not the practice of freedom, the conscious [*réfléchie*] practice of freedom."[45]

In the years that followed structuralism, as feminist thinkers began to receive attention, issues of gender ethics and the position of women in society and the academy came into focus in the works of Cixous, Le Doeuff, Irigaray, and Kristeva. In the latter two, the focus on ethics led to reflections on religion, and there is a marked turn toward the religious in their later works. A similar turn can be seen in Derrida's career, as the metaphysical and phenomenological interests of his early works are increasingly replaced by political, ethical, and religious reflections in his later writings.[46] Where questions of religion were always central to

---

45 Michel Foucault, "The Ethics of Concern for the Self as a Practice of Freedom," trans. P. Aranov and D. McGrawth, in *The Essential Works of Michel Foucault, 1954–1988. Vol. 1: Ethics: Subjectivity and Truth*, ed. Paul Rabinow (New York: New Press, 1997), p. 284.

46 By Derrida's early works, I have in mind primarily the texts before 1974: *Edmund Husserl's Origin of Geometry: An Introduction* (1962), *Of Grammatology* (1967), *Speech and Phenomena, and Other Essays on Husserl's Theory of Signs* (1967), *Writing and Difference* (1967), *Dissemination* (1972), *Margins of Philosophy* (1972), and *Glas* (1974). By the later, more ethical, political, and religious works, I have in mind *The Other Heading: Reflections on Today's Europe* (1991), *The Gift of Death* (1992), *Specters of Marx: The State of the Debt, the Work of Mourning, and the New International* (1993), *Politics of Friendship* (1994), *Monolingualism of the Other, or, The Prosthesis of Origin* (1996), *Religion* (1996, with Gianni Vattimo), *Of Hospitality* (1997), *On Cosmopolitanism and Forgiveness* (1997), *Adieu to Emmanuel Levinas* (1997), *The Work of Mourning* (2001), *Acts of Religion* (2002), *Ethics, Institutions, and the Right to Philosophy* (2002), and *Philosophy in a Time of Terror: Dialogues with Jürgen Habermas and Jacques Derrida* (2003). For full publication information, see the bibliography.

the writings of Paul Ricoeur and questions of politics were always central in the works of Lyotard, they too found a much broader audience for their later works as these topics found themselves becoming more central to the philosophical concerns of French readers. In addition, within the phenomenological tradition itself, as noted by Dominique Janicaud in his 1991 text *Le Tournant théologique de la phénoménologie française*, we find a distinct turn toward religion in several of its leading practitioners in the later decades of the twentieth century, including Jean-Luc Marion, Michel Henry, and Jean-Louis Chrétien.[47]

The years following structuralism also saw the emergence of two groups of thinkers whose critiques of the more dominant philosophical positions were grounded primarily on ethical, sometimes very traditional ethical, positions. Though they had a relatively short-lived influence that drew attention from readers of popular rather than academic journals, the *Nouveau Philosophes*, led by André Glucksmann and Bernard-Henri Lévy,[48] challenged what they believed to be the amoral stance from which they saw the French philosophical left justifying philosophical and ethical decisions that they regarded as dangerous. A similar perspective was adopted in the last decades of the twentieth century by a group of thinkers who put forward a neoliberal politics grounded on a return to Kantian ethical theory. While best known to English readers for their journalistic critique of what they called "sixties anti-humanism" in *La Pensée 68: Essai sur l'anti-humanisme contemporain*,[49] Luc Ferry and Alain Renaut, along with fellow travelers Alain Finkelkraut, Gilles Lipovetsky,

---

[47] In Janicaud's text, which is translated in Janicaud et al., *Phenomenology and the "Theological Turn": The French Debate* (New York: Fordham University Press, 2000), he is quite critical of this turn, arguing that insofar as phenomenology must renounce metaphysics "to explore experience in its phenomenal limits," while theology is essentially metaphysical in going beyond finitude and opening itself to the invisible, "phenomenology and theology make two" (p. 103).

[48] See André Glucksmann, *The Master Thinkers*, trans. Brian Pearce (New York: Harper and Row, 1980) and Bernard-Henri Lévy, *Barbarism with a Human Face*, trans. George Holoch (New York: Harper and Row, 1979). Both works were published originally in 1977. While their influence on French philosophy was short-lived, the influence of some of the *Nouveau Philosophes* on French culture can be argued to have been much more enduring. For a powerful critique of the anti-left politics and political motivations of the *Nouveau Philosophes*, see Kristin Ross, *May '68 and its Afterlives* (Chicago: University of Chicago Press, 2002), pp. 169–81.

[49] Paris: Éditions Gallimard, 1985; for English translation, see note 3 above.

André Comte-Sponville, and others produced a number of works that, while largely overlooked in American, British, and French academic circles, were a dominant presence in Parisian left-bank bookstores in the closing years of the twentieth century. And, whatever their philosophical talents might be, several of these philosophers have come to hold significant institutional power. Luc Ferry is Professor of Philosophy at the University of Paris VII-Jussieu, served as Chairman of the National Curriculum Council at the Ministry of National Education from 1994 to 2002 and, following the conservative landslide in the 2002 election, was named by Prime Minister Jean-Pierre Raffarin to replace Jack Lang as the Minister for Youth, National Education and Research, a position that put him at the center of government policy concerning school teaching and higher education as well as decisions concerning government funding for research and technology.[50] Alain Renaut is Professor of Philosophy at the University of Paris IV-Paris-Sorbonne, and was asked in 2001 by the Ministry of National Education to chair a group of experts who would examine and report on whether French universities are successful in achieving their three primary goals: the transmission of specialized knowledge, the promotion of *"culture générale,"* and the preparation of students for entering specialized professions (e.g., law, medicine, pharmacy, etc.). André Comte-Sponville is *Maître de Conférences* in Philosophy at the University of Paris I-Panthéon-Sorbonne, and has written or edited a number of "popular" philosophy texts on topics in ethics and politics that have reached a wide audience outside the academy.[51]

[50] In his position as Minister for Youth, National Education and Research, Luc Ferry put forward perhaps the most successful arguments ever made against maintaining the *classe de philosophie* as part of all *baccalauréat* programs. One is reminded here of the idea that "only Nixon could go to China."

[51] Although Comte-Sponville has authored several more academic works, he is best known as the author of *Petit Traité des grandes vertus* (Paris: Presses universitaires de France, 1995), which spent 14 months on the French bestsellers list and has been translated into over twenty languages, including English as *A Small Treatise on Great Virtues: The Uses of Philosophy in Everyday Life*, trans. Catherine Temerson (New York: Henry Holt, 2001). He has also edited over a dozen small (60–65 page) anthologies of *Pensées sur...* for publisher Albin Michel on such topics as love, freedom, morality, wisdom, death, consciousness, man, and God.

6

Conclusion

If there is a single conclusion that I hope this story of the unfolding of philosophy in France in the twentieth century supports, it is that French philosophy has been badly misunderstood when it is seen simply as a response and reaction to a number of significant German philosophical thinkers. In particular, it seems that the American reception of French philosophy has grossly over-estimated the role that Heidegger's philosophy has played, with the result that for much of the twentieth century, "French philosophy" meant Sartre's philosophy, and when it no longer meant Sartre's, it meant Derrida's. While Sartre and Derrida are both significant philosophical voices, they are not the only voices, nor were they ever the exclusive, or in Derrida's case, even dominant, voices. Because the American reception has been so heavily invested in Heidegger and a certain version of the phenomenological tradition, what resulted was an almost total blindness to important trends within French philosophy that are not amenable to being framed as Gallic Heideggerianism.

Most notable here is the French epistemological tradition, represented by Bachelard, Canguilhem, Cavaillès, and more recently, Michel Serres, a major French philosopher whose work is virtually ignored by American Continental philosophers. Author of more than thirty books, Serres is only the tenth philosopher to be elected to the *Academie Française* since 1900, and the only one since 1979. The English-speaking philosophical community's relative indifference and inattention to Serres is reflected as well by its failure to note that some of the most influential philosophers of the last two decades of the twentieth century work in what can only be called the analytic tradition. In fact, since Foucault's death in 1984, all of the Chairs in Philosophy at the Collège de France have been held by philosophers who work in the analytic tradition:[1] Jules Vuillemin, Gilles-Gaston Granger, Jacques Bouveresse, Anne Fagot-Largeault, and Ian Hacking. And since Merleau-Ponty's death in 1961, only Foucault and Jean Hyppolite have held Chairs in Philosophy at the Collège de France in which they did work that one in the English-speaking philosophical world would commonly associate with "French" philosophy.

Beyond this blindness to the French epistemological tradition, there have been other consequences of the general view of philosophy in France as Gallic Heideggerianism that inform the way French philosophy has been read and taught. Bergson, for example, has been largely overlooked, with the notable exception of those who follow Deleuze's work, for whom Bergson is an essential reference. And Deleuze, for his part, was "discovered" by English-speaking philosophers long after his impact on French thought was made. Where Derrida's early works of the 1960s were translated into English usually within 5–10 years of their appearance in France, Deleuze's major works took three to four times as long to appear in English. For example, Derrida's *Of Grammatology*, *Speech and Phenomena*, and *Writing and Difference*, all published in France in 1967, appear in English translation six, nine, and eleven years later. By contrast, although Deleuze's early text on Proust appeared in English in 1972,[2] eight years after its French publication, none of Deleuze's important historical studies of the 1960s (on Hume, Nietzsche, Kant, Bergson, and Spinoza) appeared in English sooner than 21 years after their French publication, and his two major works,

---

[1] While I am characterizing these philosophers as "analytic," this means something different in the French context than the American one. In "Continental Insularity: Contemporary French Analytical Philosophy," Pascal Engel notes that both Vuillemin and Granger are, for different reasons, not easily situated within more mainstream analytic philosophy (in *Contemporary French Philosophy*, ed. A. Phillips Griffiths [Cambridge: Cambridge University Press, 1987], pp. 6–7). The same can also be said for Bouveresse, Fagot-Largeault, and Hacking.

[2] This points to a factor other than the Heideggerianism I am highlighting in the reception of recent French theory, namely, that the initial positive responses to French theory have consistently come from departments of literature rather than departments of philosophy. With very few exceptions, the translators of the works by recent French theorists, and especially the early translations, were done by scholars trained in literature, not philosophy, and the history of the early and enthusiastic response to Derrida's work by faculty and students in departments of French, English, and Comparative Literature, is well known. To substantiate this, consider the following: from 1963 to 1980, the number of journal articles published on Derrida's work in France was 110, with 53 in journals of philosophy and 57 in journals of literary criticism; during the same period in the United States, 133

Difference and Repetition (1968) and *The Logic of Sense* (1969), appear in English translation in 1994 and 1990, respectively.[3] And while the translation of Deleuze's book on Proust was initially well received and continues to be an important resource for scholars of French literature, his series of historical monographs, which offer as significant a rereading of modern philosophy as has appeared in recent years, is largely overlooked by those philosophers who consider themselves specialists in recent French philosophy.[4]

Even Foucault, who would be regarded by many as the most dominant philosophical presence in France in the latter half of the twentieth century, was initially read far less enthusiastically by American "Continental" philosophers than he was by historians, social scientists, and feminist theorists. In fact, much of the early *philosophical* reception of Foucault's works came precisely from philosophers whose interests were in feminist theory.[5] But the fact that feminist philosophers as well as other feminist theorists were interested in Foucault's work

journal articles on Derrida were published, with 35 in philosophy and 98 in literary criticism. In the next four years (1981–4), five additional articles on Derrida were published in France (4 in philosophy, 1 in literary criticism); in the US, on the other hand, from 1981–4, 130 articles were published, with 5 in philosophy and 125 in literary criticism. These figures come from Michèle Lamont, "How to Become a Dominant French Philosopher: The Case of Jacques Derrida," *American Journal of Sociology* Vol. 93, No. 3 (November 1987): 584–622. Since 1984, however, it should be noted that the trend Lamont chronicles is not so clear: from 1984 to 2000, the MLA database lists 304 book or journal titles in English with Derrida's name in the title, while the Philosophers Index database lists 181.

3   Even more striking is the reception of Derrida's later works, which often appear in English before they appear in French or are translated almost immediately after their French publication, and would seem to have a far larger audience of English than French readers.

4   Gilles Deleuze, *David Hume, sa vie, son oeuvre* (Paris: Presses universitaires de France, 1952); *Empirisme et subjectivité* (Paris: Presses universitaires de France, 1953; English translation: 1991); "Lucrèce et le naturalisme" in *Études philosophiques*, No. 1 (Jan.–May 1961); *Nietzsche et la philosophie* (Paris: Presses universitaires de France, 1962; English translation: 1983); *La Philosophie critique de Kant* (Paris: Presses universitaires de France, 1963; English translation: 1984); *Le Bergsonisme* (Paris: Presses universitaires de France, 1966; English translation: 1988); *Spinoza et le problème de l'expression* (Paris: Éditions de Minuit, 1968; English translation: 1990); *Spinoza, philosophie pratique* (Paris: Éditions de Minuit, 1981; English translation: 1988). Publication information for the English translations can be found in the bibliography.

5   I am thinking here of the work of people like Linda Martín Alcoff, Sandra Bartky, Judith Butler, Nancy Fraser, and Jana Sawicki.

from its first appearance does not alter the fact that the "mainstream" Continental philosophical establishment and most of the large graduate programs in Continental philosophy were slow to warm to Foucault's importance, and his position in these programs remains far less important than the position of several other French philosophers who are more easily assimilated into the phenomenological–Heideggerian tradition, broadly construed.[6]

One last significant philosophical development that has received little attention outside France, again because it does not fit the dominant model of what the English-speaking philosophical community considers "French" philosophy, is the work that brings a Spinozist approach to Marxian theory. This work reflects the long tradition of Spinoza scholarship in France in the twentieth century, beginning with Alain, Lagneau, Delbos, and Brunschvicg,[7] and continuing in more recent years with the teaching and writing of Ferdinand Alquié, Martial Guéroult, Gilles Deleuze, and Louis Althusser.[8] Spinoza has been, throughout the century, one of the authors whose works were most often part of the required reading for the *agrégation*,[9] and while today the English-speaking philosophical world has all but given up on political theories that don't in some way ground themselves in Kant, whether in a Habermasian or Rawlsian guise, many of the politically engaged students who

---

[6] A similar point could be made by examining the English-speaking philosophical community's response to the two most productive of the French philosophers associated with Derrida: consider the relative indifference to the work of Sarah Kofman, who always maintained her distance from the work of Heidegger, in comparison to the relatively enthusiastic reception of Jean-Luc Nancy's work, which maintains a consistent engagement with Heidegger's *oeuvre*.

[7] Alain (Émile-Auguste Chartier), *Les Philosophes* (Paris: P. Delaplane, 1901); Victor Delbos, *Le Problème moral dans la philosophie de Spinoza et dans l'histoire du spinozisme* (Paris: Félix Alcan, 1893); Léon Brunschvicg, *Spinoza* (Paris: Félix Alcan, 1894) and *Spinoza et ses contemporains* (Paris: Félix Alcan, 1923).

[8] Ferdinand Alquié, *Nature et vérité dans la philosophie de Spinoza* (Paris: Centre de documentation universitaire, 1965) and *Le Rationalisme de Spinoza* (Paris: Presses universitaires de France, 1981); Martial Guéroult, *Spinoza 1. Dieu (Éthique, I)* (Paris: Aubier-Montaigne, 1968) and *Spinoza II. L'Âme (Éthique, II)* (Paris: Aubier-Montaigne, 1974). For Deleuze's texts, see note 4, above.

[9] From 1900 to 1958, Spinoza's texts, sometimes in French and sometimes in Latin, are part of the program for the *concours* in 1900–3, 1906, 1908, 1913–14, 1919, 1923–4, 1926, 1928–31, 1933–4, 1936–9, 1942–4, 1948, 1951–2, 1954–6, and 1958. Only Plato and Kant (who appear almost every year), Aristotle (44 times), Descartes (41 times), Leibniz (33 times), and Hume (32 times) appear on the program more frequently. The somewhat unexpected presence of Hume is in part a consequence

came under Althusser's influence in his years at the École Normale Supérieure have followed his turn away from Kantian transcendental philosophy and toward a Spinozist immanentism.

One place to locate this turn from Kant to Spinoza is in terms of how the French Spinozists avoid the Kantian assumption that the individual autonomy of the isolated subject is the *summum bonum*, an assumption that leads to the modern idea that politics begins with the problem of balancing the rights of the individual against the needs of society. For Deleuze as well as French Marxists like Althusser, Alain Badiou, Jacques Rancière, Pierre Macherey, Pierre-François Moreau, Alexandre Matheron, or Étienne Balibar,[10] the political attractiveness of Spinoza is due in part to the fact that his metaphysics of the subject can avoid this problem by allowing the subject to see him- or herself as *one* with the public rather than a *part* of the public. As Antonio Negri has argued, in a book well known in French philosophical circles,[11] contrary to the

---

of selections from Hume's *Treatise on Human Nature* being one of the two choices for the English language oral explication 17 times between 1937 and 1958. Spinoza's centrality to the French canon should be compared to his role in US philosophical instruction, where he is by far the most often marginalized or overlooked of the "Gang of Seven" that typically comprise the syllabi for courses in the History of Modern Philosophy.

[10]   Among the significant texts by this group are the following: Étienne Balibar, *Spinoza et la politique* (Paris: Presses universitaires de France, 1985); Pierre Macherey, *Hegel ou Spinoza* (Paris: F. Maspero, 1979); *Avec Spinoza: Études sur la doctrine et l'histoire du spinozisme* (Paris: Presses universitaires de France, 1992); *Introduction à l'"Ethique" de Spinoza, 5 Vols: 1. ptie. La Nature des choses; 2. ptie. La Réalité mentale; 3. ptie. La Vie affective; 4. ptie. La Condition humaine; 5. ptie. Les Voies de la libération* (Paris: Presses universitaires de France, 1994–8); Alexandre Matheron, *Individu et communauté chez Spinoza* (Paris: Éditions de Minuit, 1969); *Individualité et relations interhumaines chez Spinoza* (Paris: Éditions de Minuit, 1969); *Le Christ et le salut des ignorants chez Spinoza* (Paris: Aubier-Montaigne, 1971); *Anthropologie et politique au XVIIe siècle: Études sur Spinoza* (Paris: Vrin, 1986); Pierre-François Moreau, *Spinoza* (Paris: Éditions du Seuil, 1975); *Spinoza: L'Expérience et l'éternité* (Paris: Presses universitaires de France, 1994).

[11]   Although written in Italian while in prison and published in 1981, Negri's text was translated into French by François Matheron in 1982 as *L'Anomalie sauvage: Puissance et Pouvoir chez Spinoza* (Paris: Presses universitaires de France, 1982), with prefaces by Gilles Deleuze, Pierre Macherey, and Alexandre Matheron. Negri had been invited by Louis Althusser to teach at the École Normale Supérieure in 1977–8. A leading figure in the Italian extreme-Left *Autonomia* movement, Negri was arrested in April 1979 and accused of having been the leader of the Red Brigades, the terrorist movement that had assassinated Aldo Moro, two-time Prime Minister of Italy (1963–8 and 1974–6) and leader of the Christian Democrat

rigid individualism that characterizes seventeenth-century thinkers like Hobbes,[12] Spinoza understands human individuality constructing itself as a collective entity.[13] "By singular things," Spinoza writes in the *Ethics*, "I understand things that are finite and have a determinate existence. And if a number of individuals so concur in one action that together they are all the cause of one effect, I consider them all, to that extent, as one singular thing."[14] This understanding of individual and collective, which Spinoza elaborates in his political works in terms of his concept of the multitude,[15] departs from both the Kantian and contract-theory traditions, and it has facilitated a continued attraction to Marxian theory that one sees in the works of Badiou, Rancière, Balibar, Macherey, and others. But insofar as these thinkers work out of a tradition that is alien both to the Heideggerian–phenomenological tradition that has dominated English-language Continental philosophy and to the neo-Kantian tradition that dominates current English-language social and political theory, their work has been all but ignored.

As I have tried to suggest throughout part I, were one familiar with the institutions that govern philosophical instruction and the indigenous developments in philosophy in France in the nineteenth and twentieth centuries, it would be harder to ignore some of the philosophical

---

Party. After awaiting trial for four and a half years, during which time most of the charges against him were dropped, Negri was released from prison in July 1983 following his election to the Italian parliament as a member of the Radical Party. Two months later, after a vote to remove his parliamentary immunity, he escaped to France and sought political asylum. From 1983 to 1997, Negri taught political philosophy at the University of Paris-VIII-Saint-Denis. In July 1997, Negri voluntarily returned to Italy to serve the remainder of his sentence at Rebibbia prison in Rome. He completed his sentence and was released on April 25, 2003.

[12] C. B. Macpherson's *The Political Theory of Possessive Individualism: Hobbes to Locke* (Oxford: Clarendon Press, 1962) is the *locus classicus* for this account of individualism in seventeenth-century thought.

[13] Antonio Negri, *The Savage Anomaly: The Power of Spinoza's Metaphysics and Politics*, trans. Michael Hardt (Minneapolis: University of Minnesota Press, 1991), p. 135.

[14] Benedict de Spinoza, *Ethics*, Book II, Definition 7. The importance of this idea for Deleuze's thinking about becoming, de- and reterritorialization, and assemblages must here also be noted.

[15] See Negri, *The Savage Anomaly*, pp. 194–210, and Étienne Balibar, "Spinoza, the Anti-Orwell," in *Masses, Classes, Ideas: Studies on Politics and Philosophy Before and After Marx*, trans. James Swenson (New York: Routledge, 1994), pp. 3–37.

positions that have been obscured by the English-language, and particularly the American, reception of a few "master thinkers." While it might not be surprising for philosophy, which has often understood itself to be the most transcendent of disciplines, to see itself as distinct from the institutional practices that form its practitioners, it is ironic that followers of trends in twentieth-century French philosophy, who pride themselves on their attentiveness to history, should be guilty of the same conceit.[16]

And, to return to an idea suggested at the outset, I hope that it is now clear that it makes sense to mean by "French philosophy" something more than simply the philosophy that is written in France or in the French language. For while there may be no unifying themes that describe what one would identify as uniquely "French" philosophy, there are certain institutions – the *lycée* education and the *classe de philosophie*, the preparation for and study at the École Normale Supérieure, the preparation for and admission into the *agrégation*, the tradition of public instruction at the University of Paris, the institutional practices at the Collège de France and the École Pratique des Hautes Études – that throughout the century and continuing to this day have marked the activity of philosophizing in France. And these institutions have created a unique philosophical sensibility that does allow one to identify developments in "French philosophy" that distinguish it from its German, British, and American counterparts. Why so many of the English-speaking "specialists" in French philosophy are unaware of these institutions and their effects on French philosophical sensibilities remains a question worth asking. This chapter closes with the hope that more attention will be spent examining the academic institutionalization of philosophy in France – and the United States – with rather less spent awaiting the next appearance of a master discourse from a master thinker.

---

[16] Soulié comes to a similar conclusion at the end of his "Anatomie du goût philosophique."

Part II

Key Biographies in Brief

Ferdinand Alquié (1906–85) was born in Carcassonne (Aude, Languedoc). He studied at the Lycée de Carcassonne, then in Paris at the Lycée Louis-le-Grand and later at the Sorbonne, where he submitted his thesis for the *Diplôme d'études supérieures* in 1929 on "L'Argument ontologique chez saint Anselme et les critiques de Gaunilon et de saint Thomas d'Aquin" ("The Ontological Argument in Saint Anselm and the Criticisms of Gaunilo and Saint Thomas Aquinas"). He passed his *agrégation* in 1931, finishing first, and taught from 1931–42 at *lycées* in Mont-de-Marsan (1931), Carcassonne (1932–6), the Lycée Saint-Louis in Paris (1937), and Lycée Rollin (1938). In 1939, Alquié was appointed as instructor of the *khâgne* at the *lycée* in Caen, but he returned to Paris the following year, and taught *hypokhâgne* or *khâgne* at the prestigious Paris Lycées Condorcet (1940), Louis-le-Grande (1941–2), and Henri-IV (1941–2). He taught briefly at the Sorbonne (1945) before joining the faculty at the University of Montpellier, where he taught until 1951. In 1950, Alquié completed his *Doctorat ès Lettres*, submitting a primary thesis, *Le Découverte métaphysique de l'homme chez Descartes* ("The Metaphysical Discovery of Man in Descartes"), along with a *thèse complémentaire La Nostalgie de l'Être* ("The Nostalgia for Being"). Alquié returned to teach at the Sorbonne in 1952, became Professor of the History of Modern Philosophy in 1953, and taught there until his retirement in 1976. He was elected to the *Académie des Sciences morales et politiques* in 1975.

Associated with the activities of the surrealist group in the 1920s and 1930s, Alquié authored over twenty books, including several important studies that focused on reason in modern philosophy (Descartes, Malebranche, Spinoza, Kant). One of his works has appeared in English translation: *Philosophie du surréalisme* (1955; English translation: *The Philosophy of Surrealism*, trans. Bernard Waldrop [Ann Arbor: University of Michigan Press, 1965]). He also served as editor of important editions of the works of Descartes and Kant. Over his two decades at the Sorbonne, he served on the juries of numerous doctoral theses and his influence can be seen on many figures, including Gilles Deleuze, whose secondary thesis for the *Doctorat d'État* on Spinoza he directed, and, most notably, Jean-Luc Marion.

Louis Althusser (1918–90) was born in Birmandreis, near Algiers. He lived in Algeria until 1930, when his family moved to Marseilles, where Althusser attended the Lycée Saint-Charles. In 1936, the family moved to Lyon, where Althusser attended the Lycée du Parc, preparing his *hypokhâgne* and *khâgne*, and studying with Jean Guitton and Jean Lacroix, among others. His plans to enroll in the École Normale Supérieure in 1939 were interrupted by the war and, having been called to military service, Althusser was captured by the Germans in June 1940. He spent the remainder of the war in a prisoner-of-war camp in Schleswig-Holstein. After the war, Althusser resumed his studies at the École Normale Supérieure, where he met Jean-Toussaint Desanti and the Vietnamese Marxist philosopher and phenomenologist Trân Duc Thao. He wrote his *Diplôme d'études supérieures*, "Du contenu dans la pensée de G. W. F. Hegel" ("On Content in the Thought of G. W. F. Hegel"), in 1947 under the direction of Gaston Bachelard. Althusser passed his *agrégation* in 1948, scoring first on the written examination and second on the oral, and was appointed *agrégé-répétiteur* or *caïman* at the École Normale Supérieure. He presented a thesis to Vladimir Jankélévitch and Jean Hyppolite on "Politics and Philosophy in the Eighteenth Century" in 1950, but this was ultimately rejected. Althusser remained as *caïman* (his official title was *Maître-assistant* and, beginning in 1954, *Secrétaire de l'École littéraire* of the École Normale Supérieure) until the end of his career in November 1980, which allowed him to befriend and influence several generations of students he coached for the *agrégation* exam (among them Michel Foucault, Jacques Derrida, Michel Serres, and Pierre Bourdieu). A later generation of students, instructed by Althusser in seminars on Marx, includes Étienne Balibar, Alain Badiou, Pierre Macherey, Dominique Lecourt, Régis Debray, Jacques Rancière, and Jacques-Alain Miller. Throughout these years, Althusser was a dominant philosophical presence at the École Normale and the conferences and lectures he organized allowed his students access to most of the important philosophers in France.[1] In

---

[1]   For a list of some of the individuals who spoke at Althusser's invitation, see Étienne Balibar's memorial note for Althusser in the 1993 issue of the *Annuaire* of the

1975, Althusser was awarded his *Doctorat d'État* at the University of Picardie on the basis of published work.

Althusser was one of the leading figures in the structuralist movement, along with Jacques Lacan and Claude Lévi-Strauss. He joined the French Communist Party (PCF) in 1948 and was one of the party's leading theoreticians for many years. Althusser's structuralist reading of Marx as a scientist rather than humanist, which was strongly influenced by the work of Jean Cavaillès and Georges Canguilhem, put him at odds not only with Sartre's existentialist reading but also with anyone whose interpretation of Marx drew heavily upon the 1844 manuscripts, which Althusser all but dismissed as non-Marxist juvenilia. The sharp distinction he drew between ideology and science, between the early Hegelian Marx and the later, scientific Marx of the *Grundrisse* and *Capital*, eventually put him at odds with the PCF establishment. In the 1970s, he became a focal point of party infighting, as a cadre of Althusser's students at the École Normale presented a Maoist challenge to the party that they saw as increasingly reactionary. Although Althusser himself, unlike many of his students, was not publicly censured and expelled from the PCF, at the session of the Central Committee devoted to questions of ideology and culture, held March 11–13, 1966, the party chose to back Roger Garaudy's position rather than Althusser's, a choice that diminished considerably his subsequent influence on party affairs.

From the late 1940s onward, Althusser suffered from serious bouts of depression and, beginning in the 1950s, he was under constant medical supervision with frequent hospitalizations and extreme treatments, including electroshock, for manic depression. In November 1980, he was arrested for the strangulation murder of Hélène Rytmann-Legotien, his long-time companion (they met in 1946) and, since 1976, his wife. Following a lengthy psychiatric examination, Althusser was declared unfit to stand trial and was confined to the Sainte-Anne psychiatric hospital. He spent most of the remainder of his life living in various public and private clinics in and around Paris.

Not surprisingly, the murder of his wife was a scandal that seriously tarnished Althusser's reputation as well as the reputation of the École Normale, where at the time he not only taught but lived on school

---

Association Amicale de Secours des Anciens Élèves de l'École Normale Supérieure, pp. 427–8; among those mentioned are Guéroult, Canguilhem, Beaufret, Gandillac, Vuillemin, Granger, Foucault, Serres, Deleuze, Vernant, Negri, and Bouveresse. It was also at Althusser's invitation and initiative that Lacan began offering his seminars at the École Normale in 1964.

premises. While the École Normale quickly regained its prestige, Althusser's prestige was not as quick to recover. Although a number of works of his have been published posthumously, he was never able to excite his readers the way he had excited the students who came under his tutelage at the École Normale Supérieure, nor were his posthumous writings able to recreate the mystique that surrounded him in earlier days, a mystique we see clearly in the following remark from one of his students during the 1960s, Dominique Lecourt:

> Such is the oblivion to which he has been brutally consigned that you will have no image of Althusser, who was my friend for over twenty years. The heavy incline of his enormous domed forehead, the bags under his eyes, his sometimes halting gait – these already attested to the atrocious suffering that ravaged his life. His intense blue eyes could be cheerful, sarcastic, arrogant; he would often become abruptly shrouded in the mists of melancholy for long periods of silence. But the pupil I then was did not possess the key to what I have just written. My friends and I discerned in it the stamp of genius. Althusser was the prince of philosophers, the hero of thought who was defying the Communist Party authorities, the one who was going to save Marx from Marxism and the Marxists.[2]

Raymond Aron (1905–83) was born in Paris. He attended *lycée* in Versailles before doing his *hypokhâgne* and *khâgne* at the Lycée Condorcet in 1922–4, where he studied philosophy with André Cresson. Aron studied at the École Normale Supérieure from 1924 to 1927, entering with the same class of 52 students (29 in arts, 23 in sciences) that included, among others, Jean-Paul Sartre, Paul Nizan, Daniel Lagache, and Georges Canguilhem. He received certificates in psychology, philosophy, history of philosophy, and morality and sociology, and submitted his thesis to Léon Brunschvicg for the *Diplôme d'études supérieures* in 1927 on "La Notion d'intemporal dans la philosophie de Kant" ("The Notion of the Atemporal in Kant's Philosophy"). Aron passed the *agrégation* in 1928, finishing first, and obtained his *Doctorat ès Lettres* from the Sorbonne in 1938, submitting his thesis *Introduction à la philosophie de l'histoire* (*Introduction to the Philosophy of History: An Essay on the Limits of Historical Objectivity*, trans. George J. Irwin [Boston, MA: Beacon Press, 1961]) along with a *thèse complémentaire*, "Essai

---

[2] Dominique Lecourt, *The Mediocracy: French Philosophy since the mid-1970s*, trans. Gregory Elliot (London: Verso, 2001), pp. 11–12.

sur la théorie de l'histoire dans l'Allemagne comtemporaine" ("Essay on the Theory of History in Contemporary Germany"). Between 1930 and 1940, he taught at the University of Cologne (1930–1), the Maison Académique Française in Berlin (1931–3), the *lycée* in Le Havre (1933–4), the École Normale Supérieure-Saint Cloud (1935–9), and as *Maître de conférences* at the University of Toulouse (1939–40). From 1940 to 1944, Aron served as editor of *La France libre* in London. After the war, he returned to Paris and taught at the Institut d'Études Politiques (Sciences Po) and the École Nationale d'Administration (1945–55) before assuming the position of Professor of Sociology at the Sorbonne, where he taught from 1957 to 1968. In 1970, he was elected to the Chair in Sociology at the Collège de France, a position he held until his death in 1983. During these years, he also served, beginning in 1960, as *Directeur d'études* of "Philosophy and Political Sociology" in the Sixth Section of the École Pratique des Hautes Études, and from 1965–70, he taught as Professor-at-Large at Cornell University.

Aron was a major figure in the introduction of German sociology, especially that of Max Weber, in France. He was elected to the *Académie des Sciences morales et politiques* in 1963. Aron was close friends with Jean-Paul Sartre and Simone de Beauvoir during the 1920s and 1930s, but after World War II, at the outset of the Cold War, they had a falling out as Aron's politics turned to the right and more classical liberalism. He came to have little sympathy for existentialism and even less sympathy for those Marxists who would not oppose the actions of Stalin. He wrote as a journalist for many years, briefly for *Les Temps modernes*, on whose original editorial board he sat, and, following the break with Sartre and Beauvoir, for the conservative daily *Le Figaro* and, later, for the more progressive *L'Express*. A prolific writer, Aron published over thirty books of philosophy, sociology, history, and political analysis, including *La Sociologie allemande contemporaine* (1936; English translation: *German Sociology*, trans. Mary and Thomas Bottomore [New York: Free Press of Glencoe, 1964]) and *L'Opium des intellectuels* (1955: English translation: *The Opium of the Intellectuals*, trans. Terence Kilmartin [New York: W. W. Norton, 1962]). In his later years, as his interests turned toward concrete political, economic, and international issues, he became one of the leading political commentators in France.

Pierre Aubenque (1929–) was born in L'Isle-Jourdain (Gers, Midi-Pyrénées). He attended *lycée* in Toulouse before entering the École Normale Supérieure in 1947. Aubenque passed his *agrégation* in 1950, finishing first, and, following a fellowship at the Fondation Thiers,[3] taught at the universities of Montpellier (1955–60), Besançon (1960–4), Aix-en-Provence (1964–6), and Hamburg (1968–9), before taking a Chair in Ancient Philosophy at the University of Paris IV-Paris-Sorbonne in 1970. While his philosophical interests are wide-ranging and his teaching has influenced several generations of Sorbonne students, Aubenque is best known for his studies of Aristotle, especially his *Le Problème de l'être chez Aristote* ("The Problem of Being in Aristotle"), submitted in 1962 for the *Doctorat d'État* and published later that year.

Gaston Bachelard (1884–1962) was born in Bar-sur-Aube (Champagne). After his military service, he worked for several years for the postal service, during which time he also completed a *licence* in mathematics in 1912 at the Lycée Saint-Louis in Paris. Bachelard began his studies in philosophy in 1919, passed his *licence* in philosophy in 1920, and passed the *agrégation* in 1922. During World War I, he served with distinction, spending 38 months at the Front, for which he was awarded the *Croix de guerre*. From 1919–30, he was professor of physics and chemistry at the Collège at Bar-sur-Aube. During this period, his interests turned toward the philosophy of science. He received his *Doctorat ès Lettres* from the Sorbonne in 1929, submitting to Abel Rey and Léon Brunschvicg his doctoral thesis *L'Essai sur la connaissance approchée* ("Essay on Approximate Knowledge") and his complementary thesis *Étude sur l'évolution d'une problème de physique: La Propagation thermique dans les solides* ("Study of the Evolution of a Physics Problem: Thermic Propagation in Solids"). From 1930–40, he was professor of philosophy at the University of Dijon. In 1940, he was named *Maître de conférences* in the Methodology and Philosophy of Science and Director of the Institut d'Histoire des Sciences et des Techniques at the Sorbonne. Soon thereafter he succeeded Abel Rey and occupied the Chair in the History and Philosophy of Science at the Sorbonne until his retirement in 1954. In 1951, he was awarded the *Légion d'honneur*; in 1955, he was elected to the *Académie des Sciences morales et politiques*; and in 1961, he received the *Grand Prix National des Lettres*.

---

[3] The Fondation Thiers, located in the 16th arrondissement of Paris, was established in 1892 through a donation by Mlle. Félicie Dosne (sister-in-law of President Adolphe Thiers [1797–1877], first president of the Third Republic, 1871–3) to provide a residence and modest financial support to young researchers for three consecutive years.

Between 1928 and 1961, Bachelard published 23 books, including 12 on the philosophy of modern science and nine on artistic and poetic imagination. Rejecting positivism, he can reasonably be regarded as the first thinker to emphasize the concept of discontinuity in the history of science. In the French context, which has only recently distinguished philosophy of science from epistemology, Bachelard's influence has been considerable, and in the second half of the century his works were often required reading for the *agrégation*. In particular, his introduction of the idea of discontinuity has influenced a number of thinkers, most notably Georges Canguilhem, Jean Hyppolite, and Michel Foucault, who came to see French philosophy in the twentieth century as divided into two traditions: one, "a philosophy of experience, of sense and of subject" that he identified with Sartre and Merleau-Ponty; the other "a philosophy of knowledge, of rationality and of concept" that he associated with Bachelard, Cavaillès, and Canguilhem.[4] Perhaps his greatest impact was on Louis Althusser, who used Bachelard's concept of the "epistemological break [*coupure épistémologique*]" to ground his claim that with *Capital*, Marx not only broke sharply with the Hegelian and Feuerbachian formulations of his youth, but also invented a new science of historical materialism.

Alain Badiou (1937–) was born in Rabat, Morocco. He did his *baccalauréat* at the experimental Lycée de Bellevue in Toulouse, *hypokhâgne* in 1954–5 at the classical Lycée Fermat in Toulouse, and his *khâgne* in 1955–6 in Paris at the Lycée Louis-le-Grand. Badiou studied at the École Normale Supérieure from 1956 to 1961, where he worked closely with Louis Althusser, and passed his *agrégation* in 1960, finishing first. After his obligatory military service, Badiou taught at the *lycée* in Reims from 1963 to 1965, then as an *Assistant* and *Maître-assistant* at the University of Reims from 1965 to 1969. In 1968, he was invited by Michel Foucault to join the faculty of the Department of Philosophy at the experimental University at Vincennes (Paris VIII), where he served as *Maître-assistant* (1969–83), *Maître de conférences* (1983–90), and, following the publication of his major work *L'Être et l'événement* in 1988 and the receipt of his *Habilitation* in 1989, as professor with a Chair in Ontology (1990–9). During his 30-year career at Paris VIII,

---

[4] Michel Foucault, "Introduction," in Georges Canguilhem, *The Normal and the Pathological*, trans. Carolyn R. Fawcett in collaboration with Robert S. Cohen (New York: Zone Books, 1989), p. 8.

Badiou's colleagues included Michel Serres, Gilles Deleuze, François
Châtelet, Jean-François Lyotard, Jacques Rancière, and Jacques-Alain
Miller. In 1999, Badiou left Vincennes to assume a chair as Professor
and Head of the Philosophy Department at the École Normale Supérieure. Since 1989, he has also been a *Directeur de Programme* at the
Collège Internationale de Philosophie. Throughout his career, Badiou
has been strongly associated with the Maoist movement in France and
he remains politically active as one of the leaders, with Sylvain Lazarus
and Natacha Michel, of *L'Organisation Politique*, an organization concerned with direct interventions in a range of controversial issues,
including current immigration and labor policies. In addition to authoring several works of fiction and theater, Badiou has produced a significant body of philosophical literature. His two most important texts are
Théorie du sujet (1982) and *L'Être et l'événement* (1988), the latter being a
work regarded by many as the most significant ontological work to
appear since Heidegger's *Being and Time*.

Badiou's work responds to what he sees as the contemporary malaise
among philosophers who regard the project of philosophy as, in some
sense, no longer possible. After so many "ends" of philosophy, "ends"
of metaphysics, and "deaths" of the subject, Badiou suggests that
philosophers no longer know what it means to do philosophy. Responding to this tendency, he calls instead for philosophy, and philosophers,
to recommit themselves to the project of systematic thinking. For
Badiou, such a project involves recognizing the compossibility of four
"generic conditions" – the matheme, the political, the poem, and love.
On Badiou's account, philosophy within modernity has tended to "su-
ture" itself to one or the other of these conditions, with the consequence
that it lost sight of its intrinsic mission, which is to think their compossibility. Badiou's project for philosophy is to de-suture thought from its
fixation on one of these generic conditions to the exclusion or devalu-
ation of the others. Today, he concludes, such a return of philosophy to
systematic thinking is possible because we are witnessing related transformations within each of the conditions. That is to say, we have
recently witnessed four events – Cantor–Gödel–Cohen's account of
multiplicity, the political upheavals between May 1968 and the Solidarity movement in Poland, Celan's call for the poem to think its other, and
Lacan's refiguring the concept of love – that make systematic philosophy possible once again. What this means for Badiou is that the time
is right for what he calls a "Platonic gesture," one that responds to
the anti-Platonism of the last century by once again thinking

Being *qua* Being, but now, *pace* Plato, thinking Being as "essentially multiple."

Étienne Balibar (1942–) was born in Avallon (Yonne, Burgundy). He studied at the Lycée Descartes in Tours from 1952 to 1958 and, following his *baccalauréat*, he attended *hypokhâgne* and *khâgne* at the Lycée Louis-le-Grand in 1958–60. Balibar continued his education at the École Normale Supérieure from 1960 to 1965, working closely with Jean Hyppolite, Louis Althusser, and Jacques Derrida. He received a *licence* in philosophy at the Sorbonne in 1962, and completed a *Diplôme d'études supérieures*, under the direction of Georges Canguilhem at the Sorbonne in 1963, submitting a thesis titled "La Technologie dans *Le Capital* de Marx" ("Technology in Marx's *Capital*"). After passing the *agrégation* in 1964, Balibar taught first as an *Assistant* at the University of Algiers (1965–7), then at the *lycée* in Savigny-sur-Orge, where he taught the *classe de lettres supérieures* from 1967 to 1969. He began his long career at the University of Paris in 1969, first as *Assistant*, then *Maître-assistant* at the University de Paris I-Sorbonne. In 1976–7, he taught at the University in Leiden in the Netherlands. He returned to the University de Paris I-Sorbonne in 1977, first as *Maître-assistant*, then *Maître de conférences*, and continued there until 1994. Balibar completed his doctorate in 1987, receiving the degree of *Docteur en philosophie* from the Katholieke Universiteit in Nijmegen, Belgium, for his thesis "La Contradiction infinie: Éléments d'une philosophie dans l'histoire" ("Infinite Contradiction: Elements of a Philosophy of History"). Following his *Habilitation à diriger des recherches* from the University de Paris I-Sorbonne in 1993, Balibar assumed the position of Professor of Political Philosophy at the University of Paris X-Nanterre, and became Professor Emeritus in 2002. Beginning in 2000, he has also taught for one quarter each year as Professor of Humanities in the Department of French and Italian and the Department of English and Comparative Literature at the University of California, Irvine.

Balibar began his career as one of the group of young scholars (including Pierre Macherey, Jacques Rancière, Roger Establet) who worked with Louis Althusser on the project that eventually became *Lire "Le Capital"* (1965; English translation: *Reading Capital*). Throughout his career, he has continued to work on issues related to Marxist thought and political theory more generally, and has made major contributions to the understanding of Spinoza as a political thinker. In the mid-1980s, he began a collaboration with Immanuel Wallerstein (1930–; sociologist and, since 1976, founding Director of the Fernand Braudel Center for the Study of Economies, Historical Systems, and Civilizations at Binghamton University), organizing several seminars at the Maison des Sciences de l'Homme in Paris on topics relating to racism, ethnicity, class, and nationalism, and resulting in their co-authored *Race, nation, classe* (1988; English translation: *Race, Nation, Class*).

Roland Barthes (1915–80) was born in Cherbourg (Manche, Normandy), grew up in Bayonne in the southwest of France, and moved to Paris in 1924. Barthes attended the Lycées Montaigne from 1924 to 1930 and Louis-le-Grand from 1930 to 1934, where he obtained *baccalauréats* in 1933 and 1934. He went on to study classics and French literature at the Sorbonne from 1935 to 1939, but his poor health made it impossible for him to study for and pass the entrance exams to the École Normale Supérieure or to take the *agrégation*. In 1939, he was awarded a *licence de lettres classiques* and began teaching at the *lycée* in Biarritz. Barthes received a *Diplôme d'études supérieures* from the Sorbonne in 1941 for his work on Greek tragedy. He taught in Paris at the Lycées Voltaire and Carnot from 1940 to 1941, but spent much of the period between 1940 and 1945 in various sanatoria in Paris suffering from tuberculosis. In the late 1940s, Barthes's health improved and he taught French at the Institut Français in Bucharest, Romania (1948), and at the University of Alexandria in Egypt (1949–50). There he met and became friends with linguist and semiotician Algirdas J. Greimas (1917–92), who first introduced him to the work of Ferdinand de Saussure. Barthes returned to France and worked from 1952 to 1959 at the Centre National de la Recherche Scientifique (CNRS). Although his failure to pass the *agrégation* prevented his obtaining a regular university appointment, he began teaching at the École Pratique des Hautes Études in 1960, becoming in 1962 the *Directeur d'études* in the Sixth Section in the "Sociology of Signs, Symbols, and Representations." With the assistance and support of his friend Michel Foucault, Barthes was elected to the chair of "Literary Semiology" at the Collège de France in 1977. He died tragically of complications after having been hit by a truck on February 25, 1980, following a luncheon at the Collège de France organized by Jack Lang for then presidential candidate François Mitterand.

Throughout his life, Barthes was active in journalism and the art scene. In the mid-1940s, he became interested in existentialism, and wrote for *Combat*, edited by Albert Camus. In the early 1950s, he co-founded *Théâtre populaire*, a radical drama review, and he wrote a regular column for *Les Lettres nouvelles*. Following the publication of his *On Racine* in 1963, he became embroiled in a very public debate with Raymond Picard, the editor of the Pléiade edition of Racine's works and a Professor of Literature at the Sorbonne.[5] In the early 1960s, Barthes associated and became friends with members of the *Tel Quel* group; he contributed frequently to their journal and was an important influence on Julia Kristeva, who studied with him at the École Pratique des Hautes Études (Kristeva herself was later an influence on Barthes as he moved away from a more narrow structural approach toward questions of intertextuality). By the mid-1960s, Barthes was among the most famous of the intellectuals associated with the structuralist movement, and several of his texts from the 1960s and 1970s were foundational in the development of structuralist literary criticism and theory. In the mid-1970s, he became one of the leading supporters of the *nouveau roman*, especially the work of Alain Robbe-Grillet and Philippe Sollers, whose work with *Tel Quel* he had long supported. Through his art criticism, his columns in *Le Nouvel Observateur*, his bestselling books, and his media appearances in radio and television interviews, Barthes was in the 1970s one of the best-known intellectuals in France, a fact reflected in his being chosen, in 1977, as the first living French non-fiction writer to be the subject of a colloquium at Cerisy-la-Salle.[6]

Georges Bataille (1897–1962) was born in Billom (Puy-de-Dôme, Auvergne). He completed a *baccalauréat* in philosophy through a correspondence course in 1914 and, after giving up plans to become a priest, he studied to be a medievalist librarian and archivist from 1918 to 1921 at the École des Chartres (School of Palaeography) in Paris. For much of the rest of his life, he worked as a librarian, first at the Bibliothèque Nationale in Paris from 1922 to 1942, then following a seven-year medical leave for tuberculosis, at the libraries at Carpentras (1949–51) and Orleans (1951–61).

---

[5] For a discussion of this debate in terms of the different "symbolic capital" possessed by Picard as an academic and Barthes as an avant garde intellectual outside the academy, see Pierre Bourdieu, *Homo Academicus*, trans. Peter Collier (Stanford, CA: Stanford University Press, 1988), pp. 115–18.

[6] Barthes was the ninth living subject of a Cerisy colloquium; previous figures who attended colloquia devoted to their work were Martin Heidegger (1955), Arnold Toynbee (1958), Giuseppe Ungaretti (1960), Raymond Queneau (1960), Michel Butor (1973), Claude Simon (1974), Alain Robbe-Grillet (1975), and Francis Ponge (1975).

Bataille was associated with many of the significant cultural developments in France during his lifetime. He was affiliated with the Surrealist movement in 1929–30, had a falling out but was reconciled with André Breton in 1935. From 1931 to 1934, he was a member of the anti-Stalinist Democratic Communist Circle, led by Boris Souvarine. In 1935, he created, with André Breton, "Contre-Attaque," an anti-fascist group of revolutionary intellectuals, and with Pierre Klossowski, he founded the journal *Acéphale* and its associated Nietzschean secret society. Bataille was, with Roger Callois and Michel Leiris, one of the founding members of the *Collège de Sociologie*, which from 1936 to 1939 brought together a group of intellectuals that also included Klossowski, Jean Wahl, Alexandre Kojève, and Jean Paulhan, among others, to share their views on contemporary society and, in particular, on the functions played by violence and the sacred in the formation of communities. Walter Benjamin attended some of these meetings, and it was to Bataille that Benjamin entrusted his manuscripts (with instructions to deliver them to Theodor Adorno) as he fled Paris in his ill-fated attempt to escape to Spain in 1940 (having been stopped at the Spanish border, Benjamin took his own life on September 26). In 1946, Bataille founded the influential journal *Critique*, which he imagined as an anti-existentialist rival to *Les Temps modernes*, and he remained its editor until his death.

In addition to these cultural associations and his fictional works, Bataille's philosophical writings have been very influential. The three major influences on his own work are, without question, his readings of Marcel Mauss's *The Gift*, which he credits with providing the basis for all understanding of what he would go on to call "general economy"; his lifelong engagement with the writings of Nietzsche ("Except for a few exceptions, my company on earth is mostly Nietzsche");[7] and Hegel (Bataille attended first Alexandre Koyré's and then Alexandre Kojève's lectures on Hegel at the École Pratique des Hautes Études). Whether through his writings or his life, Bataille is perhaps more closely associated than anyone else in France with the notion of transgression. His own work was one of the first to blur the boundaries between philosophy and the human sciences (in particular, ethnology) and, as such, he stands as an important figure in the developments of structuralism and

---

[7]   Georges Bataille, *On Nietzsche*, trans. Bruce Boone (New York: Paragon House, 1992), p. 3.

poststructuralism. Michel Foucault, Maurice Blanchot, and the *Tel Quel* group (Philippe Sollers, Julia Kristeva, et al.) are among those upon whom Bataille's influence is most readily apparent.

Jean Beaufret (1907–82) was born in Mars, a rural village near Auzances (Creuse, Limousin). He completed his *baccalauréat* at the *lycée* in Montluçon, where he studied from 1919 to 1925 and attended *hypokhâgne* and *khâgne* at the Lycée Louis-le-Grand before entering the École Normale Supérieure in 1928, where his classmates included Simone Weil. He also followed Léon Brunschvicg's course on rationalism at the Sorbonne, and submitted his thesis for the *Diplôme d'études supérieures* on "Les Rapports du droit et de las morale d'après Fichte" ("The Idea of Law and the Theory of the State in Fichte's Practical Philosophy") in 1931. Beaufret passed his *agrégation* on his second attempt in 1933, and taught at *lycées* in Auxerre, Alexandria, Grenoble, and Lyon before returning to Paris in 1944. He taught in Paris at the Lycées Saint-Louis and Jacques-Decour before being named to teach *khâgne* (*première supérieure*) at Henri-IV in 1946. Beaufret taught at Henri-IV until 1952, at which time he took up a research post at the Centre Nationale de la Recherche Scientifique. He left the CNRS in 1955 and resumed his teaching in the influential position of teacher of the *première supérieure* at the Lycée Condorcet from 1955 to 1972. During much of this period, Beaufret also lectured regularly at the École Normale Supérieure.

Beaufret read Husserl in 1941 and he discovered the work of Heidegger soon thereafter. He first met Heidegger in 1946 and later that year, Heidegger wrote his "Letter on Humanism," in response to questions posed to him by Beaufret. Beaufret remained the foremost French Heideggerian for many years. He was the individual primarily responsible for organizing and directing the ten-day colloquium at Cerisy that brought Heidegger to France in 1955. While Beaufret himself was active in the Resistance, he felt an apolitical reading of Heidegger was possible and thought one could read Heidegger's anti-humanism without tying it to his association with National Socialism. Others disagreed, and already by 1955, many were troubled by the revelations of Heidegger's links with Nazism, as evidenced by the fact that both Sartre and Merleau-Ponty refused to attend the Cerisy colloquium. Although Beaufret did not publish much, through his influential teaching at the Lycée Condorcet and the long-lasting relations he developed with his *khâgne* students, as well as his frequent lectures at the École

Normale, he had a tremendous influence on both the introduction and dissemination of Heidegger's thought in France.

Simone de Beauvoir (1908–86) was born in Paris. Beginning at the Institut Adeline-Désir, a Catholic girls' school that sought to prepare young girls for their proper stations in life, Beauvoir began the serious study of philosophy on her own initiative in 1925, first at the Institut Sainte-Marie at Neuilly, then the Institut Catholique in Paris. She eventually ended up at the Sorbonne, where she studied with Léon Brunschvicg, one of the few supporters at the time of the idea that women should study philosophy. There she met Simone Weil, Maurice Merleau-Ponty, Henri Lefebvre, and Georges Politzer, and in 1929, she submitted her thesis for the *Diplôme d'études supérieures* on "Le concept chez Leibniz" ("The Concept in Leibniz"). Beauvoir registered for some classes at the École Normale Supérieure that same year, only the third year in which women were permitted to study at the Letters Section of the École Normale (at the time, Simone Weil was the only woman enrolled as a full-time student, with three other women students attending part-time), and it was here that she first met Jean-Paul Sartre, with whom the rest of her life would be intimately intertwined. She prepared for the *agrégation* with fellow École Normale students Sartre and Paul Nizan and passed the exam in 1929 (scoring second to Sartre's first, though some have suggested that sexism might have been responsible for this ranking).[8] In the spring of 1929, she, along with Claude Lévi-Strauss and Maurice Merleau-Ponty, began her teaching practicum at the Lycée Janson-de-Sailly, becoming in the process the first woman in France to teach at a boys' *lycée*. She taught philosophy at *lycées* in Marseilles, Rouen, and Paris until 1943, when her contract was terminated by the administration following complaints from the mother of one of her female students. Although reappointed to the faculty after

---

[8] See the interview with Maurice de Gandillac by Ingrid Galster, " 'Ils auraient pu les mettre *ex aequo*': Entretien avec le philosophe Maurice de Gandillac sur l'agrégation de Beauvoir et d'autres sujets," *Lendemains* 94 (1999): 19–36, in which he comments that Beauvoir and Sartre should have been awarded the first rank together. Gandillac passed the *agrégation* that same year, and he suggests that the jury might have awarded the first rank to Sartre because he was an older and more experienced student. The *jury de l'agrégation de philosophie* that year was presided over by André Lalande, and included Dominique Parodi, Charles Lalo, Georges Davy, Jean Laporte, and Jean Wahl.

the war, Beauvoir never returned to teaching, supporting herself instead by her writing.

In 1946, Beauvoir was, with Sartre and Merleau-Ponty, one of the founding editors of the influential left-wing journal *Les Temps modernes*. In the years between 1947 and her death, she engaged in many political activities, campaigning against the Algerian war in the late 1950s, supporting the student demonstrations in May 1968, and working for the legalization of contraception and abortion in France in the 1970s and 1980s. She was the author of several philosophical works, numerous novels, and a series of diaries that chronicle much of the French intellectual left during her lifetime. Her magnum opus, *The Second Sex*, is rightfully regarded as the first major work of philosophical feminism and for many remains one of the founding works of feminism in the twentieth century. Her other influential philosophical work, *The Ethics of Ambiguity*, is generally regarded as the first work of existentialist ethics. Long overlooked by philosophers as little more than Sartre's girlfriend and follower (she is, for the most part, completely ignored by French studies of twentieth-century philosophy written before 1970, and is dismissed or disparaged by many of the early, and sympathetic, treatments of existentialism), her own contributions to existentialist and moral philosophy have more recently begun to attract the serious philosophical attention they deserve.

Henri Bergson (1859–1941) was born in Paris. He studied first at the Lycée Bonaparte (subsequently renamed the Lycée Condorcet) and later at the École Normale Supérieure from 1878 to 1881, passing his *agrégation* in 1881. He completed his doctorate *Essai sur les données immédiates de la conscience* (*Time and Free Will: An Essay on the Immediate Data of Consciousness*) in 1889, submitting his *thèse secondaire* in Latin on "The Aristotelian Theory of Place" (*Quid Aristoteles de loco senserit*). From 1881 to 1898, he taught at *lycées* in Angers, Clermont-Ferrand, and Paris, including the prestigious Lycée Henri-IV (where he taught the *première supérieure* from 1890 to 1898). In 1898, he was appointed to a senior teaching position as *Maître de conférences* at the École Normale Supérieure, and from 1900 to 1921, he held a Chair in Philosophy at the Collège de France: from 1900 to 1904, the "Chair in Greek and Latin Philosophy," and from 1904 to 1921, the "Chair in Modern Philosophy." Bergson suffered from a debilitating form of arthritis, and because of his poor health, he stopped teaching in 1914. Following his retirement, Bergson's health left him in relative seclusion and he had difficulty working. Twenty-five years separate Bergson's final two significant texts: *Creative Evolution* was published in 1907, while *Two Sources of Morality and Religion* did not appear until 1932. He became a member of the *Académie des Sciences morales et politiques* in 1901, was elected to the *Académie Française* in 1914, and was awarded the Nobel Prize for Literature in 1927.

Bergson's activities were not restricted to the writing and teaching of philosophy. In 1917, he traveled to America as part of a diplomatic mission to persuade the United States to enter the war. After the war, he served from 1918 to 1925 as chairman of an educational body created within the League of Nations, the *Commission Internationale de Coopération Intellectuale* (a forerunner of UNESCO). Although born to Jewish parents, Bergson became in later life spiritually committed to Catholicism. As indicated in his 1937 will, he would most likely have converted, though he refused to renounce his commitment to his Jewish background at a time when French Jews were most seriously threatened. In fact, this moral commitment to his Jewish heritage may very well have played a significant role in his death: by virtue of his contributions to French intellectual culture, Bergson was made an "Honorary Aryan" by the Vichy government and given an exemption to their law requiring all Jews to register. He refused this special treatment and, in solidarity with his fellow Jews, he stood in line for several hours in frigid weather; he died of pulmonary complications two days later in early January, 1941.

During much of his lifetime, Bergson was perhaps the most dominant figure in French philosophy and one of the best-known philosophers in the world. When he studied at the École Normale Supérieure, French philosophy was divided between neo-Kantianism, represented at the École Normale by Émile Boutroux, and evolutionism, represented by the writings of Herbert Spencer. Unlike many of his fellow *normaliens*, Bergson was inclined toward Spencer rather than Kant, a choice that not only directed his future writing but also produced dismissive or hostile responses to his work from within the French academic philosophical establishment. This response, not coincidentally, put the philosophical academicians at odds with the broader Paris society, where Bergson's originality, his accessible writing style, and his public lectures at the Collège de France made him enormously popular.

In his early works, Bergson addressed more psychological themes, and his ideas on *durée* (duration), the experience of time and memory, and freedom, with which his friend William James located strong connections to his own work, would influence phenomenological and existential philosophy. In his later work, he turned toward more meta-physical, moral, and religious issues, and his vitalism, spiritualism, and idea of *élan vital* (vital force) had a powerful influence on many French Catholic thinkers, including Charles Péguy, Emmanuel Mounier, Pierre Teilhard de Chardin, and Gabriel Marcel. Bergson's importance and influence was eclipsed with the rise of existentialist philosophy in the 1930s, but his work experienced a revival in the last decades of the twentieth century, in large part because of the place it occupies in the thinking of Gilles Deleuze.

Maurice Blanchot (1907–2003) was born in Quain (Sâone-et-Loire, Burgundy). He received his *baccalauréat* in 1922, and began his studies with an emphasis on German and philosophy at the University of Strasbourg in 1923. It was two years later that he met and began a lifelong friendship with Emmanuel Levinas. After Strasbourg, he traveled to Paris and enrolled in the Sorbonne, where he received his *Diplôme d'études supérieures* in 1930 for a thesis on "La Conception du Dogmatisme chez les Sceptiques anciens d'après Sextus Empiricus" ("The Conception of Dogmatism in the Ancient Sceptics According to Sextus Empiricus"). While in Strasbourg, Blanchot became interested in the extreme right-wing Action Française and in the 1930s he wrote for several right-wing journals, including *Journal des Débats*, *Réaction*, *Le Rempart*, *Combat*, and *L'Insurgé*. After France's defeat in 1940, however, he refused to collaborate with the Vichy government, renounced politics, and all but retired from public life (his only public appearance since then was during the events of May 1968, though he is widely believed to have been the author of the "Manifeste de 121," a manifesto declaring the "right to insubordination" in protest of the war in Algeria, signed by 121 intellectuals, most from the left). Through his novels, his literary critical essays, and his theoretical and fragmentary writings on language, death, totalitarianism, the Holocaust, anti-Semitism, and community, Blanchot has had a profound impact on many French philosophers, including Georges Bataille, Emmanuel Levinas, Michel Foucault, Gilles Deleuze, Jacques Derrida, Sarah Kofman, and Jean-Luc Nancy.

Maurice Blondel (1861–1949) was born in Dijon. He attended the Lycée de Dijon, completing his *baccalauréat* in law in 1879. After a year at the University of Dijon, he entered the École Normale Supérieure, where he studied from 1881 to 1884, working closely with Émile

Boutroux. He passed the *agrégation* in 1886, after having failed in two previous attempts, and then taught at *lycées* in Chaumont (1884–5), Montauban (1886–9), and Aix-en-Provence (1886–9). In 1893, he received his *Doctorat ès Lettres*, submitting to Boutroux his doctoral thesis and most famous work, *L'Action: Essai d'une critique de la vie et d'une science de la pratique* (English translation: *Action: Essay on a Critique of Life and a Science of Practice*, trans. Oliva Blanchette [Notre Dame, IN: University of Notre Dame Press, 1984]), as well as a *thèse complémentaire* in Latin on Leibniz (*De vinculo substantiali et de substantia composita apud Leibnitium*). He taught as *Maître de conférences* in 1895 at the University at Lille and from 1896 to 1927 at the University at Aix-en-Provence, where he assumed a Professor's chair in 1899. During his career, which was cut short because of health problems, Blondel was known as one of the leading Christian philosophers working outside the Thomist tradition.

Célestin Bouglé (1870–1940) was born in Saint-Brieuc (Côtes-d'Armor, Brittany). He came to Paris in 1884, where he studied at the Lycée Henri-IV from 1884 to 1890 before entering the École Normale Supérieure in the fall of 1890. In 1891, Bouglé received his *licence ès lettres*; in 1893, he completed his studies at the École Normale and he passed his *agrégation* that same year, finishing first. After spending a year studying in Germany on a fellowship, he taught at the *lycée* in Saint-Brieuc (1894–7) and as *Maître de conférences* at Montpellier (1897–1900) and Toulouse (1900–8), where he was promoted to Professor of Social Philosophy in 1901. Bouglé received his *Doctorat ès Lettres* in 1899, following the submission of his thesis *Les Idées égalitaires, étude sociologique* ("Egalitarian Ideas: A Sociological Study"). In 1909, he returned to Paris to take a position at the Sorbonne as *chargé de cours* (assistant lecturer) in the history of social economy and assumed a Chair as Professor of the History of Social Economy in 1919. Bouglé served as adjunct director of the École Normale Supérieure from 1927 to 1935, and as Director from 1935 until his death. Throughout his career, Bouglé was associated with the sociological school of Émile Durkheim, though he often departed from the positions held by more orthodox Durkheimians. His commitment to empirical research had a strong influence on many who worked in the departments of philosophy during his more than thirty years at the Sorbonne and École Normale.

Pierre Bourdieu (1930–2002) was born in Denguin (Pyrénées-Atlantique, Aquitaine). He attended the Lycée de Pau (1941–7), did his *hypokhâgne* and *khâgne* at the Lycée Louis-le-Grand (1948–51), and then attended the École Normale Supérieure (1951–4). In 1953, he submitted a thesis for the *Diplôme d'études supérieures* to Henri Gouhier that included an annotated translation from the Latin, with preface and commentary, on Leibniz's *Animadversiones in partem generalem principiorum Cartesianorum* (*Critical Remarks Concerning the General Part of Descartes's Principles*). He passed his *agrégation* in philosophy in 1954. Bourdieu taught first at the *lycée* in Moulins (1954–5), and from 1955–7 worked on a thesis for the *Doctorat d'État* under the direction of Georges Canguilhem which was to have been titled *Structures temporelles de la vie affective* ("Temporal Structures of Affective Life") and was focused on Husserl as well as recent work in biology and psychology.

During this period, Bourdieu grew increasingly uncomfortable with the field of philosophy, and he left France for Kabylia, a mountainous coastal region in northern Algeria, in the midst of the Algerian War to work on a phenomenological analysis of the social world that quickly became sociological fieldwork on what he called a theory of practice. He taught from 1958 to 1960 at the University of Algiers, offering courses on indigenous Algerian culture at a time when the question of whether Algeria really had an indigenous culture was politically charged. He returned to France in 1960, teaching first in Paris at the Sorbonne, as the assistant of Raymond Aron (1960–1), then as *Maître de conférences* at the University of Lille (1961–4). In 1964, he returned to Paris to assume the position of *chargé de cours* at the École Normale Supérieure (1964–84) and, with the support of Claude Lévi-Strauss, Raymond Aron, and Fernand Braudel, became a *Directeur d'études* of the Sixth Section of the École Pratique des Hautes Études (which became in 1975 the École des Hautes Études en Sciences Sociales), a position that he held until his death. In 1982, he assumed the Chair in Sociology at the Collège de France and he served as Director of the Centre de Sociologie Européenne (CSE) of the Collège de France and the École des Hautes Études en Sciences Sociales from 1985 to 1998. In 1993, the Centre National de la Recherche Scientifique (CNRS) awarded Bourdieu its highest distinction, the *Médaille d'or* (Gold Medal).

Like Claude Lévi-Strauss, Bourdieu's education was philosophical, and like Lévi-Strauss, a propensity toward empirical studies conjoined with a fortuitous appointment allowed Bourdieu to move away from the narrowly philosophical world into the social sciences. Also like Lévi-Strauss, he never completed his *Doctorat d'État*, which is required for presiding over dissertation defense committees. One final point of similarity with Lévi-Strauss is worth noting: both continued to address philosophical issues within their anthropological and sociological research and both have, as a consequence, had a large influence upon and following among philosophers. Among those whom Bourdieu cites as formative influences on his thinking are to be found, in addition to Marx and sociologists like Émile Durkheim, Max Weber, and Lévi-Strauss, phenomenological philosophers like Husserl, Schutz, Heidegger, Sartre, and Merleau-Ponty, and epistemologists-cum-philosophers of science Gaston Bachelard, Alexandre Koyré, George Canguilhem, and Jules Vuillemin. His career and life have also intersected both Michel Foucault's and Jacques Derrida's. He and Derrida were peers at the École Normale Supérieure, while he and Foucault were colleagues at the Collège de France. All three have been to some extent "outsiders" to the French academic establishment (their all having been born far from Paris is not inconsequential to this fact, as Bourdieu explains in *Homo Academicus*), though all three have at the same time been profoundly influential on the very institutions to which they position themselves as outsiders. While he avoided intervening in political affairs early in his career, Bourdieu became a more public intellectual in the 1990s, so much so that the French cultural magazine *Magazine littéraire* could title its October 1998 issue *Pierre Bourdieu: L'Intellectuel dominant?* ("Pierre Bourdieu: The Dominant Intellectual?").

Émile Boutroux (1845–1921) was born in Montrouge, near Paris. He studied at the Lycée Henri-IV and entered the École Normale Supérieure in 1865, where he studied with Jules Lachelier. In 1868 he passed his *agrégation*, studied for a year at Heidelberg, and began teaching at the *lycée* in Caen in 1871. Boutroux defended his thesis *De la contingence des lois de la nature* (English translation: *The Contingency of the Laws of Nature*, trans. Fred Rothwell [Chicago: Open Court, 1916]) in 1874 at the Sorbonne, along with a *thèse complémentaire* in Latin on Descartes (*De veritatibus aeternis apud Cartesium*). Following his *doctorat*, Boutroux taught at the universities of Montpellier (1874–6) and Nancy (1876–7) before returning to the École Normale Supérieure, where he taught from 1877 to 1886, and where his students included Jean Jaurès (1859–1914), Émile Durkheim, Pierre Janet (1859–1947), and Henri Bergson. In 1888, he became Professor of the History of Modern Philosophy at the Sorbonne, a position he held until his retirement in 1907. He was elected to the *Académie des Sciences morales et politiques* in 1898, served as

President of the Fondation Thiers in 1902, and was elected to the *Académie Française* in 1914.

Boutroux sought to challenge the tendency toward materialist metaphysics while recognizing the relevance of the natural sciences. A specialist in Leibniz and seventeenth-century German philosophy, he thought that a historically informed philosophy of nature could reconcile the tensions between metaphysics and science. Drawing upon resources within Leibnizian rationalism, French spiritualism, and the natural sciences, Boutroux anticipates and influences the work of both Henri Bergson and Gaston Bachelard. In addition to his thesis, his major works include *Idée de loi naturelle dans la science et la philosophie contemporaines* (1895; English translation: *Natural Law in Science and Philosophy*, trans. Fred Rothwell [New York: Macmillan, 1914]) and *Science et religion dans la philosophie contemporaine* (1908; English translation: *Science and Religion in Contemporary Philosophy*, trans. Jonathan Nield [London: Duckworth, 1909; New York: Macmillan, 1911]).

Jacques Bouveresse (1940–) was born in Epenoy (Doubs, Franche-Comté). He received his *baccalauréat* from a seminary in Besançon and did his *hypokhâgne* and *khâgne* at the Lycée Lakanal in Sceaux before entering the École Normale Supérieure in 1961, where he was one of the few students in his years there who remained outside the scope of influence of Louis Althusser and structuralism more generally. In 1964, he received his *Diplôme d'études supérieures* for a project on Fichte's philosophy of law and political philosophy, directed by Raymond Aron, but chose to continue his philosophy studies in epistemology rather than political philosophy. Bouveresse passed his *agrégation* in 1965 and completed his *Doctorat d'État* in 1975 with the submission of *Le Mythe de l'intériorité. Expérience, signification et langage privé chez Wittgenstein* ("The Myth of Interiority: Experience, Signification, and Private Language in Wittgenstein"), directed by Yvon Belaval at the University of Paris I-Paris-Sorbonne. From 1969 to 1971, he served first as *Assistant*, then *Maître-assistant* at the Faculté de Lettres et Sciences Humaines at the University of Paris I-Paris-Sorbonne. He worked at the Centre National de la Recherche Scientifique (CNRS) from 1971 to 1975, then rejoined the faculty of the University of Paris I-Paris-Sorbonne as *Maître-assistant*, but was quickly promoted to *Maître de conférences*, then Professor from 1976 to 1979. He taught at the University of Geneva from 1979 to 1983, returned to teach at the Sorbonne from 1983 to 1995, and was elected to the Collège de

France in 1994 to the newly created "Chair of Philosophy of Language and Consciousness," which he has occupied since 1995.

Bouveresse is France's leading Wittgenstein scholar. Among his more than twenty books are nine on Wittgenstein, including works on his philosophy of language (*La Parole malheureuse* [1971] and *Herméneutique et linguistique. Suivi de Wittgenstein et la philosophie du langage* [1991]), ethics and aesthetics (*Wittgenstein: La Rime et la raison. Science, éthique et esthétique* [1973]), philosophy of psychology (*Le Mythe de l'intériorité. Expérience, signification et langage privé chez Wittgenstein* [1976]), philosophy of mathematics and logic (*La Force de la règle. Wittgenstein et l'invention de la nécessité* [1987] and *Le Pays des possibles. Wittgenstein, les mathématiques et le monde réel* [1988]), his relationship with psychoanalysis (*Philosophie, mythologie et pseudoscience. Wittgenstein lecteur de Freud* [1991; English translation: *Wittgenstein Reads Freud: The Myth of the Unconscious*]), and two collections of essays [*Essais I. Wittgenstein, la modernité, le progrès et le déclin* [2000] and *Essais III. Wittgenstein et les sortilèges du langage* [2003]).

Bouveresse is, by his own admission, "very unFrench" in the sense that he works primarily in analytic philosophy and shows little interest in the intellectual resources to which most recent French philosophers appeal (Hegel, Nietzsche, Heidegger, structuralism). His work largely has been overlooked by the more well-known philosophers in France of the last three decades of the twentieth century and, for his part, he is largely dismissive of much of the philosophical work produced in France since the 1960s, which he regards as "quite simply unreadable [whose] interest has seemed . . . in many cases to be of a documentary or sociological rather than of a properly philosophical nature."[9] While very critical of what he sees as the irrationalism of contemporary French philosophy that calls for the kind of demythologizing that he associates with Wittgenstein, Bouveresse is not, however, the sort of narrowly analytic philosopher one finds working in other countries, as his long-standing interests in relating Wittgenstein's thought to Freud or Frazer, or his work on the novelist Robert Musil (*L'Homme probable. Robert Musil, le hasard, la moyenne et l'escargot de l'Histoire* [1993]) makes clear. He has been a major influence in the rise in importance of analytic philosophy in contemporary French philosophy, as evidenced by his being elected to the primary chair in philosophy at the Collège de

---

9   Jacques Bouveresse, "Why I am so very unFrench," trans. Kathleen McLaughlin in *Philosophy in France Today*, ed. Alan Montefiore (Cambridge: Cambridge University Press, 1983), p. 9.

France and his being named in 1989 to co-chair, along with Jacques Derrida, a Commission de philosophie et d'épistémologie charged with formulating a response to the 1975 "Réforme Haby," which sought to seriously reduce the number of hours of philosophy required to graduate from a *lycée*.[10]

Émile Bréhier (1876–1952) was born in Bar-le-Duc (Meuse, Lorraine). He attended *lycée* in Versailles, then Louis-le-Grand, where he completed his *baccalauréat* in letters in 1893, and a second *baccalauréat* in sciences in 1896. Bréhier studied at the Sorbonne from 1896 to 1900, passed the *agrégation* in 1900, and received his *Doctorat ès Lettres* in 1908, submitting theses *Les Idées philosophiques et religieuses de Philon d'Alexandrie* ("The Philosophical and Religious Ideas of Philo of Alexandria") and *La Théorie des incorporels dans l'ancien stoïcisme* ("The Theory of Incorporeals in Ancient Stoicism"). Bréhier taught as Professor of Philosophy at *lycées* in Coutances (1900–2), Laval (1903–8), and Beauvais (1908–9) before being named *Maître de conférences* at the University in Rennes (1909–11) and Professor of Philosophy at the University of Bordeaux (1912–14). Seriously wounded in World War I, he was appointed *Maître de conférences* in the History of Philosophy at the Sorbonne in 1919, promoted to Professor without Chair in 1923, and named Professor of Philosophy and the History of Philosophy in 1930, a position he held until his retirement in 1946. Bréhier also served for one year (1925–6) as Professor and Associate Dean of the Faculty at the University of Cairo. In 1944, Bréhier was elected to the *Académie des Sciences morales et politiques*, and became its president in 1950. He is best known for his five-volume *Histoire de la philosophie* (1926–32; English translation: *The History of Philosophy, 7 vols.*, trans. Joseph Thomas [Chicago: University of Chicago Press, 1963–9]), as well as a number of works on ancient and German philosophy.

Léon Brunschvicg (1869–1944) was, along with Henri Bergson, one of the dominant philosophical figures in France in the first three decades of the twentieth century. He was born in Paris, studied at the Lycée

---

[10] The report of Bouveresse and Derrida's commission is published as an appendix to Jacques Derrida, *Du droit à la philosophie* (Paris: Galilée, 1990). It appears in English translation as "Report of the Committee on Philosophy and Epistemology" in Jacques Derrida, *Eyes of the University: Right to Philosophy 2*, trans. Jan Plug (Stanford, CA: Stanford University Press), pp. 250–82. For more about the Réforme Haby, see Appendix 1 of this volume.

Condorcet and later at the École Normale Supérieure from 1888 to 1891, where he followed the courses of Émile Boutroux. Brunschvicg passed his *agrégation* in 1891, finishing first, and presented his doctoral thesis *La Modalité du jugement* ("The Modality of Judgment") and Latin *thèse complémentaire* on Aristotle (*Qua ratione Aristoteles metaphysicam vim syllogismo inesse demonstraverit*) to the Sorbonne in 1897. He taught at *lycées* in Lorient, Tours, Rouen, and in Paris at the Lycées Condorcet (1900–3) and Henri-IV, where he replaced Henri Bergson and taught the *première supérieure* from 1903 to 1909. In 1909, Brunschvicg began a 30-year career at the Sorbonne as *Maître de conférences*, being promoted to Professor without Chair in 1921 and Professor of the History of Modern Philosophy in 1927. He retired from teaching in 1940. Brunschvicg was elected to the *Académie des Sciences morales et politiques* in 1920, and was co-founder in 1893 (with Xavier Léon and Élie Halévy) of the *Revue de métaphysique et de morale*.

In the twentieth century, Brunschvicg was the figure most closely identified with French neo-Kantianism, heir to the legacy of nineteenth-century idealists Maine de Biran, Renouvier, Cournot, Ravaisson, Lachelier, and Lagneau. He published widely on both idealism and the history of philosophy, in particular, Descartes, Spinoza, and Pascal. Although his work was never translated into English, through his position at the Sorbonne, as an influential presence in the early years of the Société Française de Philosophie (founded in 1901 by Xavier Léon and André Lalande), and as frequent member of the *jury d'agrégation* and its president from 1936 to 1938, he exerted enormous influence on French academic philosophy in the first four decades of the twentieth century. For example, it was primarily through Brunschvicg's urging that a certificate in science was made a requirement for sitting for the *agrégation* in philosophy.[11] Among his more significant writings are *Spinoza et ses contemporains* (1894; "Spinoza and his Contemporaries"), *Les Étapes de la philosophie mathématique* (1912; "The Stages in the Philosophy of Mathematics"), *L'Expérience humaine et la causalité physique* (1922; "Human Experience and Physical Causality"), *La Génie de Pascal* (1924; "Pascal's Genius"), and *Le Progrès de la conscience dans la philosophie occidentale* (1927; "The Development of Consciousness/Conscience in Western Philosophy").

Albert Camus (1913–60) was born in Mondovi, Algeria. He was educated in Algiers, where he attended *lycée* from 1923 to 1930. He

---

[11]   See René Boirel, *Brunschvicg, sa vie, son oeuvre* (Paris: Presses universitaires de France, 1964), p. 19.

attended the University of Algiers from 1930 to 1933, where his studies focused on literature and philosophy. In 1934, he joined the Algerian Communist Party, but he resigned the following year. In 1936, he received a *Diplôme d'études supérieures* for a thesis on the "Rapports de l'hellénisme et du christianisme à travers les oeuvres de Plotin et de saint Augustin" ("Relationship of Greek and Christian thought in Plotinus and St. Augustine"). He intended to proceed to the *agrégation*, but an attack of tuberculosis forced him to interrupt his studies. Camus went to Paris in the late 1930s and, in the years before the war, he wrote for the theater and as a journalist. During the war, he was active in the Resistance, editing a flyer that evolved after the war into the Parisian daily *Combat*, which Camus continued to edit until 1947. In 1957, Camus received the Nobel Prize for Literature. A few years later, he was killed in an automobile accident.

With his first novel, *The Stranger* (1942; *The Outsider* in the UK), Camus assured himself a place as a major representative of the genre of existential literature, and this text remains perhaps the single best-known work of existential fiction. His other two novels, *The Plague* (1947) and *The Fall* (1956), are also classics within that genre. But Camus's non-fiction prose also has had its influence. *The Myth of Sisyphus* (1942) is a powerful reflection on nihilism and the absurd. He was, for a time, associated with the editorial group of *Les Temps modernes* and, while not becoming himself a member of the editorial collective, he assisted them by making available to them the resources of his own, much larger journal, *Combat*. His friendship with Sartre and Beauvoir in particular was quite strong until the appearance in 1951 of *The Rebel*. The basic moral, political, and philosophical themes of this work ran counter to the positions associated with Sartre and his circle, and following a very harsh review by Francis Jeanson, then managing editor of *Les Temps modernes*, Camus's relations with Sartre, Beauvoir, and the other existentialists were irreparably sundered. Camus held Sartre responsible for Jeanson's critical review, and the two traded public letters in *Les Temps modernes* in the summer of 1952 that often blurred the line between the political and the personal. While Camus remained committed both to anti-Soviet and liberal humanist values, as did Raymond Aron, who also broke with Sartre during this period for many of the same reasons, his influence on the French scene was much diminished in the final years of his life.

Georges Canguilhem (1904–95) was born in Castelnaudary (Aude, Languedoc). He studied at the Collège and Lycée in Castelnaudary, where he received his *baccalauréat*. Canguilhem then attended the Lycée Henri-IV in Paris from 1921 to 1924, where he did his *khâgne* with Émile Chartier (Alain), before entering the École Normale Supérieure with the class that included Raymond Aron, Paul Nizan, and Jean-Paul Sartre. In 1926, he completed his thesis, directed by Célestin Bouglé, for the *Diplôme d'études supérieures* on "La Notion d'ordre et de progrès chez Comte" ("The Theory of Order and Progress in Auguste Comte"), and he passed the *agrégation* the following year. In the 1930s, he taught at *lycées* in Charleville (1929–30), Albi (1930–1), Douai (1932–3), Valenciennes (1933–5), Béziers (1935–6), and the Lycée Pierre de Fermat (1936–40) in Toulouse.

While in Toulouse, he began his study of medicine, while working also for various pacifist and anti-fascist causes, and from 1940 to 1944, he was active in the Resistance, eventually occupying a position of leadership. Early in 1941, his friend Jean Cavaillès, having been called to the Sorbonne, proposed Canguilhem as his replacement in the Faculty of Letters at the University of Strasbourg, which at that time had been relocated in Clermont-Ferrand. At Clermont-Ferrand, Canguilhem was able to continue his medical studies and, in 1943, he submitted a thesis in medicine: *Essai sur quelques problèmes concernant le normal et le pathologique* (*Essay on Some Problems Concerning the Normal and the Pathological*). After the war, from 1945 to 1948, he taught history and philosophy of science at the University of Strasbourg. In 1948, he took up the administrative post of *Inspecteur Générale de Philosophie* (the "inspector general" was a very powerful position, whose responsibilities included evaluating the pedagogy of secondary school teachers of philosophy), a position he occupied until 1955. That year, he completed his *Doctorat d'État*, submitting to Gaston Bachelard a principal thesis on "La Formation du concept de réflexe aux XVIIe et XVIIIe siècles" ("The Formation of the Concept of Reflex in the Seventeenth and Eighteenth Centuries"), with a *thèse complémentaire* "La Connaissance de la Vie" ("The Knowledge of Life"), after which he replaced Bachelard as Director of the Institut d'Histoire des Sciences et des Techniques and Chair in the History and Philosophy of Science at the Sorbonne, positions he held until his retirement in 1971. In 1987, the Centre National de la Recherche Scientifique (CNRS) awarded Canguilhem its highest distinction, the *Médaille d'or*, making him the only recipient of this award for work done in philosophy since it was first awarded in 1954 (to mathematician Émile Borel [1871–1956]).

Like Bachelard, Canguilhem's work moves between epistemology and philosophy of science, though unlike Bachelard, his interests lie primarily in the biological and medical sciences. His account of the history of science made use of Bachelard's notion of the epistemological break, but he also emphasized the institutions and social forces that inform the scientific construction of knowledge as he investigated the shifting relations between the normal and the pathological. His influence can be seen in all the developments of structuralism, especially Louis Althusser's reinterpretation of Marx. But his most significant impact was on the career of Michel Foucault, whose thesis on the history of madness he directed and whose ideas on epistemic ruptures and normalization can be traced directly to the work of Canguilhem. Foucault often acknowledged Canguilhem's importance for his own development, and acknowledged Canguilhem's influence on French philosophy more generally when he introduced the English translation of *On the Normal and the Pathological*:

> Let us not forget this fact which depends, as you will, on the sociology of French intellectual environments, the functioning of our university institutions or our system of cultural values: in all the political or scientific discussion of these strange sixty years past, the role of the "philosophers" – I simply mean those who had received their university training in philosophy departments – has been important: perhaps too important for the liking of certain people. And, directly or indirectly, all or almost all these philosophers have had to "come to terms with" the teaching and books of Georges Canguilhem.[12]

Cornelius Castoriadis (1922–97) was born in Constantinople, Turkey. His family moved to Athens to avoid the political unrest accompanying the foundation of the modern Turkish state, and there he studied economics, philosophy, and law. He was involved with several leftist political groups, joining the Greek Communist Youth in 1941 (a group formed in opposition to the Greek Communist Party) and the Trotskyists in 1942. Threatened by both fascists and Stalinists, he left

---

[12] Foucault, "Introduction," in *The Normal and the Pathological*, p. 7. Louis Althusser makes a similar comment, noting that he "cannot over-emphasize the importance for all of us of Canguilhem's influence" in leading French philosophy away from an idealist approach, in *The Future Lasts Forever: A Memoir*, ed. Olivier Corpet and Yann Moulier Boutang, trans. Richard Veasey (New York: New Press, 1993), p. 184.

Greece for Paris in December 1945. Initially aligned with the Trotskyist
Fourth International, he broke with them in 1948 and, with Claude
Lefort, Castoriadis founded in 1949 the revolutionary group and journal
Socialisme ou Barbarie, serving as its intellectual leader and dominant
force until it disbanded in 1965.

Staunchly anti-Stalinist and anti-Soviet, *S ou B* became one of, if not
the most influential non-communist Marxist groups in France and was
one of the intellectual sources for the student revolts of May 1968.
Castoriadis worked as an economist for the Organization of Economic
Cooperation and Development from 1948 to 1970. In 1973, he became a
practicing psychoanalyst, and in 1979 he was named *Directeur de
recherches* at the École des Hautes Études en Sciences Sociales. The
following year, he assumed the position of *Directeur d'études* in "Institution of Society and Historical Creation" at the EHESS. In 1980, he
was awarded the *Doctorat d'État* from the University of Paris X-
Nanterre for a thesis titled *L'Élément imaginaire de l'histoire*, directed
by Paul Ricoeur. Castoriadis's writings draw heavily from classical
Greek philosophy, as well as the writings of Marx and Freud, but
never lose sight of the need to merge theory with practice and to ground
theory in the materiality of historical conditions. In addition to his long
collaboration with Claude Lefort, Castoriadis was also a major influence
on the early political thinking of Jean-François Lyotard, who was
associated with *S ou B* from 1955 to 1963. As the leading theoretician
of *Socialism ou Barbarie* and one of the dominant Marxist voices who
saw the Stalinist-Soviet bureaucratization not as a betrayal but as an
outgrowth of communism, his impact on the student rebel leaders in
1968 was profound, as attested to by Daniel Cohn-Bendit, who commented in the theoretical section of his chronicle of the student revolt
that "the views we have been presenting are those of P. Chaulieu" (one
of several pen-names under which Castoriadis wrote for *Socialisme ou
Barbarie*).[13]

Jean Cavaillès (1903–44) was born in Saint-Maixent (Deux-Sèvres,
Poitou-Charentes). After completing *baccalauréat*s in both mathematics

---

[13]   Daniel Cohn-Bendit and Gabriel Cohn-Bendit, *Obsolete Communism: The Left-
        Wing Alternative*, trans. Arnold Pomerans (New York: McGraw Hill, 1968),
        p. 133. A sociology student at the University of Paris-Nanterre and one of the
        leaders of the student rebellion, Cohn-Bendit was expelled from France in 1968. He
        was active in various political movements in Germany and France and, since 1994,
        has served as a member of the European Parliament for the Green Party.

and philosophy, he attended *hypokhâgne* and *khâgne* at the Lycée Louis-le-Grand from 1920 to 1922. After finishing first in the entrance examination, Cavaillès studied at the École Normale Supérieure from 1923 to 1926. He completed his *Diplôme d'études supérieures* under Léon Brunschvicg at the Sorbonne, submitting his thesis "La Philosophie et les applications du calcul des probabilité chez Bernoulli" ("Philosophy and the Applications of Probability Calculus in Bernoulli") in 1926, and he passed his *agrégation* in 1927. Following his years of military service (1927–8), Cavaillès's interests in mathematics and logic led him to make several trips to Germany, funded by a fellowship from the Rockefeller Foundation (1929–30), where he met and worked with Husserl as well as several German mathematicians while visiting universities in Berlin, Hamburg, Göttingen, Munich, and Freiburg. From 1931 to 1935, Cavaillès held the position of *agrégé-répétiteur* ("*caïman*") at the École Normale Supérieure. He taught at the *lycée* in Amiens in 1937 while working on his doctoral thesis, and received his *Doctorat ès Lettres* for a thesis on set theory and the foundations of mathematics, *Méthode axiomatique et formalisme* ("Axiomatic Method and Formalism"), submitted in 1938, along with a *thèse complémentaire*, "Remarques sur la formation de la théorie abstraite des ensembles" ("Remarks on the Formation of Abstract Set Theory"). With his *Doctorat*, he held various positions at the University of Strasbourg and the Sorbonne. One of the founders of the French Resistance, Cavaillès was captured by the Nazis and executed.

During his short lifetime, Cavaillès only published two works, though he also made a major contribution to the history of mathematics and set theory by editing the correspondence between Cantor and Dedekind (*Briefwechsel Cantor-Dedekind* [1938]). His last work, written while in prison, was edited by his friends Georges Canguilhem and Charles Ehresmann and published in 1947 under the title *Sur la logique et la théorie de la science* ("On the Logic and Theory of Science"). In it, Cavaillès introduces the concept of structure as a challenge to phenomenological theories of subjectivity, a concept that would lie dormant for several decades before being rediscovered in his work by thinkers like Michel Foucault and Louis Althusser. His commitment to the idea that epistemology has an essential historical dimension likewise had a profound influence on the thinking of his friends Gaston Bachelard and Georges Canguilhem. Cavaillès's significance and influence on subsequent French philosophy is attested to by both Foucault and Canguilhem. The former divides French philosophy in the twentieth century along a "line that separates a philosophy of experience, of sense and of subject and a philosophy of knowledge, of rationality and of concept. On the one hand, one network is that of Sartre and Merleau-Ponty; and then another is that of Cavaillès, Bachelard, and Canguilhem."[14] And Canguilhem, for his part, credits Cavaillès for setting for philosophy this task: "to substitute for the primacy of a lived, or reflected consciousness the primacy of concept, system, or structure."[15]

Émile Chartier (1868–1951), better known under his pseudonym "Alain," was born in Mortagne-au-Perche (Orne, Normandy). In 1886, he entered the Lycée Michelet in Vanves, where he was introduced to philosophy in the class of Jules Lagneau (1851–94). Alain went on to study philosophy and literature at the École Normale Supérieure from 1889 to 1892, passed his *agrégation* in 1892, and taught in Pontivy, Lorient, and Rouen before returning to Paris in 1903 to begin what became a celebrated career teaching first at the Lycée Condorcet (1903–6), then the Lycée Michelet (1906–9), where he taught the class previously taught by his mentor Lagneau. In 1909, he joined the faculty at the prestigious Lycée Henri-IV, where aside from the war years that he spent at the front (1914–17), he taught the class *première supérieure* ("*khâgne*") from 1909 to 1933, a position held before him by Léon Brunschvicg, Victor Delbos, and Henri Bergson. Simone Weil, Georges Canguilhem, and Mikel Dufrenne are three of the students upon whom he exerted a profound influence. Alain wrote a number of books on art, aesthetics, ethics, humanism, and philosophy, but he is best known for the more than 5,000 short essays, which he called "*Propos*" or "Remarks," for various newspapers and journals on topics concerning politics, ethics, and aesthetics. In 1951 he became the first recipient of the *Grand Prix National des Lettres*.

François Châtelet (1925–85) was born in Paris. He studied at the Lycée Janson-de-Sailly before entering the Sorbonne in 1943, where he worked with Gaston Bachelard and Jean Wahl and began a close friendship with Gilles Deleuze. He completed his studies at the

---

[14] Foucault, "Introduction," in *The Normal and the Pathological*, p. 8.
[15] Georges Canguilhem, "Mort de l'homme ou épuisement du cogito," *Critique* (July 1967), quoted in Didier Eribon, *Michel Foucault*, trans. Betsy Wing (Cambridge, MA: Harvard University Press, 1991), p. 165.

Sorbonne in 1948, passed the *agrégation* that same year, and began teaching at the *lycée* in Oran, Algeria. After a few years teaching in Tunis, Châtelet returned to Paris in 1954 and spent the next four years as a researcher at the Centre National de la Recherche Scientifique (CNRS). He resumed his teaching career in 1958 at the Lycée Saint-Louis, and the following year, Châtelet submitted his thesis for his *Doctorat d'État* to his director, Jean Hyppolite, on *La Naissance de l'histoire: La Formation de la pensée historique en Grèce* ("The Birth of History: The Formation of Historical Thought in Greece"), with a secondary thesis "Logos et praxis: Recherches sur la signification théoretique du marxisme" ("Logos and Praxis: Investigations of the Theoretical Significance of Marxism"). Châtelet left the Lycée Saint-Louis for the Lycée Louis-le-Grand, before being asked in 1968 to join the new Philosophy Department being set up by Michel Foucault at the University at Vincennes. Châtelet replaced Foucault as head of the Philosophy Department in 1970, and continued at Vincennes until illness forced his retirement in 1982. In addition to his own works in the history of philosophy, informed as they are by his commitment to Marxism, Châtelet also oversaw a number of important editions of essays on the history of philosophy and political thought, including the eight-volume *Histoire de la philosophie* (Hachette, 1972). He was, with Jacques Derrida, Jean-Pierre Faye, and Dominique Lecourt, one of the founders of the Collège International de Philosophie in 1982.

Hélène Cixous (1937–) was born in Oran, Algeria; her mother was Austro-German, her father a Sephardic Jew. She studied at the Lycée Fromentin in Algiers from 1947 to 1953, did her *hypokhâgne* at the Lycée Bugeaud in Algiers in 1954, and, traveling with her husband to Paris in 1955, her *khâgne* at the Lycée Lakanal in the suburbs of Paris. From 1956 to 1959, she studied at the University of Bordeaux, and she passed her *agrégation* in English in 1959 (at age 22, she was the youngest *agrégée de lettres* in France). She taught English for several years in Bordeaux before becoming an *Assistante* at the University of Bordeaux in 1962. In 1965, she was appointed *Maître-assistante* at the Sorbonne, and in 1967 was named *Maître de conférences* at the University at Nanterre. In 1968, she defended her doctoral thesis in English on *L'Exil de James Joyce ou l'art du remplacement* ("The Exile of James Joyce, or The Art of Replacement"), thereby becoming the youngest person in France to have received a *Doctorat d'État*. In 1968, Cixous was asked by the Minister of Education to help organize the faculty of the experimental university at Vincennes (now University of Paris VIII). Michel Foucault had a similar position, having been invited to organize the Department of Philosophy, and the two became close friends. Among the figures Cixous recruited to Vincennes were Michel Butor, Michel Deguy, Lucette Finas, Gérard Genette, and Tzvetan Todorov. In 1970, with Genette and Todorov, she founded the influential literary journal *Poétique*. She has remained a Professor of English at the University of Paris VIII, moving with the campus to Saint-Denis in 1978.

In addition to being a prolific author of works of poetry, fiction (in 1969, she won the Prix Médicis for her novel *Dedans*), theater, and literary criticism, Cixous has been an influential figure in the women's movement in France. In 1974, she created the first doctoral program in women's studies in Europe, the *Centre de recherches en études féminines*, at the University of Paris VIII-Vincennes, offering degrees in *Études Féminines*. Over the years, this center has been threatened with disaccreditation several times, but in each case, Cixous has managed to bring enough pressure to bear on the government to keep the program in existence or, when it was abolished in 1980, to bring it back to life the following year. This program remains the only doctoral program in women's studies in France. Cixous has also been associated with the MLF (*Mouvement de Libération des Femmes*), founded by Antoinette Fouque in 1968, and for many years published her works with their press *Éditions des Femmes*. In addition to her friendship with Foucault (with whom she participated in the activities of the GIP [*Groupe d'information sur les prisons*] in 1971), she has been most closely associated in philosophical circles with Jacques Derrida, with whom she shares Algerian Jewish roots. The two collaborated on several projects and continued to work closely on both academic and political projects.

As a theorist, Cixous is perhaps the figure most closely associated with *écriture féminine*. Her widely read essay "The Laugh of the Medusa" (1975), which appeared first in an issue of the French journal *L'Arc* devoted to Simone de Beauvoir (whose name is never mentioned in Cixous's essay), is generally viewed as the manifesto for "feminine writing." Drawing upon Hegel, Nietzsche, Freud, Heidegger, and most especially Derrida, Cixous's critical writings have been at the forefront of demonstrating how logocentrism easily elides into phallogocentrism as the modern move to the subject as center invariably engenders this subject as male.

Georges Davy (1883–1976) was born in Bernay (Eure, Normandy). He attended the Lycée de Coutances, then the Lycée Michelet, and received his *baccalauréat* in 1902. From 1905 to 1908, Davy studied at the École Normale Supérieure, and he passed the *agrégation* in 1908. Davy spent 1908–9 studying in Germany, then was supported by a fellowship from the Fondation Thiers from 1909 to 1912. After a year at the French Institute in London (1913–14), Davy taught at *lycées* in Saint-Omer (1914), Nice (1915–16), and the Lycée Parc in Lyon (1917–19), before being named to the faculty of letters at the University of Dijon in 1920. Davy received his *Doctorat ès Lettres* in 1922 following the submission of his thesis *La Foi jurée* ("Juror's Faith"), and took his place as one of the leading figures in the Durkheimian school. For the next four decades, Davy occupied a number of important administrative positions in addition to teaching. He served first as Dean of the Faculty of Letters at Dijon (1922–30), then Recteur at the Academie de Rennes (1931–8), before also taking on the administrative position of *Inspecteur Générale*, a position he held from 1933 to 1944. Davy returned to teaching in 1944, becoming first *Maître de conférences* in the History of Social Economy, then Professor without Chair (1945), then Professor of Sociology (1945) at the Sorbonne. In 1950, Davy was named Dean of the Faculty of Letters at the Sorbonne, and he retired in 1955, at which time he became Director of the Fondation Thiers. He was elected to the *Académie des Sciences morales et politiques* in 1952, and presided over L'Institut International de Philosophie Politique from 1953 to 1967. Although Davy's own scholarly interests focused on the sociology of law and legal institutions, his influence on French philosophy is not insignificant insofar as, in addition to the administrative positions already mentioned, he served for almost thirty years as a member of the *jury de agrégation de philosophie*, including serving as president of the jury from 1940 to 1956.

Gilles Deleuze (1925–95) was born in Paris. He studied from primary school through his *baccalauréat* at the Lycée Carnot, the school in his quartier of the 17th Arrondissement, from 1932 to 1943, after which he did his *khâgne* at the Lycée Henri-IV (1943–4). Deleuze studied philosophy at the Sorbonne from 1944 to 1948, receiving his *Diplôme d'études supérieures* in 1947 for a project on Hume supervised by Jean Hyppolite and Georges Canguilhem. This would later become his first book, *Empiricism and Subjectivity*, published in 1953. He passed the *agrégation* in 1948. Deleuze taught at *lycées* in Amiens (1948–52) and Orléans

(1953–5) before returning to Paris to teach at the Lycée Louis-le-Grand (1955–7). He left Louis-le-Grand for the Sorbonne, where he taught as *Maître-assistant* in the history of philosophy from 1957 to 1960. From 1960 to 1964, Deleuze was *attaché de recherches* at the Centre National de la Recherche Scientifique (CNRS), and he taught at the University of Lyon from 1964 to 1969. His thesis, *Difference and Repetition*, supervised by Maurice de Gandillac, was submitted in 1968 for the *Doctorat d'État*, along with a secondary thesis, *Spinoza and the Problem of Expression*, supervised by Ferdinand Alquié. Both were published in 1968. That same year, he was invited by Michel Foucault to become Professor of Philosophy at the University of Paris VIII-Vincennes, but illness prevented him from joining the faculty until 1969. He remained at Paris VIII, moving with the campus from Vincennes in 1978 to the new campus at Saint Denis, until his retirement in 1987. In his later years, Deleuze's pulmonary condition became so debilitating that it became difficult for him to work or socialize with friends. He committed suicide on November 4, 1995.

Deleuze had several strong friendships with many of France's leading intellectuals. In 1943, he met Michel Tournier; while studying at the Sorbonne, he became friends with François Châtelet, Jean-François Lyotard, Michel Butor, Pierre Klossowski, and Claude and Jacques Lanzmann. In 1962, during his time at the CNRS, he met Michel Foucault, with whom he would remain close both personally and intellectually until 1977. And in 1969, he met Félix Guattari, with whom he would work closely for the remainder of his life, collaborating together on four books.

In the 1970s, Deleuze was involved in a number of activities in support of leftist political groups and organizations, including the *Groupe d'information sur les prisons* (GIP), formed by Foucault and Daniel Defert, the "Front Homosexuel d'Action Révolutionnaire (FHAR, an ultra-leftist gay rights group, whose "theorist" was philosopher Guy Hocquenghem). He also associated with the Maoists, and supported the Italian autonomy movement (whose theoretical leader was Antonio Negri) and the Palestinian Liberation movement. It was also in the 1970s that Deleuze's health began to deteriorate. His pulmonary problems, which began in the late 1960s and led to a lung operation in 1970, made it difficult for him to travel. He was, however, able to oversee, beginning in February 1966 with Foucault and later Maurice de Gandillac, the French translation of the Colli-Montinari critical edition of Nietzsche's works and to participate in the 1972 colloquium on Nietzsche at Cerisy.

The range of Deleuze's literary production from his 1953 text on Hume, which he dedicated to Jean Hyppolite, to his final work, the collection of essays on philosophy and literature, *Critique et clinique*, in 1993, is truly astounding. He produced a series of studies in the history of philosophy, with books on Spinoza, Leibniz, Hume, Kant, Nietzsche, and Bergson. His 1962 work on Nietzsche, in particular, was a major factor in the development of interest in Nietzsche in France in the 1960s. And his little book on Kant was one of the first to argue that Kant's third critique, *Critique of Judgment*, should be read not as an aesthetic appendix to the epistemological and ethical revolutions of the first two critiques but as the *telos* toward which Kant's entire critical project was directed. His 1964 study of Proust remains a classic of Proust scholarship, as are his two works on cinema in the field of film studies. Deleuze first became known to most English readers through his work co-authored with radical psychoanalyst Félix Guattari. Most significant in this regard was the first volume of their *Capitalism and Schizophrenia: Anti-Oedipus*, which was read as a manifesto of the May 1968 movement, a major articulation of the philosophy of desire, and a profound critique of psychoanalysis. *Difference and Repetition*, on the other hand, stands as one of the foundational texts of the philosophy of difference and it was in his review of this book, along with *The Logic of Sense*, that Foucault made his often quoted remark that "perhaps one day, this century will be known as Deleuzian."[16]

Unlike many of his well-known peers, Deleuze preferred to avoid publicity and rarely accepted invitations to publish or appear in various media venues. In a 1988 *Magazine littéraire* special issue on his work, his biographical notice concluded with the following: "Traveled little, never belonged to the Communist Party, never was a phenomenologist or Heideggerian, did not renounce Marx, did not repudiate May '68."[17]

Jacques Derrida (1930–2004) was born in El-Biar, a suburb of Algiers, into a Sephardic Jewish family. He began his *lycée* education there in 1941, but his education was disrupted during World War II by local restrictions on Jews. He passed his *baccalauréat* on his second try in

---

[16] Michel Foucault, "Theatrum Philosophicum," trans. Donald F. Bouchard and Sherry Simon, in *Language, Counter-Memory, Practice: Selected Essays and Interviews*, ed. Donald F. Bouchard (Ithaca, NY: Cornell University Press, 1977), p. 165. Foucault's review appeared originally in *Critique*, no. 282 (1970): 885–908.

[17] *Magazine littéraire*, no. 259 (September 1988): 19.

1948 and began reading philosophy seriously while completing his *hypokhâgne* at the Lycée Bugeaud in Algiers. In 1949, he moved to Paris and did his *khâgne* at the prestigious Lycée Louis-le-Grand in preparation for the entrance examination for the École Normale Supérieure. Although he failed on his first attempt, he passed the exam in 1952 and entered the École Normale, where he studied with Louis Althusser, Jean Hyppolite, and Michel Foucault. In 1953, he traveled to the Husserl Archive in Louvain to research for his thesis, and he submitted his *Diplôme d'études supérieures*, directed by Hyppolite and Maurice de Gandillac, on *The Problem of Genesis in Husserl's Philosophy* in 1954 (it was not published until 1990). This early work shows the influence not only of Hyppolite but also of Jean Cavaillès and the Vietnamese Marxist phenomenologist Trân Duc Thao (Derrida often cites Trân Duc Thao in interviews when he reviews his philosophical development).

Following his *Diplôme*, Derrida began work again under Hyppolite on a doctoral thesis on "The Ideality of the Literary Object." In part because of Hyppolite's death, Derrida abandoned the project. He passed his *agrégation* in 1956 and, in 1959, he began his teaching career in the *hypokhâgne* at the *lycée* in Le Mans. From 1960 to 1964, as assistant to Suzanne Bachelard, Georges Canguilhem, Paul Ricoeur, and Jean Wahl, he taught "general philosophy and logic" at the Sorbonne. In 1964, he was invited by Althusser and Hyppolite to lecture at the École Normale Supérieure, where he taught until 1983, serving as *agrégé-répétiteur* (*caïman*) in philosophy from 1965 until his promotion to *Maître-assistant* in 1967. Derrida submitted *De la grammatologie* (the full, recorded title was *De la grammatologie: Essai sur la permanence de concepts platonicien, aristotélicien et scolastique de signe écrit*), directed by Maurice de Gandillac, for his *Doctorat du troisième cycle* in 1967, and he eventually was awarded his *Doctorat d'État* in 1980, where he defended several of his earlier texts (refraining specifically from presenting and defending some of his more stylistically transgressive texts like *Glas* and *The Post Card*)[18] before a jury at the Sorbonne that included Pierre Aubenque, Maurice

---

[18] Titled officially *L'Inscription de la philosophie: Recherches sur l'interprétation de l'écriture*, Derrida's *Doctorat* was awarded for a collection of ten already published works: *Edmund Husserl's Origin of Geometry: An Introduction*, *Writing and Difference*, *Speech and Phenomena*, *Of Grammatology*, *Dissemination*, *Margins of Philosophy*, *The Archeology of the Frivolous*, *Fors*, *Scribble*, and *The Truth in Painting*.

de Gandillac, Jean-Toussaint Desanti (who served as the thesis Director), Henri Joly, Gilbert Lascault, and Emmanuel Levinas.

From the mid-1960s, Derrida had regular appointments at several American universities, including Johns Hopkins (1966–75, affiliated with the Humanities Center), Yale (1975–86, affiliated with the English Department), and SUNY at Buffalo (affiliated with the Comparative Literature Department). From 1987, he spent one quarter each year as a Visiting Professor of French and Comparative Literature at the University of California at Irvine, a position he shared for many years with Jean-François Lyotard and then with Étienne Balibar. For reasons that have much more to do with academic philosophy in the United States than with Derrida's work, for all his time teaching in the United States, he never had a regular appointment in a Department of Philosophy, having spent time instead in Departments of English, French, Humanities, and Comparative Literature. He has been associated, since 1975, with GREPH (*Le Groupe de Recherche sur l'Enseignement Philosophique*), a group that has examined how philosophy is taught in French secondary schools and universities.[19] And in 1982, he was one of the founders, with François Châtelet, Jean-Pierre Faye, and Dominique Lecourt, of the Collège Internationale de Philosophie, serving as its first Director from 1982 to 1984. In 1983, he also left the École Normale Supérieure following his election as *Directeur d'études* in "Philosophical Institutions" at the École des Hautes Études in Sciences Sociales, a position he held until his death.

The major influences on Derrida's intellectual development are numerous, as are those upon whom he has been a significant influence. Clearly, Heidegger, Husserl, Hegel, and Nietzsche appear in many of his works, as do Rousseau, Kant, Freud, and Lacan. Of a more personal nature, his work reflects the influence of his friends and sometimes mentors Emmanuel Levinas, Louis Althusser, Paul DeMan, and Maurice Blanchot. Among those upon whom his influence is most apparent, one must include, restricting the list to France, Jean-Luc Nancy,

---

[19] Many of the founding documents of GREPH are published in their collective work *Qui a peur de la philosophie?* (Paris: Flammarion, 1977). Parts of this text have been translated in Jacques Derrida, *Who's Afraid of Philosophy? Right to Philosophy I*, trans. Jan Plug (Stanford, CA: Stanford University Press, 2002) and *Eyes of the University: Right to Philosophy 2*, trans. Jan Plug and others (Stanford, CA: Stanford University Press, 2004).

Philippe Lacoue-Labarthe, Sarah Kofman, Jean-François Lyotard, and Hélène Cixous.

While somewhat marginalized, for most of his career, from the real sites of academic institutional power in France, Derrida has nevertheless been at the cutting edge of intellectual developments for much of the last four decades of the twentieth century. He was, from the mid-1960s to 1972, associated with Philippe Sollers and the *Tel Quel* group, publishing several of his essays in the journal (the first, in 1965, was "La Parole souflée" on Georges Bataille) as well as two of his books under its "Collection *Tel Quel*" label (*Writing and Difference* in 1967 and *Dissemination* in 1972). He broke definitively with Sollers and the group in 1972 over what he saw as their rigid, pro-PCF and dogmatic Marxist and Maoist positions. At the invitation of René Girard, he attended the important 1966 colloquium at Johns Hopkins University on structuralism – "The Languages of Criticism and the Sciences of Man" – which was instrumental in bringing some of the leading figures in French theory (including Jacques Lacan, Jean Hyppolite, and Roland Barthes) to the attention of the American intellectual community. While this conference was, to some extent, intended to introduce structuralism to America, it turned out, in no small part thanks to Derrida's presentation of "Structure, Sign, and Play in the Discourse of the Human Sciences," to announce the beginning of the end of structuralism and the emergence of a new discourse that came, in the United States, to be called "poststructuralism." Derrida's highlighting of the "question of style" in Nietzsche played a large part in initiating the blossoming of Nietzsche scholarship in the 1970s and 1980s (his text *Spurs: Nietzsche's Styles* was a revised version of the paper titled "La Question du style" ["The Question of Style"] that he presented at the momentous Colloquium on Nietzsche held at Cerisy-la-Salle in 1972)[20] and has permanently altered the way Nietzsche's texts are read. His work had a profound impact on literary studies and scholarship in the last decades of the century and, in his later works, as his interests turned toward questions of politics, ethics, and religion, he continued to influence those fields as well.

---

[20] The papers and subsequent discussions from this conference are published in *Nietzsche aujourd'hui*, 2 vols. (Paris: Union générale d'Éditions, 1973). Among those who presented papers, in addition to Derrida, were Gilles Deleuze, Pierre Klossowski, Sarah Kofman, Jean-François Lyotard, and Jean-Luc Nancy.

Jean-Toussaint Desanti (1914–2002) was born in Corsica. He left Corsica after *lycée*, and did his *khâgne* at the Lycée Lakanal, where he discovered Spinoza and Marx, two figures who were to engage his thought for the entirety of his career. Desanti attended the École Normale Supérieure from 1935 to 1938, where he was introduced by Merleau-Ponty to Husserl and phenomenology, and was influenced by Jean Cavaillès to look to mathematics as an object of philosophical reflection. During these years, he also followed the courses of Léon Brunschvicg at the Sorbonne. He submitted his thesis for the *Diplôme d'études supérieures* in 1938 on "L'Être et la relation dans la philosophie platonicienne" ("Being and Relation in Platonic Philosophy"). In the 1940s, he was influenced by the work of Gaston Bachelard. Desanti taught for many years at the Lycée Lamartine and at the École Normale Supérieure-Saint Cloud, where he served as *agrégé-répétiteur* from 1958 to 1971. In 1968, he received his *Doctorat d'État* for theses examining the epistemological implications of topics in mathematics (real variables and set theory), *Recherches épistémologiques sur le développement de la théorie des fonctions de variables réelles: Essai sur le statut des idéalités mathématiques* and "Recherches sur la formation du concept de mesure des ensembles (de Riemann, 1866 à Lebesgue, 1918)." Soon thereafter, in 1971, he became Professor of Philosophy at the Sorbonne, where he taught until his retirement. A committed communist, Desanti joined the French Communist Party in 1943, broke with the party in 1958, but remained one of the principal figures among communist intellectuals. Drawing upon phenomenological and structuralist paradigms, Desanti had a profound influence upon students at the ENS-Saint Cloud, comparable to that of Louis Althusser at the ENS-rue d'Ulm. Desanti's best-known work is his doctoral thesis *Les Idéalities mathématiques* (1968; "Mathematical Idealities").

Mikel Dufrenne (1910–95) was born in Clermont (Oise, Picardie). He studied with Alain for his *khâgne* at the Lycée Henri-IV, then at the École Normale Supérieure from 1929 to 1932, where he submitted his thesis for the *Diplôme d'études supérieures* in 1931 on "La Nature de la connaissance sensible chez Descartes" ("The Nature of Sensible Knowledge in Descartes"). Dufrenne passed his *agrégation* in 1932. He was captured during the war and spent five years in the same prisoner of war camp with Paul Ricoeur, with whom he became close friends. Together with Ricoeur, Dufrenne worked on the philosophy of Karl Jaspers, and the two published *Karl Jaspers et la philosophie de* *l'existence* in 1947. His two-volume *Phénoménologie de l'expérience esthé-tique* (English translation: *The Phenomenology of Aesthetic Experience*, trans. Edward S. Casey [Evanston, IL: Northwestern University Press, 1973]), submitted for his *Doctorat d'État* in 1953 along with a *thèse complémentaire* titled *Notion de personnalité de base et son contexte dans l'anthropologie américaine*, was the second major work in phenomenology to be produced in France, second only to Merleau-Ponty's *Phenomen-ology of Perception* (1945). It remains one of the most significant phe-nomenological reflections on aesthetics. Dufrenne was named Professor of Philosophy at the University of Poitiers in 1953 and taught there until 1963, when he became one of the founding faculty members of the University of Nanterre (later Paris X), where he taught until his retire-ment in 1974. As an author of several works on aesthetics, as an editor of the *Revue d'esthétique*, and as director of the Esthétique series for the publisher Klincksieck (which oversaw the publication of Jean-François Lyotard's *Discours, figure: Un essai d'esthétique* in 1971), Dufrenne was perhaps the best-known philosopher of art and aesthetics in France for much of the second half of the twentieth century.

Frantz Fanon (1925–61) was born in Martinique in the French Antil-les. He attended grade school and the Lycée Schoelcher in Fort-de-France, Martinique, where he first met and studied with Aimé Césaire, one of the founding figures of the negritude movement (with Léon Damas and Léopold Sédar Senghor). During World War II, he served in the Free French army both in north Africa and in Europe. After the war, he returned to Martinique to work for the campaign of his former *lycée* teacher Césaire, then a parliamentary candidate from the Com-munist Party for a delegate's seat at the French National Assembly. After Césaire's unsuccessful campaign, Fanon completed his *baccalaur-éat* in 1946, during the final year of which he concentrated on the philosophies of Césaire and Jean-Paul Sartre. He continued his educa-tion in France, studying medicine and psychiatry at the University of Lyon from 1947 to 1951. Fanon served as head of the psychiatry department of Blida-Joinville Hospital in Algeria from 1953 to 1956. In 1954, Fanon joined the Algerian liberation movement (the FLN, or Front de Libération Nationale) and his sympathies toward the FLN led to his expulsion from Algeria in January 1957. He moved to Tunis, where he became an editor of the FLN's newspaper, *El Moudjahid*. Under Fanon's editorial guidance, the paper became more radical and he published in it articles on Black Africa and African unity. While

Fanon's political activities became increasingly revolutionary, he continued to practice medicine and teach at the University of Tunis. From 1957 to 1960, Fanon played a role in Algerian and Antillean diplomacy, representing one or the other group at meetings of African leaders. In 1960 he was appointed ambassador to Ghana by the rebel Algerian Provisional Government. Fanon died of leukemia in a hospital in Washington, DC in 1961.

Philosophically, Fanon draws upon five central resources: Hegel and the struggle for recognition, which he used to frame his analyses of colonialism and racism; psychoanalysis, which he used in his psychiatric practice and in his theoretical practice for analyzing the psychology of racism; existentialist philosophy, both in terms of the writings of Kierkegaard, Nietzsche (Fanon began his medical thesis with a quotation from Nietzsche: "I dedicate myself to living beings, not to introspective mental process."), Heidegger, Jaspers, and Merleau-Ponty; the writings and intellectual figure of Sartre, whose *Anti-Semite and Jew* served as a significant model for analyzing racism, whose journal *Les Temps modernes* was engaged in political analyses with which Fanon could sympathize, and whose exemplification of the engaged intellectual provided Fanon with a model; and the negritude movement, which initially inspired him insofar as it allowed for the construction of a positive image of native peoples that could challenge their construction by their colonial masters. He came to criticize the negritude movement, however, arguing that it assumed a solidarity among black peoples that was a political mistake that distracted attention from the real plight of black people under colonial and racist regimes.

Fanon's relation to Sartre is a complex one. On the one hand, the analysis of the look from *Being and Nothingness* had a large impact on Fanon's first work, *Black Skin, White Masks*, as did the analysis of anti-Semitism in *Anti-Semite and Jew*. On the other hand, "Black Orpheus," Sartre's controversial introductory essay to Léopold Sédar Senghor's important 1948 literary anthology, *Anthologie de la nouvelle poésie nègre et malgache de langue française*, in which he criticized the negritude movement, distressed Fanon greatly when it first appeared. Fanon went on to share some of Sartre's political concerns about the negritude movement, and he eventually approached Sartre for an introductory essay to his last work, *The Wretched of the Earth*, which Sartre was happy to provide.

When he died, Fanon was more widely known as a political revolutionary and advocate of Algerian independence than a theorist and philosopher. But in the years since his death, his psycho-political analysis of the construction of the colonial subject and his class analysis of colonialism and the relations between racism and colonialism have had a profound effect on many Third World intellectuals and on several fields of postcolonial studies.

Michel Foucault (1926–84) was born in Poitiers (Vienne, Poitou-Charentes). He attended elementary and secondary school at the Lycée Henri-IV in Poitiers from 1932 to 1940. Performing badly on his end-of-year examinations in 1940, Foucault remained in Poitiers but transferred to the Collège Saint-Stanislaus for two years, completing his *baccalauréat* in 1942. Conditions in Paris during the war made it unwise for Foucault to travel to Paris to continue his education, and he returned to the Lycée Henri-IV in Poitiers in 1943 to begin his *hypokhâgne*. Instruction at the Poitiers *lycée* was somewhat disorganized and after he failed the competitive entrance exam to the École Normale Supérieure, Foucault in 1945 went to study at the Lycée Henri-IV in Paris. Here he first met Jean Hyppolite, who was then teaching the *khâgne* at Henri-IV and who would remain in Paris long enough to introduce Foucault to Hegel's *Phenomenology of Spirit* before leaving for the University of Strasbourg. Foucault entered the École Normale Supérieure in 1946, passing the examination monitored by Georges Canguilhem and Pierre-Maxime Schuhl. Among his professors at the École Normale, Foucault worked most closely with Louis Althusser, with whom he became good friends. Foucault obtained the *licence de philosophie* in 1948. He was also quite interested in psychology, and attended the lectures of Daniel Lagache at the Sorbonne, where he obtained a *licence de psychologie* in 1949. During this time, he also attended Maurice Merleau-Ponty's lectures on the mind–body relation and on the human sciences, Jean Beaufret's lectures on Heidegger, as well as the lectures of Jean Hyppolite and Jacques Lacan. For his thesis for the *Diplôme d'études supérieures* in 1949, Foucault wrote on "La Constitution d'un transcendental dans *La Phénoménologie de l'esprit* de Hegel" ("The Constitution of a Historical Transcendental in Hegel's *Phenomenology of Spirit*") under the direction of Hyppolite. In July 1951, he passed the *agrégation* on his second try, finishing third.

Foucault was named *répétiteur* of psychology at the École Normale Supérieure in 1951, where Jacques Derrida, Gérard Genette, and Paul Veyne were among his students. Poor health exempted him from his obligatory military service. He passed his *diplôme de psychopathologie* at the Institute of Psychology of Paris in June 1952 and, upon the recommendation of Jules Vuillemin, he began teaching psychology at the University of Lille in addition to his position at the École Normale. He merged his interests in Heidegger and psychology by studying with Ludwig Binswanger in Switzerland in 1953, and one of his first publications was a translation and introduction to Binswanger's *Dream and Existence*. From 1955 to 1958, he taught in Sweden at the University of Uppsala, where he met and became friendly with historian of religion Georges Dumézil (1898–1986), who spent his summers in Uppsala following the completion of his courses at the Collège de France.

After working briefly at the Centre Français in Warsaw and the Institut Français in Hamburg, Foucault returned to France in 1960 and began teaching philosophy and psychology at the University of Clermont-Ferrand. Here he began a friendship with Vuillemin, who would remain at Clermont-Ferrand until he replaced Merleau-Ponty at the Collège de France, and first met Gilles Deleuze and Michel Serres. At Clermont-Ferrand, he also met Daniel Defert, a young philosophy student and activist who became his companion in 1963 and remained with Foucault until the end of his life. (Defert became a Professor of Sociology at the University of Paris XIII and, following Foucault's death, founded in 1984 and was president of AIDES, the oldest and most prominent AIDS group in France.) In 1961, Foucault submitted to Georges Canguilhem his thesis for the *Doctorat d'État* – *Folie et déraison. Histoire de la folie à l'âge classique* ("Madness and Irrationality: A History of Insanity in the Classical Age of Reason") – which he defended before a jury that was presided over by Henri Gouhier and included Canguilhem as reporter, Daniel Lagache, Jean Hyppolite, and Maurice de Gandillac. A second *thèse complémentaire*, "Introduction à l'*Anthropologie* de Kant," was submitted the same year, and included a translation of Kant's *Anthropology* into French, prefaced by a lengthy, and heretofore unpublished introduction that showed the influence of Heidegger's *Kant and the Problem of Metaphysics*.[21]

In the early 1960s, Foucault was a member of the editorial committee led by Georges Bataille of the journal *Critique*, and he was also associated with the *Tel Quel* group. Along with Deleuze, he organized the famous Royaumont colloquium on Nietzsche in July 1964, and in

---

[21] First published in German in 1929, a French translation by Alphonse de Waelhens and Walter Biemel, *Kant et le problème de la métaphysique*, was published by Éditions Gallimard in 1953.

February 1966 Foucault and Deleuze accepted responsibility for over-seeing the French translation of the Colli-Montinari critical edition of Nietzsche's works. Foucault lived in Tunisia from 1966 to 1968, and so was out of Paris during the events of May '68. In late 1968, he returned to France at the request of Georges Canguilhem, who, on behalf of the Orientation Committee selected to organize the faculty of the experimental university at Vincennes (University of Paris VIII), extended an invitation to Foucault to form a new department of philosophy. Hélène Cixous had a similar position, having been invited to organize the department of English, and the two became close friends. Gilles Deleuze was Foucault's first selection, but because of his poor health, Deleuze would not in fact join the faculty for two years, by which time Foucault had already left. Others Foucault invited who did join the faculty included Alain Badiou, Étienne Balibar, François Châtelet, Daniel Defert (a controversial choice, given his relationship with Foucault and his relative lack of philosophical credentials at the time), Judith Miller (daughter of Jacques Lacan), Jacques Rancière, René Schérer, and Michel Serres. Foucault was also instrumental in the negotiations that allowed for the creation of a department of psychoanalysis distinct from the department of psychology. Under the direction of Serge Leclaire, the department of psychoanalysis was initially a part of Vincennes's philosophy department, and was historically significant insofar as it provided an institutional base for Lacanian academicians. Foucault left Vincennes in 1970, having been proposed by Jules Vuillemin and elected to the Chair of the History of Systems of Thought at the Collège de France, a position he would hold until his death.

Foucault was very much at the center of the intellectual scene in Paris from the mid-1960s to the end of his life. He became interested in prison reform and, with Jean-Marie Domenach and Pierre Vidal-Naquet, he co-founded GIP (*Groupe d'information sur les prisons*) in 1971. In addition to his close friendship with Althusser, he was friends with Roland Barthes, and played an important role in Barthes's election to the Collège de France in 1977, as he did as well for Pierre Bourdieu's election in 1982. He was also an important influence on Derrida, though the two were estranged from one another for almost twenty years, following an exchange over Foucault's *History of Madness*; their reconciliation was facilitated by Foucault's active intervention on Derrida's behalf following Derrida's false arrest on drug charges in Prague in 1982. He was also, for many years, close to Deleuze, though they too went their separate ways over complicated political and philosophical disagreements in the late 1970s. Foucault lectured frequently in Brazil and, from 1972, increasingly in the United States, first at the University of Buffalo and, beginning in 1975, at Berkeley, where he was initially invited by Leo Bersani to join the French Department. While Foucault continued to lecture at a number of other American universities, Berkeley became something of a second institutional home, and the freedom afforded him in San Francisco was a welcome change from the demands of Paris. Foucault's health declined during the early 1980s and he died of AIDS in the summer of 1984, just weeks after the publication of the second and third volumes of *The History of Sexuality*.

Maurice Patronnier de Gandillac (1906–) was born in Paris. He studied at the Lycée Pasteur de Neuilly and did his *khâgne* at the Lycée Louis-le-Grand before entering the École Normale Supérieure in 1925, in the class that included Jean Hyppolite and followed the entering class that included Sartre, Aron, and Canguilhem. While at the École Normale, Gandillac studied medieval philosophy at the Sorbonne with Étienne Gilson, and a year after receiving his *licence ès lettres*, Gandillac submitted to Gilson his thesis for the *Diplôme d'études supérieures* in 1928 on "La Critique du principe de causalité chez Pierre D'Ailly" ("The Critique of the Principle of Causality in Pierre D'Ailly"). Gandillac passed his *agrégation* in 1929, and wrote his doctoral thesis on *La Philosophie de Nicolas de Cues* ("The Philosophy of Nicholas of Cusa"), which was published in 1941. He taught at the University at Lille before coming to the Sorbonne, where he replaced Émile Brehier in 1946 as Professor of History of the Philosophy of the Middle Ages and Renaissance. Gandillac taught at the Sorbonne until the end of his career, and created there a Center for Research on Medieval Thought.

In addition to his important work in Medieval philosophy, Gandillac also had interests in modern and contemporary, especially German, philosophy; these dual interests are reflected in an extraordinary collection of translations, including translations of Nicholas of Cusa, the complete works of Pseudo-Dionysius the Areopagite, and Peter Abelard, as well as Hegel, Novalis, Nietzsche (in addition to translating *Thus Spoke Zarathustra* and two volumes of his correspondence, Gandillac served with Gilles Deleuze as General Editor of the translation into French of the Colli-Montinari Critical Edition of Nietzsche's Collected Works), Walter Benjamin, Ernst Bloch, and Georg Lukács. Gandillac's wide-ranging interests are also reflected in his many years as *animateur* and participant in the events organized at the International Cultural Center at Cerisy-la-Salle and his service, since 1964, as President of the Association des Amis de Pontigny-Cerisy. A sense of the scope of figures who engaged with Gandillac can be seen in the volume of essays organized in his honor, *L'Art des confins: Mélanges offerts à Maurice de Gandillac*,[22] which includes essays by Gilles Deleuze, Jacques Derrida, Pierre Hadot, Eugene Ionesco, Jean-François Lyotard, Albert Memmi, Jean-Luc Nancy, and Paul Ricoeur, among others.

Roger Garaudy (1913–) was born in Marseilles. He studied at the Lycée Henri-IV and the Sorbonne, completed an *agrégation* in philosophy in 1953, and a *Doctorat d'État* also in 1953 with a thesis *La Théorie matérialiste de la connaissance* (*The Materialist Theory of Consciousness*). Garaudy taught at the Lycée Buffon (1958–9), was *Maître de conférences* at the University of Clermont-Ferrand (1962–5), and taught aesthetics at the University of Poitiers as *Maître de conférences* (1965–9) and professor (1969–73). From the late 1940s to the late 1960s, he was a leading theorist for the French Communist Party, advocating an increasingly humanist version of Marxism following the fall of Stalin. He served as a *député* to the Assemblée Nationale from 1946 to 1951 and was vice-president of the Assemblée from 1956 to 1958. Garaudy was involved in several significant Marxist polemics, first with Jean-Paul Sartre and later with Louis Althusser. Among his more than twenty books are *Les Sources françaises du socialisme scientifique* (1949; "French Sources of Scientific Socialism") and *Perspectives de l'homme: Existentialisme, pensée catholique, marxisme* (1959; "Perspectives on Man: Existentialism, Catholic Thought, Marxism"). Late in his life, Garaudy gained notoriety in a different way, as a Holocaust denier: on February 27, 1998, a French court found the 84-year-old Garaudy guilty of violating a law that prohibits the questioning of crimes "against humanity." Also convicted for "racial defamation," Garaudy was fined 240,000 francs (roughly $40,000) for claims made in his 1995 book *Les Mythes fondateurs de la politique israélienne* (English translation: *The Founding Myths of Israeli Politics*, trans. Theodore J. Okeefe [Newport Beach, CA: Institute for Historical Review, 2000]), in which he denied that the Holocaust had occurred.

---

[22]   Annie Cazenave and Jean-François Lyotard, *L'Art des confins: Mélanges offerts à Maurice de Gandillac* (Paris: Presses universitaires de France, 1985).

Étienne Gilson (1884–1978) was born in Paris. He studied at the seminary at Notre-Dame-des-Champs (1895–1902) and completed his *baccalauréat* at the Lycée Henri-IV (1902–3). Following his military service, he began his studies at the Sorbonne in 1905, where he worked with Victor Brochard, Victor Delbos, Lucien Lévy-Bruhl, and André Lalande. He also followed Henri Bergson's course at the Collège de France on "L'Effort intellectuel." In 1906, he submitted his thesis for the *Diplôme d'études supérieures* "Sur l'origine scolastique de quelques theories cartésiennes" ("On the Scholastic Origin of Some Cartesian Theories"), passed the *agrégation* in 1907, and taught at *lycées* in Bourg-en-Bresse (1907–8), Rochefort-sur-Mer (1908–10), Tour (1910–11), Saint-Quentin (1911–12), and Angers (1912–13) prior to World War I. In 1913, Gilson submitted his thesis *La Liberté chez Descartes et la théologie* ("Freedom in Descartes and Theology"), along with *Index scolastico-cartésian*, a dictionary of scholastic terminology in Descartes's work as his *thèse complémentaire*, for the *Doctorat ès Lettres* to his Director, Lucien Lévy-Bruhl, with whom he worked closely at both Henri-IV and the Sorbonne. He served during World War I, spending three years (1916–18) in a prisoner of war camp. In 1919, he was appointed Professor of the History of Philosophy at the University of Strasbourg. From 1921 to 1926, Gilson served as *Maître de conférences* in the History of Medieval Philosophy at the Sorbonne, was promoted and taught as Professor without Chair from 1926 to 1931, and from 1932 to 1951, he held the Chair of History of Medieval Philosophy at the Collège de France. He was elected to the *Académie Française* in 1947. Gilson retired from his Chair at the Collège de France in 1951 to devote all his time to the direction of research at the Pontifical Institute of Medieval Studies at the University of Toronto, which he had helped to establish in 1929.

Gilson was the author of over thirty books, among which are major studies of many of the leading medieval theologians and philosophers, including St. Augustine (*Introduction a l'étude de saint Augustin* [1929; English translation: *The Christian Philosophy of Saint Augustine*, trans. L. E. M. Lynch (New York: Random House, 1960)]), St. Bonaventure, St. Thomas Aquinas (*Le Thomisme: Introduction au système de Saint Thomas D'Aquin* [first edition 1919, revised and enlarged through six editions; English translations: third edition: *The Philosophy of St. Thomas Aquinas*, trans. Edward Bullough (Cambridge, MA: Heffer and Sons, 1924); fifth edition: *The Christian Philosophy of St. Thomas Aquinas*, trans. L. K. Shook (New York: Random House, 1956)]; *Saint Thomas d'Aquin*

[1931; English translation: *Moral Values and the Moral Life*, trans. Leo R. Ward (St. Louis: B. Herder, 1931)]), and Duns Scotus. He is generally regarded as one of the most influential neo-Thomist scholars and historians of medieval philosophy of the twentieth century.

Henri Gouhier (1898–1994) was born in Auxerre (Yonne, Burgundy). He studied at the École Normale Supérieure from 1919 to 1922, submitted his thesis in 1920 for the *Diplôme d'études supérieures* "Rapports de la raison et de la foi, selon Descartes" ("The Relations of Reason and Faith according to Descartes"), and passed the *agrégation* in 1921, finishing first. In 1923, he completed a *Diplôme* in the Fifth Section of the École Pratique des Hautes Études, was a fellow at the Foundation Thiers from 1922 to 1925, and completed his *Doctorat ès Lettres* in 1926, submitting his thesis *La Vocation de Malebranche* ("Malebranche's Calling") and *thèse complémentaire La Philosophie de Malebranche et son expérience religieuse* ("Malebranche's Philosophy and his Religious Experience"). Gouhier taught from 1925 to 1928 at the *lycée* at Troyes before joining the faculty at the University of Lille, where he served as *chargé de cours* (1929–30), *Maître de conférences* (1930–3), Professor of the Philosophy and Science of Education (1933–6), and Professor of Philosophy (1936–40). After a brief time at the Académie de Bordeaux, Gouhier came to the Sorbonne as *chargé de l'enseignement de la maîtrise de conférences d'histoire de la philosophie moderne* in 1941, and, in 1948, became Chair of the History of Religious Thought in France since the Sixteenth Century, a position he held until he retired in 1968. He was elected to the *Académie de Sciences morales et politiques* in 1961 and to the *Académie Française* in 1979. Gouhier published a number of books on the history of French philosophy, including several books on Descartes as well as books on Malebranche, Pascal, Rousseau, Maine de Biran, Comte, and Bergson.

Gilles-Gaston Granger (1920–) was born in Paris. He did his *khâgne* at the Lycée Henri-IV, and studied at the École Normale d'Instituteurs de la Seine before entering the École Normale Supérieure in 1940. At the École Normale, he began a lifelong friendship with Jules Vuillemin, and studied with and was deeply influenced by Jean Cavaillès. Granger submitted his thesis for the *Diplôme d'études supérieures* on "L'Homme chez Aristotle" ("Man in Aristotle's Work") to Emile Bréhier in 1942, received a *licence* in mathematics in 1946, and received his *Doctorat d'État* in 1955, following the submission of his primary thesis "Concept, structure, et loi en science économique" ("Concept, Structure, and Law in Economic Science") and his *thèse complémentaire* "La Mathématique sociale du Marquis de Condorcet" ("The Social Mathematics of the Marquis de Condorcet"). After completing his *agrégation* in 1943, Granger taught at the Lycée Carnot in Dijon (1943–4), served in the armed forces in 1944–5, and taught the *Première Supérieure* at the Lycée Thiers in Marseille (1945–6). He took a position as an adjunct professor at the University of São Paulo (1947–53), taught as *Maître de conférences* at the University of Rennes (1955–9), then was promoted to Professor first at São Paulo (1959–60) and then Rennes (1960–2). Granger left Rennes to serve as Director of the École Normale Supérieure in Brazzaville (1962–4) before being named to a professorship at the University of Aix. He taught at Aix from 1964 to 1986, during which time he also directed a seminar in Comparative Epistemology. In 1986, he was elected to a Chair in Comparative Epistemology at the Collège de France, a position he held until 1991. In addition to important historical studies of Wittgenstein (1969) and Aristotle's theory of science (1976), Granger's works are primarily in philosophy of language and epistemology. The fundamental theses of his comparative epistemology are put forward in his important 1955 work *Méthodologie économique*, a revision of his thesis for the *Doctorat d'État*. To date, one of his works has appeared in English: *Pensée formelle et sciences de l'homme* (1960; *Formal Thought and the Sciences of Man* [Boston, MA: D. Reidel, 1983]).

Félix Guattari (1930–92) was born in Villeneuve-les-Sablons (Oise, Picardie). He studied pharmacy and philosophy at the University of Paris in the early 1950s. In the 1950s, he was active in the French Communist Party (PCF) and engaged in activities with several other leftist political groups, several of which led him to break with the PCF in 1958. In 1953, he co-founded, along with Lacanian psychiatrist Jean Oury, the Clinique at La Borde and was associated with the "anti-psychiatry" movement. The clinic was an experimental hospital that challenged many of the traditional approaches to treating mental patients – in particular, the treatment of psychotics – and questioned the necessity of a hierarchical relationship between patient and therapist. Guattari's work there explored the links between psychological repression and social oppression and the relations between institutions and analysis. In 1953, Guattari began attending Jacques Lacan's seminars; from 1962 to 1969 he underwent analysis with Lacan and, in 1969, he joined Lacan's École Freudienne de Paris, remaining a member until Lacan himself dissolved the group in 1980.

Guattari was a longtime political activist and he played an active role in the events of May 1968. In 1968, he met Gilles Deleuze and it is his work with Deleuze that has had the greatest philosophical impact. Together, they wrote four books, including *Anti-Oedipus*, the single work which many feel best represents the spirit of the time that animated May '68. Guattari produced several works of his own that blur the line between the psychological and the political and, in his final works, turned his political attentions toward ecological questions. Among his more significant works are *Psychanalyse et transversalité: Essais d'analyse institutionnelle* (Paris: F. Maspero, 1972), *La Révolution moléculaire* (Fontenay-sous-Bois: Recherches, 1977) (parts of these two works appear in English in *Molecular Revolution: Psychiatry and Politics*, trans. Rosemary Sheed [London: Penguin, 1980]), *Les Trois écologies* (Paris: Galilée, 1989; English translation: *The Three Ecologies*, trans. Ian Pindar and Paul Sutton [London: Athlone Press, 2000]), and *Chaosmose* (Paris: Galilée, 1992; English translation: *Chaosmosis: An Ethicoaesthetic Paradigm*, trans. Paul Bains and Julian Pefanis [Bloomington: Indiana University Press, 1995]).

Martial Guéroult (1891–1976) was born in Le Havre (Seine Maritime, Normandy). He entered the École Normale Supérieure in 1913 and worked closely with Léon Brunschvicg, Léon Robin (1866–1947), and especially Victor Delbos, but his studies were interrupted by World War I, during which he was seriously wounded. Guéroult returned to resume his studies, graduated from the École Normale in 1920, and passed the *agrégation* in 1919. He taught at the *lycée* in Chartres (1921–2) before becoming *Maître de conférences d'histoire generale de la philosophie* at the University of Strasbourg in 1922. Guéroult taught at the *lycée* in Vendôme from 1923 to 1929, but returned to Strasbourg as *Maître de conférences* in 1929. In 1930, Guéroult submitted his thesis for the *Doctorat ès Lettres* on *L'Évolution et la structure de la doctrine de la science chez Fichte* ("The Evolution and Structure of Fichte's Doctrine of Science"), with a second thesis on "La Philosophie transcendentale de Salomon Maïmon" ("The Transcendental Philosophy of Salomon Maïmon"), and was named in 1933 to a Professor's Chair at Strasbourg. He taught at the University of Strasbourg until 1945, at which time he joined the faculty of the Sorbonne as Chair of the History of Modern Philosophy. Guéroult taught there until his election in 1951 to the Chair in the History and Technology of Philosophical Systems at the Collège de France, which he held until his retirement in1962. Elected to the

Académie de Sciences morales et politiques in 1957, Guéroult wrote several important works on the history of philosophy, including texts on Descartes, Berkeley, Malebranche, Spinoza, and Fichte.

Jean Guitton (1901–99) was born in Saint-Étienne (Loire, Rhône-Alpes). He attended *lycée* in Saint-Étienne (1908–17), did his *hypokhâgne* at the Lycée Louis-le-Grand (1917–18), and received a *licence* from the Sorbonne (1918), before entering the École Normale Supérieure in 1920. He completed his studies at the Sorbonne in 1923, obtaining a *Diplôme d'études supérieures* for a thesis on "L'Idée de signe chez Berkeley" ("The Idea of the Sign in Berkeley"). Guitton passed his *agrégation* in 1923, and submitted his doctoral thesis for the *Doctorat ès Lettres* in 1933, influenced by the thought of Maurice Blondel, *Le Temps et l'éternité chez Plotin et saint Augustin* ("Time and Eternity in Plotinus and Saint Augustine"), with a *thèse secondaire* on *La Philosophie de Newman*. He taught at the *lycée* in Troyes (1924–5), held a fellowship at the Fondation Thiers (1925–8), returned to teach at the *lycée* in Moulins (1930–4), then Lyon (1935–7), where he replaced Vladimir Jankélévitch as the teacher of the *khâgne* and had a profound influence on Louis Althusser, who was his student in 1937.

Guitton began his university career in 1937 at the University of Montpellier, where he taught until 1939. During the war, he was a prisoner in Germany from 1940 to 1945, and following the war, he was prohibited in 1946 by the "comité d'épuration" ("Committee for Purification") from university teaching because of his publications in support of Marshall Pétain. He taught at the *lycée* in Avignon from 1946 to 1949 and the Lycée Montaigne in Dijon from 1949 to 1950, before resuming his university career at the University of Dijon (1950–4). In 1954, Guitton was appointed to a professorship at the Sorbonne, where he held the Chair in Philosophy and the History of Philosophy from 1955 to 1968. In 1961, he was elected to the *Académie Française*, and in 1987 to the *Académie des Sciences morales et politiques*. Guitton was the author of 54 books, including the eight-volume *La Pensée moderne et le catholicisme* ("Modern Thought and Catholicism"), published between 1934 and 1948. One of the best-known Christian philosophers of his day, Guitton was a personal friend of Pope Paul VI and one of the few laymen authorized to take part in the Second Vatican Council in 1963.

Pierre Hadot (1922–) was born in Reims (Marne, Champagne). He attended seminary in Reims before entering the Sorbonne, where he submitted his thesis for the *Diplôme d'études supérieures* in 1947. From 1949 to 1964, he did research at the Centre National de la Recherche Scientifique (CNRS). In 1964, he became *Directeur d'études* in the Fifth Section of the École Pratique des Hautes Études in "Patristique latine" ("Latin Patristics"). He submitted his thesis for the *Doctorat ès Lettres* in 1968 on *Porphyre et Victorinus* ("Porphyry and Victorinus"). In 1972, the title of his chair was changed to "Théologies et mystiques de la Grèce hellénistique et de la fin de l'Antiquité" ("Theologies and Mysticisms of Hellenistic Greece and the End of Antiquity"). He served from 1976 to 1983 as the Director of the Centre d'études des religions du livre. In 1982, he was elected to the Chair in the History of Hellenistic and Roman Thought at the Collège de France, a position he held until 1991. Long respected as a scholar of antiquity in France, Hadot came to the attention of the English-speaking world as an influential figure in Foucault's revision of his "History of Sexuality" project in the late 1970s. Among his many works are several translated into English, including *La Citadelle Intérieure: Introduction au Pensées de Marc Aurèle* (1992; English translation: *The Inner Citadel: The Meditations of Marcus Aurelius*, ed. and trans. Michael Chase [Cambridge, MA: Harvard University Press, 1997]); *Exercices spirituels et philosophies antiques*, 2nd edn. (1987; English translation: *Philosophy as a Way of Life: Spiritual Exercises from Socrates to Foucault*, ed. Arnold Davidson, trans. Michael Chase [Oxford: Blackwell, 1995]); *Plotin ou la simplicité du regard* (1997; English translation: *Plotinus or the Simplicity of Vision*, trans. Michael Chase [Chicago: University of Chicago Press, 1998]), and *Qu'est-ce que la philosophie antique?* (1995; English translation: *What is Ancient Philosophy?* trans. Michael Chase [Cambridge, MA: Harvard University Press, 2002]).

Michel Henry (1922–2002) was born in Haïphong, Vietnam. He spent his childhood in Lille, where his family relocated following his father's death. Henry did his *hypokhâgne* and *khâgne* at the Lycée Henri-IV, studying philosophy with René Bertrand, before returning to Lille to attend the university there. In 1943, he submitted his thesis for the *Diplôme d'études supérieures* on "La Bonheur de Spinoza" ("Spinoza's Happiness") to Maurice de Gandillac, and passed the *agrégation* in 1945. After a brief post as Professor of Philosophy in Casablanca, Henry worked for ten years in relative isolation and poverty on his thesis *L'Essence de la manifestation* (English translation: *The Essence of Manifestation*, trans. Girard Etzkorn [The Hague: Martinus Nijhoff,

1973]), which was received enthusiastically by his examining jury at the Sorbonne, which included Jean Hyppolite, Jean Wahl, Paul Ricoeur, Ferdinand Alquié, and Henri Gouhier, and was published in 1963. Because of the positive response to his thesis, Henry was offered several university positions in Paris, which he declined, preferring the relative quiet and isolation of a provincial campus in order to write. He spent four years as a researcher at the Centre National de la Recherche Scientifique before joining the faculty at the Université Paul-Valéry in Montpellier, where apart from brief periods as a guest professor at the École Normale Supérieure and the Sorbonne in Paris, the Catholic University of Louvain, the University of Washington at Seattle, and the University of Tokyo, he spent the entirety of his career, retiring from teaching in 1987.

Michel Henry is generally regarded as one of France's most important phenomenological thinkers in the second half of the twentieth century, and he is one of the major proponents of the so-called "theological turn" in French phenomenology. Called the "new Bergson" – but a "Bergson who had read Heidegger"[23] – following the publication of his thesis, Henry's work sought to redefine "subjectivity" and "life" through analyses of the lived body, immanence, and bodily feeling (*le sentiment corporel*). In addition to his doctoral thesis, several of Henry's other major works have appeared in English translation, including *Philosophie et phénoménologie du corps. Essai sur l'ontologie biranienne* (1965; English translation: *Philosophy and Phenomenology of the Body*, trans. Girard Etzkorn [The Hague: Martinus Nijhoff, 1975]); *Généalogie de la psychanalyse. Le Commencement perdu* (1985; English translation: *The Genealogy of Psychoanalysis*, trans. Douglas Brick [Stanford, CA: Stanford University Press, 1998]); *C'est moi la vérité. Pour une philosophie du christianisme* (1996; English translation: *I am the Truth: Toward a Philosophy of Christianity*, trans. Susan Emanuel [Stanford, CA: Stanford University Press 2002]); and an important two-volume study of Marx: *Marx. I. Une philosophie de la réalité; II. Une philosophie de l'économie* (1976; abridged English translation: *Marx: A Philosophy of Human Reality*, trans. Kathleen McLaughlin [Bloomington: Indiana University Press, 1983]).

Jean Hyppolite (1907–68) was born in Jonzac (Charente-Maritime, Poitou-Charentes). He studied at the *lycée* in Rochefort and did his

---

[23] These remarks are attributed to Jean Lacroix in Robert Maggiori's obituary "Michel Henry ravi à la Vie," *Liberation*, July 8, 2002: 34.

khâgne at the *lycée* in Poitiers (where he first began his study of Hegel with Georges Bénézé [1888–1978], a disciple of Alain)[24] before entering the École Normale Supérieure in 1925, where he was profoundly influenced by his *caïman* Jean Cavaillès, and studied with fellow *normaliens* Jean-Paul Sartre, Georges Canguilhem, Raymond Aron, and Maurice Merleau-Ponty. In 1928, he submitted his thesis for the *Diplôme d'études supérieures* on "Mathématique et méthode chez Descartes des *Regulae* au *Discours*" ("Mathematics and Method in Descartes from the *Regulae* to the *Discourse*") and, the following year, he passed his *agrégation*, finishing third following Sartre's first and Beauvoir's second. His principal thesis for the *Doctorat ès Lettres*, completed in 1946, was a 600-page commentary on the *Genesis and Structure of Hegel's Phenomenology of Spirit* that remains perhaps the dominant Hegel interpretation in French philosophy. He received his *Doctorat ès Lettres* in 1947 following the submission of his *thèse complémentaire*, a French translation of Hegel's *Phenomenology of Spirit*, which had been published previously in two parts between 1939 and 1941. Hyppolite taught at various *lycées* from 1929 to 1945, including the prestigious Paris Lycées Louis-le-Grand (1939–41) and Henri-IV (where he taught the class *première supérieure* from 1941 to 1945) before becoming Professor of Philosophy at the University of Strasbourg in 1945. He taught at Strasbourg until 1949, when he was appointed to a Chair in History of Philosophy at the Sorbonne. In 1954, Hyppolite became Director of the École Normale Supérieure and served in that position until his election to the Collège de France in 1963, where he held the Chair in the History of Philosophical Thought until his death.

Along with Alexandre Kojève, Hyppolite stands at the center of the Hegel revival in France. Unlike Kojève, whose interpretation was directed toward showing how Hegel leads to Marx, Hyppolite's interpretation remains closer to Hegel's text, presenting it as Hegel's "voyage of discovery" from empirical consciousness to absolute knowledge. While their interpretive approaches differ, Kojève and Hyppolite both have exerted a profound influence on how Hegel was read in France: where Kojève taught the generations of the 1940s and 1950s how to read Hegel, Hyppolite did the same for the students of the 1960s and after. His influence on structuralist and poststructuralist thinkers is extensive: Michel Foucault, who replaced him at the Collège de France, credits

---

[24] See "Témoignage de Jean Hyppolite" in *Bulletin de l'Association des Amis d'Alain* no. 27 (December 1968): 57.

him in his inaugural address, while Gilles Deleuze's first book, *Empiricism and Subjectivity* (1953), was dedicated to him. At a memorial in his honor at the École Normale Supérieure on January 19, 1969, Foucault expressed the effect of Hyppolite as a teacher this way: "All the problems which are ours – we his former students or his students of today – all these problems are ones that he has established for us."[25]

Luce Irigaray (1930–) was born in Blaton, Belgium. She received her *licence* in philosophy from the University of Louvain in 1954 and, the following year, submitted her thesis "La Notion de pureté chez Paul Valéry, le mot pur, la pensée pure, la poésie pure" ("The Notion of Purity in Paul Valéry: Pure Word, Pure Thought, Pure Poetry") for a masters in philosophy also at the University of Louvain. From 1956 to 1959, she taught in Brussels. In 1960, Irigaray moved to Paris and studied at the University of Paris, where she completed her masters in psychology in 1961 and her *Diplôme* in psychopathology from the Institut de Psychologie de Paris in 1962. She returned to Belgium and worked for the Fondation Nationale de la Recherche Scientifique from 1962 to 1964 before returning to Paris as a research assistant at the Centre National de la Recherche Scientifique (CNRS). She has worked on psycholinguistics at the CNRS since 1964 and was appointed subsequently a Director of Research there in 1986. Irigaray completed a *Doctorat du troisème cycle* in linguistics at Nanterre in 1968, submitting her thesis *Approche psycholinguistique du langage des déments* (published in 1973 as *Le Langage des déments*) ("The Language of the Mad"). In 1974, she submitted *Speculum. La Fonction de la femme dans le discours philosophique* ("Speculum: The Function of Woman in Philosophical Discourse"; English translation: *Speculum of the Other Woman*) to her Director, François Châtelet, for her *Doctorat d'État* in philosophy at the University of Paris VIII-Vincennes, where she had been teaching in the Department of Psychoanalysis since 1970. Although Irigaray had participated in Jacques Lacan's psychoanalytic seminars in the 1960s and had trained as and become a psychoanalyst, the radical challenge to both Lacan and the psychoanalytic establishment posed by her argument in *Speculum* led shortly after its publication to her expulsion from Lacan's École Freudienne de Paris and her dismissal from her position at the

---

[25] Michel Foucault, "Jean Hyppolite. 1907–1968," in *Dits et écrits I* (Paris: Éditions Gallimard, 1994), p. 785.

University of Paris VIII-Vincennes.[26] She has taught at Erasmus University in Rotterdam in 1982, the University of Bologna in 1985, the École des Hautes Études en Sciences Sociales (1985–7), and the Collège Internationale de Philosophie (1988–92).

Since the appearance of the English translations of her two early works *Speculum* and *This Sex Which Is Not One* in 1985, Irigaray has been a leading voice of French feminist thought, along with Julia Kristeva and Hélène Cixous. Her early interests in arguing for sexual difference led to charges of "essentialism," and much of the early discussion of her work centered on either accusing or defending her of this charge. In 1982, she held the Jan Tinbergen Chair at Erasmus University in Rotterdam, and the lectures she delivered that spring on Plato, Aristotle, Descartes, Spinoza, Merleau-Ponty, and Levinas reflect the increasingly philosophical focus of her research, as evidenced in their subsequent publication as *An Ethics of Sexual Difference*. More recently, her writings reflect both her empirical research in linguistics, where questions of sexual difference are again explored, and her continued interest in politics, where she has influenced the feminist movements in France and Italy. In addition, several of her most recent writings reflect a religious turn characteristic of many French philosophers and theorists in the final years of the twentieth century.

Vladimir Jankélévitch (1903–85) was born in Bourges (Cher, Val de Loire) into a family of Russian origin. His father, a doctor, translated a number of works of German and Russian into French and was one of the first of Freud's French translators. He studied at the Lycée Montaigne, did his *khâgne* at the Lycée Louis-le-Grand, and attended the École Normale Supérieure from 1922 to 1925, where he submitted his thesis to Émile Bréhier for the *Diplôme d'études supérieures* in 1924 on

---

[26]   In addition to Irigaray's dismissal, 1974 marked the year the Vincennes Department of Psychoanalysis was renamed "Le Champ freudien," with Lacan as Director and Jacques-Alain Miller as President. These events led to concerns that the independence of the university was being threatened, concerns voiced in a public letter written by two prominent members of Vincennes's Department of Philosophy, Gilles Deleuze and Jean-François Lyotard, and published in December 1974 in *Les Temps modernes*. In their letter, they suggest that the Department of Psychoanalysis's actions, insofar as it is following the orders of someone not officially a member of the university faculty (Lacan), remind one "of a Stalinist operation" ("Sur le Département de psychanalyse de Vincennes," trans. Bill Readings in Jean-François Lyotard, *Political Writings* [Minneapolis: University of Minnesota Press, 1993], pp. 68–9).

"La Dialectique de Plotin" ("The Dialectic of Plotinus"). He passed his *agrégation* in 1926, finishing first, and received his *Doctorat ès Lettres* from the Sorbonne in 1933, submitting his principal thesis on "L'Odyssée de la conscience dans la dernière philosophie de Schelling" ("The Odyssey of Consciousness in Schelling's Late Philosophy," submitted in 1932) and a *thèse complémentaire* "Valeur et signification de la mauvaise conscience" ("Value and Significance of Bad Conscience"). From 1927 to 1932, Jankélévitch taught at the French Institute in Prague, taught briefly in 1933 at the *lycée* in Caen, and from 1933 to 1936 taught *khâgne* at the Lycée in Lyon. In 1936, he taught at the University of Toulouse and in 1937 was named Professor at the University of Lille. From 1940 to 1944, Jankélévitch was prohibited from teaching because of the anti-Semitic restrictions of the Vichy government, but following the war, he returned to teach at Lille from 1947 to 1951. In 1952, he assumed the Chair in Moral Philosophy at the Sorbonne, replacing René Le Senne, and he held this position until his retirement in 1978.

While largely unknown in the English-speaking world (only one of his philosophical texts have been translated into English), Jankélévitch has had a profound influence, as writer and teacher, on several generations of French philosophers. Influenced by Bergson and Kierkegaard, his 800-plus page *Traité des vertus* (1949; "Treatise on the Virtues") is one of the most important works of ethics and moral psychology to appear in France in the twentieth century. Similarly, his 1933 text on Bergson and his numerous writings on music (including texts on Debussy, Liszt, and Ravel) have been widely read. But it is his ethical writings and his reflections on moral psychology, the Holocaust, and other events of the twentieth century that have had the greatest impact on French philosophy, and it would not be overstating the case to say that with Emmanuel Levinas, he stands as something of a moral icon among the French philosophical world. That said, it is important to note that for most of his 26 years as a Sorbonne professor, Jankélévitch occupied the only chair in moral philosophy, and interest in his classes was affected during these years both by the general drift away from philosophy toward the human sciences and a tension within Sorbonne philosophy between the fields perceived to be "rigorous" and "hard philosophy" (epistemology and philosophy of the natural sciences, associated with Georges Canguilhem, whose tenure at the Sorbonne overlaps that of Jankélévitch from 1955 to 1971) and those fields thought of as "soft" or passé (most notably, ethics). Among the writers on whom his influence can be most directly seen are Louis Althusser, whose thesis he co-directed with Jean Hyppolite, Sarah Kofman, Michèle Le Doeuff, Catherine Clément, and Elisabeth de Fontenay. Only one of Jankélévitch's important ethical works has appeared in English translation: *Forgiveness*, trans. Andrew Kelley (Chicago: University of Chicago Press, 2005 [*Le Pardon*. Paris: Aubier-Montaigne, 1967]). In addition, two of his texts on music have also been translated into English: *Ravel* (1956; *Ravel*, trans. Margaret Crosland [Westport, CN: Greenwood Press, 1959]) and *La Musique et l'ineffable* (1961; *Music and the Ineffable*, trans. Carolyn Abbate [Princeton, NJ: Princeton University Press, 2003]).

Pierre Klossowski (1905–2001) was born in Paris into an artistic family of Polish origin: his father was a painter and art historian, his mother a painter and student of Pierre Bonnard, and his younger brother was the important painter Balthus (Balthasar Klossowski, 1908–2001). From 1914 to 1923, his family lived in Switzerland, Germany, and Italy. In 1923, after returning to Paris, he was introduced by the German poet Rainer Maria Rilke (with whom his mother was lover) to André Gide, for whom he worked as a private secretary while pursuing his studies at the Lycée Janson-de-Sailly and École Pratique des Hautes Études. In the 1930s, Klossowski was associated with the Surrealists; he was also friends with Georges Bataille, Roger Caillois, and André Masson, and was an active participant in the *Collège de Sociologie*. With Bataille's encouragement, he joined the anti-fascist group "Contre-Attaque" and he also worked with Bataille in the creation in 1935 of the journal *Acéphale* and its associated Nietzschean secret society. In 1939, Klossowski began a period of religious investigations that included a stay with the Benedictines in Hautecombe and entering the Dominican noviciate in Lesse. He continued his study of theology in Saint-Maximin, then in Lyon, then at the seminary at Fourvière. Klossowski returned to Paris in 1943, and participated in the meetings of the group "Dieu vivant" ("Alive God") with, among others, Maurice de Gandillac and Jacques Lacan.

Klossowski began his activities as a translator in 1928 with a translation of Hölderlin's *Poèmes de la folie*. In addition to a wide range of literary translations from German and Latin, including works by Kafka, Hamann, Tertullien, and Virgil's *Aenied*, Klossowski was also responsible for several significant philosophical translations into French, including his friend Walter Benjamin's essay "The Work of Art in the Age of Mechanical Reproduction" (1936), Nietzsche's *The Gay Science* (1954) and associated unpublished notes, Wittgenstein's *Tractatus*

(1961), and Heidegger's two-volume *Nietzsche* (1971). Klossowski authored a number of fictional works as well as several important theoretical works, including *Sade, mon prochain* (1947; English translation: *Sade My Neighbor*, trans. Alphonso Lingis [Evanston, IL: Northwestern University Press, 1991]); *Le Bain de Diane* (1956; English translation: *Diana at Her Bath: The Women of Rome*, trans. Stephen Sartarelli and Sophie Hawkes [New York: Marsilio Publishers, 1990]), *Un si funeste désir* (1963; English translation: *Such a Deathly Desire*, trans. Russell Ford [Albany: State University of New York Press, 2006]); and *Nietzsche et le cercle vicieux* (1969; English translation: *Nietzsche and the Vicious Circle*, trans. Daniel W. Smith [Chicago: University of Chicago Press, 1998]). After 1970, Klossowski stopped most of his writing activities and devoted himself entirely to drawing, for which he attracted increasing attention in his final years. Among those on whose work Klossowski's influence can be seen are Michel Foucault, Gilles Deleuze, and Maurice Blanchot.

Sarah Kofman (1934–94) was born in Paris, her family having emigrated from Poland in 1929. In 1942, her father, a rabbi, was arrested and deported to Auschwitz, where he died. No longer safe in Paris, Kofman's mother dispatched her children to various locations throughout France, where they spent the rest of the war in hiding. After the war but still separated from her mother, Kofman lived in different institutions for children. She eventually returned to Paris and was rejoined with her mother. Kofman attended the Lycée Jules-Ferry, did her *hypokhâgne* and *khâgne* at the Lycée Fénelon, then enrolled at the Sorbonne, where she obtained a *Diplôme d'études supérieures* for a thesis on Plato and language. Kofman passed her *agrégation* in 1959, and taught in Toulouse at the Lycée Saint-Sernin (1960–3) and in Paris at the Lycée Claude Monet (1963–70). She began her doctoral dissertation in 1966, "The Concept of Culture in Nietzsche and Freud," working with Jean Hyppolite, and continued under Gilles Deleuze, who took over for Hyppolite after his death in 1968. Kofman eventually abandoned her original dissertation project, and submitted *L'Enfance de l'art: Une interpretation de l'esthétique Freudienne*, directed by Mikel Dufrenne, in 1970 (English translation: *The Childhood of Art: An Interpretation of Freud's Aesthetics*, trans. Winifred Woodhull [New York: Columbia University Press, 1988]) for a *Doctorat du troisième cycle* at the University of Paris X-Nanterre. In 1976, she was awarded a *Doctorat d'État* from the University of Paris VIII-Vincennes, directed by Gilles Deleuze, on the basis of six already published works on Nietzsche and Freud.[27] In 1970, Kofman began as a *Maître-assistante* at the University of Paris I-Sorbonne. Soon thereafter, she was promoted to *Maître de conférences* and remained in that position until being appointed to a Professor's chair in 1991.

Sarah Kofman met Jacques Derrida in 1969 and was closely associated with him for many years. She frequently attended his seminars at the École Normale Supérieure, and several of her texts were presented originally as papers at Derrida's seminar. Along with Derrida, Jean-Luc Nancy, and Philippe Lacoue-Labarthe, Kofman was a member of GREPH (*Groupe de Recherches sur l'Enseignement Philosophique*) in the mid-1970s and published essays in several collected texts with this group. Kofman authored over twenty books on philosophy, psychoanalysis, literature, and art. In almost all of them, Nietzsche and Freud figure as major references, and they figure as the central foci of ten of them – five each on Freud and Nietzsche. Derrida would write, in a memorial essay, that she knew "both Nietzsche and Freud . . . whose bodies of work she had read inside and out. Like no one else in this century, I dare say. She loved them pitilessly, and was implacable towards them . . . at the very moment when, giving them without mercy all that she could, and all that she had, she was inheriting from them and was keeping watch over what they had – what they still have – to tell us."[28] Kofman incarnated a Freudo-Nietzscheanism, reading Freud as a Nietzschean and Nietzsche as a Freudian, while at the same time showing the influence of years associating with Derrida. Unlike most other members of the GREPH group, Heidegger was an insignificant figure in Kofman's thinking,[29] which might explain in part

---

[27] Titled *Travaux sur Nietzsche et sur Freud*, Kofman presented for her *Doctorat: Vatour Rouge* (Paris: Aubier-Flammarion, 1975), *Nietzsche and Metaphor, Freud and Fiction, The Childhood of Art, Camera Obscura*, and her presentation at the 1972 Cerisy Colloquium on Nietzsche, "Le/Les 'Concepts' de culture dans les *Intempestives* ou la double dissimulation" (published in *Nietzsche aujourd'hui* [Paris: Union générale d'Éditions, 1973]).

[28] Jacques Derrida, ". . . . ." in *The Work of Mourning*, ed. and trans. Pascale-Anne Brault and Michael Naas (Chicago: University of Chicago Press, 2001), p. 173.

[29] At a conference on her work that was planned for the University of Warwick and that, following her death, became a memorial conference, Kofman's good friend Jean-Luc Nancy told the story that he had accepted Kofman's invitation to speak at the conference under one condition: that he would use the occasion to speak on Heidegger and that she would promise to offer her own thoughts on Heidegger, something he said she had steadfastly refused to do for over two decades.

why she often seemed an outsider within this group. Suffering from ill-health, Kofman took her own life on October 15, 1994, the 150th anniversary of Nietzsche's birth.

Alexandre Kojève (1902–68) was born Aleksandr Vladimirovich Kozhevnikov in Moscow. Kojève's family was wealthy and prominent; the painter Wassily Kandinsky was his uncle. He was arrested after the Russian Revolution and, although he eventually became a committed communist, he left Russia with his family in 1920 for Germany. He studied at the University of Heidelberg (1920–2, 1924–6) and Berlin (1922–4), and completed a dissertation under Karl Jaspers at the University of Heidelberg in 1926 on the Russian religious philosopher Vladimir Sergeevich Soloviev (1853–1900). In 1927, Kojève moved to Paris to continue his studies at the Sorbonne. While studying at the Sorbonne, he was invited by fellow Russian émigré Alexandre Koyré (1882–1964) to take over his course on Hegel's religious philosophy at the École Pratique des Hautes Études while Koyré took a leave to teach at the University of Cairo. Kojève lectured on Hegel from 1933 to 1939 to a seminar audience that included several individuals who would be among those who dominated the French intellectual scene for the remainder of the century. One of Kojève's seminar students, Robert Marjolin, went on to become the Minister of Foreign Economic Affairs under Charles de Gaulle and Kojève was invited by Marjolin after the war to join the finance ministry, where he continued as an advisor to some of France's most important financial ministers until his death.

Along with Jean Hyppolite, the French translator of Hegel's *Phenomenology of Spirit*, and, to a lesser extent, Jean Wahl, the author of the first important twentieth-century French study of Hegel (*Le Malheur de la conscience dans la philosophie de Hegel* [1929: "The Unhappiness of Consciousness in the Philosophy of Hegel"]), Kojève stands at the center of the revival of interest in France in Hegel's thought. Although he did not publish much, his lectures on Hegel, edited and published in 1947 with his approval by one of his seminar participants, the surrealist poet and writer Raymond Queneau, proved to be one of the most significant events in twentieth-century French thought. This was in part due to the participants in Kojève's seminar, which included, in addition to Queneau, Raymond Aron, Georges Bataille, André Breton, Jean-Toussaint Desanti, Aron Gurwitsch, Jacques Lacan, Maurice

Merleau-Ponty, and Eric Weil.[30] But it was also due to the power of Kojève's reading which, focused on the *Phenomenology*, drew out the Marxist implications of Hegel's account of the dialectic of master and slave as a dialectic of human history and the existential implications of the struggle for recognition as the fundamental dynamic of the relation between self and other. It would not be overstating the facts to say that Kojève taught the French how to read Hegel and his influence on French philosophy between 1940 and 1960 is unsurpassed.

Alexandre Koyré (1892–1964) was born in Taganrog, Russia, and attended *lycée* in Rostov-on-the-Don. Between 1908 and 1911, he studied in Göttingen with Edmund Husserl and mathematician David Hilbert (1862–1943). He then moved to Paris and from 1911 to 1914 studied with Léon Brunschvicg at the Sorbonne, to whom he submitted in 1913 his thesis for the *Diplôme d'études supérieures*, "Étude sur l'argument ontologique de saint Anselme" ("Study of St. Anselm's Ontological Argument"). During these years, he also followed closely Henri Bergson's lectures at the Collège de France. Koyré's interest in phenomenology also led him to study scholastic theology with Étienne Gilson and François Picavet (1851–1921). During World War I, he served at the Russian front as an officer in the Foreign Legion. Koyré emigrated to Paris in 1919 and taught philosophy in Montpellier. He resumed his studies at the École Pratique des Hautes Études and received from the Sorbonne his *Doctorat d'Université* for a thesis, submitted to François Picavet, on *L'Idée de Dieu dans la philosophie de saint Anselme* ("The Idea of God in Saint Anselm's Philosophy"). In 1929, Koyré submitted his thesis for the *Doctorat ès Lettres*, dedicated to Léon Brunschvicg and Étienne Gilson, on *La Philosophie de Jacob Boehme* ("The Philosophy of Jacob Boehme") along with a *thèse complémentaire* on *La Philosophie et le problème national en Russie au début du XIXe siècle* ("Philosophy and the National Problem in Russia at the Beginning of the Nineteenth Century"). In addition to teaching for several years at the University of Cairo, from 1931 to the 1950s Koyré was *Directeur d'études* of "History of Religious Ideas in Modern Europe" at the Fifth Section of the École Pratique des Hautes Études, a

---

30   Sartre, who was clearly influenced by Kojève's reading of Hegel, appears not to have actually attended the seminars, according to the fairly detailed records of registered students kept by the École Pratique des Haute Études.

position he held concurrently with a Chair at the Princeton Institute for Advanced Study.

Koyré played major roles in several developments in philosophy in both France and Germany. He was the person who first introduced Bergson's work in Germany in 1911 at the Göttingen Circle and was the first to bring Husserl's phenomenology to France. His emphasis on the role of phenomenology in the interpretation of Hegel was influential for the Hegelianism of Alexandre Kojève and Jean-Paul Sartre, and it was he who invited his fellow Russian émigré Kojève to take over his Hegel lectures at the École Pratique des Hautes Études. From 1931 to 1937, he served as one of the editors of the journal *Recherches philosophiques*, which played an important role in the introduction of phenomenology and existentialism in France between the wars. Along with Jacques Maritain, Koyré founded the École Libre des Hautes Études in New York, and he facilitated the meeting between Roman Jakobson and Claude Lévi-Strauss in New York that many regard as the inaugural moment in the evolution of French structuralism. After World War II, he assumed in 1948 a second position at the École Pratique des Hautes Études in the Sixth Section as *Directeur d'études* in the "History of Scientific Thought." Soon thereafter, he was considered for a chair at the Collège de France in the "History of Scientific Thought" and, when he failed to get this position, he returned in 1955 to the United States and the Princeton Institute for Advanced Study. While best known for his work on Descartes and Hegel, Koyré also made important contributions to the history of science insofar as he argued that historical analysis was in fact an important factor in the understanding of science. This idea would influence both Thomas Kuhn and Michel Foucault. His most important text, *Études galiléennes*, was published in three volumes in 1939 (*1. A l'aube de la science classique. 2. La Loi de la chute des corps. Descartes et Galilée. 3. Galilée et la loi d'inertie*) ("1. The Dawn of Classical Science. 2. The Law of Falling Bodies: Descartes and Galileo. 3. Galileo and the Law of Inertia") and dedicated to Émile Meyerson (1859–1933), whose own work on epistemology played a significant role in Koyré's thinking.

Julia Kristeva (1941–) was born in Sliven, Bulgaria. She studied at the University of Sophia before emigrating to Paris in 1965, where she began studying at the École Pratique des Hautes Études, first with Lucien Goldmann, then Roland Barthes, and finally Claude Lévi-Strauss. That same year, she joined the *Tel Quel* group, headed by novelist and theorist Philippe Sollers, who she married in 1967, and she became part of the editorial board of *Tel Quel* in 1970. Kristeva completed a *Doctorat du troisième cycle* at Nanterre in 1968, submitting her thesis *Le Texte du roman: Approche sémiologique d'une structure discursive transformelle* (published in 1970). At the suggestion of Sollers and her friend and fellow linguist Émile Benveniste, she began studying Freud; like most of the *Tel Quel* group, she attended Lacan's seminars, and in 1979 became a practicing psychoanalyst. In 1973, she received her *Doctorat ès Lettres*, having submitted as her thesis *La Révolution du langage poétique: L'Avant-garde à la fin du XIXe siècle, Lautréamont et Mallarmé* (English translation: *Revolution in Poetic Language*). The following year, she took up a chair in linguistics at the University of Paris VII-Denis Diderot, and she is currently Director of the doctoral program in Langue, Littérature, Civilisation. Kristeva has worked at the Centre National de la Recherche Scientifique (CNRS) and, since 1997, has been a member of the CNRS's *Conseil Scientifique*. In 2000, she co-founded the Institut Roland Barthes.

Kristeva emerged as one of the leading feminist theorists in France in the last decades of the twentieth century. Her early work, informed by Barthes's structuralism and semiology, was an important influence on literary studies, as was the attention she drew to the work of Russian literary theorist Mikhail Bakhtin. In these early works, most notably *Revolution in Poetic Language*, she introduced the distinction between the "semiotic" and the "symbolic" as a way to bring the body (and in particular, the maternal body) to the heart of the processes of signification. Kristeva's other major contribution to recent philosophical and critical theory has been her work on abjection, which she describes as a psychic process in which the subject's identity is first constituted and later preserved by means of excising those characteristics, attachments, individuals, etc., that come to be seen as a threat to one's psychic integrity but to which one nevertheless remains in some sense attracted and attached. In Kristeva's later work, which has become increasingly political, she has expanded her earlier analyses of abjection to offer a psychoanalytic account of oppression, and in particular, patriarchal oppression insofar as the maternal body has emerged for her as the paradigm of the abject.

Jacques Lacan (1901–81) was born in Paris. He attended the Jesuit Collège Stanislaus and began his clinical training in 1927 at the Hôpital Sainte-Anne, central Paris's major psychiatric hospital. He submitted his thesis, "On Paranoid Psychosis and its Relation to Personality," and was awarded his *Doctorat en Médecine* in psychiatry in 1932. In 1934, he joined the Société psychanalytique de Paris ("Psychoanalytic Society of Paris," founded in 1925) and, in 1952, he resigned from the Society over its position that only medical doctors should be allowed to become psychoanalysts. With his friend Daniel Lagache (1903–72; later holder of the Chair in Psychopathology at the Sorbonne) and Françoise (Marette) Dolto (1908–88; a specialist in the psychoanalysis of childhood and a leading figure in the French psychoanalytic establishment), Lacan founded the Société française de psychanalyse ("French Psychoanalytic Society") in 1953. Later that year, Lacan became an internationally known and controversial figure following his delivery of the new Society's report to the Congrès des psychanalystes de langue française at the Psychological Institute of the University of Rome. This report, the so-called "Rome Discourse," is for all practical purposes the manifesto of the structuralist reinterpretation of Freud. Here Lacan draws upon his various philosophical influences (Heidegger, Hegel [through Koyré and Kojève, whose lectures at the École Pratique des Hautes Etudes he attended]) as well as Saussurean linguistics to explore the function of language in psychoanalysis.

In 1953, Lacan began his public seminars, which he would continue for 26 years. These seminars grew to be immensely popular and influential and, over the years, many of France's leading writers and intellectuals attended, including Roland Barthes, Julia Kristeva, Michel Leiris, Claude Lévi-Strauss, and Philippe Sollers. Among the philosophers who attended at various times were Louis Althusser, Alain Badiou, Jacques Derrida, Michel Foucault, Jean Hyppolite, Maurice Merleau-Ponty, and Paul Ricoeur. In 1963, Lacan was expelled from the International Psychoanalytic Association and the following year, he began his own school, L'École Freudienne de Paris, which he led until he disbanded the school in 1980. With the support of Lévi-Strauss and Althusser, Lacan was given a lecturer's position at the École Pratique des Hautes Études in 1964, where he lectured to increasingly large audiences at one of the prestigious seminar rooms at the École Normale Supérieure, a possibility facilitated by Althusser in his position as *Secrétaire de l'École littéraire*. The publication of *Écrits* in 1966 brought Lacan to the attention of a much wider audience. In 1974, he was named the Scientific Director of the Department of Psychoanalysis at the University of Paris VIII-Vincennes, which was renamed Le Champ freudien. His already controversial practices became even more controversial at Vincennes, as his emphasis on mathesis and the matheme became an orthodoxy for all who wished to work with him.

As one of the figures most closely associated with the rise of structuralism, Lacan's influence on French literary and philosophical culture has been extensive. His introduction of the "mirror stage" (first presented in 1936 to the Fourteenth Congress of the International Psychoanalytic Association in Marienbad), use of Saussurean linguistics to argue that the unconscious is structured like a language, and introduction of the thematics of the Symbolic, the Imaginary, and the Real in his reinterpretation of Freudian theory, have informed much that has gone on in French theory in the last four decades of the twentieth century. In fact, it would not be overstating his impact to say that the force of his writings and the influence of his teachings in his seminars bear primary responsibility for the omnipresence of Freud in contemporary French theory, placing Lacan among the most dominant figures in French intellectual culture.

André Lalande (1867–1963) was born in Dijon. He studied at *lycées* in Reims, Digne, Montpellier, and Toulouse before beginning his philosophical studies with Émile Durkheim at the *lycée* in Sens in 1882–4. After completing his *baccalauréat* in Sens, Lalande attended *khâgne* at the Lycée Henri-IV in Paris before entering the École Normale Supérieure, where he studied from 1885 to 1888. At the École Normale, he worked with Victor Brochard (1848–1907) and Léon Ollé-Laprune (1839–98), and received his *licence ès lettres* in 1886, and, as was customary, in his third year took courses at the Sorbonne, where he worked with Émile Boutroux and Théodule Ribot (1839–1916). He passed the *agrégation* in 1888, finishing first. Lalande taught at the École Monge (renamed the Lycée Carnot in 1895) from 1888 to 1895, the Lycée Michelet (1895–6), and the Lycées Louis-le-Grand, Henri-IV, and Condorcet (1896–7) before returning to the Lycée Michelet, where he taught as Professor of Philosophy from 1897 to 1904. Lalande received his *Doctorat ès Lettres* in 1899 for a thesis *L'Idée de dissolution opposée à celle d'évolution* ("The Idea of Dissolution opposed to that of Evolution"), in which he engaged, and at times challenged, the evolutionary philosophy of Herbert Spencer, along with a *thèse complémentaire Quid de mathematica senserit Baconus Verulamius* ("What Bacon, Baron Verulam, Thought about Mathematics"). His university career began in 1904 as *chargé de conférences* at the Sorbonne; from 1906 to 1909, he served as *Maître de conférences de logique et méthodologies des sciences*. In 1909, Lalande became Adjunct Professor at the Sorbonne; in 1915, he was named *Directeur des études* for the Philosophy section, and he was elected to a chair as Professor of Philosophy in 1918, a position he held until his retirement in 1937. Lalande also taught at the University of Cairo in 1926–8, 1929–30, and following his retirement from the Sorbonne, from 1937 to 1940, and he gave weekly lectures at the École Normale Supérieure de Sèvres from 1901 to 1934 (except those years he was in Egypt).

Throughout his career, Lalande played an important role in a number of philosophical events. He was a co-founder, along with Léon Brunschvicg and Xavier Léon, in 1901 of the Société Française de Philosophie, and served as it General Secretary from 1901 to 1937. He served as well as President of the *jury d'agrégation de philosophie* from 1920 to 1927, 1929, and from 1931 to 1934. Lalande wrote a number of works on epistemology in which he defended the universality of reason, but he is best known as the author of the leading dictionary of philosophy in the French language, *Vocabulaire technique et critique de la philosophie*. From 1902 to 1923, Lalande organized regular sessions of the Société Française de Philosophie during which the members of the Société met to discuss the meanings of key philosophical terminology. The proceedings of these meetings were published in two issues each year of the *Bulletin de la Société Française de Philosophie* and collected together and annotated by Lalande for their first complete publication by Félix Alcan in 1925–6. Lalande continued to oversee the subsequent editions of the dictionary until the ninth edition, published in 1962; the latest edition, the eighteenth, was published by Presses universitaires de France in 1996.

Louis Lavelle (1883–1951) was born in Saint-Martin-de-Villeréal (Lot-et-Garonne, Aquitaine). He studied at *lycées* in Saint-Étienne and Lyon. Unable to enter the École Normale Supérieure, Lavelle studied at the University of Lyon. He passed the *agrégation* in 1909 and was named to the Lycée de Vendôme and later, in 1911, to the Lycée de Limoges. His teaching was interrupted during the war, but was resumed in 1919 at the Lycée Fustel-de-Coulanges in Strasbourg, where he taught until 1925. Lavelle was awarded his doctorate in 1921 by the Sorbonne for the thesis *La Dialectique du monde sensible* ("The Dialectic of the Sensible World"). He left Strasbourg for Paris in 1925, and taught at the leading Paris *lycées* (Saint-Louis, Condorcet, Louis-le-Grand, Henri-IV) until 1940. During these years, Lavelle also held many important administrative positions, including *chargé d'enseignement* at the Sorbonne from 1934 to 1936 and *Inspecteur Générale* in 1940. He was named to the Chair in Modern Philosophy at the Collège de France in 1941 and taught there until his death. Elected to the *Académie de Sciences morales et politiques* in 1947, Lavelle authored over twenty-five books, the most important of which is the four-volume *La Dialectique de l'éternal présent: De l'être* (1928), *De l'acte* (1937), *Du temps et de l'éternité* (1945), and *De l'âme humaine* (1951) ("The Dialectic of the Eternal Present: On Being, On the Act, On Time and Eternity, On the Human Soul"). Several of his works have appeared in English translation, including *Evil and Suffering*, trans Bernard Murchland (New York: Macmillan, 1963), *Four Saints*, trans. Dorothea O'Sullivan (Notre Dame, IN: University of Notre Dame Press, 1963), and *The Dilemma of Narcissus*, trans William Gairdner (New York: Humanities Press, 1973).

Michèle Le Doeuff (1948–) was born in Motreff (Brittany). She attended *lycée* in Quimper, did her *khâgne* at the *lycée* in Brest, and entered the École Normale Supérieure-Fontenay in 1966. She later attended the Sorbonne, submitting to Hélène Védrine her thesis *Recherches sur L'Imaginaire philosophique* for the *Doctorat du troisième cycle* in 1980, and completed her *Habilitation à diriger des recherches* in 1993. Le Doeuff passed her *agrégation* in 1971 and began teaching as an *Assistante*, then *Maître de conférences*, at the ENS-Fontenay in 1973. She has also been *Directrice de recherche* at the Centre National de la Recherche Scientifique in Paris and taught for several years, beginning in 1995, as Professor of Women's Studies at the University of Geneva. In addition to her doctoral thesis, translated into English as *The Philosophical Imaginary*, trans. Colin Gordon (Stanford, CA: Stanford University Press, 1989), Le Doeuff has published two other important works, both of which have appeared in English translation: *Des femmes, de la philosophie, etc.* (1989; *Hipparchia's Choice: An Essay Concerning Women, Philosophy, etc.*, trans. Trista Selous [Oxford: Blackwell, 1991]), and *Le Sexe du savoir* (1998; *The Sex of Knowing*, trans. Kathryn Hamer and Lorraine Code [New York: Routledge, 2003]).

Henri Lefebvre (1901–91) was born in Hagetmau (Landes, Aquitaine). He studied at the Lycée Louis-le-Grand in Paris, completed his *licence* in philosophy in 1918, working with Maurice Blondel, at the University of Aix-en-Provence. In 1920, he submitted his thesis for the *Diplôme d'études supérieures* from the Sorbonne on "Pascal et Jansénius" to Léon Brunschvicg. Lefebvre's interests soon turned from philosophy to more social and political issues, and he eventually completed his *Doctorat d'État* at the Sorbonne in 1954, submitting a historical sociological thesis on rural communities in the Pyrenees. He taught and worked in broadcasting in Toulouse from 1930 to 1949, was a *Maître de recherches* at the CNRS from 1949 to 1961, Professor of Sociology at the University of Strasbourg from 1961 to 1965 (where he established the first Institute of Sociology), and Professor of Sociology at the University of Paris X-Nanterre from 1965 to 1973.

In the 1920s, Lefebvre was associated with the Surrealist movement in Paris. He was one of the founders, in 1924, along with Paul Nizan, Georges Politzer, Pierre Morhange, Georges Friedmann, and Norbert Guterman, of the "Philosophies" group, a collection of leftist intellectuals who, responding to World War I and influenced by Pascal, Spinoza, and Nietzsche as well as Schelling and Hegel, were the first group of innovative Marxist theorists in France. Lefebvre's writings from this period show signs of the existentialist ideas that would come into prominence a decade later. He joined the Parti Communiste Français (PCF) in 1929 and was the party's leading intellectual voice in the 1940s. Lefebvre was, with Norbert Guterman, the first to translate the works of the young Karl Marx into French (1933), and his *Le Matérialisme dialectique* (1939; *Dialectical Materialism*, trans. John Sturrock [London: Cape, 1968]) was one of the first works to introduce Marxist dialectics into France. He was also one of the first writers in France before World War II to publicly criticize nationalism and National Socialism and one of the first to question the fascist reading of Nietzsche that was being promulgated in Germany.

Over the years, Lefebvre's position within Marxist circles changed radically. In the 1940s, he was a prominent critic of Sartrean existentialism. In the 1950s, his humanistic approach and criticism of Stalinism led to his exclusion in 1957 from the PCF and his reconciliation with Sartre. In the 1960s, he was influential on several avant-garde movements, including Guy Debord and the Situationniste Internationale, and Daniel Cohn-Bendit and the student revolutionaries of 1968. Lefebvre's influence can also be seen on Jean Baudrillard, who served as his assistant at Nanterre during these years. In the 1970s, he was a vocal critic of structuralism and his humanist Marxism was one of the positions directly challenged by Althusser's scientific approach to Marxism. The author of over forty books, including several on philosophers and philosophical topics, Lefebvre is best known as one of the founders of rural sociology and applied sociology in France. His best-known works include *Logique Formelle, Logique Dialectique* (1947; "Formal Logical, Dialectical

Logic"), *Critique de la vie quotidienne* (1947; *Critique of Everyday Life*, trans. John Moore [London: Verso, 1991]), *Critique de la vie quotidienne. 2. Fondements d'une sociologie de la quotidienneté* (1962; *Critique of Everyday Life. Volume 2: Foundations for a Sociology of the Everyday*, trans. John Moore [London: Verso, 2002]), and *La Production de l'espace* (1974; *The Production of Space*, trans. Donald Nicholson-Smith [Oxford: Blackwell, 1991]).

Claude Lefort (1924–) was born in Paris. He studied at the Lycée Carnot during the Occupation, where he first became a student of Maurice Merleau-Ponty, an encounter that would inform the rest of his career, and at the Lycée Henri-IV, before entering the Sorbonne. Lefort passed his *agrégation* in 1949, and taught at *lycées* in Nîmes (1949) and Reims (1950). From 1951 to 1989, his career alternated between research at the CNRS (1951–3, 1956–65, and 1971–6) and university appointments at São Paulo (1953–4), the Sorbonne (1954–6), and Caen (1966–71). In 1973, he received his *Doctorat d'État* for his thesis "La Travail de l'oeuvre, Machiavel," and from 1976 to 1989, he served as *Directeur d'études* in "The Problems of Politics" at the École des Hautes Études en Sciences Sociales. An active Trotskyite since 1943, Lefort was the co-founder, with Cornelius Castoriadis, of the militant group *Socialisme ou barbarie* in 1948. He worked for several years as part of the editorial group at *Les Temps modernes*, during which time he engaged in several significant polemics. Two of the most important were a critique of Claude Lévi-Strauss's structuralist introduction to the edition of Marcel Mauss's work in *Sociologie et anthropologie* (1952) for reducing the individual to little more than an effect of social structures and, from an opposite direction, a very visible dispute with what he regarded as Jean-Paul Sartre's overly subjectivist position in the essay "The Communists and Peace" (1952), which he felt gave individuals too much power to impose their own meanings on events. This latter debate led to Lefort's breaking with *Les Temps modernes* in 1953, though he continued collaborating with several other journals (*Arguments*, *Textures*, *Libre*, *Passé présent*) throughout the following four decades. Through his sustained critique of totalitarianism and bureaucratic rationality, Lefort was one of the most widely read French political philosophers of the second half of the twentieth century. In addition to his important works in political philosophy, Lefort is best known for editing the notes and drafts of Merleau-Ponty's last, posthumously published text *The Visible and the Invisible* (1964).

Édouard Le Roy (1870–1954) was born in Paris. He was educated at the École Normale Supérieure, science section, from 1892 to 1895, where he concentrated in mathematics, passed the *agrégation* in mathematics in 1895, and received his doctorate in science in 1898. He taught mathematics at the Lycée de Versailles and the Lycée Saint-Louis before substituting for his friend Henri Bergson at the Collège de France from 1914 to 1921, at which time he was formally elected to replace Bergson at the Collège as possessor of the Chair in Modern Philosophy, a position he held until 1940. In 1919, he was elected to the *Académie des Sciences morales et politiques* and in 1941 to the *Académie Française* (again replacing Bergson). Le Roy is associated with the Bergsonian critique of science, and he followed Bergson as well in seeing that there could be no ultimate rational understanding of the relations between philosophical reason and faith. His interests in and sympathy for "creative evolution" also led to a long friendship with Pierre Teilhard de Chardin, while his radical version of scientific conventionalism produced an extended critical response from Henri Poincaré (1854–1912) and a sympathetic rejoinder from Pierre Duhem (1861–1916). Among his best-known works are "Science et philosophie" (1899–1900), *Dogme et critique* (1906; "Dogma and Criticism," condemned by Pope Pius X), *L'Exigence idéaliste et la fait de l'évolution* (1927; "The Exigency of Idealism and the Fact of Evolution"), *Les Origines humaines et l'évolution de l'intelligence* (1928; "Human Origins and the Evolution of Intelligence"), and *La Pensée intuitive* (1929–30; "Intuitive Thought," 2 vols.).

René Le Senne (1882–1955) was born in Elbeuf-sur-Seine (Seine-Maritime, Normandy). He studied at the Collège Sainte-Croix de Neuilly from 1892 to 1896, then the Lycée Condorcet from 1896 to 1899, completing his *baccalauréat* in rhetoric in 1898, in philosophy in 1899, and in science, also in 1899. From 1899 to 1903, he did his *hypokhâgne* and *khâgne* at the Lycée Henri-IV, studying philosophy with Victor Delbos and Léon Brunschvicg, and completing his *licence* in philosophy in 1902. From 1903 to 1906, Le Senne studied at the École Normale Supérieure, completing a *licence* in science in 1905. He passed the *agrégation* in 1906 and worked from 1907 to 1910 with the support of a fellowship from the Fondation Thiers. He taught from 1910 to 1914 at the Lycée de Chambéry, and from 1914 to 1923 at the Lycée Thiers in Marseille, with an interruption from 1914 to 1917 during which he served in the infantry and later the postal service.

From 1923 to 1925, he taught in Paris at the Lycées Condorcet and Victor-Duruy, where he had as a student Simone Weil. From 1925 to 1941, Le Senne taught at the Lycée Louis-le-Grand, beginning with the *classe de philosophie* (1925–9), then *hypokhâgne* (1929–30), and *khâgne* (1930–41), and also taught occasionally during this period at the Lycée Condorcet and the Sorbonne. Le Senne was awarded his doctorate in 1931 following the submission of his thesis *Le Devoir* ("Duty"), with a *thèse complémentaire Le Mensonge et le Caractère* ("Falsehood and Character"). From 1931 to 1946, Le Senne taught at the École Normale Supérieure at Sèvres, and began teaching at the Sorbonne in 1942 as *Maître de conférences* in Pedagogical Psychology, then Professor of Pedagogical Psychology before being named Professor of Ethics in 1949. He retired from the Sorbonne in 1952. Elected to the *Académie des Sciences morales et politiques* in 1948, Le Senne is the founder of French characterology (a pyschological theory that divides people into types based on certain character triats), and author of several works in ethics, the history of philosophy, and spiritualism, one of which has appeared in English translation: *Obstacle and Value*, trans. Bernard P. Dauenhauer (Evanston, IL: Northwestern University Press, 1972).

Claude Lévi-Strauss (1908–) was born in Brussels. In 1914, his family moved to Versailles. When his family moved to Paris, he completed his *baccalauréat* at the Lycée Janson-de-Sailly and attended *hypokhâgne* at the Lycée Condorcet in 1926, where he studied with André Cresson (1869–1950). After deciding not to continue to prepare for the entrance exam to the École Normale Supérieure, Lévi-Strauss enrolled in the University of Paris as a law student. While at the University of Paris from 1927 to 1932, Lévi-Strauss completed a *licence* in philosophy, taking classes from the neo-Kantian Léon Brunschvicg and completing his thesis for the *Diplôme d'études supérieures* under sociologist Célestin Bouglé on "The Philosophical Postulates of Historical Materialism." He also completed a second *licence* in law in 1927. Lévi-Strauss began student teaching at the Lycée Janson-de-Sailly in the spring of 1929, along with Simone de Beauvoir and Maurice Merleau-Ponty.

Although he passed his *agrégation* in philosophy in 1931 and taught for a year at the Lycée Mont-de-Marsan in 1932 and for two more years in Laon (1933–5), Lévi-Strauss had little enthusiasm for philosophy. At the suggestion of Célestin Bouglé, then Director of the École Normale Supérieure, he traveled to Brazil and served from 1935 to 1939 as Professor of Sociology at the University of São Paulo, a position that afforded him the opportunity to do field work on the Indians of the Brazilian interior. He returned to France in 1939 but fled the German occupation for New York, where from 1942 to 1945 he was a visiting professor at the École Libre des Hautes Études, the French university-in-exile associated with the New School for Social Research. During this time, he met another exile, linguist Roman Jakobson, with whom he became good friends and from whom he learned the basics of structural phonology. In 1946–7, he worked at the French Embassy to the United States, returning to France in 1948 where he served briefly as Assistant Director of the Musée de l'Homme. He submitted his thesis for the *Doctorat ès Lettres*, *Les Structures élémentaires de la parenté* (*The Elementary Structures of Kinship*), along with a *thèse complémentaire La Vie familiale et sociale des Indiens Nambikwara* ("The Family and Social Life of the Nambikwara Indians"), in 1948 and was named by historian Lucien Febvre (1878–1956) to be a *Directeur d'études* at the newly formed Sixth Section of the École Pratique des Hautes Études. In 1950, Lévi-Strauss was elected to replace Maurice Leenhardt (1878–1954) as *Directeur d'études* at the Fifth Section of the École Pratique, holding the chair, originally held by Marcel Mauss, in "Comparative Religions of Non-Civilized Peoples," which he soon renamed "Religions of Peoples without Writing Systems."[31] He retained his position at the Sixth Section in "Social Anthropology" and offered a single seminar, under the auspices of the two institutions, that was attended by French ethnologists for the next thirty years. In 1959, with the strong support of Maurice Merleau-Ponty, he was named to the Chair of Social Anthropology at the Collège de France, a position he held until his retirement in 1982.[32] In 1967, the Centre National de la Recherche Scientifique (CNRS) awarded Lévi-Strauss its highest distinction, the *Médaille d'or*, and in 1973, he was elected to the *Académie Française*.

Lévi-Strauss is regarded by many to be the dominant figure in the rise of structuralism, and a leading figure in the fall from centrality both of existentialism and Sorbonne philosophy. As a student, however, Lévi-Strauss was part of the same circle that included all the major existentialists, and his connections with them were cordial. In fact, Lévi-Strauss sent Simone de Beauvoir an unpublished draft of his

---

[31] See François Dosse, *History of Structuralism, Vol. 1*, trans. Deborah Glassman (Minneapolis: University of Minnesota Press, 1997), p. 13.

[32] Earlier nominations to the Collège de France by psychologist Henri Piéron in 1949, and Émile Benveniste and Georges Dumézil in 1950, had been unsuccessful.

doctoral thesis *The Elementary Structures of Kinship*, for which she wrote a strongly positive review for *Les Temps modernes* in 1949, crediting Lévi-Strauss for his "brilliant awakening" of French sociology from its long sleep.[33] Quite likely, Beauvoir did not read the thesis carefully, for she goes on to claim that Lévi-Strauss's "thinking is clearly inscribed in that great humanist mainstream that considers human existence as bearing within itself its own justification," and that she found "singularly striking the agreement between certain descriptions and the theses put forward by existentialism: existence, in a single movement, in establishing itself establishes its laws; it is not governed by any internal necessity, and yet it escapes contingency by assuming the conditions of its springing forth."[34] It soon became apparent, however, that Lévi-Strauss's philosophical position was fundamentally opposed to existentialism. Jean-Paul Sartre, in particular, was the object of Lévi-Strauss's polemics and he addressed critically Sartre's work on a number of occasions, most notably in the closing chapter of *The Savage Mind* (1962), where he was perhaps the first to put forward the rhetoric of the "death of the subject," writing that "I believe the ultimate goal of the human sciences to be not to constitute, but to dissolve man."[35] He did remain friendly with Maurice Merleau-Ponty, to whose memory *The Savage Mind* was dedicated and with whom he was colleagues at the Collège de France for several years, and Merleau-Ponty's late turn toward structuralism is in part due to his relationship with Lévi-Strauss. He was also influential on, and was influenced by, the work of the other major figures in the structuralist movement – Jacques Lacan, Roland Barthes, Louis Althusser – and Michel Foucault no doubt has his work in mind when, in the closing pages of *The Order of Things*, he cites ethnology, along with psychoanalysis, as occupying a "privileged position" in our knowledge of the human sciences.

Emmanuel Levinas (1906–95) was born in Kaunas, Lithuania into an orthodox Jewish family. In 1916, his family moved to the Ukraine, but returned to Lithuania in 1920. In 1923, he went to the University of

---

[33] Simone de Beauvoir, "Review of *Les Structures élémentaires de la parenté*," *Les Temps modernes* (November 1949): 943.

[34] Beauvoir, "Review of *Les Structures élémentaires de la parenté*," p. 949.

[35] Claude Lévi-Strauss, *The Savage Mind* (Chicago: University of Chicago Press, 1966), p. 247.

Strasbourg, where he became acquainted with the thought of Durkheim and Bergson, and studied with Maurice Halbwachs (1877–1945), Maurice Pradines (1874–1958), Charles Blondel, and Henri Carteron. At Strasbourg, he met and became lifelong friends with Maurice Blanchot, and it was here that he completed his *licence* in philosophy. He traveled to Germany, where he studied phenomenology with one of Husserl's early students, Jean Héring (1890–1966), at Göttingen. In 1928, he spent two semesters at the University of Freiburg, where he was able to attend Husserl's last seminars on phenomenological psychology and intersubjectivity and Heidegger's first seminars as Husserl's successor. Here he read Heidegger's *Being and Time*, to which he was to say he gained access via Bergson's thought, and which was to remain one of his most significant intellectual references, even after Heidegger's Nazi connections and later philosophy turned Levinas in other directions. In 1930, he received his *Doctorat d'Université* from Strasbourg for his thesis *La Théorie de l'intuition dans la phénoménologie de Husserl* (*The Theory of Intuition in Husserl's Phenomenology*) and, later that year, he became a naturalized French citizen.

Levinas moved to Paris as an administrator for the *Alliance Israélite Universelle*, an organization that assisted eastern European Jews in gaining access to educational institutions. In Paris, he attended Léon Brunschvicg's lectures at the Sorbonne and was a regular visitor to Gabriel Marcel's weekly meetings. He also became close friends with Jean Wahl, with whom he frequently discussed Hegel, and in 1961 he dedicated to Marcelle and Jean Wahl *Totality and Infinity*, his *Doctorat d'État*, which he submitted along with a *thèse complémentaire Études sur la phénoménologie*. More interested in Heidegger's phenomenology than Husserl's, in 1932 he published one of the first articles in France on Heidegger, "Martin Heidegger et l'ontologie" (*Revue philosophique de la France et de l'etranger* 113 [1932]: 395–431). During the war, Levinas served in the French Army as an interpreter; he became a prisoner of war in 1940 but his status as a French officer protected him from the fate of many of his fellow Jews, including almost all of his immediate family (parents, grandparents, two younger brothers), who died in the anti-Jewish genocide in the Ukraine. Levinas would often allude to the guilt of the survivor in his later writings, and there is little question that his account of the obligation to the other is inflected in part by his experiences as a European Jew. Following the war, Levinas was appointed to the École Normale Israélite Orientale, where he had taught briefly in the 1930s; he helped develop its program in Jewish studies and served as its Director from 1945 to 1961. Having spent most of his life outside the world of formal academics, following the publication of *Totality and Infinity*, an academic career became possible, and Levinas became Professor of Philosophy first at Poitiers (1964–7; colleagues included Mikel Dufrenne and Jeanne Delhomme), then the University of Paris X-Nanterre (1967–73), and finally the University of Paris IV-Paris-Sorbonne (1973–6; Emeritus 1976–9).

Although Levinas did not publish much until late in life (only four books before he turned 55), he has played a significant role in the unfolding of philosophy in France. He has credited Edmund Husserl (1859–1938), Martin Buber (1878–1965), and Franz Rosenzweig (1886–1929) as the major influences on his own thinking, and is generally recognized as the figure most responsible for first introducing phenomenology to France, both in its Husserlian and Heideggerian forms. His 1930 work on *The Theory of Intuition in Husserl's Phenomenology* had a profound effect on many, including Jean-Paul Sartre in particular. But this was not to be his only impact, for his deep reflection on ethics as philosophically fundamental ("ethics as first philosophy") has been of prime importance in the turn toward ethics in the last two decades of the twentieth century. Likewise, his reflections on Judaism and the Talmud (which he came to know after he came to France, having grown up reading the Hebrew Bible rather than the Aramaic Talmud) have also been influential in the turn toward theology that characterizes the later writings of Jacques Derrida, upon whom Levinas's influence has been consistent and significant throughout his career. Others clearly influenced by Levinas include Jean-François Lyotard and Maurice Blanchot.

Lucien Lévy-Bruhl (1857–1939) was born in Paris. He was a student at the Lycée Charlemagne before entering the École Normale Supérieure in 1876. He received his *agrégation* in 1879, finishing first. Lévy-Bruhl taught at *lycées* in Poitiers (1879–82) and Amiens (1882–5), and at the Lycée Louis-le-Grand (1886–95). He received his *Doctorat ès Lettres* in 1884 for a thesis on *L'Idée de responsabilité* ("The Idea of Responsibility"), with a *thèse complémentaire* in Latin on "The Idea of God in Seneca" (*Quid de deo Seneca Senserit*). In 1895, he became *Maître de conférences* at the École Normale Supérieure, where he taught until 1902. In 1902, he became *chargé du cours* for the History of Modern Philosophy at the Sorbonne, and was promoted to the Chair in History of Modern Philosophy in 1908, replacing Émile Boutroux. He retired from that position in 1926, having included among his friends Émile

Durkheim, Henri Bergson, and Jean Jaurès, and among the students he influenced, Étienne Gilson and Georges Davy. While Lévy-Bruhl's early works were on philosophical topics (Jacobi, Comte, the history of French philosophy), he is best known for his anthropological works on "primitive mentality," most of which were translated into English within a few years of their French publication, including *Les Fonctions mentales dans les sociétés inférieures* (1912; *How Natives Think*, trans. Lilian A. Clare [New York: A. A. Knopf, 1925]), *La Mentalité primitive* (1922; *Primitive Mentality*, trans. Lilian A. Clare [New York: Macmillan, 1923]), and *Le Surnaturel et la nature dans la mentalité primitive* (1931; *Primitives and the Supernatural*, trans. Lilian A. Clare [New York: E. P. Dutton, 1935]).

Jean-François Lyotard (1924–98) was born in Versailles. He attended the Lycées Buffon and Louis-le-Grand in Paris and, after twice failing the entrance exam to the École Normale Supérieure, Lyotard enrolled at the Sorbonne, where he was classmates with Michel Butor, François Châtelet, Gilles Deleuze, and Roger Laporte. Lyotard's thesis for his *Maîtrise*, "L'Indifférence comme notion éthique" ("Indifference as an Ethical Notion"), was submitted in the late 1940s. He passed the *agrégation* in 1950 and submitted *Discours, figure*, directed by Mikel Dufrenne, to the faculty at the University of Paris X-Nanterre for his *Doctorat d'État* in 1971. From 1950 to 1952, Lyotard taught at a boys' *lycée* in Constantine, Algeria, after which he took up a teaching position at La Flèche, a school for the sons of military personnel, where he taught until 1959. From 1959 to 1966, Lyotard was *Maître-assistant* at the Sorbonne; he then joined the philosophy department at the University of Nanterre (later Paris X), where he taught from 1967 to 1972. He was active during the 1968 demonstrations in support of the "March 22 Movement," the movement associated most notably with Daniel Cohn-Bendit and credited with starting the chain of events that resulted in the student uprising of May 1968. From 1968 to 1970, he was *chargé de recherches* at the Centre National de la Recherche Scientifique. In 1972, Lyotard joined the faculty at the University of Paris VIII-Vincennes, where he became *Maître de conférences* and taught at Vincennes until he retired as Professor Emeritus in 1987. He was an enthusiastic supporter of the Collège International de Philosophie, serving as its second President from 1984 to 1986. Beginning in the 1970s, Lyotard taught often at a number of American universities, including Johns Hopkins University, the University of California (at San Diego and at

Berkeley), and the Center for Twentieth Century Studies at the University of Wisconsin-Milwaukee. From 1987 to 1994, he was a regular member of the French and Italian Department at the University of California at Irvine and he taught from 1994 until his death in the French Department at Emory University.

Throughout the 1950s, Lyotard was actively engaged in politics. He joined *Socialisme ou barbarie*, a political organization founded by Claude Lefort and Cornelius Castoriadis that was perhaps the most influential Marxist group in France not aligned with the communists; in 1955, he joined the editorial board of its journal as its principal spokesperson on Algeria. Lyotard remained with *Socialisme ou barbarie* until 1963, when several tensions within the group led to an amicable split, with Lyotard and others taking over the publication of *Pouvoir Ouvrier* (1964–6), the group's monthly worker's newspaper, and Castoriadis's majority faction retaining control of the primary journal *Socialisme ou barbarie* (which also continued until 1966). During the 1960s and until the end of his life, Lyotard was also active in the art world as the author of many books and essays, as well as contributor to several exhibition catalogues, including the exhibition he organized in 1985, "Les Immatériaux," at the Centre Pompidou in Paris.

Lyotard's name, more than any other, is associated with philosophical postmodernism, in part a result of his first widely read work, *The Postmodern Condition*. In this occasional text, written at the request of the Quebec government, Lyotard first introduced his definition of the postmodern as "incredulity toward metanarratives": rather than naming a specific epoch, the postmodern names, instead, an anti-foundationalist attitude that seeks to go beyond the legitimating orthodoxy of the moment. Postmodernity, then, resides constantly at the heart of the modern, challenging those totalizing and comprehensive master narratives (like the Enlightenment narrative of the emancipation of the rational subject or the Marxist narrative of the emancipation of the working class) that serve to legitimate its practices. In place of these master narratives, Lyotard suggests we look instead to less ambitious *petits récits* or "little narratives" that refrain from totalizing claims in favor of recognizing the specificity and singularity of events.

Beyond his writing on the postmodern, *The Différend* remains in the view of many, including Lyotard himself, his most original and important work. Drawing heavily from Wittgenstein's *Philosophical Investigations* and Kant's *Critique of Judgment* and political writings, Lyotard here reflects on how one can make judgments (political as well as aesthetic) in cases where there is no rule of judgment to which one can appeal. This is the *différend*, a dispute between (at least) two parties in which the parties operate within radically heterogeneous language games that are so incommensurate that they cannot even come to a consensus on the principles or rules that could govern how their dispute might be settled. In contrast to litigations, in which the disputing parties share a language in which rules of judgment can be justly appealed to in order to resolve the dispute, *différends* (examples might be the conflicting claims to land rights by aboriginal peoples and current residents, or disputes concerning the right of a woman to maintain control over her body and the right of a fetus to reside in that body until viable) are such that our task is not to resolve them but to express them in a way that does not do unjustifiable violence to one or more of the parties by posing the dispute in a way that delegitimates their claim. In other words, our political task, if we are to be just, is to phrase the dispute in a way that respects the difference between the competing claims.

Pierre Macherey (1938–) was born in Belfort (Franche-Comté). He attended the École Normale Supérieure from 1958 to 1963. In 1961, he completed his *maîtrise*, "Philosophie et politique chez Spinoza" ("Philosophy and Politics in Spinoza"), directed by Georges Canguilhem. He worked as *Maître de conférences* at the Sorbonne from 1966 to 1992 and as Professor at the University of Lille III since 1992. After his *maîtrise*, Macherey began working closely with Louis Althusser and was part of a group of students (including Étienne Balibar and Jacques Rancière) who collaborated with Althusser in developing the structuralist reading of Marx. His most important work, *Pour une théorie de la production littéraire* (1966; English translation: *A Theory of Literary Production*, trans. Geoffrey Wall [London: Routledge and Kegan Paul, 1978]), is generally regarded as the best representation of Althusserian literary criticism. Macherey was awarded his *Doctorat d'État*, under the title *A quoi pense la littérature?* ("About What Is Literature Thinking?"), from the University of Paris I-Panthéon-Sorbonne for work produced in 1991 and, since then, has produced a massive five-volume interpretation of Spinoza's *Ethics* (Paris: Presses universitaires de France, 1994–8).

Gabriel Marcel (1889–1973) was born in Paris. His father, a career diplomat, was posted to Stockholm and Marcel spent some of his childhood in Sweden. He returned to France for schooling at the Lycée Carnot and received his *baccalauréat* in 1906. After deciding not to compete for a place in the École Normale Supérieure, Marcel attended the Sorbonne, where he worked with André Lalande and Victor Delbos, and completed his *licence* in philosophy in 1907. While the philosophers at the Sorbonne did not impress him, Marcel was greatly influenced by Henri Bergson's lectures at the Collège de France and his philosophical interests during these years focused primarily on Anglo-American idealists like Josiah Royce and F. H. Bradley. His thesis for the *Diplôme d'études supérieures* on "The Metaphysical Ideas of Coleridge and their Relationship to the Philosophy of Schelling" was completed in 1909. Marcel passed the *agrégation* in 1910, along with his good friend Jean Wahl, and in 1911, he submitted a proposal for the *Doctorat*, "Essai sur les fondements métaphysiques de l'intelligibilité religieuse. La Théorie de la finalité chez Spinoza" ("Essay on the Metaphysical Foundations of Religious Intelligibility: The Theory of Finality in Spinoza"), though he never completed this work. He taught intermittently between 1912 and 1940 at the *lycée* in Vendôme (1911–12), the Lycée Condorcet in Paris (1915–18), the *lycée* in Sens (1918–22), the Lycée Louis-le-Grand (1939), and, during the war, the *lycée* in Montpellier. During his lifetime, Marcel was widely known as a man of letters who wrote plays, reviews, and essays as well as philosophy. He received the *Académie Française*'s *Grand prix de Littérature* in 1949, and was elected to the *Académie des Sciences politiques et morales* in 1952. He lectured widely around Europe, and was invited to Aberdeen to deliver the prestigious Gifford lectures in 1949–50 (subsequently published as the two-volume *Mystery of Being*).

Although he preferred to be called a "neo-Socratic," Marcel is mainly known as the foremost Christian existentialist. Raised agnostic, Marcel converted to Catholicism in 1929, though his affinities for Bergson left him unattracted to Thomism. It could be claimed that Marcel published the first work of existential philosophy in the twentieth century: his *Metaphysical Journal* was published in 1927, the same year as Martin Heidegger's *Being and Time*, with which it shares many themes, if not the same mode of exposition. As far as French existentialism is concerned, Marcel's *Being and Having* was published in 1935, the year before Sartre's *Transcendence of the Ego* and eight years before *Being and Nothingness*, and in it Marcel emphasized such existential themes as being-in-the-world, facticity, embodiment, and freedom, while keeping in sight the mystery of being and the necessity of transcendence. Beyond his writings, Marcel also played a personal role in the intellectual development of a number of thinkers, as the weekly Friday gatherings at his home on the Rue de Tournon brought together for philosophical conversation such figures as Emmanuel Levinas, Louis Lavelle, Rene Le Senne, Jean Wahl, and Paul Ricoeur. In the 1940s, as existentialism became increasingly identified with Sartre's atheistic version, Marcel came to reject any association of his work with existentialism. Despite his protests, however, the label of "Christian existentialist" continued to be applied to him.

Jean-Luc Marion (1946–) was born in Meudon, just outside of Paris. He studied at the Lycée international de Sèvres, did his *hypokhâgne* and *khâgne* under Jean Beaufret at the Lycée Condorcet, studied at the École Normale Supérieure from 1967 to 1970, and then at the University of Paris IV-Paris-Sorbonne, where he worked closely with Ferdinand Alquié, who directed his *Doctorat du troisième cycle*, a new annotated translation of Descartes's *Les Regulae ad Directionem ingenii* (*Rules for the Direction of the Mind*) with a commentary, "La Chose et le savoir. Essai sur la thématique et la topique aristotelicienne de certains concepts des regulae" ("Thing and Knowledge: Essay on Aristotelian Themes and Topics of Certain Concepts in the *Regulae*"), submitted in 1974. Marion passed the *agrégation* in 1971 and received his *Doctorat d'État* in 1981, having submitted his thesis *Le Fondement du savoir dans la pensée de Descartes* ("The Foundation of Knowledge in the Thought of Descartes") to Alquié the previous year. He taught as *Assistant* at the University of Paris IV-Paris-Sorbonne (1973–81), and as Professor at the University of Poitiers (1981–8) and University of Paris X-Nanterre (1988–95) before returning to Paris IV-Paris-Sorbonne in 1995 as Professor and Director of the Centre d'études cartésiennes. Since 1994, Marion has also taught regularly at the University of Chicago in the School of Divinity. In addition to authoring a number of works on Descartes, Marion has emerged as the dominant thinker at the intersection of phenomenology and religion.

Jacques Maritain (1882–1973) was born in Paris. He did his *hypokhâgne* and *khâgne* at the Lycée Henri-IV (1898–1900), and then studied at the Sorbonne (1901–5), but was also greatly influenced by Henri Bergson's lectures at the Collège de France. He passed his *agrégation* in 1905, and then went to Heidelberg to study biology (1906–8) before returning to Paris to begin the serious study of Thomism. In 1912, he began teaching philosophy at the Collège Stanislaus in Paris, and in 1914, he became Professor of Modern Philosophy at the Institut Catholique de Paris, where he taught until 1939. In 1932, he began a regular visiting appointment at the Pontifical Institute of Medieval Studies in Toronto, where he taught during the war, teaching also at Princeton (1941–2) and Columbia (1941–4). After the war, Maritain served as French ambassador to the Vatican from 1945 to 1948, then returned to Princeton as Professor of Philosophy from 1948 until he retired in 1960.

Maritain was one of the foremost Thomist scholars and philosophers of the first half of the twentieth century, and many regard him to be the twentieth century's leading interpreter of St. Thomas Aquinas. He was influential in theological existentialism (he referred to Thomism as "Existentialist Intellectualism") and his thought intersected with and engaged themes from Emmanuel Mounier's personalism and Gabriel Marcel's Catholicism. His more than fifty books addressed a wide range of issues in science, poetry, mysticism, and politics, and among his better known works are *Art et Scholastique* (1920; *Art and Scholasticism, with Other Essays*, trans. J. F. Scanlan [London: Sheed & Ward, 1946]); *Distinguer pour unir ou les degrés du savoir* (1932; English translation: *Distinguish to Unite, or The Degrees of Knowledge*, trans. supervised by Gerald B. Phelan [New York: Charles Scribner's Sons, 1959]); *Sept leçons sur l'être et les premiers principes de la raison spéculative* (1934; English translation: *A Preface to Metaphysics* [London: Sheed & Ward 1939]); *Court traité de l'existence et de l'existant* (1947; English translation: *Existence and the Existent*, trans. Lewis Galantiere and Gerald B. Phelan [New York: Pantheon, 1948]).

Maurice Merleau-Ponty (1908–61) was born in Rochefort-sur-Mer (Charente-Maritime, Poitou-Charentes). He studied in Paris at the Lycée Janson-de-Sailly and did his *khâgne* at the Lycée Louis-le-Grand before entering the École Normale Supérieure in 1926. He completed his studies at the École Normale in 1930, submitting his thesis in 1929 for the *Diplôme d'études supérieures* on "La Notion du multiple intelligible chez Plotin" ("The Notion of the Intelligible Multiple in Plotinus") under Émile Brehier, and passed the *agrégation*, finishing second, in 1930. Merleau-Ponty began student teaching at the Lycée Janson-de-Sailly in the spring of 1929, along with Simone de Beauvoir and Claude Lévi-Strauss. He taught at *lycées* in Beauvais (1931–3) and Chartres (1934–5), spending the intermediate year (1933–4) at the Caisse des Recherches Scientifiques (precursor to the Centre Nationale de la Recherche Scientifique). From 1935 to 1939, he served as *agrégé-répétiteur* (*caïman*) at the École Normale Supérieure. It was while at the École Normale Supérieure that Merleau-Ponty conducted his postgraduate research on perception, and during these years he also attended Alexandre Kojève's lectures on Hegel at the École Pratique des Hautes Études. From 1940 to 1944, he taught at the Lycée Carnot, then assumed the position of teaching the *première supérieure* at the Lycée Condorcet in 1944–5. After the war, he completed his *Doctorat ès Lettres* in 1945, submitting as his principal thesis *Phenomenology of Perception*, and his *thèse complémentaire The Structure of Behavior* (which was completed in 1938 and first published in 1942), and was appointed *Maître de conférences* (1945), then Professor of Philosophy (1948) at the University of Lyon. Merleau-Ponty left Lyon in 1949 to assume a position at the Sorbonne (made possible through the strong support of Jean Wahl),[36] where he taught until 1952 with a Chair not in Philosophy but in Child Psychology and Pedagogy, a chair later held by Jean Piaget. Along with Jean-Paul Sartre and Simone de Beauvoir, he was a founding editor in 1946 of the influential journal *Les Temps modernes,* though he resigned as editor in late 1952 over disagreements with Sartre and the other editors concerning, among other things, their support of the Soviet Union's backing the North Korean invasion of South Korea.[37] Never entirely comfortable with a chair in psychology rather than philosophy, Merleau-Ponty left the Sorbonne in 1952 when he was elected to replace Louis Lavelle in the Chair in Modern Philosophy at the Collège de France, a position he held until his untimely death.

Like many of his generation, Merleau-Ponty was educated in a philosophical tradition dominated by Cartesianism and the critical idealism of Léon Brunschvicg. Also like many of his generation, Merleau-Ponty reacted strongly against these traditions, turning instead to psychology and phenomenology, especially Husserl's later work *The Crisis of European Sciences and Transcendental Phenomenology* (1936), where he introduced the idea of the *Lebenswelt* or "Life-World." Merleau-Ponty was, in fact, the first scholar to visit the newly founded Husserl Archive in Louvain, Belgium in 1939, and he can be credited as the principal discoverer of the so-called "later Husserl" of *Ideen II* and the *Krisis.* Merleau-Ponty was reported to have been in the audience when Husserl presented his "Paris Lectures" at the Sorbonne in 1929

---

[36] See the "Notice Nécrologique" for Wahl by Pierre-Maxime Schuhl in *Revue philosophique* 164 (1974): 400.

[37] The most detailed account of the specific events leading up to Merleau-Ponty's resignation is found in Sartre's memorial essay "Merleau-Ponty," in *Situations,* trans. Benita Eisler (New York: G. Braziller, 1965), pp. 204–6.

and, with Emmanuel Levinas, he is one of the two people most responsible for developing interest in Husserl's phenomenology in France.

From their days at the École Normale Supérieure until a falling-out
over politics in the early 1950s, Merleau-Ponty and Sartre were close
colleagues and, in many respects, their careers parallel one another's.
Like Sartre, Merleau-Ponty's first work, his 1942 thesis *The Structure of
Behavior*, was a philosophical analysis of psychological phenomena. His
major work, *Phenomenology of Perception*, was published in 1945, two
years after Sartre's *Being and Nothingness* and, while broadly sympathetic to the existentialist project, it offered important corrections to
what he regarded as Sartre's extreme account of freedom and his overly
dualistic approach to human being. Also like Sartre, he wrote numerous
essays on literary and aesthetic topics, and in the late 1940s and 1950s
wrote increasingly on political topics. Indeed, it was their respective
commitments to communism that, in some respects, first brought them
together and that led to their ultimate split. At *Les Temps modernes*,
Merleau-Ponty was officially the editor in charge of political affairs. He
and Sartre both strongly backed the French Communist Party (though
neither was an official member of the party) and its solidarity with the
Soviet Union, even going so far as to support Stalin and the Soviet
Union in some of its most excessively repressive actions. But they split
over the Korean War, as Merleau-Ponty found unconvincing the argument that solidarity among the left required supporting North Korea in
what he regarded as its blatantly aggressive invasion of the South. The
publication of Sartre's essay "Les Communistes et la paix" in *Les Temps
modernes* in July 1952 without consulting with Merleau-Ponty, who was
the journal's political editor, and Merleau-Ponty's subsequent critique
of Sartre and Soviet communism in *Adventures of the Dialectic*, cemented their breach.

In his last decade, Merleau-Ponty became increasingly interested in
language and was one of the first to discuss and lecture on the work
of Ferdinand de Saussure. As he moved away from existentialism,
Merleau-Ponty found himself at home with the early developments of
structuralism. He became good friends with Claude Lévi-Strauss,
whose candidacy he promoted at the Collège de France, and he lectured
frequently on topics in the human sciences. When he died, Merleau-
Ponty left several unfinished manuscripts, the most important of which,
The Visible and the Invisible, edited by his assistant Claude Lefort, was
envisioned to be a major revision of several of the themes articulated in
Phenomenology of Perception. In addition to his profound influence on

the phenomenological and existential traditions in France, Merleau-Ponty also figures as a powerful influence on the development of structuralism: his early lectures on Saussure informed Jacques Lacan's appropriation of Saussurean linguistics, and he was an important influence on Louis Althusser.

Emmanuel Mounier (1905–50) was born in Grenoble. He began his education at the University of Grenoble in 1924 with the intention of studying medicine, but by the time he completed his degree in 1927, his interest in becoming a physician had passed. Instead, at Grenoble he began the serious study of philosophy under the tutelage of the Bergsonian philosopher Jacques Chevalier (1882–1962), and moved to Paris in 1927, where he completed his *agrégation* in philosophy in 1928, receiving the second highest scores that year (Raymond Aron received the highest score that year, while Jean-Paul Sartre failed the exam, passing it the following year). Between 1928 and 1933, Mounier was a regular visitor to the home of Jacques Maritain, whose monthly gatherings of intellectuals and artists provided Mounier the opportunity to meet and converse with several of the leading theological thinkers in Europe, including Russian émigré Nicholai Berdyaev (1874–1948) and Gabriel Marcel. The other major influence on Mounier's thinking was Charles Péguy (1873–1914), whose socialism and Bergsonism were to inform all Mounier's later thought. Péguy's rejection of the academic world and his literary ambitions (nearly all Péguy's work first appeared in the journal *Cahiers de la Quinzaine*, which he founded and directed until his death) also were to influence Mounier, whose first important work, *La Pensée de Charles Péguy* (1931; *The Thought of Charles Péguy*), was the first work to explore Péguy as a philosophical thinker.

Following his *agrégation*, Mounier proposed a thesis on the relatively obscure Spanish mystic John of the Angels (1536–1609), but his plans met with resistance at the Sorbonne and his thesis was never completed. Instead, Mounier began formulating his own thoughts on the connections between humanism, communitarianism, and religion and, in 1932, he founded the journal *Esprit*, which he edited until his death, to give voice to a philosophical position he called "Personalism." Bringing together Catholic spiritualism with socialist materialism, a strong sense of the value of community with a commitment to recognizing the value of the individual, *Esprit* soon became one of the most influential cultural journals of its day (Maurice Merleau-Ponty served for a time as its correspondent in Chartres and director of its psychology research group; he resigned in 1937 as rivals to Mounier within the editorial board drew the journal toward the political right.). During the 1930s, Mounier became one of the leading spokespersons for personalism, which Paul Ricoeur, upon whom Mounier was to be a profound influence, called "a pedagogy concerning communal life linked to an awakening of the person."[38] From 1933 to 1939, Mounier taught at the French *lycée* in Brussels; he returned to France for military service in 1939, saw *Esprit* banned by the Vichy government from 1941 to 1944, and was imprisoned in 1942 for suspicion of subversive activities. After ten months and following a brief trial, Mounier was acquitted for lack of evidence. He spent the remainder of the war writing under assumed names and, following the war, immediately resumed publishing *Esprit*. While appealing to many of the same themes as existentialism, Mounier was one of the leading theological critics who objected to the identification of existentialism with the work of Sartre; along with Marcel, he is one of the primary figures in France from whom Sartre sought to distinguish his atheistic existentialism.

Jean Nabert (1881–1960) was born in Izeaux (Isère, Rhône-Alpes). He attended *lycée* in Grenoble, then studied at the University in Lyon. Nabert passed his *agrégation* in 1910, after which he taught at *lycées* in Saint-Lô, Brest, and Metz. He received his *Doctorat ès Lettres* in 1924, following the submission of his *thèse principale L'Expérience intérieure de la liberté* ("The Inner Experience of Freedom") and *thèse secondaire* "L'Expérience interne chez Kant" ("Inner Experience in Kant"). In 1926, Nabert came to Paris and taught at the Lycée Saint-Louis, then Louis-le-Grand, before beginning to teach *khâgne* at Lycée Lakanal and, in 1931, Lycée Henri-IV. In 1944, Nabert was named *Inspecteur Générale* and served as Director of the Bibliothèque Victor Cousin until his death. Working within the tradition of reflexive philosophy, Nabert is best known for his *L'Expérience intérieure de la liberté*, published in 1924, which anticipates in several ways Sartre's account of freedom, and he was an important influence on Paul Ricoeur. Only one of Nabert's works has been translated into English: *Éléments pour une éthique* (1943; English translation: *Elements for an Ethic*, trans. William J. Petrek [Evanston, IL: Northwestern University Press, 1969]).

---

[38] Paul Ricoeur, "Emmanuel Mounier: A Personalist Philosopher," in *History and Truth*, trans. Charles A. Kelbley (Evanston, IL: Northwestern University Press, 1965), p. 136.

Jean-Luc Nancy (1940–) was born in Caudéran, near Bordeaux (Gironde, Aquitaine). He studied at the Lycée Charles-de-Gaulle in Baden-Baden and the Lycée Henri-IV in Bergerac, then did his *hypokhâgne* and *khâgne* first at the Lycée Pierre de Fermat in Toulouse, then the Lycée Louis-le-Grand in Paris and Lycée Lakanal in Sceaux. Nancy pursued his university studies first at Toulouse (1958–9), then at the Sorbonne (1960–4), where he received his *Licence de philosophie* in 1962, his *Diplôme d'études supérieures de philosophie* in 1963, and his *Certificat* in General Biology, also in 1963. He worked closely at the Sorbonne with Georges Canguilhem and, because of his strong interest in religion, with Paul Ricoeur, who served as the director of his *maîtrise* on Hegel's philosophy of religion ("La Religion de Hegel"). Also influential on Nancy was the Jesuit philosopher Georges Morel (1921–89), who met informally with a group of Christian students to discuss Hegel. Nancy passed the *agrégation* in 1964, after which he requested an appointment in Strasbourg, where he intended to pursue further study leading to a *Doctorat d'État* in theology. His request was granted and he taught *hypokhâgne* at the Lycée Bartholdi in Colmar (Alsace) from 1964 to 1968 (interrupted in 1966 by his military service, during which he served as Professor of Philosophy at the École Militaire in Strasbourg).

In 1968 Nancy became an assistant at the Institut de Philosophie in Strasbourg. In 1973, he received his *Doctorat de troisième cycle* for a thesis on "Le Discours analogique de Kant" ("Kant's Analogical Discourse"), completed again under the supervision of Paul Ricoeur. Soon after, he became first *Maître-assistant*, then *Maître de conférences* at the Université des Sciences Humaines in Strasbourg, where he was promoted to Professor in 1988. During this period, he also served as *Chargé de cours et conférences* at the École Normale Supérieure (Ulm) from 1972 to 1979. In 1987, Nancy received his *Doctorat d'État* from the University in Toulouse, following the submission of his thesis on freedom in the work of Kant, Schelling, and Heidegger, *L'Expérience de la liberté* (*The Experience of Freedom*), supervised by Gérard Granel. Jacques Derrida, Jean-Toussaint Desanti, and Jean-François Lyotard also served as members of the examining jury. Throughout the 1970s and 1980s, he taught frequently as a visiting professor at the Freie Universität in Berlin (1974–5, 1981, 1982–3) and the University of California at Irvine (1976–8, 1984), at San Diego (1985–7), and at Berkeley (1987–90). In addition to a long association with Jacques Derrida, with whom he has collaborated in the context of the activities of GREPH and the Collège Internationale de Philosophie, Nancy has also had a long collaboration with Philippe Lacoue-Labarthe, his colleague at the Université des Sciences Humaines in Strasbourg, with whom he has co-authored several books and articles. He retired from active teaching and was named Professor Emeritus at Strasbourg in 2002.

Paul Ricoeur (1913–) was born in Valence (Drôme, Rhône-Alpes). Orphaned at the age of two, he was raised by his paternal grandparents and studied as a ward of the state at the *lycée* in Rennes, where he worked closely during his *classe terminale*, *hypokhâgne*, and *khâgne* (1930–3) with Roland Dalbiez (1893–1975). He then enrolled at the University of Rennes, passed his *licence* in 1933, and following his failure of the entrance examination for the École Normale Supérieure,[39] he submitted his *maîtrise*, *Problème de Dieu chez Lachelier et Lagneau* ("The Problem of God in Lachelier et Lagneau") in 1934. In 1934–5, Ricoeur studied at the Sorbonne with Henri Bréhier, Léon Robin, and Léon Brunschvicg. He passed his *agrégation* in 1935, finishing second. During the 1930s, Ricoeur was a regular at the weekly Friday gatherings at the home of Gabriel Marcel, who he met in 1934, and it was here that he was introduced to the major themes of existential philosophy and theology. He was also a friend and collaborator with the personalist philosopher Emmanuel Mounier, and many of his early essays were published in the left-wing Christian journal *Esprit*, founded by Mounier in 1932. Jean Nabert, a leading representative of the tradition of French reflexive philosophy, also was a major influence on Ricoeur, both in his early years and especially during the 1950s and 1960s.

Ricoeur was captured during the war and spent time in the same prisoner of war camp with Mikel Dufrenne, with whom he became close friends. While in the camp, Ricoeur read the works of Husserl, Heidegger, and Marcel, and with Dufrenne, he worked intensely on the philosophy of Karl Jaspers (to which he had first been introduced by Marcel), the result of which was their jointly authored *Karl Jaspers et la philosophie de l'existence* in 1947. In 1950, Ricoeur submitted his doctoral thesis, the first volume of his *Philosophie de la volonté: Le Volontaire et l'involontaire* (*Philosophy of the Will: The Voluntary and the Involuntary*),

---

[39] Charles E. Reagen relates the following story: "[Ricoeur] did very well on the Latin and Greek parts of the exam, but, ironically, he failed the philosophy section. The question was, 'The mind is easier to know than the body.' Paul did not recognize this as a thesis of Descartes' and gave the Aristotelian answer to it which he had learned from his provincial professors." (Charles E. Reagen, *Paul Ricoeur: His Life and his Work* [Chicago: University of Chicago Press, 1996], p. 5.)

while submitting as his *thèse complémentaire* a French translation of
Husserl's *Ideen I*. From 1945 to 1948, Ricoeur taught at the Collège
Cévenol at Chambon-sur-Lignon while also working as a researcher at
the Centre Nationale de Recherche Scientifique. In 1948, when Hyppolite left for the Sorbonne, Ricoeur assumed his Chair in the History of
Philosophy at the University of Strasbourg, where he taught until 1957.
He was elected Professor of Philosophy at the Sorbonne in 1957, where,
among other courses, he taught a seminar on phenomenology, assisted
by Jacques Derrida, from 1960 to 1964. In 1967, disturbed by the
increasing overcrowding at the Sorbonne, Ricoeur chose to leave and
participate in the creation of the new university at Nanterre. In 1969, he
was appointed Dean of the Faculty of Letters at Nanterre, a position he
resigned from under pressure from the student revolutionaries in April
1970. He left Nanterre for three years (1970–3) to teach at the Catholic
University of Louvain (before its split into the Dutch university at
Leuven and the French university at Louvain-la-neuve), and returned
in 1974 to the University of Paris X-Nanterre (which by then had
become officially a part of the University of Paris), where he taught
until his retirement in 1980. Since 1970, Ricoeur also held Professor-
ships in the Department of Philosophy and the Divinity School at the
University of Chicago, where he taught for several weeks each year.

Ricoeur's career in many ways spans the entire evolution of French
philosophy in the twentieth century. He was a student when phenomenology and existentialism were first becoming popular and his earliest
works fall within the concerns of these philosophical positions. While
dedicated to Marcel, he described his *Philosophy of the Will: The
Voluntary and the Involuntary* as "a meditation on Gabriel Marcel's
work" that at the same time wanted to place itself "at the intersection
of two demands: that of a thought nourished [like Marcel's] by the
mystery of the body, and that of a thought concerned with the distinctions inherited from Husserlian descriptive method."[40] When psychoanalysis become influential in French philosophical circles, Ricoeur
addressed Freud's work, arguing for its hermeneutic and philosophical
importance. When structuralism appeared on the scene in the 1960s,
Ricoeur engaged it directly: through several balanced yet critical essays,
he brought forward both the strengths and limitations of the structuralist

[40] Paul Ricoeur, *Freedom and Nature: The Voluntary and the Involuntary*, trans.
      Erazim V. Kohák (Evanston, IL: Northwestern University Press, 1966), p. 15.
      Translation altered.

approach, arguing that its tendency toward an absolute formalism left it looking like "a Kantianism without a transcendental subject."[41] At the same time, he tried to mediate between what he felt was valuable within phenomenology, hermeneutics, and structuralism. He performed a similar role in the debate between Hans-Georg Gadamer and Jürgen Habermas, trying to bridge the developing gap between the hermeneutic and critical theory traditions. He has, in this regard, been an important and respected facilitator of dialogue among the conflicting philosophical positions during the 1960s and 1970s and remained one of the staunchest defenders of the importance of both phenomenology and hermeneutics. In Ricoeur's later work, as his interests turned to metaphor, narrative, time, and ethics, he addressed and drew from philosophers working in the Anglo-American analytic tradition, particular analytic philosophy of language and action, but even here, his commitment to and reliance on the phenomenological and hermeneutic traditions remained foundational for his thinking.

Jean-Paul Sartre (1905–80) was born in Thiviers (Dordogne, Aquitaine), but moved to Paris as a young child with his mother. He studied at the prestigious Lycée Henri-IV from 1915 to 1922 (his education being interrupted in 1917–20 when he moved with his family to the port town of La Rochelle), and prepared for the entrance exam to the École Normale Supérieure at Lycée Louis-le-Grand from 1922 to 1924. It was in his *khâgne*, taught by François Colonna d'Istria (1864–1929), that he changed his orientation from literature to philosophy, a result of his encounter with a text by Bergson: *Essai sur les données immédiates de la conscience* (*Time and Free Will: An Essay on the Immediate Data of Consciousness*). Sartre studied at the École Normale Supérieure from 1924 to 1928, entering in the famous class that included Raymond Aron, Paul Nizan, Georges Canguilhem, and Daniel Lagache; Jean Hyppolite and Maurice de Gandillac entered the following year; Maurice Merleau-Ponty entered the year after that. Although the interest in psychological experience that was sparked by Bergson remained, Sartre quickly moved away from the Bergsonian position. While at the École Normale, he obtained certificates in psychology, history of philosophy, logic and

---

[41] Paul Ricoeur, "Structure and Hermeneutics," trans. Kathleen McLaughlin, in *The Conflict of Interpretations: Essays in Hermeneutics*, ed. Don Ihde (Evanston, IL: Northwestern University Press, 1974), p. 52.

general philosophy, ethics and sociology, and physics, and he received his *Diplôme d'études supérieures* in 1928 for a thesis on "L'Image dans la vie psychologique: rôle et nature," directed by Henri Delacroix (1873–1937), a professor of psychology.

Although perhaps the most distinguished member of his class at the École Normale in the eyes of both his teachers and fellow students, Sartre failed in his first attempt at the *agrégation* in 1928. In fact, he received the lowest score among the fifty who took the exam, though his friend, Raymond Aron, who received the highest score, claimed that Sartre was failed because he took the opportunity to present some of his own ideas on the nature of existence.[42] He passed his *agrégation* the following year, this time receiving the highest score (Beauvoir finished second, Hyppolite third). From 1929 to 1931, he did his military service in the meteorological corps in St-Cyr, a position he acquired through the help of Aron. It was Aron who first introduced Sartre to phenomenology. According to a story related by Simone de Beauvoir,[43] Aron returned to Paris for a break from his studies at the French Institute in Berlin and spoke to Sartre and Beauvoir about Husserl. Sartre was apparently so inspired that he stopped at a bookshop on the walk home and purchased Emmanuel Levinas's new book on Husserl.[44]

From 1933 to 1935, inspired by Levinas and Aron, he followed Aron to Berlin, where he was a research student first at La Maison Académique Française and later at the University of Freiburg. It was here that he first read the work of Husserl and Heidegger. From 1934 to 1939, he taught at *lycées* in Le Havre, Laon, and Neuilly, outside Paris. He joined the French Army at the outbreak of World War II in 1939, and was captured by the Germans in 1940. After the armistice was signed between France and Germany, he returned to Paris and resumed teaching the *khâgne* (*première supérieure*) at the Lycée Condorcet from 1941 to 1944, at which time he gave up his teaching career to devote his time exclusively to writing literature and philosophy. With Maurice Merleau-Ponty and Simone de Beauvoir, he was a founding editor in 1946 of the influential left-wing journal *Les Temps modernes* (other

---

[42] Raymond Aron, *Memoirs: Fifty Years of Political Reflection*, trans. George Holoch (New York: Holmes and Meier, 1990), p. 25.

[43] Simone de Beauvoir, *The Prime of Life*, trans. Peter Green (New York: World Publishing, 1962), p. 112.

[44] Beauvoir does not mention which book of Levinas's, but it could only have been *The Theory of Intuition in the Phenomenology of Husserl*, first published in 1930.

members of the inaugural editorial committee included Raymond Aron, Michel Leiris, Albert Olivier, and Jean Paulhan). In addition to his many important philosophical writings, Sartre was a world-famous playwright and novelist; he also authored numerous essays on literary, aesthetic, and cultural issues. He was awarded the Nobel Prize for Literature in 1962, but he refused to accept it for political reasons.

Sartre's writings span a wide array of topics, approaches, and genre. In addition to his twelve plays, five novels, and numerous essays, Sartre published three significant literary biographies, on Baudelaire, Genet, and Flaubert (the latter in three volumes and over 2,000 pages); a fourth manuscript, on Mallarmé, was published posthumously. Restricting our focus to his philosophical texts, Sartre's writings can be organized roughly into four periods. In his earliest period (1936–40), he works primarily within the phenomenological tradition, examining psychological topics concerning consciousness, the ego, imagination, and emotions. In the 1940s, he articulates the basic themes of existentialism, most notably in his *magnum opus Being and Nothingness* (1943). In the 1950s, he moves toward more explicitly social and political issues, and much of the work of this period, including the biography of Genet, attempts to expand the existential account so as to accommodate social and political factors. From the late 1950s until his death, his writings are more explicitly political and Marxist, and questions can and have been raised about his last major work, *The Critique of Dialectical Reason* (1960), in terms of whether it involves a renunciation of his existentialist themes or whether its accounting for the ontology of groups remains compatible with the individualism of his existential ontology.

Sartre is more closely associated with French existentialism than any other figure. In fact, his identification with existentialism led several other existentialists – most notably Gabriel Marcel, Karl Jaspers, and Martin Heidegger – to dissociate themselves from the movement (in Marcel and Jaspers's cases, because of Sartre's atheism, while in Heidegger's case, the reasons have more to do with what he regarded as Sartre's humanism). But it is a mistake to see Sartre as the sole founder of philosophical existentialism: although he did not attend Alexandre Kojève's lectures on Hegel's *Phenomenology of Spirit*, there is little question that Kojève's existential and Marxist interpretation of Hegel had a profound influence on Sartre, especially in terms of Kojève's reading of the "master–slave dialectic." Similarly, it would be a mistake to see Sartre's relations with his longtime companion Simone de Beauvoir and his colleague Maurice Merleau-Ponty as one in which he exclusively influenced them. Rather, examining their respective texts shows Beauvoir to have been a constant interlocutor with and influence on Sartre, while one can see Sartre continually developing his ideas in response to criticisms placed to them in the texts of Merleau-Ponty, most notably in *Phenomenology of Perception* (1945) and *Adventures of the Dialectic* (1955).

Although Sartre remained largely outside the academic world, his influence on French intellectual life during the twentieth century is second to none. Aside from his influence on his fellow French existentialists, he had a profound impact on the postcolonial critiques of Frantz Fanon, Albert Memmi (1920–), Aimé Césaire (1913–), and others, in some cases – Fanon and Memmi in particular – writing prefaces to their works and assisting them in finding an audience. Sartre also wrote a preface to the landmark literary collection *Anthologie de la nouvelle poésie nègre et malgache de langue française*, edited in 1948 by Léopold Sédar Senghor (1906–2001), and he served on the initial editorial board of the important journal *Présence Africaine*, founded in 1947. Similarly, the persona he cultivated of the engaged intellectual became a part of the collective unconscious of French intellectuals; no less a critic of Sartre than Michel Foucault could, thus, respond in 1968 in *La Quinzaine littéraire* to the airing of an unedited radio interview he gave on Sartre from which he wished to have some comments removed, that "I think that Sartre's immense *oeuvre* and his political action will mark an epoch. It is true that several today work in another direction. I will never accept that one can compare – even in order to oppose them – the limited work of historical and methodological groundbreaking [*défrichement*] that I have undertaken with an *oeuvre* like his."[45]

While Sartre continued writing until his death, his impact on French philosophy dropped precipitously with the emergence of structuralism, a philosophical and methodological approach that positioned itself explicitly in opposition to Sartrean existentialism, humanism, and subjectivism. While the structuralists (in particular, Claude Lévi-Strauss; see, for example, the final chapter of *The Savage Mind*) responded

---

[45] Michel Foucault, "Une mise au point du Michel Foucault," *Dits et écrits I* (Paris: Éditions Gallimard, 1994), pp. 669–70. Foucault was not always so generous. In an interview a few years earlier, when asked to situate himself in relation to Sartrean humanism, he referred to *The Critique of Dialectical Reason* as "the magnificent and pathetic effort of a man of the nineteenth century to think the twentieth century" ("L'homme est-il mort?" *Dits et écrits I*, pp. 541–2).

critically to Sartre, the poststructuralists all but ignored him, rarely acknowledging his influence or challenging his ideas. Gilles Deleuze was one exception to this trend, commenting on several occasions on Sartre's work, which he appears to have known well, and going so far as to remark in 1977 that, in the context of the scholasticism of the Sorbonne and the phenomenology of the École Normale Supérieure, "Fortunately there was Sartre. Sartre was our Outside, he was really the breath of fresh air from the backyard . . . And Sartre has never stopped being that, not a model, a method or an example, but a little fresh air . . . an intellectual who singularly changed the situation of the intellectual. It is idiotic to wonder whether Sartre was the beginning or the end of something. Like all creative things and people, he is in the middle, he grows from the middle."[46] While there may have been something of an Oedipal situation working itself out among many of the poststructuralists, who sometimes speak about the overpowering cultural figure of Sartre in terms reminiscent of discourses on the Oedipal father, it would appear that Sartre's work may be due for a revival as the influence of the dominant figures within poststructural French philosophy itself begins to wane.

Ferdinand de Saussure (1857–1913) is widely regarded as the founder of modern linguistics. Born in Geneva, he studied at the Universities of Geneva, Berlin, and Leipzig, and taught first at the École Pratique des Hautes Études in Paris, and later as Professor of Linguistics at the University of Geneva, where he lectured on comparative grammar, Sanskrit, and general linguistics. While a student at Leipzig, Saussure published a monumental study of the vowel system in Indo-European languages (1878). This was to be his only work published during his lifetime. His tremendous influence is largely the result of the three lecture courses on general linguistics he gave in 1906–7, 1908–9, and 1910–11 at the University of Geneva, for which an account was put together from student notes following his death and published in 1916

---

[46]   Gilles Deleuze, *Dialogues*, trans. Hugh Tomlinson and Barbara Habberjam (New York: Columbia University Press, 1987), p. 12. See also Deleuze's refreshing appreciation of Sartre's importance in " 'Il a été mon maître,' " written a month after Sartre refused to accept the Nobel Prize for Literature, originally published in *Arts* (November 1964) and reprinted in Gilles Deleuze, *L'Île déserte et autres textes: Textes et entretiens 1953–1974*, ed. David Lapoujade (Paris: Éditions de Minuit, 2002), pp. 109–13. (" 'He Was My Teacher,' " trans. Mike Taormina, in *Desert Islands and Other Texts (1953–1974)*, ed. David Lapoujade [Cambridge, MA: MIT Press, 2003], pp. 77–80).

as the *Cours de linguistique générale* (English translation: *Course in General Linguistics*, ed. Charles Bally and Albert Sechehaye with the collaboration of Albert Riedlinger, trans. Wade Baskin [New York: Philosophical Library, 1959]).

Saussure's influence on linguistics and twentieth-century intellectual history has been profound. He is generally credited with having established linguistics as a science in which language is treated as a complete and closed system. In addition, he is credited with first introducing the term "semiology" as the science which studies the life of signs (*sēmeîon*) within society. (It should be noted that, in the American context, C. S. Peirce (1839–1914) was working at roughly the same time on a similar program that he called "semiotics.") Linguistics, for Saussure, was to be understood as a part of semiology, that part which studied signs within the system of language as a self-contained whole.

From the perspective of twentieth-century French philosophy, Saussure is credited with introducing the basic conceptual vocabulary of structuralism, though it should be noted that the term "structuralism" itself never appears in his *Cours*. What one does find is Saussure introducing the distinctions between *langue* (language) and *parole* (speech), between the synchronic and the diachronic, and between the signifier (*signifiant*) and the signified (*signifié*). By emphasizing the underlying structural features of a language and privileging the signifier over the signified and the synchronic over the diachronic, Saussure's work set the stage for the structuralist interventions of the 1950s and 1960s, as Claude Lévi-Strauss used the structural analysis of myth to found structural anthropology, Jacques Lacan offered a structural re-reading of Freudian psychoanalysis in which the unconscious was viewed to be structured like a language, Roland Barthes and others undertook the structural analysis of literature, and Louis Althusser sought to challenge orthodox and humanist readings of Marx in the name of a structural Marxism. One might also argue that, when Saussure wrote that "in language, there are only differences, *without positive terms*," he set the stage for all of those philosophers of difference that came to dominate the years following the rise and fall of structuralism.

Michel Serres (1930–) was born in Agen (Lot-et-Garonne, Aquitaine). He completed his *lycée* education and passed the *baccalauréat* examinations in both philosophy and elementary mathematics. He continued to work in both the arts and sciences, completing *licences* in math (1950), classics (1952), and philosophy (1953), and, quite exceptionally, took the entrance exam for the *grand écoles* in both science and literature. Serres attended the École navale from 1949 to 1952 and the École Normale Supérieure from 1952 to 1955. He completed his thesis for the *Diplome d'études supérieures*, directed by Gaston Bachelard, in 1954 on the difference between the Bourbaki algebraic method and the method of classical mathematicians. He passed the *agrégation* in 1955, finishing second, after which he served from 1956 to 1958 as an officer in the French National Maritime Service. During the 1960s, Serres taught with Michel Foucault, whose pupil he had been at the École Normale, at the University of Clermont-Ferrand and was invited by Foucault to join the Faculty of Philosophy at the experimental University of Paris VIII-Vincennes in 1968. That same year, he submitted his thesis for the *Doctorat d'État*, *Le Système de Leibniz et ses modèles mathématiques* ("Leibniz's System and its Mathematical Models"). He left Vincennes and his position in a Department of Philosophy for a Chair in the History of Science in the Department of History at the University of Paris I-Panthéon-Sorbonne, where he taught until his retirement in 1996. Serres also has taught regularly in North America since 1971: from 1971 to 1978, he was a Visiting Professor at Johns Hopkins University; from 1978 to 1981, a Visiting Professor at the University of Montreal; from 1981 to 1984, a Visiting Professor at the State University of New York at Buffalo; and, since 1984, Serres has been a Professor in the Department of French and Italian at Stanford University. Author of over thirty books of philosophy, science, and fiction, Serres was elected to the *Académie Française* in 1990, only the 39th philosopher to be included among the more than 700 "Immortals."

Serres has remained very much of an outsider to many of the developments associated with late twentieth-century French philosophy. As he puts it, there were four basic paths in philosophy that one could take, once having entered the academic world of the École Normale: Marxism, phenomenology, epistemology, or the human sciences.[47] He felt little attraction to either Marxism or phenomenology, and his strong background in mathematics and physics made him suspicious of both the epistemological and social scientific traditions. Where the human scientists grounded their structuralism in Saussurean linguistics, Serres's structuralism emerges from his knowledge of alge-

---

[47] Michel Serres and Bruno Latour, *Conversations on Science, Culture, and Time*, trans. Roxanne Lapidus (Ann Arbor: University of Michigan Press, 1995), pp. 7–8.

bra and topology; and where an epistemologist like Bachelard sought to keep his scientific and literary interests separate, Serres sees the literary and the scientific as mutually constitutive. In this sense, Hermes, the messenger of the gods and title of five of Serres's volumes, stands as an appropriate figure for Serres's work insofar as he continues to explore the communication that takes place between science and the arts. He also has been attentive to the moral responsibilities of the scientist and the relations between science and violence, and he credits Simone Weil, "the first philosopher really to speak of violence in all its dimensions,"[48] with being a major influence on this thinking.

Among his friends was Michel Foucault, with whom he worked at Clermont-Ferrand while Foucault was writing *The Order of Things*, and the two frequently discussed the structural relations that existed among the sciences, with Foucault focused on the human sciences and Serres more interested in the natural sciences. He was also close with René Girard, who he met at Johns Hopkins and with whom he was colleagues in the Department of French and Italian at Stanford.

Pierre Teilhard de Chardin (1881–1955) was born in Sarcenat (Puy-de-Dôme, Auvergne). He was educated in Jesuit schools and entered the Jesuit order in 1899. From 1905 to 1908, he taught physics and chemistry in a Jesuit college in Cairo. He was ordained in 1912, taught geology at the Institut Catholique de Paris from 1920 to 1928, and completed his doctorate in paleontology at the Sorbonne in 1922. From 1929 to 1945, he worked in various capacities as part of the geological service in China, where he was part of the group that discovered the skull of Peking man. He was named in 1938 Director of the Laboratory of Applied Geology at the École Pratique des Hautes Études in Paris, though the war prevented his returning to Paris until 1945. Although he was forbidden from putting forward his candidacy for a chair at the Collège de France, Teilhard was made Director of Research at the Centre National de la Recherche Scientifique in 1947 and member of the *Académie des Sciences* in 1950. While committed to showing that evolution was not incompatible with Christian doctrine, during his lifetime he was prohibited by the Vatican from publishing his philosophical works. Following his death, several of Teilhard's texts, most notably *The Phenomenon of Man* (1955), found a broad audience.

---

[48]   Serres and Latour, *Conversations on Science, Culture, and Time*, p. 18.

Part paleontology, part evolutionary biology, part Christian mysticism, part deist metaphysics, Teilhard's work bears some analogy with Bergson's – Bergson's associate Édouard Le Roy was Teilhard's close friend and frequent interlocutor – though Teilhard's commitment to the convergence of material evolution with the perfection of individual and social consciousness in the end probably bears closer analogy to so-called "new age metaphysics" than to Bergson's ideas about "creative evolution."

Trân Duc Thao (1917–93) was born in Vietnam into a family that worked for the colonial administration. After studying at the French *lycée* and one year studying law in Hanoi, he traveled to Paris, where he did his *hypokhâgne* at the Lycée Louis-le-Grand in 1936 and his *khâgne* at the Lycée Henri-IV. Thao studied at the École Normale Supérieure from 1939 to 1942, entering in the same class with Louis Althusser, Henri Birault (1918–90), and Jules Vuillemin. He submitted his thesis for the *Diplôme d'études supérieures* on "La Méthode phénoménologique chez Husserl" ("The Phenomenological Method in Husserl") to Jean Cavaillès in 1942, and passed his *agrégation* in philosophy the following year. His first-place finish in the *agrégation* exam that year, sharing the highest score with Jules Vuillemin, was an event celebrated by the press as a sign of the advantages brought by colonization. The irony of this fact was not lost on Thao, who when he eventually returned to Vietnam in 1950 participated actively in the movement for Vietnam's liberation.

In 1944, Thao traveled to Louvain to work at the Husserl Archives and was appointed as an attaché at the Centre National de la Recherche Scientifique. During the late 1940s, Thao wrote several articles on Indochina that were published in *Les Temps modernes*, and he was associated with that journal until 1950, when his growing dissatisfaction with existentialism led to a rupture with Sartre. After returning to Vietnam, Thao was named Professor in 1954, then Dean of the Faculty of History at the University of Hanoi. In 1958, however, he was accused of "Trotskyism" and subsequently forbidden from further teaching. His important works were written in Vietnam, as he sought to position Marxism as a solution to inconsistencies internal to the phenomenological commitment to idealism. In particular, Thao saw the privileging of phenomenological constitution as incapable of avoiding relativism and subjectivism unless it was grounded in materialism. By understanding constitution as a moment of production, Thao argued that dialectical materialism was the necessary solution to the problems faced by

Husserlian phenomenology's commitment to transcendental idealism. Thao's two major works, written in Vietnamese and translated into French (and then English) – *Phenomenology and Dialectical Materialism* (1951) and *Investigations into the Origins of Language and Consciousness* (1973) – were widely read and commented upon in France. Ricoeur felt it necessary to respond to Thao's critique of phenomenology,[49] while Lyotard noted the importance of Thao's attempt to conjoin phenomenology with Marxism,[50] and Derrida comments on several occasions about the influence Thao's work had on himself and other younger scholars of phenomenology in the 1950s and 1960s.[51]

Jules Vuillemin (1920–2001) was born in Pierrefontaine-les-Varans (Doubs, Franche-Comté). He studied at the Collège Saint-Clément in Metz and then the Lycée Louis-le-Grand, where he did his *khâgne* in 1937–8, before entering the École Normale Supérieure in 1939. In addition to his work at the École Normale, he also attended the classes of Bachelard, Bréhier, and Gouhier at the Sorbonne. Vuillemin submitted his thesis for the *Diplôme d'études supérieures* in 1942 to Jean Cavaillès on "The Problem of Method in Philosophy," and passed his *agrégation* in 1943, sharing the honor of finishing first with Trân Duc Thao. From 1943 to 1944, he taught at the *lycée* in Besançon. After the war, he returned to Paris and worked for five years as a researcher at the Centre National de la Recherche Scientifique. Vuillemin received his *Doctorat ès Lettres* in 1949, submitting two texts that explored existential questions: his principal thesis *Essai sur la signification de la mort* ("Essay on the Significance of Death") in 1948 and his *thèse complémentaire* on *L'Être et le travail. Les Conditions dialectiques de la psychologie et de la sociologie* ("Being and Work: The Dialectical Conditions of Psychology and Sociology"). He taught as *Maître de conférences* and Professor at the University of Clermont-Ferrand (1950–62) before being named, with the encouragement of Martial Guéroult, to the Chair in Philosophy of

---

[49]   See Paul Ricoeur's 1953 review of *Phenomenology and Dialectical Materialism*, translated as "Phenomenology" by Daniel J. Herman and Donald V. Morano, in *Southwestern Journal of Philosophy* 5:3 (1975): 149–68.

[50]   See Jean-François Lyotard, *Phenomenology*, trans. Brian Beakley (Albany: State University of New York Press, 1991), pp. 124–5, 128–9.

[51]   See, for example, his comments in "The Time of a Thesis: Punctuations," trans. Kathleen McLaughlin, in *Philosophy in France Today*, ed. Alan Montefiore (Cambridge: Cambridge University Press, 1983), p. 38.

Consciousness at the Collège de France in 1962, replacing Maurice Merleau-Ponty. He retired from teaching at the Collège in 1990.

Vuillemin was one of France's foremost historians of philosophy. Strongly influenced by the work of Martial Guéroult, his guiding interpretive thesis was that most important philosophical work was done in relation and response to the science of its time, and his work sought to demonstrate how the histories of science and philosophy illuminate each other. Vuillemin's interests in Kant and in epistemology and the philosophy of science led him to draw upon developments in the analytic tradition (Russell, Moore, Carnap, Goodman) in his effort to show how the metaphysical theories and scientific work of a particular age influenced and affected each other. He was sympathetic to the work of Foucault and was a significant supporter of Foucault's efforts to be named to a Chair in the Collège de France. Among his influential works are texts on the Kantian heritage in Fichte, Cohen, and Heidegger (1954), Kant's physics and metaphysics (1955), Aristotle (1967), Russell (1968), and contemporary theories of abstraction (1971). Two of Vuillemin's works have appeared in English translation: *Nécessité ou contingence. L'Aporie de Diodore et les systèmes philosophiques* (1984; English translation: *Necessity or Contingency: The Master Argument* [Stanford, CA: Center for the Study of Language and Information, 1996]), and *What are Philosophical Systems?* (Cambridge: Cambridge University Press, 1986).

Jean Wahl (1888–1974) was born in Marseilles. He studied at the Lycée Janson-de-Sailly and did one year of *khâgne* at the Lycée Louis-le-Grand (1906–7) before entering the École Normale Supérieure, where he studied from 1907 to 1910. In 1909, he submitted his thesis for the *Diplôme d'études supérieures*, "Contribution to the Study of Pluralist Tendencies in Contemporary English and American Philosophies," passed his *agrégation* in 1910, finishing first, and completed his *Doctorat ès Lettres* in 1920 with the submission of a principal thesis on *Les Philosophies pluralistes d'Angleterre et d'Amérique* ("Pluralist Philosophies in England and America"), and a *thèse complémentaire* on "Le Rôle de l'instant chez Descartes" ("The Role of the Idea of the Moment in the Philosophy of Descartes"). Wahl taught at *lycées* in Saint-Quentin, Nancy, Tours, and Mans before joining the philosophy faculties at the Universities of Besançon (1918), Nancy (1920), Lyon (1923), and, in 1927, the Sorbonne, where he taught the history of philosophy, assuming a professor's chair in 1936. Wahl fled Paris in 1940, when Vichy anti-Semitism made it impossible for him to continue teaching. He was arrested in 1941, but friends intervened and he was able to leave France for the United States in 1942, where he taught at Mount Holyoke (1942–5) and Smith (1944–5) Colleges. He returned to Paris in 1945, resumed his Chair in Philosophy at the Sorbonne, and became an important figure in the French philosophical world. In 1946, Wahl founded the Collège Philosophique – an organization outside the university that provided a forum and audience for controversial and non-institutionally sanctioned thinkers to present their work – and he served as President of the Société Française de Philosophie from late 1960, following the death of Gaston Berger, until his own death.

Although few of his important works have been translated into English, Wahl has been a dominant figure in the history of twentieth-century French philosophy. His *La Malheur de la conscience dans la philosophie de Hegel* (1929; "The Unhappiness of Consciousness in the Philosophy of Hegel") is rightly credited as marking the beginning of the Hegel renaissance in France, as it drew attention away from the Hegel of the System and paid attention instead to the early, more existential Hegel. His *Vers le concret* (1932; "Toward the Concrete"), with its three chapters on William James, Gabriel Marcel's *Metaphysical Journal*, and Alfred North Whitehead, was one of the first works to move away from the spiritualism that dominated French philosophy toward the concrete data of human experience that would characterize existentialism, and his *Études kierkegaardiennes* (1938; "Kierkegaardian Studies") introduced Kierkegaard's work to France and was one of the first important works of French existentialism. But Wahl's greatest influence was as a teacher, educating students at the Sorbonne for almost forty years. Lecturing on Hegel, Kierkegaard, Nietzsche, Bergson, Husserl, Heidegger, and Plato, among others, those who worked closely with him and credited him with an influence upon their thinking, include Claude Lévi-Strauss, Michel Foucault, Jacques Derrida, Michel Butor, and Gilles Deleuze. His good friend Emmanuel Levinas speaks eloquently of Wahl's impact on himself and others:

> Jean Wahl – to whom I owe much – was on the lookout for everything that had a meaning, even outside the forms traditionally devoted to its manifestation. He was especially interested in the continuity between art and philosophy [Wahl himself was an accomplished poet]. He thought it necessary, besides the Sorbonne, to give the opportunity for non-academic discourses to be heard. For this he thus founded this College

in the Latin Quarter. It was a place where intellectual non-conformism –
and even what took itself to be such – was tolerated and expected.[52]

Simone Weil (1909–43) was born in Paris to agnostic, middle-class
Jewish parents. After completing her first *baccalauréat* at the Lycée
Fenelon in 1924, she enrolled in the Lycée Victor-Duruy to study
philosophy with René Le Senne. She received her *baccalauréat* in
philosophy in 1925, and did her *hypokhâgne* and *khâgne* (1925–8) at
the Lycée Henri-IV with Emile Chartier (better known by his pseudonym "Alain"), who would be an important influence on her later
thought. Weil entered the École Normale Supérieure in 1928, the only
woman to enter that year and only the fourth woman to enroll in the
Letters Section at the École Normale Supérieure-Rue d'Ulm (the first
three, Suzette Molino, Simone Pétrement, and Cleménce Ramnoux,
had enrolled in 1927).[53] She submitted her thesis for the *Diplôme
d'études supérieures* in 1930 on "Science et perfection dans Descartes"
("Science and Perfection in Descartes"), completed her degree at the
École Normale in 1931, and passed the *agrégation* that same year, the
thirteenth woman to pass the *agrégation* in philosophy.[54] Between 1931
and 1936, she taught at various *lycées* in Le Puy, Auxerre, Roanne, and
Bourges, taking a leave of absence for a year in 1934–5 to work in the
Renault factory at Billancourt, outside Paris.[55] Weil spent a short time

52   Emmanuel Levinas, *Ethics and Infinity*, trans. Richard A. Cohen (Pittsburgh, PA:
     Duquesne University Press, 1985), p. 55. Levinas's own text *Time and the Other*
     (trans. Richard A. Cohen [Pittsburgh, PA: Duquesne University Press, 1987]) was
     constructed from four lectures he gave at Wahl's *Collège*.
53   Simone Pétrement, *La Vie de Simone Weil* (Paris: Fayard, 1973), p. 94. Weil was in
     fact the ninth woman to enroll in the École Normale Supérieure, as five women had
     been admitted into the Sciences Section by 1928, the first being Marguerite
     Rouvière, who enrolled in 1910. (Nicole Hulin, "La Section des sciences de
     l'ENS," in *École Normale Supérieure: Le Livre du bicentenaire*, ed. Jean-François
     Sirinelli [Paris: Presses universitaires de France, 1994], p. 345.)
54   Three other women also passed the *agrégation* that year: Mlles. Pétrement and
     Ramnoux, and Mme. Gauclère (Centre d'Accueil et de Recherche des Archives
     Nationales (CARAN), Paris, carton AJ/16/8488).
55   Opened at the beginning of the twentieth century, the Renault factory at Billancourt
     was for over half a century the largest factory in France. With over 30,000 workers,
     it was also a center for union militancy and was the site of many violent confron-
     tations between workers and police throughout the century. Weil's 1934 *La Con-
     dition ouvrière* (Paris: Éditions Gallimard, 1951) was the first of many testimonial
     texts written about life on the assembly line. In later years Billancourt figures as a

in Spain in 1936 observing and participating with the republicans in the Civil War, but returned to Paris later that year. In 1940, she and her family left Paris for Marseilles, where she met the major influence in her later years, the Dominican priest Father Perrin. Although she began considering herself a Christian in 1939, her intimate conversations and correspondence about God, faith, and moral and social issues with Father Perrin never persuaded her to be baptized. In 1942, she traveled with her parents to America, but soon returned to London, where she joined the Free French Forces. She contracted tuberculosis and, refusing to eat more than the amount allotted to her countrymen in France, she died in a sanatarium on August 24, 1943.

Weil published none of her work while alive. Deeply influenced by the thought of Plato, Pythagoras, the Stoics, and Eastern philosophy, her published works are editions drawn from her letters, diaries, essays, and notebooks. These do not present any systematic doctrines. Instead, they offer a profound reflection on the "needs of the soul" informed by deep theological reflection and humanistic concern for the material and spiritual needs of others. These writings, along with the figure of Simone Weil as something of a modern saint, introduce several themes into French philosophy that have inspired many, including Emmanuel Levinas, Michel Serres, and Julia Kristeva, among others.

---

metonymy for the working class in Sartre's play *No Exit* ("Il ne faut pas désespérer Billancourt [One must not despair Billancourt]"), and played a crucial role as one of the centers of worker unrest during the events of May 1968. The factory was closed on May 27, 1992. For a discussion of the significance of the Renault factory at Billancourt, see Kristin Ross, *Fast Cars, Clean Bodies: Decolonization and the Reordering of French Culture* (Cambridge, MA: MIT Press, 1995), pp. 15–26.

Appendix 1

Understanding French Academic Culture

It is impossible to understand the evolution of French philosophy in the twentieth century without understanding some of the unique aspects of French academic culture that distinguish its educational institutions from those of countries like the United States or Great Britain. The centralization of its institutions, their administration through several extremely influential bodies, many of which are organs of the state apparatus, its smallness in terms of the number of schools to which one had to attend, almost all in Paris, if one was to have a successful career in academia, make it quite unique among western countries. In addition, among the three most influential educational institutions – the Sorbonne, the *Grandes Écoles*, and the Collège de France – the changes in their respective organizations and the different relations among their faculties and students over the century have marked several generations of French philosophy students.

Equally important in terms of its effects on developments in French philosophy is a corollary of this centralization and smallness, namely, that many of the leading philosophical figures had very similar educational upbringings: they often went to the same schools, sat in the same classrooms, studied with the same professors, took the same state examinations, and competed for and often occupied the same faculty positions. A few of the more famous and significant examples: the 1924 entering class at the École Normale Supérieure included among the 29 students admitted in arts and letters Raymond Aron, Georges Canguilhem, Daniel Lagache, Paul Nizan, and Jean-Paul Sartre; in spring 1929, the philosophy faculty at the Lycée Janson-de-Sailly included Simone de Beauvoir, Claude Lévi-Strauss, and Maurice Merleau-Ponty; the audience for Alexandre Kojève's Hegel lectures at the École Pratique des Hautes Études between 1933 and 1939 included Raymond Aron, Georges Bataille, André Breton, Jean-Toussaint Desanti, Aron Gurwitsch,

Jacques Lacan, Maurice Merleau-Ponty, Raymond Queneau, and Eric Weil; in 1942–3, Jean Hyppolite, Ferdinand Alquié, and Jean-Paul Sartre all taught the very same class (the *khâgne* or *première supérieure*) at the three most prestigious Paris *lycées* – the Lycées Henri-IV, Louis-le-Grand, and Condorcet, respectively – while Maurice Merleau-Ponty was himself teaching at another Paris *lycée* that did not at that time offer the *première supérieure*, the Lycée Carnot, and Mikel Dufrenne would have been teaching at yet another Paris *lycée*, the Lycée Charlemagne, were he not in a prisoner of war camp in 1942.[1] To understand the intellectual formation of the important French philosophers of the twentieth century, it is important to understand the academic institutions in which they studied, taught, and worked, and to that end, I will here explain briefly some of the academic institutions and their features as well as some of the basic terminology of the French educational system.

Let us begin with a few words about some of the significant academic institutions in France. The first is the Sorbonne and the University of Paris, whose histories are closely intertwined. One of the first universities, whose history dates to the twelfth century, the University of Paris was first officially recognized in 1200 by King Philippe-Auguste and its importance was proclaimed in a papal decree by Gregory IX in 1231. The university was organized originally around four faculties: three "superior" faculties – Theology, Canon Law, and Medicine – and one "inferior" faculty – Arts. In 1257, Robert de Sorbon (1201–74), chaplain and confessor of King Louis IX, founded for poor theology students a college named "La Communauté des Pauvres Maîtres Étudiants en Théologie" that, by the end of the thirteenth century, was popularly known as "La Sorbonne." While technically only a single college within the larger University of Paris, the Sorbonne's Faculty of Theology was unquestionably the most powerful association within the university and through it, the Sorbonne came to be identified as early as the fifteenth century with the entire university.

During these years, the Sorbonne's Faculty of Theology was a site of theological, educational, and political power, having been granted the right to censure (i.e., to suppress works in the name of the king and the

---

[1] I am here leaving aside other features of this smallness, like having the same lovers, friends, and enemies (e.g., Jacques Lacan married the ex-wife of Georges Bataille), which also frequently had some significant effects on what happened philosophically. For a sociological account of the French academic world, see the analyses by Pierre Bourdieu in *Homo Academicus*, trans. Peter Collier (Stanford, CA: Stanford University Press, 1988).

pope). One might recall here Descartes's *Meditations on First Philosophy*, which opens with a plea "To those most learned and distinguished men, the Dean and Doctors of the sacred Faculty of Theology at Paris," that they take his work under their protection. The Sorbonne retained its influence as the center of Christian education – and higher learning in France in general – until the French Revolution. But while the Sorbonne was a dynamic site of higher education and the unrivaled center of orthodox theological teaching from the thirteenth to fifteenth centuries – its faculty during this period included, among others, Albertus Magnus, St. Bonaventure, and Thomas Aquinas – religious disputes and the conservative orthodoxy of the Theological Faculty led to a decline in the reputation of the Sorbonne during the sixteenth and seventeenth centuries. One result of this decline was the formation in 1530 of a new institution that would become the Collège de France.

Following the Revolution, the Sorbonne was closed from 1793 until it was reinstated by Napoleon in 1806 as an imperial, and more secular, university. Following Napoleon's wishes, a centralized administration governed the Sorbonne, and the Faculties of Law and Medicine regained their prominence. The Faculty of Theology was also reinstated, and two new faculties, of Letters and of Sciences, were established with decidedly secondary positions relative to the other three faculties.[2] In the humanities in particular, the primary function of the Sorbonne evolved toward the training of teachers, and a very powerful professoriat developed a system that allowed it to reproduce itself quite effectively. For example, until 1968, the Philosophy Faculty at the Sorbonne was always well represented on the juries that judged the *agrégation de philosophie* and the presiding officers of these juries were exclusively drawn from the Sorbonne faculty.[3]

[2] Among the first eight Chairs in the Faculty of Letters created on May 6, 1809 was one in philosophy, the Chair de Philosophie et Opinions des Philosophes, held initially by Claude-Emmanuel Pastoret (1755–1840). It was renamed the Chair de la Histoire de la Philosophie when it was transferred to its second holder, Pierre-Paul Royer-Collard (1763–1845), on October 24, 1810. The ninth Chair in the Faculty of Letters, created on September 19, 1809, was also in philosophy, the Chair de Philosophie, whose first holder was Pierre Laromiguière (1756–1837).

[3] In 1971, François Dagognet (1924–), a professor at the University of Lyon, became the first president of the *jury d'agrégation* for philosophy not to be simultaneously affiliated with the University of Paris. Dagognet, whose work concentrated in aesthetics and ethics, taught at Lyon from 1953 to 1986 before moving to a position at the University of Paris I-Panthéon-Sorbonne, where he taught until becoming Emeritus Professor in 1995.

During the student uprisings of May 1968, the Sorbonne was a major focus of attention and it was substantially decentralized in 1971 in accordance with a plan (the "Law of Orientation") devised in 1968 by Minister of Education Edgar Faure. Prior to 1968, several changes in the structure of the faculties of the University of Paris had already taken place, two of which are particularly relevant to French philosophy. First, the Faculty of (Catholic) Theology had been officially disbanded in 1885, with religion eventually reassigned the following year as a subject for scientific investigation at the new Fifth Section of the École Pratique des Hautes Études. Second, the "Faculté des lettres" had been officially renamed the "Faculté des lettres et sciences humaines" by a ministerial decree in July 1958, three months after the creation of a *licence* and *Doctorat de troisième cycle* in sociology in April 1958. Prior to 1958, sociology had been institutionally situated as a sub-field within philosophy, and sociologists typically taught as members of departments of philosophy.[4]

According to Faure's reorganization, the five faculties of the former university – Law and Economic Sciences, Medicine, Sciences, Letters and Human Sciences, and Pharmacy – were divided and redistributed among thirteen campuses of the University of Paris. Among these, the old Sorbonne facilities in the Latin Quarter were divided into four campuses, three of which continue to bear the Sorbonne name: University of Paris I-Panthéon-Sorbonne (primary site of the former Faculty of Law and now the largest campus, with disciplinary emphases in law, politics, humanities, and economics), Paris III-Sorbonne Nouvelle, Paris IV-Paris-Sorbonne (primary site of the former Faculty of Letters and Human Sciences), and Paris V-René Descartes (originally a university of human and life sciences and primary site of the former Faculty of Medicine). Other campuses in the present University of Paris include Paris II-Panthéon-Assas, Paris VI-Pierre et Marie Curie (Jussieu), Paris VII-Denis Diderot (Jussieu), Paris VIII-Vincennes-St. Denis (the experimental campus established to satisfy student demands for more interdisciplinary courses of study; originally established in Vincennes

---

[4] For an interesting discussion of sociology in the context of the French university, see Alain Drouard, "A propos du statut de la sociologie et du sociologue en France," in *Le Personnel de l'enseignement supérieur en France aux XIXe et XXe siècles*, the proceedings of a colloquium organized by the Institut d'Histoire Moderne et Contemporaine and the École des Hautes Études en Sciences Sociales, June 25–26, 1984 (Paris: Editions du CNRS, 1985), pp. 167–75.

in 1968, the campus moved to St. Denis in 1978), Paris IX-Paris-Dau-phine, Paris X-Nanterre (founded in 1964 to supplement the Sorbonne's Faculty of Letters and Human Sciences, it was at the origin of the student revolts of 1968 and became part of the University of Paris during the 1971 reorganization), Paris-Sud XI-Orsay, Paris XII-Val de Marne, and Paris XIII-Villetaneuse, Saint-Denis, Bobigny.

In the preceding pages, two points regarding the Sorbonne are most important. First, prior to the 1968 reorganization, the "Sorbonne" is roughly equivalent to the "University of Paris," and its faculty domin-ated academic philosophy in France. Second, after the reorganization of the 1960s, the Sorbonne was not nearly as central to French philo-sophical life as it had been. While Paris I-Panthéon-Sorbonne and Paris IV-Paris-Sorbonne remained the largest humanities campuses with the largest philosophy faculties, Paris X-Nanterre – whose faculty included Paul Ricoeur (who taught at Nanterre from 1966 until the end of his career and served for a time as Dean of the Faculty of Arts), Mikel Dufrenne (1965–74), Henri Lefebvre (1965–73), Jean-François Lyotard (1967–72), and Emmanuel Levinas (1967–73) – also attracted large numbers of philosophy students. So too did the experimental campus at Paris VIII-Vincennes-St. Denis, where many of the best-known French philosophers of the past four decades have taught, including Gilles Deleuze (from 1968–87), Jean-François Lyotard (1972–87), Alain Badiou (1968–99), François Châtelet (1969–82), and Michel Serres (1968–76).

In addition to the Sorbonne and the University of Paris, there are two other important academic institutions that have had a significant influ-ence on the history of philosophy in France. The oldest is the Collège de France, founded by François I in 1530 as a forum for "Royal Lectur-ers." The original "faculty" included three lecturers for Hebrew, two for Greek, and one for mathematics, whose function was to instruct in fields not included among the regular curriculum of the University of Paris. The lectures were intended to be open to the public and free. In 1542, the first philosopher, Franciscus Vicomercatus (Francesco Vimer-cati, 1512?–71?), was named to the faculty of the Collège Royal with a chair in Greek and Latin philosophy, which he held until 1567. In 1551, Henri II expanded the curriculum with the appointment of a second chair in Greek and Latin philosophy, given to the logician and rhetor-ician Petrus Ramus (Pierre de la Ramée, 1515–72), whose unorthodox and critical approach to Aristotle had led to his banishment from teaching at the University of Paris by the more orthodox Aristotelians.

The faculty expanded to twenty in the eighteenth century and forty at the end of the nineteenth century. First called the Collège Royal, then the Collège Impérial, the name was changed officially to the Collège de France in 1870. The Collège is not part of the regular university system, and it offers no diplomas[5] and gives no exams. Instead, the faculty of the Collège, upon election by current faculty members, offer public lectures and seminars. Election to a chair at the Collège is evidence that one has risen to the very top of one's field of expertise, and many of France's greatest scientists and scholars have taught there, including, among a very distinguished list, Georges Cuvier (1800–32), Jules Michelet (1838–52), Claude Bernard (1855–78), Ernest Renan (1862–4, 1870–92), Marcel Mauss (1931–42), Émile Benveniste (1937–72), Paul Valéry (1937–45), Georges Dumézil (1949–68), Fernand Braudel (1950–72), Claude Lévi-Strauss (1959–82), Jean-Pierre Vernant (1975–84), Roland Barthes (1977–80), and Pierre Bourdieu (1981–2002)

In the twentieth century, there have been several chairs in philosophy at the Collège de France. At the start of the century, there were three chairs: Jean Izoulet held a Chair in Social Philosophy from 1897 to 1929, after which it became the Chair in Sociology first held by Marcel Mauss (1931–42); Gabriel Tarde held the Chair in Modern Philosophy, created in 1874 for Jean Nourrisson, from 1900 to 1904, and Henri Bergson held

---

[5] Because the Collège de France grants no degrees, the prestige of a Chair at the Collège comes at the expense of directing student research and, thereby, influencing careers and exerting direct influence on the academic world. One could argue that while Michel Foucault's influence on culture was enhanced by his position at the Collège, the relative absence of Foucault's influence on academic philosophy in France is a direct consequence of his leaving the university system for the Collège. A similar claim could be made, earlier in the century, for Bergson's relative lack of influence within the academy, when compared to Brunschvicg or Durkheim. Pierre Bourdieu, on the other hand, retained his academic influence by virtue of his position as *Directeur d'études* at the École Pratique des Hautes Études and the École des Hautes Études en Sciences Sociales, and the students whose work he directed and helped publish will guarantee his influence on subsequent generations of students of sociology. One must wonder whether the relatively rapid decline of influence in France of the best-known poststructuralist philosophers (Foucault, Deleuze, Lyotard, Derrida) is in large part a consequence of their not having been institutionally empowered, by virtue of teaching at the Sorbonne, to direct the dissertations of those students who would themselves come to occupy significant seats of academic influence. Quite the opposite is the case among those with whom these poststructuralist philosophers worked in the United States and the United Kingdom.

the Chair in Greek and Latin Philosophy from 1900 to 1904.[6] Following
Tarde's death in 1904, Bergson took over the Chair in Modern Philosophy, which he held until 1921. After Bergson's retirement, the Chair
in Modern Philosophy was held in subsequent years by Édouard Le Roy
(1921–40), Louis Lavelle (1941–51), and Maurice Merleau-Ponty
(1952–61). In 1962, this chair was renamed the Chair in the Philosophy
of Consciousness upon the election of Jules Vuillemin, who held
the chair until 1990. After his retirement, Vuillemin's chair was not
replaced by a Chair in Philosophy.

For much of the twentieth century, a second chair in philosophy was
traditionally held by a historian of philosophy. The first possessor of
this chair was Étienne Gilson, who was Chair in the History of Philosophy of the Middle Ages from 1932 to 1950. Gilson's chair was
renamed by its next three possessors. Martial Guéroult held the Chair
in the History and Technology of Philosophical Systems from 1951 to
1962, Jean Hyppolite held his Chair in the History of Philosophical
Thought from 1963 to 1968, and Michel Foucault held the Chair in the
History of Systems of Thought from 1970 to 1984. After Foucault's
death, the chair was redefined[7] with the election of Gilles-Gaston
Granger in 1986 as the Chair in Comparative Epistemology. Following
Granger's retirement in 1991, there was no holder of a chair in phil-
osophy at the Collège until the analytic philosopher and Wittgenstein
scholar Jacques Bouveresse was elected in 1994 to the newly created
Chair in the Philosophy of Language and Consciousness, which he
began to occupy in 1995. In addition to Bouveresse's chair, two new
chairs in philosophy were created in 1999 – in Philosophy of the
Biological and Medical Sciences and in Philosophy and History of
Scientific Concepts – though neither had been filled by century's end.
The initial holders of these chairs, both elected in 2000 and delivering

---

[6]   After Bergson moved to the Chair in Modern Philosophy, the Chair in Greek and
      Latin Philosophy was eliminated, though a new chair was created in 1981 for Pierre
      Hadot in "History of Hellenistic and Roman Thought," which he occupied from
      1982 to 1991.

[7]   Since around the middle of the twentieth century, it has become increasingly the
      case that chairs are not associated with a particular field of inquiry, but are created
      anew to fit the research interests of its new occupant. So, while it is accurate to say
      that Merleau-Ponty held the chair formerly held by Bergson, or that Foucault held
      the chair formerly held by Guéroult and Hyppolite, it is not really accurate to say
      that Bouveresse holds the chair formerly held by Foucault. Foucault's chair lapsed
      after his death, and an entirely new chair was created for Bouveresse.

their inaugural lectures in 2001, were Anne Fagot-Largeault and Ian Hacking, respectively.

The other important academic institution is in fact a group of institutions known as the *Grandes Écoles*. The designation *grande école* applies to several public or private institutions of higher education whose students are admitted following a rigorous preparatory course (typically lasting two years) and a competitive examination. *Grandes écoles* provide high-level education in humanities, social sciences, engineering, business, and civil service subjects. The first of the *grandes écoles*, the École Nationale des Ponts et Chaussées, was set up in 1747, followed by the École des Mines in 1783. In addition to these two schools specializing in engineering studies, other influential *grandes écoles* include the École Centrale (also specializing in engineering), the École Polytechnique (familiarly known as l'X, which has a reputation for educating senior civil servants), the École de Gestion et de Commerce (specializing in management and business studies), the École Nationale d'Administration (specializing in national administration for aspiring senior civil servants), and the Institut d'Études Politiques (familiarly known as Sciences Po, which emphasizes issues in the social sciences and public policy). In the context of philosophy, and the academic world more generally, without question the most important *grande école* is the École Normale Supérieure (ENS), which was founded following the French Revolution in 1794 and has been traditionally the school that recruits the most promising *lycée* graduates in the liberal arts with the expectation that its graduates will enter the intellectual elite following completion of their course of study.

Until the middle of the twentieth century, it was a virtual requirement for academic success in France for one to attend the École Normale Supérieure on the rue d'Ulm in Paris, and this was particularly true for academic success in a department of philosophy.[8] The ENS–rue d'Ulm was founded in 1794 on the basis of a report issued on October

[8]   Paul Ricoeur, Gilles Deleuze, and Jean-François Lyotard are perhaps the only three major French philosophers of the past half century to have had successful academic careers and *not* to have studied at the École Normale Supérieure. (In Ricoeur's and Lyotard's cases, it was because they were unable to pass the competitive entrance exam. Deleuze, on the other hand, appears to be one of the very few important French philosophers not to have tried to enter the ENS.) In addition to the institutional links between the École Normale and the Sorbonne, the faculty of the Sorbonne has always had a high percentage of *normaliens*: in 1910, 80 percent of the Sorbonne's faculty of letters were former students of the École Normale; in

30 by Joseph Lakanal, then President of the National Convention's Committee of Public Instruction. In its first article, Lakanal's report called for the founding "in Paris of a *Normal School* to which would be called from all parts of the Republic citizens already instructed in useful branches of knowledge, so that they might learn, from the most skilled professors, the *art of teaching*."[9] Originally independent from the University of Paris, the ENS was attached to the University of Paris through the Decree of November 10, 1903, which specified that students at the ENS (*normaliens*) could, like other University of Paris students, enroll in courses taught by the Faculty of Letters and the Faculty of Sciences. While *normaliens* had always done this informally, the 1903 decree set up an official structure, and the director of the École Normale Supérieure now began issuing an annual report under the auspices of the University of Paris, much like the reports of the Deans of the other five faculties.[10] Because the École itself awards no university diplomas, *normaliens* must also enroll at a university in order to obtain their graduate and postgraduate university degrees, and the vast majority of *normaliens* have received their *Doctorats* from the University of Paris.

The size of the entering class at the ENS has always been quite small,[11] with the result that intense friendships and rivalries often

---

1946, the percentage had dropped, but it was still 44 percent. (These figures come from Jean-François Sirinelli, *Génération intellectuelle: Khâgneux et Normaliens dans l'entre-deux-guerres* [Paris: Presses universitaires de France, 1994], p. 158.) Today, the role of the École Normale may not be as essential to academic success in France as it once was, but its impact on French intellectual culture is still profound. For example, in 1985, 23 of the 49 professors at the Collège de France were former *normaliens*, as were 9 of the 40 members of the *Académie Française*. For an interesting account of the intellectual impact of the École Normale Supérieure, see Rémy Rieffel, "Les Normaliens dans la société intellectuelle," in Jean-François Sirinelli, ed., *École Normale Supérieure: Le Livre du bicentaire* (Paris: Presses universitaires de France, 1994), pp. 215–39.

9   Quoted in Sirinelli, ed., *École Normale Supérieure: Le Livre du bicentaire*, pp. 14–15.
10   See André Tuillier, *Histoire de l'Université de Paris et de la Sorbonne. Vol. 2: De Louis XIV à la crise de 1968* (Paris: Nouvelle Librarie de France, 1994), p. 445.
11   For example, the ENS Lettres section admitted only 23 students in 1900; in 1930, 32 students enrolled; in 1958, 38 students enrolled. More recently, the ENS has accepted a larger entering class: in 1970, 50 students were accepted into the ENS-rue d'Ulm, with an additional 35 accepted at the ENS for women at Sèvres, and in both 1998 and 1999, following the merger of the ENS-rue d'Ulm and Sèvres, 100 students were admitted to the Lettres section. These figures come from the *Supplément Historique* to the *Annuaire de l'Association des anciens élèves de l'École*

develop. As was already mentioned, the entering class or *promotion* of the 1924 Lettres section included among the 29 students admitted Raymond Aron, Georges Canguilhem, Daniel Lagache, Paul Nizan, and Jean-Paul Sartre. Jean Hyppolite and Maurice Patronnier de Gandillac entered the following year, and Maurice Merleau-Ponty entered the year after that. The limited places at the ENS are won by means of a grueling competitive examination – the *concours* – for which students prepare over two years following their *baccalauréat*, in classes designed specifically for the entrance examinations (known in ENS slang as the *hypokhâgne* and *khâgne*).[12] While students from all over France compete for these limited places, the vast majority of students admitted have traditionally come from Paris, and from the *khâgne* in two particular *lycées*: Louis-le-Grand and Henri-IV.[13] In 1938, Célestin Bouglé, Director of the ENS, described the *concours* this way: of the six written exams, "there is a Latin translation, a Latin composition, a Greek translation (which may be replaced by a translation from a modern language by the minority who intend to teach modern languages in a secondary school), then three essays, one on French literature, one on philosophy, and one on a historical subject." These papers are written over eight days, with four hours for the translations and six hours for the essays. For those who pass the written part of the *concours*, there remained an oral examination to be passed before entrance into the ENS was assured.[14]

---

normale supérieure, published every five years. It is worth noting that there are at present four Écoles Normales Supérieures, which were reorganized in 1985. In addition to the ENS-rue d'Ulm (which alone is referred to simply as the École Normale Supérieure), there are also the ENS-Fontenay-St. Cloud (the ENS-Fontenay was created for female students in 1880 and the ENS-St. Cloud was created for male students in 1882; they were united in 1985), ENS-Cachan (created in 1912), and ENS-Lyon (created in 1985).

[12]   The origin of the term *khâgne* is unclear. Sometimes spelled *Cagne*, the *Dictionnaire Robert* claims that the word first appears in 1888 and suggests that it was a term expressing contempt used by the students in the preparatory classes in the sciences for the École Polytechnique or the École Spéciale Militaire de Saint-Cyr to refer to literature students whose "aptitudes physiques" were not of the highest quality.

[13]   From 1921 to 1956, of the 1,082 students admitted into the ENS Lettres section, 799 did their *khâgne* in Paris, 283 at *lycées* outside of Paris. And from Paris, 461 of those admitted did *khâgne* at Lycée Louis-le-Grand and 251 at Lycée Henri-IV. These figures come from *Revue Universitaire* 65, No. 5 (Nov.-Dec. 1956): 290–1.

[14]   Célestin Bouglé, *The French Conception of "Culture Générale" and its Influence upon Instruction* (New York: Columbia University Press, 1938), p. 15. For more information about the *concours*, see Robert J. Smith, *The Ecole Normale Supérieure and the Third Republic* (Albany: State University of New York Press, 1982), ch. 2.

In 1985, the ENS took on a new structure with the merger of the ENS-rue d'Ulm and École Normale Supérieure for Girls at Sèvres, which was founded in 1881 as part of a series of initiatives to advance the cause of women's education in France.[15] In the words of article two of the Decree of August 26, 1987 that established the new ENS, it would "provide a cultural and scientific training of the highest standard for pupils intending to pursue careers in research, whether pure or applied; in university and secondary school teaching; and, more generally, in public service and administration."[16] In addition to philosophy, the ENS is currently comprised of five other humanities departments (History, Classics, Literature and Languages, Social Sciences, Geography) and seven science departments (Pure and Applied Mathematics, Cognitive Studies, Computer Science, Physics, Chemistry, Biology, Earth–Atmosphere–Ocean). The primary mission of the ENS remains the training of future teachers and professors, though today more non-academic careers are launched at the ENS than has been the case in past years.

One other educational institution has also had a large impact on philosophical developments in France in the twentieth century: the École Pratique des Hautes Études (EPHE). The EPHE was created by a decree issued by the Minister of Public Education, Victor Duruy, in 1868 as an experimental research institution that would operate autonomous from the Sorbonne and would not be a diploma-granting institution. The EPHE was organized initially around four thematic sections: mathematics, physics and chemistry, natural history and physiology,

---

[15]   Although the ENS for Girls at Sèvres had existed since 1881, women had been studying in the Science section at the ENS-rue d'Ulm since Marguerite Rouvière passed the *concours* in 1910. According to an official decree by the Ministry of Public Instruction, however, "girls" were not to be granted the title of "student" (*élève*), but were to be considered *boursières d'études*. This was the situation for the next four women admitted into the Science section: Jeanne Rouvière (1912), Georgette Parize (1917), Madeleine Chaumont (1919), and Marie-Louise Jacotin (1926, who entered with the second highest score on the *concours*). The situation changed in 1927, as Rouvière, Parize, and Chaumont asked for, and were granted, the title of "former student" (*ancien élève*), with all the accompanying rights and privileges, and the title "student" was extended as well to Jacotin, and to the first three women accepted that year into the Lettres section at the ENS: Suzette Molino, Simone Pétrement, and Clémence Ramnoux. This information is drawn from Nicole Hulin, "La Section des sciences de l'ENS," in Sirinelli, ed., *Ecole Normale Supérieure: Le Livre du bicentenaire*, pp. 344–5.

[16]   The full text of the statute of the École Normale Supérieure, Decree No. 87–695 of August 26, 1987 can be found at www.ens.fr/ecole/statut_en.php.

and history and philology. Over the years, the EPHE evolved through the creation of two additional sections that have had more direct and significant influence on philosophical developments: the Fifth Section, for the scientific study of religion, was created in 1886, the year following the dissolution of the Faculty of Theology at the Sorbonne, and its faculty has included Marcel Mauss, Étienne Gilson, Georges Dumézil, and Claude Lévi-Strauss. The Sixth Section, created in 1947, was organized around the social or human sciences.[17] The first president of the Sixth Section was the *Annales* historian Lucien Febvre, who along with Fernand Braudel (the Sixth Section's second president, serving from 1956 to 1972), both founded the *Annales* school and were the prime movers behind the creation of the Sixth Section.

In 1975, the Sixth Section of the École Pratique was renamed the École des Hautes Études in Sciences Sociales (EHESS), and it was authorized to grant recognized doctoral diplomas (*Doctorat de troisième cycle* and *Doctorat d'État*). While associated with historians for much of its existence (to date, five of its six presidents have been historians), the EHESS has always been an institution that welcomed interdisciplinary research. It also allowed intellectuals to teach who were not necessarily credentialed in ways that would permit them to hold university posts. As a consequence, in addition to being the site for established professors like Pierre Bourdieu, Jacques Derrida, François Furet, and Alain Touraine, the EPHE and EHESS have also hosted seminars by such important intellectual figures as Roland Barthes, Michel de Certeau, Lucien Goldmann, Georges Gurvitch, Alexandre Kojève, Alexandre Koyré, Milan Kundera, and Herbert Marcuse. The EPHE has continued to evolve, and today only the third (life and earth sciences), fourth (historical and philological sciences), and fifth (religious sciences) sections still exist as part of the EPHE.

Before turning away from academic institutions, a few words are in order regarding a recently created philosophical institution: the Collège International de Philosophie. Founded on October 10, 1983, the Collège is an autonomous, state-supported research and teaching institution

---

[17]   Victor Duruy had originally intended there to be a Fifth Section, for the economic sciences, as part of the initial organization of the EPHE, but his hope for this section remained unfulfilled until the creation of the Sixth Section in 1947. For further discussion of the EPHE, see Terry Nichols Clark, *Prophets and Patrons: The French University and the Emergence of the Social Sciences* (Cambridge, MA: Harvard University Press, 1973), pp. 42–51.

proposed by a government "mission" composed of Jacques Derrida, François Châtelet, Jean-Pierre Faye, and Dominique Lecourt in response to a request from the Minister of Research and Industry, Jean-Pierre Chevènement. Chevènement charged the mission with investigating the possibility of creating an institution that would allow for experimental and interdisciplinary work in philosophy that could not be accommodated within the more constraining structures of the university. Free and open to the public, the Collège began operations in late 1983 with Derrida as its first director, and it supports research, organizes colloquia and lectures, and offers courses in six areas of intersection with philosophy: science; art and literature; law and economics; politics; psychoanalysis; and philosophy.

One additional uniquely French institution, though not strictly speaking an educational institution, that plays a role in the lives of several philosophers, especially early in the twentieth century, should also briefly be mentioned: the Institut de France. Created in 1795 to "protect and perfect the arts and sciences," the Institut de France is today the union of five learned societies that had been suppressed following the French Revolution: the *Académie Française* (founded in 1635 under the regime of Louis XIII by Cardinal Richelieu); the *Académie des Inscriptions et Belles-Lettres* (founded as the *Académie Royale des Inscriptions et Médailles* in 1663 by Jean-Baptiste Colbert, a leading advisor of Louis XIV and Controller General of Finance from 1665, renamed in 1716); the *Académie des Sciences* (founded in 1666 by Colbert); the *Académie des Beaux-Arts* (the union in 1816 of the *Académie de Peinture et de Sculpture*, founded in 1648 by Charles Le Brun, and the *Académie d'Architecture*, founded by Colbert in 1671); and the *Académie des Sciences morales et politiques* (founded in 1795, abolished by Napoleon as dangerous to the state in 1803, and reinstated in 1832).

While many philosophers have, over the years, been elected "Members of the Institute" into the *Académie des Sciences morales et politiques*, some also have been elected to the more prestigious *Académie Française*. With membership limited at any one time to 40, selection as one of the "Immortals" is considered to be a recognition of supreme achievement. Of the approximately 700 members of the *Académie Française* since its founding in 1635, 30 are classified as philosophers, including Fontenelle (elected 1691), Montesquieu (1728), Voltaire (1746), D'Alembert (1754), Condillac (1768), Condorcet (1782), and Destutt de Tracy (1808). In the twentieth century, ten philosophers have been elected to the *Académie*

Française: Émile Boutroux (1912), Henri Bergson (1914), Paul Hazard (1940), Édouard Le Roy (1945), Ernest Seillière (1946), Étienne Gilson (1946), Jean Rostand (1959), Jean Guitton (1961), Henri Gouhier (1979), and Michel Serres (1990). In addition to Serres, the twentieth century ended with two other members of the *Académie* whose work has informed and been informed by philosophy in France: Claude Lévi-Strauss (1973) and Léopold Sédar Senghor (1983; died 2001).

One final organization worth mentioning that, over the years, has supported the work of many of the philosophers mentioned in the preceding pages is the Centre National de la Recherche Scientifique (CNRS, the French National Center for Scientific Research). The origin of the CNRS can be traced to 1901 and the creation of the Caisse des Recherches Scientifiques (CRS). The Caisse Nationale de la Recherche Scientifique was created in 1935, bringing together both the CRS and the CNS, the Caisse Nationale des Sciences, which had been founded in 1930. The organization expanded again in 1938, as the Caisse Nationale de la Recherche Scientifique merged with the Office National des Recherches Scientifiques. This organization, then named the Centre National de la Recherche Scientifique Appliquée, was re-organized by official decree of President Albert Lebrun on October 19, 1939 as the Centre National de la Recherche Scientifique or the CNRS, with the explicit aim of bringing together both pure and applied re-search in a single institution under the authority of the Ministry of National Education. Although the primary focus of research at the CNRS has been in the sciences, its funds have supported the work of many social scientists and philosophers, including Roland Barthes, Pierre Bourdieu, Georges Canguilhem, Pierre Hadot, Luce Irigaray, Michèle Le Doeuff, Trân Duc Thao, and Jules Vuillemin.

In addition to these academic and research institutions, the most important and unique French institutional practice that has had a significant impact on French philosophy, one with no equivalent in the English-speaking academic system, is the *agrégation*. The *agrégation* was established in 1766 under Louis XV as a competitive examination to certify secondary school teachers. The original *agrégation* sought to credential teachers in three areas: philosophy, letters, and grammar. Its creation had important political implications, however, especially for the teaching of philosophy insofar as it took the power to credential these teachers out of the hands of an examining jury selected by the Faculty of Theology and gave it to a jury under the exclusive control of the Faculty of Arts.[18] In 1821, three distinct competitive examinations were organized, one for sciences, one for letters (including philosophy), and one for grammar. Four years later, in 1825, a fourth competitive examination was created specifically for classes in philosophy. In subsequent years, many other specific competitive examinations have also been created, including examinations in history and geography (1831), mathematics (1841), German (1849), and English (1849).

In its modern form, the philosophy *agrégation* is a competitive exam that licenses students for teaching philosophy in secondary schools. The content of the exam is chosen by a *jury d'agrégation*, acting under the auspices of the Ministry of Public Instruction (now the Ministry of National Education), on the basis of the philosophy syllabus determined for the preceding year. The structure and content of the philosophy *agrégation* has been a subject of almost constant review and debate throughout the twentieth century.[19] In the early years of the twentieth century, the exam consisted of two parts: a written part, consisting of three essays, each allotted seven hours, often scheduled for a single week, with two questions on general philosophy and one on the history of philosophy. Following the written examination, of which typically

---

[18] André Chervel, *Histoire de l'agrégation: Contribution à l'histoire de la culture scolaire* (Paris: Éditions Kimé, 1993), p. 18. Most of the following details concerning the history of the *agrégation* come from this work.

[19] For a fascinating discussion of the philosophy *agrégation*, see the proceedings of the May 7, 1938 meeting of the Société Française de Philosophie, which was devoted to this topic: "L'Agrégation de philosophie," *Bulletin de la Société Française de Philosophie* vol. 38 (1938): 117–58. In this discussion, one sees many of the perennial problems raised: questions concerning the stress of such a rigorous examination, the problem of a "generation gap" between examiners and students, the relative importance of demonstrating technical knowledge versus pedagogic ability, the importance of knowledge of the philosophical canon, etc. Another issue that emerges in this discussion points directly to tensions between the Sorbonne and the École Normale Supérieure. This concerns whether the *agrégation*, whose purpose is to identify good teachers who know the material they will be required to instruct, discriminates against more creative philosophizing. While the Sorbonne establishment (Brunschvicg, Roustan, Parodi) question whether the École Normale is concentrating enough on making sure its students know the material, the representatives from the ENS, Célestin Bouglé, the Director, and Maurice Merleau-Ponty, the *agrégé-répétiteur*, suggest that insofar as the ENS encourages independence of thought, their students may be discriminated against by the more conservative Sorbonne jurors. Bouglé in particular is quite defensive, suggesting at one point that the session be subtitled "How to explain the failure of the *normaliens* at the *agrégation*" (p. 138).

only one in four applicants passed, several oral examinations were required. In the first oral examination, applicants were given three philosophical texts with one hour each to prepare a thirty-minute explication. The second oral required applicants to prepare a "lesson" on an assigned topic, given six hours' access to the Sorbonne library to prepare the lesson. The number of applicants who ultimately were admitted into the *agrégation* was determined by the state in accordance with the number of teaching posts available. The *agrégation* results of 1913 are typical of these early years: of 66 students who registered for the exam, 17 passed the written examination and were "admittable" to the oral examination; of these, ultimately seven were admitted as *agrégés*. In its more recent incarnations, both the length of the written exams and the number of oral presentations have been reduced, in part in response to claims that the examination was too difficult, in part in response to the need for more individuals to fill the available teaching posts. The first teaching jobs following the *agrégation* are typically in provincial *lycées*, with the best students returning soon thereafter to Paris to teach in the more prestigious *lycées*.

Prior to the educational reorganization in 1968, the *agrégation* typically was taken immediately upon completion of one's formal schooling (usually at the Sorbonne or the École Normale Supérieure), and the instructors assigned to prepare students for this exam, called the *agrégé-répétiteur* (or *caïman* in ENS slang),[20] often had profound influences on the students who come to depend on them.[21] Over the years, some of

---

[20]   The precise origin of the term *caïman* is contested. It might be related to the Cayman Islands (*Îles caïman*), or to a species of alligator that, because of its reputed cruelty, came to be the ironic nickname attributed to a former ENS *agrégé-répétiteur*. Alain Peyrefitte, in *Rue d'Ulm: Chroniques de la vie normalienne*, 4th edn. (Paris: Fayard,1994), suggests its usage dates from 1852 (p. 615).

[21]   The role of the *agrégé-répétiteur* is not unproblematic, however, as Jacques Derrida has forcefully noted: "A repeater, the *agrégé-répétiteur* should produce nothing, at least if to produce means to innovate, to transform, to bring about the new. He is destined to repeat and make others repeat, to reproduce and make others reproduce: forms, norms, and a content. He must assist students in the reading and comprehension of texts, help them interpret and understand what is expected of them, what they must respond to at the different stages of testing and selection, from the point of view of the contents or logico–rhetorical organization of their exercises (*explication de texte*, essays, or *leçons*). With his students he must therefore make himself the representative of a system of reproduction ... Or, rather, he must make himself the expert who, passing for knowing better the demand to which he first had to submit, explains it, translates it, repeats and re-presents it, therefore, to the

the most influential philosophy professors at the École Normale Supérieure have served as *agrégé-répétiteur* or *caïman*, including Jean Cavaillès (1931–5), Maurice Merleau-Ponty (1935–9), Georges Gusdorf (1939–48), and Louis Althusser (1948–80). Today, one can take the *agrégation* examination with a *maîtrise* or diploma from a *grande école*, although it is no longer necessary to pass the *agrégation* in order to teach in a secondary school. Students can, instead, take an examination for a secondary school teaching diploma called the *Certificat d'Aptitude au Professorat de l'Enseignement Secondaire* (CAPES), created in 1950 to meet the need for more secondary education teachers without diminishing the prestige of the *agrégation*. In contrast to the CAPES, *agrégation* holders (known as *agrégés*; feminine *agrégées*) enjoy certain privileges (higher salaries and shorter working hours), and they are also qualified to teach at universities after a few years of teaching experience at a *lycée*.

Before concluding this appendix, it will be helpful to clarify some basic pedagogic and institutional terminology, with the intention of comparing, as closely as possible, these terms with their American or British equivalents. At the level of university instruction, faculty ranks in France fall into four basic classes: an *Assistant* is roughly the equivalent of an Assistant Professor (US) or Lecturer (UK); a *Maître-assistant* is roughly the equivalent of an Associate Professor (US) or Senior Lecturer or Reader (UK); a *Maître de conférences*, for which the *Doctorat d'État* or *Doctorat de troisième cycle* is required, has approximately the same privileges and responsibilities of a Full Professor (US) or Senior Lecturer (UK); and a *Professeur* typically is elected by his or her peers to possess one of a limited number of chairs, with roughly the responsibilities and privileges of a Full Professor (US) or Professor with a Personal Chair (UK).

In France, the first four years of secondary education are spent at a *collège*; the last three years at a *lycée*, studying for the *baccalauréat* (*le bac*), which names both the series of examinations the passing of which certifies the successful completion of one's secondary education and the diploma awarded for passing this series of examinations. The *bac* is thus comparable to a high school diploma. Since 1863, the *classe de philosophie* has been a required subject of the final year at *lycée*,[22] and continues to be a

---

young candidates." Jacques Derrida, "When a Teaching Body Begins," in *Who's Afraid of Philosophy? Right to Philosophy I*, trans. Jan Plug (Stanford, CA: Stanford University Press, 2002), p. 75. Derrida's text first appeared in *Politiques de la philosophie*, ed. Dominique-Antoine Grisoni (Paris: Grasset, 1976).

22 For this reason, it is often referred to as the *classe terminale*.

major component of most students' *baccalauréat* examinations. Insofar as the *baccalauréat* was necessary for most civil service jobs, and passing the *classe de philosophie* and its associated examination was required for receiving the *baccalauréat*, the syllabus for the *classe de philosophie* has been, and continues to be, one of the most hotly contested issues in French public education. The *classe de philosophie* existed prior to 1863; in fact, it was reinstated in 1863, following its abolition ten years earlier, by Minister of Public Instruction Victor Duruy, who commented that "the true cause of the spread of negative doctrines among certain young people is the declines in philosophy teaching in our *lycées* . . . The study of philosophy is the best remedy for materialism."[23] Challenges to, and defenses of, the *classe de philosophie* have continued through the twentieth century, often in conjunction with changes in the French political landscape. One of the most famous of these appears in the "Instructions du 2 septembre 1925" issued by Minister of Public Instruction Anatole de Monzie, in which he summarizes the importance of instruction in philosophy for those about to complete their *lycée* education. The *classe de philosophie*, Monzie writes, will provide students with "a method of reflection and general principles of intellectual and moral life that may support them in their new existence, make them craftsmen capable of seeing beyond their crafts, citizens capable of exercising the enlightened and independent judgment required by our democratic society."[24] More recently, the challenge to the *classe de philosophie* posed by the "Réforme Haby" in 1975 was one of the prime factors leading to the creation by Derrida and others of GREPH, *Groupe de Recherches sur l'Enseignement Philosophique*.[25]

---

[23] Quoted by Jacques Derrida in "La Philosophie et ses classes," in *Qui a peur de la philosophie* (Paris: Flammarion, 1977), p. 447.

[24] Anatole de Monzie's "Instructions du 2 septembre 1925" is available from several websites, including www2.ac-lyon.fr/enseigne/philosophie/txteoff/monzie.html. For a detailed discussion of the *classe de philosophie*, see Michel Jamet, "La Classe de philosophie hier et aujourd'hui et l'enseignement de la philosophie," *Revue de l'Enseignement Philosophique*, 35ème Année, No. 2 (1984): 73–87, and No. 3 (1984): 81–90. For another eloquent defense of the *classe de philosophie* as an important transitional step between secondary and higher education in which young people are encouraged both to think in terms of general ideas and to think for themselves, see Bouglé's *The French Conception of "Culture Générale,"* esp. pp. 34–42.

[25] Derrida addresses the political importance of the *classe de philosophie* and the politics behind the "Réforme Haby" in "La Philosophie et ses classes." Noting that there are many different motivations behind the defense of the *classe de philosophie*, the attack on the class, when it comes from those in power, is not ambiguous: "The

Although the *lycée* is the equivalent of a high school, there are more and less prestigious *lycées*, and in the first half of the century, it was not uncommon for important philosophers to spend much if not all their career teaching at the more prestigious *lycées*, including the Lycées Louis-le-Grand, Henri-IV, and Condorcet, all in Paris. Among the philosophers who spent a significant part of their careers teaching philosophy in these *lycées* are Alain (from 1903–33, including 21 years at the Lycée Henri-IV), Henri Bergson (1881–97), Simone de Beauvoir (1929–43), Jean Hyppolite (1929–45), Maurice Merleau-Ponty (1931–45), and Jean Beaufret (1946–52, 1955–72). For those students who intend to go on to a career teaching, it is common to spend an additional two years at the *lycée* following the *baccalauréat* studying in a particular field for the rigorous entrance exams into one of the *grandes écoles*, typically the École Normale Supérieure. The first of these years for humanities and social science students is known as the *hypokhâgne* (officially, this course was called the *Lettres Supérieures*) and the second the *khâgne* (officially, the *Première Supérieure*).[26] The instructors in these courses often have profound effects on the subsequent careers of these students, and Alain, Brunschvicg, Hyppolite, and Jean Beaufret are among those who are often mentioned as influential instructors for these courses.

The system of post-secondary education in France has undergone numerous revisions since the French Revolution. In the cases of most of the figures discussed in this volume, especially those whose education was completed prior to the changes made to the University of Paris following 1968, the educational path they followed was fairly standard:

---

destruction of the *classe de philosophie*, since that is what is at issue, is meant to stop most *lycée* students from exercising philosophical and political critique. Historical critique as well, since history is once again the target associated with philosophy. In the *lycées*, at the age when one begins to vote, is the *classe de philosophie* not, with the exception of history, the only place in which, for example, texts on theoretical modernity, those on Marxism and psychoanalysis in particular, have some chance of being read and interpreted? And there is nothing fortuitous in the fact that the pressure from those in power has become continually more pronounced against this class and certain of its instructors and students since 1968 and the 'protests' that developed in the *lycées*." (Derrida, "La Philosophie et ses classes," p. 447; this essay appears in English in Derrida's *Who's Afraid of Philosophy? Right to Philosophy I*, pp. 158–63.)

[26] For students hoping to enter a *grand école scientifique* like the Science section of the École Normale Supérieure or the École Polytechnique, the preparatory classes are called the *hypotaupe* and *taupe*.

after *lycée*, they attend *hypokhâgne* and *khâgne* (usually in Paris, at the Lycée Louis-le-Grand or Lycée Henri-IV).[27] They then attend the École Normale Supérieure or the University of Paris and continue their studies, completing work in four fields (each resulting in receipt of a *certificat*), and obtaining a *licence* (roughly the equivalent of a master's degree).[28] University education is completed with the submission of a thesis, usually to the Faculty of Letters at the Sorbonne, for which they are awarded a *Diplôme d'études supérieures*.[29] After successfully passing the *agrégation*, they begin their careers teaching in provincial *lycées* for several years before returning to Paris to teach in a *lycée* or university, and following the submission of a *thèse principale* and a *thèse*

[27] Since the inception of these preparatory classes for entry into the École Normale Supérieure, there has been an intense rivalry between these two *lycées* – the most prestigious in Paris – in terms of their students' success on the exam. The first *Première Supérieure* was offered at Henri-IV in 1883. Between 1890 and 1904, the overwhelming majority of students entering the Lettres section at the École Normale came from these classes, with 102 students from Henri-IV and 76 from Louis-le-Grand. As noted earlier, from 1921 to 1956, almost 66 percent of the students admitted into the ENS Lettres section came from these two *lycées*, with 461 from Louis-le-Grand and 251 from Henri-IV. More recently, these schools continue to be dominant. In 1985, the last year that the ENS-rue d'Ulm had an admission separate from ENS for Girls at Sèvres, 33 of the 39 entering students came from these two *lycées* (18 from Henri-IV, 15 from Louis-le-Grand). And in the first ten years following the fusion of the ENS-Ulm and Sèvres (1986–95), almost 63 percent of the 767 entering students came from the Lycées Henri-IV (337) and Louis-le-Grand(144). These figures are drawn from Jacques Bouillon, Isabelle Brian, Ghislain Brune, and Bernard Roussel, *Le Lycée Henri-IV, Paris* (Thionville: G. Klopp, 1996).

[28] Following the educational reforms of 1973, the French undergraduate educational system has been divided into cycles and the successful completion of each cycle is typically assessed via an examination or thesis, followed by the awarding of a diploma. At the university level, the *premier cycle*, typically two or sometimes three years, terminates with a DEUG (*Diplôme d'Études Universitaires Générales*). The *deuxième cycle* terminates with a *licence* (after one year) or a *maîtrise* (after two years). The *licence* now is roughly equivalent to an American college diploma and the *mâitrise* can be compared to an American masters degree. The *troisième cycle* varies with the subject and academic level that the student seeks. After one year of the *troisième cycle*, the student can receive a research-oriented diploma called a *Diplôme d'Études Approfondies* (DEA) and can continue on to do two to four years of additional research work in pursuit of a *Doctorat de troisième cycle*.

[29] In 1963, the Fouchet Reform eliminated the *Diplôme d'études supérieures*, effectively replacing it with the *maîtrise*. See Tuillier, *Histoire de l'Université de Paris et de la Sorbonne, Vol. 2*, p. 526.

secondaire or *thèse complémentaire*,[30] they are awarded a *Doctorat*, which allows them to occupy a professor's chair in a university.

The *Doctorat* has changed several times during the twentieth century. During the first half of the century, following the submission of the two theses to the Faculty of Letters at the University of Paris, the individual was awarded a *Doctorat ès Lettres*.[31] There was also a less rigorous, and less prestigious, *Doctorat d'Université* which could be received for the submission of a single thesis. By the 1950s, the *Doctorat ès Lettres* was renamed the *Doctorat d'État*, with little change in the work required. In 1954 (for the sciences) and 1958 (for letters and human sciences), a less grueling *Doctorat de troisième cycle* was created on the model of the American Ph.D. to lessen what had become an increasingly long period of time between the typical students' completion of their *Diplôme d'études supérieures* and their *Doctorat d'État*.[32] During the latter half of the century, it became increasingly common for the *Doctorat d'État* to be awarded in recognition of the publication of a significant body of work rather than the presentation and defense of a single thesis. Among those who received their *Doctorat d'État* for a body of work are Louis Althusser, Jacques Derrida, Sarah Kofman, and Pierre Macherey. To clarify the confusion that existed between the relative prestige of the three existing doctoral degrees (*Doctorat d'Université*, *Doctorat de troisième cycle*, and *Doctorat d'État*), and to make the French *Doctorat* more easily comparable to doctorates acquired in other countries, the system was again revised in 1984, at which time the *Doctorat de troisième cycle* became the only doctoral degree granted, and a *Habilitation* (officially, the *Habilitation à diriger des recherches*) was created for those possessors of a *Doctorat* who were deemed qualified to occupy a chair as a university professor and themselves direct doctoral students' research.

[30]   Which, until 1903, had to be written in Latin. See Tuillier, *Histoire de l'Université de Paris et de la Sorbonne, Vol. 2*, p. 446.

[31]   Although some other French universities were approved to grant *Doctorats* prior to 1968, with very few exceptions, the recipients of the highest *Doctorats* have always submitted their theses to the faculty at the University of Paris.

[32]   Antoine Prost, *L'École et la famille dans une société en mutation*, vol. 4 of *Histoire Générale de l'enseignement et de l'éducation en France*, ed. Louis-Henri Parais (Paris: Nouvelle Librairie de France, 1981), p. 270. The creation of the *Doctorat de troisième cycle* also met the increasing need for more university teachers. With a *Doctorat de troisième cycle*, one could teach in a university as an *Assistant* or *Maître-assistant*, while a *Doctorat d'État* was still required to hold a position as *Maître de conférences* or *Professeur*. See Tuillier, *Histoire de l'Université de Paris et de la Sorbonne, Vol. 2*, pp. 519–20.

Appendix 2

Bibliography of French Philosophy in English Translation

Louis Althusser

Essays in Self-Criticism. Trans. Grahame Lock. London: New Left Books, 1976 [*Réponse à John Lewis*. Paris: F. Maspero, 1973; *Éléments d'autocritique*. Paris: Hachette, 1974].

Essays on Ideology. London: Verso, 1984 [*Éléments d'autocritique*. Paris: Hachette, 1974].

For Marx. Trans. Ben Brewster. London: Verso, 1990 [*Pour Marx*. Paris: F. Maspero, 1965].

The Future Lasts Forever: A Memoir. Ed. Olivier Corpet and Yann Moulier Boutang. Trans. Richard Veasey. New York: New Press, 1993 [*L'Avenir dure longtemps; suivi de Les Faits*. Paris: Le Grand livre du mois, 1992].

The Humanist Controversy and Other Writings (1966–67). Ed. François Matheron. Trans. and intro. G. M. Goshgarian. London: Verso, 2003.

Lenin and Philosophy and Other Essays. Trans. Ben Brewster. London: New Left Books, 1971 [*Lénine et la philosophie*. Paris: F. Maspero, 1969].

Machiavelli and Us. Ed. François Matheron. Trans. Gregory Elliot. London: Verso, 1999 [1972, revised 1986; first published in *Écrits philosophiques et politiques. Tome 2*. Paris: Stock/IMEC, 1995].

Montesquieu, Rousseau, Marx: Politics and History. Trans. Ben Brewster. London: New Left Books, 1972 [*Montesquieu, la politique et l'histoire*. Paris: Presses universitaires de France, 1959].

Philosophy and the Spontaneous Philosophy of the Scientists and Other Essays. Ed. and intro. Gregory Elliott. Trans. Ben Brewster, et al. London: Verso, 1990 [*Philosophie et philosophie spontanée des savants.* Paris: F. Maspero, 1974].

The Spectre of Hegel: Early Writings. Ed. and intro. François Matheron. Trans. G. M. Goshgarian. London: Verso, 1997 [*Écrits philosophiques et politiques. Tome 1.* Paris: Stock/IMEC, 1994].

Writings on Psychoanalysis: Freud and Lacan. Ed. Olivier Corpet and François Matheron. Trans. Jeffrey Mehlman. New York: Columbia University Press, 1996 [*Écrits sur la psychanalyse: Freud et Lacan.* Paris: Stock/IMEC, 1993].

And Étienne Balibar. *Reading Capital.* Trans. Ben Brewster. London: New Left Books, 1970 [*Lire "Le Capital."* 2 Vols. Paris: F. Maspero, 1965].

Gaston Bachelard

Air and Dreams: An Essay on the Imagination of Movement. Trans. Edith R. Farrell and C. Frederick Farrell. Dallas, TX: Dallas Institute Publications, 1988 [*L'Air et les songes: Essai sur l'imagination du mouvement.* Paris: J. Corti, 1943].

Dialectic of Duration. Trans. Mary McAllester Jones. Manchester: Clinamen Press, 2000 [*La Dialectique de la durée.* Paris: Société française d'imprimerie et de librairie, 1936].

Drawings for the Bible. Illustrated by Marc Chagall. Trans. Stuart Gilbert. New York: Harcourt, Brace, 1960 [*Marc Chagall. Dessins pour la Bible. Introduction à la Bible de Chagall, par Gaston Bachelard.* Paris: Éditions de la revue "Verve," 1960].

Earth and Reveries of Will: An Essay on the Imagination of Matter. Trans. Kenneth Haltman. Dallas, TX: Dallas Institute of Humanities and Culture, 2002 [*La Terre et les rêveries de la volonté.* Paris: J. Corti, 1948].

The Flame of a Candle. Trans. Joni Caldwell. Dallas, TX: Dallas Institute Publications, 1988 [*La Flamme d'une chandelle.* Paris: Presses universitaires de France, 1961].

The Formation of the Scientific Mind. Trans. Mary McAllester Jones. Manchester: Clinamen Press, 2003 [*La Formation de l'esprit scientifique*. Paris: J. Vrin, 1938].

Fragments of a Poetics of Fire. Ed. Suzanne Bachelard. Trans. Kenneth Haltman. Dallas, TX: Dallas Institute Publications, 1990 [*Fragments d'une poétique du feu*. Paris: Presses universitaires de France, 1988].

Gaston Bachelard, Subversive Humanist: Texts and Readings. Ed. and trans. Mary McAllester Jones. Madison: University of Wisconsin Press, 1991.

Lautréamont. Trans. Robert S. Dupree. Dallas, TX: Dallas Institute Publications, 1986 [*Lautréamont*. Paris: J. Corti, 1939].

The New Scientific Spirit. Trans. Arthur Goldhammer. Boston, MA: Beacon Press, 1984 [*Le Nouvel esprit scientifique*. Paris: Presses universitaires de France, 1934].

On Poetic Imagination and Reverie: Selections from the Works of Gaston Bachelard. Trans. and intro. Colette Gaudin. Indianapolis, IN: Bobbs–Merrill, 1971.

The Philosophy of No: A Philosophy of the New Scientific Mind. Trans. G. C. Waterston. New York: Orion Press, 1968 [*La Philosophie du non. Essai d'une philosophie du nouvel esprit scientifique*. Paris: Presses universitaires de France, 1940].

The Poetics of Reverie. Trans. Daniel Russell. New York: Orion Press, 1969 [*La Poétique de la reverie*. Paris: Presses universitaires de France, 1960].

The Poetics of Space. Trans. Maria Jolas. New York: Orion Press, 1964 [*La Poétique de l'espace*. Paris: Presses universitaires de France, 1957].

The Psychoanalysis of Fire. Trans. Alan C. M. Ross. Boston, MA: Beacon Press, 1964 [*La Psychanalyse du feu*. Paris: Éditions Gallimard, 1938].

The Right to Dream. Trans. J. A. Underwood. New York: Grossman, 1971 [*Le Droit de rêver*. Paris: Presses universitaires de France, 1970].

Water and Dreams: An Essay on the Imagination of Matter. Trans. Edith R. Farrell. Dallas, TX: Pegasus Foundation, 1983 [*L'Eau et les rêves. Essai sur l'imagination de la matière*. Paris: J. Corti, 1942].

Alain Badiou

Being and Event. Trans. Oliver Feltham. London: Continuum, 2005 [*L'Être et l'événement*. Paris: Éditions du Seuil, 1988].

Can Politics Be Thought? Trans. Bruno Bosteels. Durham, NC: Duke University Press, 2004 [*Peut-on penser la politique?* Paris: Éditions du Seuil, 1985].

The Century. Trans. Alberto Toscano. Cambridge, MA: MIT Press, 2005 [*Le Siècle*. Paris: Éditions du Seuil, 2004].

Deleuze: The Clamor of Being. Trans. Louise Burchill. Minneapolis: University of Minnesota Press, 2000 [*Deleuze: La Clameur de l'être*. Paris: Hachette, 1997].

Ethics: An Essay on the Understanding of Evil. Trans. Peter Hallward. London: Verso, 2001 [*L'Éthique: Essai sur la conscience du mal*. Paris: Hatier, 1993].

Handbook of Inaesthetics. Trans. Alberto Toscano. Stanford, CA: Stanford University Press, 2005 [*Petit manuel d'inesthétique*. Paris: Éditions du Seuil, 1998].

Infinite Thought: Truth and the Return to Philosophy. Trans. and ed. Oliver Feltham and Justin Clemens. London: Continuum, 2003.

Manifesto for Philosophy. Trans. and ed. Norman Madarasz. Albany: State University of New York Press, 1999 [*Manifeste pour la philosophie*. Paris: Éditions du Seuil, 1989].

On Beckett. Trans. Alberto Toscano. Manchester: Clinamen Press, 2003 [*Beckett: L'Increvable désir*. Paris: Hachette, 1995].

On Metapolitics. Trans. Jason Barker. London: Verso, 2004 [*Abrégé de métapolitique*. Paris: Éditions du Seuil, 1998].

Saint Paul: The Foundation of Universalism. Trans. Ray Brassier. Stanford, CA: Stanford University Press, 2003 [*Saint Paul: La Fondation de l'universalisme*. Paris: Presses universitaires de France, 1997].

Theoretical Writings. Trans. and ed. Alberto Toscano and Ray Brassier. London: Continuum, 2004.

Étienne Balibar

Masses, Classes, Ideas: Studies on Politics and Philosophy Before and After Marx. Trans. James Swenson. New York: Routledge, 1994 [1982–91].

On the Dictatorship of the Proletariat. Trans. and intro. Grahame Lock. Afterword by Louis Althusser. Atlantic Highlands, NJ: Humanities Press, 1977 [*Sur la dictature du prolétariat.* Paris: F. Maspero, 1976].

The Philosophy of Marx. Trans. Chris Turner. London: Verso, 1995 [*La Philosophie de Marx.* Paris: Éditions la Découverte, 1993].

Politics and the Other Scene. Trans. Christine Jones, James Swenson, and Chris Turner. London: Verso, 2002 [*Droit de cité.* La Tour-d'Aigues: Éditions de l'Aube, 1998].

Spinoza and Politics. Trans. Peter Snowdon. London: Verso, 1998 [*Spinoza et la politique.* Paris: Presses universitaires de France, 1985].

We, the People of Europe? Reflections on Transnational Citizenship. Trans. James Swenson. Princeton, NJ: Princeton University Press, 2004 [*Nous, citoyens d'Europe? Les Frontières, l'État, le peuple.* Paris: Éditions la Découverte, 2001].

And Louis Althusser. *Reading Capital.* Trans. Ben Brewster. London: New Left Books, 1970 [*Lire "Le Capital."* 2 vols. Paris: F. Maspero, 1965].

And Immanuel Wallerstein. *Race, Nation, Class: Ambiguous Identities.* Trans. Chris Turner. London: Verso, 1991 [*Race, nation, classe: Les Identités ambiguës.* Paris: Éditions la Découverte, 1988].

Roland Barthes

All Except You. Trans. Saul Steinberg. Paris: Galerie Maeght, 1983 [*All except you.* Paris: Repères, 1983].

Arcimboldo. Trans. John Shepley. Milan: F. M. Ricci, 1980 [*Arcimboldo.* Paris: F. M. Ricci, 1978].

A Barthes Reader. Ed. and intro. Susan Sontag. New York: Hill and Wang, 1982.

Camera Lucida: Reflections on Photography. Trans. Richard Howard. New York: Hill and Wang, 1981 [*La Chambre claire: Note sur la photographie.* Paris: Éditions Gallimard, 1980].

Critical Essays. Trans. Richard Howard. Evanston, IL: Northwestern University Press, 1972 [*Essais critiques.* Paris: Éditions du Seuil, 1964].

Criticism and Truth. Trans. and ed. Katrine Pilcher Keuneman. Minneapolis: University of Minnesota Press, 1987 [*Critique et vérité.* Paris: Éditions du Seuil, 1966].

The Eiffel Tower, and Other Mythologies. Trans. Richard Howard. New York: Hill and Wang, 1979.

Elements of Semiology. Trans. Annette Lavers and Colin Smith. New York: Hill and Wang, 1968 [*Eléments de sémiologie.* Paris: Éditions du Seuil, 1964].

Empire of Signs. Trans. Richard Howard. New York: Hill and Wang, 1982 [*L'Empire des signes.* Geneva: Skira, 1970].

The Fashion System. Trans. Matthew Ward and Richard Howard. New York: Hill and Wang, 1983 [*Système de la mode.* Paris: Éditions du Seuil, 1967].

The Grain of the Voice: Interviews 1962–1980. Trans. Linda Coverdale. New York: Hill and Wang, 1985 [*Le Grain de la voix: Entretiens, 1962–1980.* Paris: Éditions du Seuil, 1981].

Image—Music—Text. Essays selected and trans. Stephen Heath. New York: Hill and Wang, 1977.

Incidents. Trans. Richard Howard. Berkeley: University of California Press, 1992 [*Incidents.* Paris: Éditions du Seuil, 1987].

A Lover's Discourse: Fragments. Trans. Richard Howard. New York: Hill and Wang, 1978 [*Fragments d'un discours amoureux.* Paris: Éditions du Seuil, 1977].

Michelet. Trans. Richard Howard. New York: Hill and Wang, 1987 [*Michelet par lui-même: Images et textes.* Paris: Éditions du Seuil, 1954].

Mythologies. Selected and trans. Annette Lavers. New York: Hill and Wang, 1972 [*Mythologies.* Paris: Éditions du Seuil, 1957].

New Critical Essays. Trans. Richard Howard. New York: Hill and Wang, 1980 [*Nouveaux essais critiques*. Paris: Éditions du Seuil, 1972].

On Racine. Trans. Richard Howard. New York: Hill and Wang, 1964 [*Sur Racine*. Paris: Éditions du Seuil, 1963].

The Pleasure of the Text. Trans. Richard Miller. New York: Hill and Wang, 1975 [*Le Plaisir du texte*. Paris: Éditions du Seuil, 1973].

The Responsibility of Forms: Critical Essays on Music, Art, and Representation. Trans. Richard Howard. New York: Hill and Wang, 1985 [*L'Obvie et l'obtus*. Paris: Éditions du Seuil, 1982].

Roland Barthes by Roland Barthes. Trans. Richard Howard. New York: Hill and Wang, 1977 [*Roland Barthes par Roland Barthes*. Paris: Éditions du Seuil, 1975].

The Rustle of Language. Trans. Richard Howard. New York: Hill and Wang, 1986 [*Le Bruissement de la langue*. Paris: Éditions du Seuil, 1984].

S/Z. Trans. Richard Miller. New York: Hill and Wang, 1974 [*S/Z*. Paris: Éditions du Seuil, 1970].

Sade, Fourier, Loyola. Trans. Richard Miller. New York: Hill and Wang, 1976 [*Sade, Fourier, Loyola*. Paris: Éditions du Seuil, 1970].

The Semiotic Challenge. Trans. Richard Howard. New York: Hill and Wang, 1988 [*L'Aventure sémiologique*. Paris: Éditions du Seuil, 1985].

Writer Sollers. Trans. and intro. Philip Thody. Minneapolis: University of Minnesota Press, 1987 [*Sollers écrivain*. Paris: Éditions du Seuil, 1979].

Writing Degree Zero. Trans. Annette Lavers and Colin Smith. New York: Hill and Wang, 1968 [*Le Degré zéro de l'écriture*. Paris: Éditions du Seuil, 1953].

And F. Bovon, F. J. Leenhardt, and R. Martin-Achard. *Structural Analysis and Biblical Exegesis: Interpretational Essays*. Trans. Alfred M. Johnson, Jr. Pittsburgh, PA: Pickwick Press, 1974 [*Analyse structurale et exégèse biblique: Essais d'interprétation*. Paris: Delachaux et Niestlé, 1972].

Georges Bataille

The Absence of Myth: Writings on Surrealism. Trans. and ed. Michael Richardson. London: Verso, 1994 [1945–51].

The Accursed Share, Vol. 1: An Essay on General Economy. Trans. Robert Hurley. New York: Zone Books, 1988 [*La Part maudite: Essai d'économie générale*. Paris: Éditions de Minuit, 1949, 1967].

The Accursed Share, Vol. 2: The History of Eroticism; Vol. 3: Sovereignty. Trans. Robert Hurley. New York: Zone Books, 1991 [*Œuvres complètes. Vol. 8. L'Histoire de l'érotisme; La Souveraineté*. Paris: Éditions Gallimard, 1976].

The Bataille Reader. Ed. Fred Botting and Scott Wilson. Oxford: Blackwell, 1997.

The College of Sociology (1937–1939). Ed. Denis Hollier. Trans. Betsy Wing. Minneapolis: University of Minnesota Press, 1988 [*Le Collège de sociologie: 1937–1939*. Paris: Éditions Gallimard, 1979].

The Cradle of Humanity: Prehistoric Art and Culture. Ed. and intro. Stuart Kendall. Trans. Michelle Kendall and Stuart Kendall. New York: Zone Books, 2004.

Encyclopædia Acephalica: Comprising the Critical Dictionary and Related Texts. Ed. Georges Bataille. Assembled and introduced by Alastair Brotchie. Trans. Iain White with additional translations by Dominic Faccini, et al. London: Atlas Press, 1995 [1929–30].

Erotism: Death and Sensuality. Trans. Mary Dalwood. [Originally published as *Death and Sensuality: A Study of Eroticism and the Taboo*.] New York: Walker, 1962 [*L'Érotisme*. Paris: Éditions de Minuit, 1957].

Georges Bataille: Essential Writings. Ed. Michael Richardson. London: Sage, 1998.

Guilty. Trans. Bruce Boone. Venice, CA: Lapis Press, 1988 [*Le Coupable*. Paris: Éditions Gallimard, 1944].

Inner Experience. Trans. and intro. Leslie Anne Boldt. Albany: State University of New York Press, 1988 [*L'Expérience intérieure*. Paris: Éditions Gallimard, 1943].

Lascaux; or, The Birth of Art: Prehistoric Painting. Trans. Austryn Wainhouse. Lausanne: Skira, 1955 [*La Peinture préhistorique. Lascaux, ou la Naissance de l'art.* Geneva: Skira, 1955].

Literature and Evil. Trans. Alastair Hamilton. New York: Urizen Books, 1981 [*La Littérature et le mal: Emily Brontë, Baudelaire, Michelet, Blake, Sade, Proust, Kafka, Genet.* Paris: Éditions Gallimard, 1957].

Manet. Trans. Austryn Wainhouse and James Emmons. New York: Skira/ Rizzoli, 1983 [*Manet.* Geneva: Skira, 1955].

On Nietzsche. Trans. Bruce Boone. New York: Paragon House, 1992 [*Sur Nietzsche, volonté de chance.* Paris: Éditions Gallimard, 1945].

The Tears of Eros. Trans. Peter Connor. San Francisco: City Lights Books, 1989 [*Les Larmes d'Eros.* Paris: J.-J. Pauvert, 1961].

Theory of Religion. Trans. Robert Hurley. New York: Zone Books, 1989 [*Théorie de la religion.* Paris: Éditions Gallimard, 1973].

The Trial of Gilles de Rais. Trans. Richard Robinson. Los Angeles: Amok, 1991 [*Le Procès de Gilles de Rais.* Paris: J.-J. Pauvert, 1965].

The Unfinished System of Nonknowledge. Ed. and intro. Stuart Kendall. Trans. Michelle Kendall and Stuart Kendall. Minneapolis: University of Minnesota Press, 2001.

Visions of Excess: Selected Writings, 1927–1939. Ed. and intro. Allan Stoekl. Trans. Allan Stoekl, with Carl R. Lovitt and Donald M. Leslie, Jr. Minneapolis: University of Minnesota Press, 1985.

Simone de Beauvoir

Adieux: Farewell to Sartre: Followed by Conversations with Jean-Paul Sartre. Trans. Patrick O'Brian. New York: Pantheon, 1984 [*La Cérémonie des adieux; suivi de Entretiens avec Jean-Paul Sartre: août-septembre 1974.* Paris: Éditions Gallimard, 1981].

After the Second Sex: Conversations with Simone de Beauvoir. Ed. Alice Schwarzer. Trans. Marianne Howarth. New York: Pantheon Books, 1984 [*Simone de Beauvoir aujourd'hui: Entretiens.* Paris: Mercure de France, 1983].

All Said and Done. Trans. Patrick O'Brian. New York: Putnam, 1974 [*Tout compte fait.* Paris: Éditions Gallimard, 1972].

America Day by Day. Trans. Patrick Dudley. New York: Grove Press, 1953 [*L'Amérique au jour le jour.* Paris: P. Morihien, 1948].

Brigitte Bardot and the Lolita Syndrome. Trans. Bernard Frechtman. New York: Arno Press, 1959 [English Original. Translated into French in *Les Écrits de Simone de Beauvoir.* Ed. Claude Francis and Fernande Gontier. Paris: Gallimard, 1979. Pp. 363–76].

The Coming of Age. Trans. Patrick O'Brian. New York: Putnam, 1972 [*La Vieillesse.* Paris: Éditions Gallimard, 1970].

The Ethics of Ambiguity. Trans. Bernard Frechtman. New York: Philosophical Library, 1949 [*Pour une morale de l'ambiguïté.* Paris: Éditions Gallimard, 1947].

Force of Circumstance: The Autobiography of Simone de Beauvoir. Trans. Richard Howard. New York: Putnam, 1965 [*La Force des choses.* Paris: Éditions Gallimard, 1963].

Letters to Sartre. Ed. and trans. Quintin Hoare. New York: Arcade Publishers, 1992 [*Lettres à Sartre.* Paris: Éditions Gallimard, 1990].

The Long March. Trans. Austryn Wainhouse. Cleveland, OH: World Publishing, 1958 [*La Longue marche: Essai sur la Chine.* Paris: Éditions Gallimard, 1957].

Memoirs of a Dutiful Daughter. Trans. James Kirkup. Cleveland, OH: World Publishing, 1959 [*Mémoires d'une jeune fille rangée.* Paris: Éditions Gallimard, 1958].

Must We Burn Sade? Trans. Annette Michelson. New York: Grove Press, 1955 [*Faut-il brûler Sade?* Paris: Les Temps Modernes, 1951–2].

Philosophical Writings. Ed. Margaret A. Simons with the assistance of Marybeth Timmermann and Mary Beth Mader. Urbana: University of Illinois Press, 2004.

The Prime of Life: The Autobiography of Simone de Beauvoir. Trans. Peter Green. Cleveland, OH: World Publishing, 1962 [*La Force de l'âge.* Paris: Éditions Gallimard, 1960].

The Second Sex. Ed. and trans. Howard Madison Parshley. New York: Alfred A. Knopf, 1952 [*Le Deuxième sexe.* Paris: Éditions Gallimard, 1949].

A Transatlantic Love Affair: Letters to Nelson Algren. Compiled and annotated by Sylvie Le Bon de Beauvoir. Trans. Ellen Gordon Reeves. New York: New Press, 1998 [*Lettres à Nelson Algren: Un amour transatlantique, 1947–1964.* Paris: Éditions Gallimard, 1997].

A Very Easy Death. Trans. Patrick O'Brian. New York: Putnam, 1966 [*Une mort très douce.* Paris: Éditions Gallimard, 1964].

And Gisèle Halimi. *Djamila Boupacha, the Story of the Torture of a Young Algerian Girl Which Shocked Liberal French Opinion.* Trans. Peter Green. New York: Macmillan, 1962. [*Djamila Boupacha.* Paris: Éditions Gallimard, 1962].

Henri Bergson

Creative Evolution. Trans. Arthur Mitchell. New York: Henry Holt, 1911 [*L'Evolution créatrice.* Paris: Félix Alcan, 1907].

The Creative Mind. Trans. Mabelle L. Andison. New York: Philosophical Library, 1946 [*La Pensée et le mouvant.* Paris: Félix Alcan, 1934].

Duration and Simultaneity, With Reference to Einstein's Theory. Trans. Leon Jacobson. Indianapolis, IN: Bobbs-Merrill, 1965 [*Durée et simultanéité à propos de la théorie d'Einstein.* Paris: Firmin-Didot, 1922].

Henri Bergson: Key Writings. Ed. Keith Ansell-Pearson and John Mullarkey. London: Continuum, 2002.

An Introduction to Metaphysics. Trans. T. E. Hulme. New York: G. P. Putnam's Sons, 1912 [*Introduction à la métaphysique.* Paris: Félix Alcan, 1903].

Laughter: An Essay on the Meaning of the Comic. Trans. Cloudesley Brereton and Fred Rothwell. New York: Macmillan, 1914 [*Le Rire: Essai sur la signification du comique.* Paris: Félix Alcan, 1900].

Matter and Memory. Trans. Nancy Margaret Paul and W. Scott Palmer. New York: Macmillan, 1911; New York: Zone Books, 1988 [*Matière et mémoire: Essai sur la relation du corps à l'esprit.* Paris: Félix Alcan, 1896].

The Meaning of the War: Life and Matter in Conflict. Intro. H. Wildon Carr. London: T. F. Unwin, 1916 [*La Signification de la guerre.* Paris: Bloud et Gay, 1915].

Mind-Energy: Lectures and Essays. Trans. H. Wildon Carr. New York: Henry Holt, 1920 [*L'Énergie spirituelle: Essais et conférences.* Paris: Félix Alcan, 1919].

The Philosophy of Poetry: The Genius of Lucretius. Ed., trans., and in part recast by Wade Baskin. New York: Philosophical Library, 1959 [*Extraits de Lucrèce, avec un commentaire, des notes et une étude sur la poésie, la philosophie, la physique, le texte et la langue de Lucrèce.* Paris: Delagrave, 1884].

Selections from Bergson. Ed. and intro. Harold A. Larrabee. New York: Appleton-Century-Crofts, 1949.

Time and Free Will: An Essay on the Immediate Data of Consciousness. Trans. F. L. Pogson. New York: Macmillan, 1910 [*Essai sur les données immédiates de la conscience.* Paris: Félix Alcan, 1889].

The Two Sources of Morality and Religion. Trans. R. Ashley Audra and Cloudesley Brereton, with the assistance of W. Horsfall Carter. New York: Henry Holt, 1935 [*Les Deux sources de la morale et de la religion.* Paris: Félix Alcan, 1932].

The World of Dreams. Trans. Wade Baskin. New York: Philosophical Library, 1958 [*Le Rêve.* Paris: Félix Alcan, 1901].

Maurice Blanchot

Awaiting Oblivion. Trans. John Gregg. Lincoln: University of Nebraska Press, 1997 [*L'Attente, l'oubli.* Paris: Éditions Gallimard, 1962].

The Blanchot Reader. Ed. Michael Holland. Oxford: Blackwell, 1995.

The Book to Come. Trans. Charlotte Mandell. Stanford, CA: Stanford University Press, 2003 [*Le Livre à venir.* Paris: Éditions Gallimard, 1959].

Faux Pas. Trans. Charlotte Mandell. Stanford, CA: Stanford University Press, 2001 [*Faux pas.* Paris: Éditions Gallimard, 1943].

Friendship. Trans. Elizabeth Rottenberg. Stanford, CA: Stanford University Press, 1997 [*L'Amitié.* Paris: Éditions Gallimard, 1971].

The Gaze of Orpheus, and Other Literary Essays. Ed. P. Adams Sitney. Trans. Lydia Davis. Barrytown, NY: Station Hill Press, 1981.

The Infinite Conversation. Trans. Susan Hanson. Minneapolis: University of Minnesota Press, 1993 [*L'Entretien infini.* Paris: Éditions Gallimard, 1969].

Lautréamont and Sade. Trans. Stuart Kendall and Michelle Kendall. Stanford, CA: Stanford University Press, 2004 [*Lautréamont and Sade.* Paris: Éditions de Minuit, 1949].

Michel Foucault as I Imagine Him. Trans. Jeffrey Mehlman. New York: Zone Books, 1987 [*Michel Foucault tel que je l'imagine.* Fontfroide-le-Haut: Fata Morgana, 1986].

The Siren's Song: Selected Essays. Ed. and intro. Gabriel Josipovici. Trans. Sacha Rabinovitch. Bloomington: Indiana University Press, 1982.

The Space of Literature. Trans. and intro. Ann Smock. Lincoln: University of Nebraska Press, 1982 [*L'Espace littéraire.* Paris: Éditions Gallimard, 1955].

The Station Hill Blanchot Reader: Fiction and Literary Essays. Ed. George Quasha. Trans. Lydia Davis, Paul Auster, and Robert Lamberton. Barrytown, NY: Station Hill/Barrytown, 1999.

The Step Not Beyond. Trans. and intro. Lycette Nelson. Albany: State University of New York Press, 1992 [*Le Pas au-delà.* Paris: Éditions Gallimard, 1973].

The Unavowable Community. Trans. Pierre Joris. Barrytown, NY: Station Hill Press, 1988 [*La Communauté inavouable.* Paris: Éditions de Minuit, 1983].

The Work of Fire. Trans. Charlotte Mandell. Stanford, CA: Stanford University Press, 1995 [*La Part du feu.* Paris: Éditions Gallimard, 1949].

The Writing of the Disaster. Trans. Ann Smock. Lincoln: University of Nebraska Press, 1986 [*L'Écriture du désastre.* Paris: Éditions Gallimard, 1980].

And Jacques Derrida. *The Instant of My Death/Demeure: Fiction and Testimony.* Trans. Elizabeth Rottenberg. Stanford, CA: Stanford University Press, 2000 [*L'Instant de ma mort.* Saint-Clément: Fata Morgana, 1994].

And Pierre Klossowski. *Decadence of the Nude/La Décadence du/Nu.* Trans. Paul Buck and Catherine Petit. London: Black Dog, 2003.

Pierre Bourdieu

Acts of Resistance: Against the New Myths of Our Time. Trans. Richard Nice. Cambridge: Polity Press, 1998. US Title: *Acts of Resistance: Against the Tyranny of the Market.* New York: New Press, 1999 [*Contre-feux, tome 1: Propos pour servir à la résistance contre l'invasion néo-libérale.* Paris: Éditions Liber-Raisons d'Agir, 1998].

Algeria 1960: The Disenchantment of the World: The Kabyle House or the World Reversed: Essays by Pierre Bourdieu. Trans. Richard Nice. New York: Cambridge University Press, 1979 [*Algérie 60: Structures économiques et structures temporelles.* Paris: Éditions de Minuit, 1977].

The Algerians. Trans. Alan C. M. Ross. Boston, MA: Beacon Press, 1962 [*Sociologie de l'Algérie.* Paris: Presses universitaires de France, 1958].

Backfire: Against the Tyranny of the Market. Trans. Chris Turner. London: Verso, 2002 [*Contre-feux, tome 2: Pour un mouvement social européen.* Paris: Éditions Liber-Raisons d Agir, 2001].

Distinction: A Social Critique of the Judgment of Taste. Trans. Richard Nice. Cambridge, MA: Harvard University Press, 1984 [*La Distinction: Critique sociale du jugement.* Paris: Éditions de Minuit, 1979].

The Field of Cultural Production: Essays on Art and Literature. Ed. and intro. Randal Johnson. New York: Columbia University Press, 1993 [1968–87].

Firing Back: Against the Tyranny of the Market. Trans. Loïc Wacquant. New York: New Press, 2003 [*Contre-feux, tome 2: Pour un mouvement social européen.* Paris: Éditions Liber-Raisons d'Agir, 2001].

Homo Academicus. Trans. Peter Collier. Stanford, CA: Stanford University Press, 1988 [*Homo academicus.* Paris: Éditions de Minuit, 1984].

In Other Words: Essays Towards a Reflexive Sociology. Trans. Matthew Adamson. Stanford, CA: Stanford University Press, 1990 [*Choses dites.* Paris: Éditions de Minuit, 1987].

An Introduction to the Work of Pierre Bourdieu: The Practice of Theory. Ed. Richard Harker, Cheleen Mahar, and Chris Wilkes. New York: St. Martin's Press, 1990.

Language and Symbolic Power. Ed. and intro. John B. Thompson. Trans. Gino Raymond and Matthew Adamson. Cambridge, MA: Harvard University Press, 1991 [*Ce que parler veut dire: L'Économie des échanges linguistiques*. Paris: A. Fayard, 1982].

The Logic of Practice. Trans. Richard Nice. Stanford, CA: Stanford University Press, 1990 [*Le Sens pratique*. Paris: Éditions de Minuit, 1980].

Masculine Domination. Trans. Richard Nice. Stanford, CA: Stanford University Press, 2001 [*La Domination masculine*. Paris: Éditions du Seuil, 1998].

On Television. Trans. Priscilla Parkhurst Ferguson. New York: New Press, 1998 [*Sur la television; suivi de L'Emprise du journalisme*. Paris: Liber, 1996].

Outline of a Theory of Practice. Trans. Richard Nice. New York: Cambridge University Press, 1977 [*Esquisse d'une théorie de la pratique: Précédé de trois études d'ethnologie kabyle*. Geneva: Droz, 1972].

Pascalian Meditations. Trans. Richard Nice. Stanford, CA: Stanford University Press, 2000 [*Méditations pascaliennes*. Paris: Éditions du Seuil, 1997].

Photography, a Middle-Brow Art. Trans. Shaun Whiteside. Stanford, CA: Stanford University Press, 1990 [*Un art moyen: Essai sur les usages sociaux de la photographie*. Paris: Éditions de Minuit, 1965].

The Political Ontology of Martin Heidegger. Trans. Peter Collier. Stanford, CA: Stanford University Press, 1991 [*L'Ontologie politique de Martin Heidegger*. Paris: Éditions de Minuit, 1988].

Practical Reason: On the Theory of Action. Stanford, CA: Stanford University Press, 1998 [*Raisons pratiques: Sur la théorie de l'action*. Paris: Éditions du Seuil, 1994].

The Rules of Art: Genesis and Structure of the Literary Field. Trans. Susan Emanuel. Stanford, CA: Stanford University Press, 1996 [*Les Règles de l'art: Genèse et structure du champ littéraire*. Paris: Éditions du Seuil, 1992].

Science of Science and Reflexivity. Trans. Richard Nice. Chicago: University of Chicago Press, 2004 [*Science de la science et réflexivité. Cours du Collège de France 2000–2001*. Paris: Éditions Raison d'Agir, 2001].

Sociology in Question. Trans. Richard Nice. Thousand Oaks, CA: Sage, 1993 [*Questions de sociologie*. Paris: Éditions de Minuit, 1984].

The State Nobility: Elite Schools in the Field of Power. Trans. Lauretta C. Clough. Stanford, CA: Stanford University Press, 1996 [*La Noblesse d'État: Grandes écoles et esprit de corps*. Paris: Éditions de Minuit, 1989].

And Alain Accardo. *The Weight of the World: Social Suffering in Contemporary Society*. Trans. Priscilla Parkhurst Ferguson and others. Stanford, CA: Stanford University Press, 1999 [*La Misère du monde*. Paris: Le Grand livre du mois, 1993].

And Jean-Claude Chamboredon and Jean-Claude Passeron. *The Craft of Sociology: Epistemological Preliminaries*. Ed. Beate Krais. Trans. Richard Nice. New York: Walter de Gruyter, 1991 [*Le Métier de sociologue: Préalables épistémologiques*. Paris: Mouton, 1968].

And Alain Darbel with Dominique Schnapper. *The Love of Art: European Art Museums and their Public*. Trans. Caroline Beattie and Nick Merriman. Stanford, CA: Stanford University Press, 1991 [*L'Amour de l'art: Les Musées d'art européens et leur public*. Paris: Éditions de Minuit, 1966].

And Hans Haacke. *Free Exchange*. Cambridge: Polity Press, 1995 [*Libre-échange*. Paris: Éditions du Seuil, 1993].

And Jean-Claude Passeron. *The Inheritors: French Students and their Relation to Culture*. Trans. Richard Nice. Chicago: University of Chicago Press, 1979 [*Les Héritiers: Les Étudiants et la culture*. Paris: Mouton, 1964].

And Jean-Claude Passeron. *Reproduction in Education, Society, and Culture*. Trans. Richard Nice. Beverly Hills, CA: Sage, 1977 [*La Reproduction: Éléments pour une théorie du système d'enseignement*. Paris: Éditions de Minuit, 1970].

And Jean-Claude Passeron and Monique de Saint-Martin. *Academic Discourse: Linguistic Misunderstanding and Professorial Power*. Trans. Richard Teese. Stanford, CA: Stanford University Press, 1994 [*Rapport pédagogique et communication*. Paris: Mouton, 1965].

And Loïc J. D. Wacquant. *An Invitation to Reflexive Sociology*. Chicago: University of Chicago Press, 1992.

Albert Camus

Albert Camus: The Essential Writings. Ed. with interpretive essays by Robert E. Meagher. New York: Harper Colophon Books, 1979.

American Journals. Trans. Hugh Levick. New York: Paragon House, 1987 [*Journaux de voyage.* Texte établi, présenté et annoté par Roger Quilliot. Paris: Éditions Gallimard, 1978].

Between Hell and Reason: Essays from the Resistance Newspaper "Combat," 1944–1947. Selected and trans. Alexandre de Gramont. Hanover, CT: Wesleyan University Press, 1991.

Lyrical and Critical Essays. Ed. Philip Thody. Trans. Ellen Conroy Kennedy. New York: Knopf, 1968 [1938–59].

The Myth of Sisyphus, and Other Essays. Trans. Justin O'Brien. New York: Knopf, 1955 [*Le Mythe de Sisyphe: Essai sur l'absurde.* Paris: Éditions Gallimard, 1942].

Notebooks, 1935–1942. Trans. Philip Thody. New York: Knopf, 1963 [*Carnets. 1. Mai 1935–février 1942.* Paris: Éditions Gallimard, 1962].

Notebooks, 1942–1951. Trans. Justin O'Brien. New York: Knopf, 1965 [*Carnets. 2. Janvier 1942–mars 1951.* Paris: Éditions Gallimard, 1964].

The Rebel: An Essay on Man in Revolt. Rev. and trans. Anthony Bower. New York: Knopf, 1954 [*L'Homme révolté.* Paris: Éditions Gallimard, 1951].

Resistance, Rebellion, and Death. Trans. and intro. Justin O'Brien. New York: Knopf, 1961.

Selected Essays and Notebooks. Ed. and trans. Philip Thody. London: Penguin, 1970.

September 15th, 1937: From the Notebooks of Albert Camus. Bronxville, NY: Valenti Angelo, 1963.

Speech of Acceptance Upon the Award of the Nobel Prize for Literature: Delivered in Stockholm on the 10th of December, 1957. Trans. Justin O'Brien. New York: Knopf, 1958.

Youthful Writings. Intro. Paul Vialleneix. Trans. Ellen Conroy Kennedy. New York: Knopf, 1976 [*Cahiers Albert Camus. 2: Le Premier Camus* par Paul Viallaneix. *Suivi d'Écrits de jeunesse* Paris: Éditions Gallimard, 1973].

And Jean Grenier. *Correspondence, 1932–1960.* Trans. and intro. Jan F. Rigaud. Additional annotations by Marguerite Dobrenn. Lincoln: University of

Nebraska Press, 2003 [*Correspondance: 1932–1960.* Avertissement et notes par Marguerite Dobrenn. Paris: Éditions Gallimard, 1981].

And Arthur Koestler. *Reflections on the Guillotine: An Essay on Capital Punishment.* Trans. Richard Howard. Michigan City, IN: Fridtjof-Karla Publications, 1959 [*Réflexions sur la peine capitale.* Paris: Calman-Lévy, 1957].

And Jean-Paul Sartre. *Sartre and Camus: A Historic Confrontation.* Ed. and trans. David A. Sprintzen and Adrian van den Hoven. Amherst, NY: Humanity Books, 2004.

Georges Canguilhem

Ideology and Rationality in the History of the Life Sciences. Trans. Arthur Goldhammer. Cambridge, MA: MIT Press, 1988 [*Idéologie et rationalité dans l'histoire des sciences de la vie: Nouvelles études d'histoire et de philosophie des sciences.* Paris: J. Vrin, 1977].

On the Normal and the Pathological. Trans. Carolyn R. Fawcett in collaboration with Robert S. Cohen. Intro. Michel Foucault. New York: Zone Books, 1989 [*Essai sur quelques problèmes concernant le normal et le pathologique.* Clermont-Ferrand: Publications de la Faculté des lettres de l'Université de Strasbourg, 1943; *Le Normal et le pathologique.* Paris: Presses universitaires de France, 1966].

A Vital Rationalist: Selected Writings from Georges Canguilhem. Ed. François Delaporte. Trans. Arthur Goldhammer. New York: Zone Books, 1994.

Cornelius Castoriadis

The Castoriadis Reader. Trans. and ed. David Ames Curtis. Oxford: Blackwell, 1997.

Crossroads in the Labyrinth. Trans. Kate Soper and Martin H. Ryle. Cambridge, MA: MIT Press, 1984 [*Les Carrefours du labyrinthe.* Paris: Éditions du Seuil, 1978].

History and Revolution: A Revolutionary Critique of Historical Materialism. London: Solidarity, 1971.

History as Creation. London: Solidarity, 1978.

The Imaginary Institution of Society. Trans. Kathleen Blamey. Cambridge, MA: MIT Press, 1987 [*L'Institution imaginaire de la société*. Paris: Éditions du Seuil, 1975].

On Plato's "Statesman." Ed. and trans. David Ames Curtis. Stanford, CA: Stanford University Press, 2002 [*Sur "le politique" de Platon*. Paris: Éditions du Seuil, 1999].

Philosophy, Politics, Autonomy. Ed. David Ames Curtis. New York: Oxford University Press, 1991.

Political and Social Writings. 3 Vols. Trans. and ed. David Ames Curtis. Minneapolis: University of Minnesota Press, 1988–93.

World in Fragments: Writings on Politics, Society, Psychoanalysis, and the Imagination. Ed. and trans. David Ames Curtis. Stanford, CA: Stanford University Press, 1997.

Hélène Cixous

"Coming to Writing" and Other Essays. Ed. Deborah Jenson. Trans. Sarah Cornell, et al. Cambridge, MA: Harvard University Press, 1991 [*La Venue à l'écriture*. Paris: Union générale d'Éditions, 1977].

The Exile of James Joyce. Trans. Sally A. J. Purcell. New York: D. Lewis, 1972 [*L'Exil de James Joyce ou l'art du remplacement*. Paris: B. Grasset, 1968].

The Hélène Cixous Reader. Ed. Susan Sellers. Preface by Hélène Cixous and foreword by Jacques Derrida. New York: Routledge, 1994.

Neuter. Trans. and intro. Lorene M. Birden. Lewisburg, PA: Bucknell University Press, 2004 [*Neutre*. Paris: B. Grasset, 1972].

Portrait of Jacques Derrida as Young Jewish Saint. Trans. Beverly Bie Brahic. New York: Columbia University Press, 2003 [*Portrait de Jacques Derrida en jeune saint juif*. Paris: Galilée, 2001].

Reading with Clarice Lispector. Ed., trans., and intro. Verena Andermatt Conley. Minneapolis: University of Minnesota Press, 1990.

Readings: The Poetics of Blanchot, Joyce, Kafka, Kleist, Lispector, and Tsve-tayeva. Ed., trans., and intro. Verena Andermatt Conley. Minneapolis: University of Minnesota Press, 1991.

Stigmata: Escaping Texts. New York: Routledge, 1998.

Three Steps on the Ladder of Writing. Trans. Sarah Cornell and Susan Sellers. New York: Columbia University Press, 1993.

Writing Differences: Readings from the Seminar of Hélène Cixous. Ed. Susan Sellers. New York: St. Martin's Press, 1988.

And Mireille Calle-Gruber. *Hélène Cixous, Rootprints: Memory and Life Writing*. Trans. Eric Prenowitz. New York: Routledge, 1997.

And Catherine Clément. *The Newly Born Woman*. Trans. Betsy Wing. Minneapolis: University of Minnesota Press, 1986 [*La Jeune née*. Paris: Union générale d'Éditions, 1975].

And Jacques Derrida. *Veils*. Trans. Geoffrey Bennington. Stanford, CA: Stanford University Press, 2001 [*Voiles*. Paris: Galilée, 1998].

Gilles Deleuze

Bergsonism. Trans. Hugh Tomlinson and Barbara Habberjam. New York: Zone Books, 1988 [*Le Bergsonisme*. Paris: Presses universitaires de France, 1966].

Cinema 1: The Movement-Image. Trans. Hugh Tomlinson and Barbara Habberjam. Minneapolis: University of Minnesota Press, 1986 [*Cinema 1: L'Image-mouvement*. Paris: Éditions de Minuit, 1983].

Cinema 2: The Time Image. Trans. Hugh Tomlinson and Robert Galeta. Minneapolis: University of Minnesota Press, 1989 [*Cinema 2: L'Image-temps*. Paris: Éditions de Minuit, 1985].

The Deleuze Reader. Ed. and intro. Constantin V. Boundas. New York: Columbia University Press, 1993.

Desert Islands and Other Texts (1953–1974). Ed. David Lapoujade. Trans. Mike Taormina. Cambridge, MA: MIT Press, 2003 [*L'Île déserte et autres textes: Textes et entretiens, 1953–1974*. Édition préparée par David Lapoujade. Paris: Éditions de Minuit, 2002.].

Difference and Repetition. Trans. Paul Patton. New York: Columbia University Press, 1994 [*Différence et répétition.* Paris: Presses universitaires de France, 1968].

Empiricism and Subjectivity: An Essay on Hume's Theory of Human Nature. Trans. and intro. Constantin V. Boundas. New York: Columbia University Press, 1991 [*Empirisme et subjectivité: Essai sur la nature humaine selon Hume.* Paris: Presses universitaires de France, 1953].

Essays Critical and Clinical. Trans. Daniel W. Smith and Michael A. Greco. Minneapolis: University of Minnesota Press, 1997 [*Critique et clinique.* Paris: Éditions de Minuit, 1993].

Expressionism in Philosophy: Spinoza. Trans. Martin Joughin. New York: Zone Books, 1990 [*Spinoza et le problème de l'expression.* Paris: Éditions de Minuit, 1968].

The Fold: Leibniz and the Baroque. Trans. Tom Conley. Minneapolis: University of Minnesota Press, 1993 [*Le Pli: Leibniz et le baroque.* Paris: Éditions de Minuit, 1988].

Foucault. Ed. and trans. Seán Hand. Minneapolis: University of Minnesota Press, 1988 [*Foucault.* Paris: Éditions de Minuit, 1986].

Francis Bacon: The Logic of Sensation. Trans. and intro. Daniel W. Smith. Minneapolis: University of Minnesota Press, 2004. [*Francis Bacon: Logique de la sensation.* Paris: Éditions de la Différence, 1981].

Kant's Critical Philosophy: The Doctrine of the Faculties. Trans. Hugh Tomlinson and Barbara Habberjam. Minneapolis: University of Minnesota Press, 1984 [*La Philosophie critique de Kant: Doctrine des facultés.* Paris: Presses universitaires de France, 1963].

The Logic of Sense. Ed. Constantin V. Boundas. Trans. Mark Lester with Charles Stivale. New York: Columbia University Press, 1990 [*Logique du sens.* Paris: Éditions de Minuit, 1969].

Masochism: An Interpretation of Coldness and Cruelty. Trans. Jean McNeil. With *Venus in Furs*, by Leopold von Sacher-Masoch. Trans. Aude Willm. New York: G. Braziller, 1971 [*Présentation de Sacher-Masoch: Le Froid et le cruel: avec le texte intégral de La vénus à la fourrure.* Paris: Éditions de Minuit, 1967].

Negotiations, 1972–1990. Trans. Martin Joughin. New York: Columbia University Press, 1995 [*Pourparlers: 1972–1990*. Paris: Éditions de Minuit, 1990].

Nietzsche and Philosophy. Trans. Hugh Tomlinson. New York: Columbia University Press, 1983 [*Nietzsche et la philosophie*. Paris: Presses universitaires de France, 1962].

Proust and Signs. Trans. Richard Howard. New York: G. Braziller, 1972 [*Marcel Proust et les signes*. Paris: Presses universitaires de France, 1964].

Pure Immanence: Essays on A Life. Ed. and intro. John Rajchman. Trans. Anne Boyman. New York: Zone Books, 2001.

Spinoza, Practical Philosophy. Trans. Robert Hurley. San Francisco: City Lights Books, 1988 [*Spinoza, philosophie pratique*. Paris: Éditions de Minuit, 1970, revd. 1981].

And Félix Guattari. *Anti-Oedipus: Capitalism and Schizophrenia*. Trans. Robert Hurley, Mark Seem, and Helen R. Lane. New York: Viking Press, 1977 [*Capitalisme et schizophrénie. 1. L'Anti-Oedipe*. Paris: Éditions de Minuit, 1972].

And Félix Guattari. *Kafka: Toward a Minor Literature*. Trans. Dana Polan. Minneapolis: University of Minnesota Press, 1986 [*Kafka: Pour une littérature mineure*. Paris: Éditions de Minuit, 1975].

And Félix Guattari. *On the Line*. Trans. John Johnston. New York: Semiotext(e), 1983.

And Félix Guattari. *A Thousand Plateaus: Capitalism and Schizophrenia*. Trans. Brian Massumi. Minneapolis: University of Minnesota Press, 1987 [*Capitalisme et schizophrénie. 2. Mille plateaux*. Paris: Éditions de Minuit, 1980].

And Félix Guattari. *What is Philosophy?* Trans. Hugh Tomlinson and Graham Burchell. New York: Columbia University Press, 1994 [*Qu'est-ce que la philosophie?* Paris: Éditions de Minuit, 1991].

And Claire Parnet. *Dialogues*. Trans. Hugh Tomlinson and Barbara Habberjam. New York: Columbia University Press, 1987. Second edition includes new essay, "The Actual and the Virtual." Trans. Eliot Ross Albert. New York: Columbia University Press, 2002 [*Dialogues*. Paris: Flammarion, 1977].

Jacques Derrida

Acts of Literature. Ed. Derek Attridge. New York: Routledge, 1992.

Acts of Religion. Ed., trans., and intro. Gil Anidjar. New York: Routledge, 2002.

Adieu to Emmanuel Levinas. Trans. Pascale-Anne Brault and Michael Naas. Stanford, CA: Stanford University Press, 1999 [*Adieu: À Emmanuel Lévinas.* Paris: Galilée, 1997].

Aporias: Dying–Awaiting (One Another At) the "Limits of Truth." Trans. Thomas Dutoit. Stanford, CA: Stanford University Press, 1993 [*Apories: Mourir—s'attendre aux "limites de la vérité."* Paris: Galilée, 1995].

The Archeology of the Frivolous: Reading Condillac. Trans. and intro. John P. Leavey, Jr. Pittsburgh, PA: Duquesne University Press, 1980 [*L'Archéologie du frivole: Lire Condillac.* Paris: Galilée, 1976].

Archive Fever: A Freudian Impression. Trans. Eric Prenowitz. Chicago: University of Chicago Press, 1996 [*Mal d'archive: Une impression freudienne.* Paris: Galilée, 1995].

Cinders. Ed., trans., and intro. Ned Lukacher. Lincoln: University of Nebraska Press, 1991 [*Feu la cendre.* Paris: Éditions des Femmes, 1987].

Deconstruction in a Nutshell: A Conversation with Jacques Derrida. Ed. John D. Caputo. New York: Fordham University Press, 1997.

A Derrida Reader: Between the Blinds. Ed. and intro. Peggy Kamuf. New York: Columbia University Press, 1991.

The Derrida Reader: Writing Performances. Ed. Julian Wolfreys. Lincoln: University of Nebraska Press, 1998.

Dissemination. Trans. and intro. Barbara Johnson. Chicago: University of Chicago Press, 1981 [*La Dissémination.* Paris: Éditions du Seuil, 1972].

The Ear of the Other: Otobiography, Transference, Translation: Texts and Discussions with Jacques Derrida. Ed. Claude Lévesque and Christie V. MacDonald. Trans. Peggy Kamuf. New York: Schocken Books, 1985 [*L'Oreille de l'autre: Otobiographies, transferts, traductions: Textes et débats avec Jacques Derrida.* Montréal: VLB, 1982].

Edmund Husserl's Origin of Geometry: An Introduction. Trans. John P. Leavey, Jr. Lincoln: University of Nebraska Press, 1989 [*Edmund Husserl. L'Origine de la géométrie*. Paris: Presses universitaires de France, 1962].

Ethics, Institutions, and the Right to Philosophy. Trans. and ed. Peter Pericles Trifonas. Lanham, MD: Rowman and Littlefield, 2002.

Eyes of the University: Right to Philosophy 2. Trans. Jan Plug and others. Stanford, CA: Stanford University Press, 2004 [*Du droit à la philosophie*. Paris: Galilée, 1990].

For Nelson Mandela. Ed. Jacques Derrida and Mustapha Tlili. New York: Seaver Books, 1987.

The Gift of Death. Trans. David Wills. Chicago: University of Chicago Press, 1995 [*Donner la mort*. In *L'Éthique du don: Jacques Derrida et la pensée du don*. Paris: Métailié-Transition, 1992].

Given Time: I. Counterfeit Money. Trans. Peggy Kamuf. Chicago: University of Chicago Press, 1992 [*Donner le temps. 1. La Fausse monnaie*. Paris: Galilée, 1991].

Glas. Trans. John P. Leavey, Jr. and Richard Rand. Lincoln: University of Nebraska Press, 1986 [*Glas*. Paris: Galilée, 1974].

Limited Inc. Trans. Samuel Weber and others. Evanston, IL: Northwestern University Press, 1988 [1977].

Margins of Philosophy. Trans. Alan Bass. Chicago: University of Chicago Press, 1982 [*Marges de la philosophie*. Paris: Éditions de Minuit, 1972].

Memoirs: For Paul de Man. Trans. Cecile Lindsay, Jonathan Culler, and Eduardo Cadava. New York: Columbia University Press, 1986 [*Mémoires: Pour Paul de Man*. Paris: Galilée, 1988].

Memoirs of the Blind: The Self-Portrait and Other Ruins. Trans. Pascale-Anne Brault and Michael Naas. Chicago: University of Chicago Press, 1993 [*Mémoires d'aveugle: L'Autoportrait et autres ruines*. Paris: Réunion des musées nationaux, 1990].

Monolingualism of the Other, or, The Prosthesis of Origin. Trans. Patrick Mensah. Stanford, CA: Stanford University Press, 1998 [*Le Monolinguisme de l'autre, ou, la prothèse d'origine*. Paris: Galilée, 1996].

Negotiations: Interventions and Interviews, 1971–2001. Ed. Elizabeth Rottenberg. Stanford, CA: Stanford University Press, 2002.

Of Grammatology. Trans. Gayatri Chakravorty Spivak. Baltimore, MD: Johns Hopkins University Press, 1976 [*De la grammatologie.* Paris: Éditions de Minuit, 1967].

Of Hospitality. Trans. Rachel Bowlby. Stanford, CA: Stanford University Press, 2000 [*De l'hospitalité.* Paris: Calmann-Lévy, 1997].

Of Spirit: Heidegger and the Question. Trans. Geoffrey Bennington and Rachel Bowlby. Chicago: University of Chicago Press, 1989 [*De l'esprit: Heidegger et la question.* Paris: Galilée, 1987].

On Cosmopolitanism and Forgiveness. Trans. Mark Dooley and Michael Hughes. New York: Routledge, 2001 [*Cosmopolites de tous les pays, encore un effort!* Paris: Galilée, 1997].

On the Name. Ed. Thomas Dutoit. Trans. David Wood, John P. Leavey, and Ian McLeod. Stanford, CA: Stanford University Press, 1995 [*Sauf le nom.* Paris: Galilée, 1993].

The Other Heading: Reflections on Today's Europe. Trans. Pascale-Anne Brault and Michael B. Naas. Bloomington: Indiana University Press, 1992 [*L'Autre cap; suivi de La Démocratie ajournée.* Paris: Éditions de Minuit, 1991].

Paper Machine. Trans. Rachel Bowlby. Stanford, CA: Stanford University Press, 2005 [*Papier Machine: Le Ruban de machine à écrire et autres réponses.* Paris: Galilée, 2001].

Points … : Interviews, 1974–1994. Ed. Elisabeth Weber. Trans. Peggy Kamuf and others. Stanford, CA: Stanford University Press, 1995 [*Points de suspension: Entretiens.* Paris: Galilée, 1992].

Politics of Friendship. Trans. George Collins. London: Verso, 1997 [*Politiques de l'amitié.* Paris: Galilée, 1994].

Positions. Trans. Alan Bass. Chicago: University of Chicago Press, 1981 [*Positions: Entretiens avec Henri Ronse, Julia Kristeva, Jean-Louis Houdebine, Guy Scarpetta.* Paris: Éditions de Minuit, 1972].

The Post Card: From Socrates to Freud and Beyond. Trans. and intro. Alan Bass. Chicago: University of Chicago Press, 1987 [*La Carte postale: De Socrate à Freud et au-delà.* Paris: Flammarion, 1980].

The Problem of Genesis in Husserl's Philosophy. Trans. Marian Hobson. Chicago: University of Chicago Press, 2003 [*Problème de la genèse dans la philosophie de Husserl.* Paris: Presses universitaires de France, 1990].

Raising the Tone of Philosophy: Late Essays by Immanuel Kant, Transformative Critique by Jacques Derrida. Ed. Peter Fenves. Trans. John Leavey, Jr. Baltimore, MD: Johns Hopkins University Press, 1993 [*D'un Ton apocalyptique adopté naguère en philosophie.* Paris: Galilée, 1983].

Resistances of Psychoanalysis. Trans. Peggy Kamuf, Pascale-Anne Brault, and Michael Naas. Stanford, CA: Stanford University Press, 1998 [*Résistances de la psychanalyse.* Paris: Galilée, 1996].

Right of Inspection. Photographs by Marie-Françoise Plissart. Trans. David Wills. New York: Monacelli Press, 1998 [*Droit de regards, suivi de Une lecture de Jacques Derrida.* Paris: Éditions de Minuit, 1985].

Rogues: Two Essays on Reason. Trans. Pascale-Anne Brault and Michael Naas. Stanford, CA: Stanford University Press, 2005 [*Voyous.* Paris: Galilée, 2003].

Signéponge/Signsponge. Trans. Richard Rand. New York: Columbia University Press, 1984 [*Signéponge.* Paris: Éditions du Seuil, 1984].

Sovereignties in Question: The Poetics of Paul Celan. Ed. Thomas Dutoit and Outi Pasanean. New York: Fordham University Press, 2005.

Specters of Marx: The State of the Debt, the Work of Mourning, and the New International. Trans. Peggy Kamuf. New York: Routledge, 1994 [*Spectres de Marx: L'État de la dette, le travail du deuil et la nouvelle Internationale.* Paris: Galilée, 1993].

Speech and Phenomena, and Other Essays on Husserl's Theory of Signs. Trans. and intro. David B. Allison. Evanston, IL: Northwestern University Press, 1973 [*La Voix et le phénomène: Introduction au problème du signe dans la phénoménologie de Husserl.* Paris: Presses universitaires de France, 1967].

Spurs: Nietzsche's Styles. Trans. Barbara Harlow. Chicago: University of Chicago Press, 1979 [*Éperons: Les Styles de Nietzsche.* Paris: Flammarion, 1978].

The Truth in Painting. Trans. Geoff Bennington and Ian McLeod. Chicago: University of Chicago Press, 1987 [*La Vérité en peinture.* Paris: Flammarion, 1978].

Who's Afraid of Philosophy? Right to Philosophy 1. Trans. Jan Plug. Stanford, CA: Stanford University Press, 2002 [*Du droit à la philosophie*. Paris: Galilée, 1990].

Without Alibi. Ed., trans., and intro. Peggy Kamuf. Stanford, CA: Stanford University Press, 2002.

The Work of Mourning. Ed. and trans. Pascale-Anne Brault and Michael Naas. Chicago: University of Chicago Press, 2001 [*Chaque fois unique, la fin du monde*. Présenté par Pascale-Anne Brault et Michael Naas. Paris: Galilée, 2003].

Writing and Difference. Ed., trans., and intro. Alan Bass. Chicago: University of Chicago Press, 1978 [*L'Écriture et la différence*. Paris: Éditions du Seuil, 1967].

And Geoffrey Bennington. *Jacques Derrida*. Trans. Geoffrey Bennington. Chicago: University of Chicago Press, 1993 [*Jacques Derrida*. Paris: Éditions du Seuil, 1991].

And Maurice Blanchot. *The Instant of My Death/Demeure: Fiction and Testimony*. Trans. Elizabeth Rottenberg. Stanford, CA: Stanford University Press, 2000 [*Demeure*. Paris: Galilée, 1998].

And Hélène Cixous. *Veils*. Trans. Geoffrey Bennington. Stanford, CA: Stanford University Press, 2001 [*Voiles*. Paris: Galilée, 1998].

And Peter Eisenman. *Chora L Works*. Ed. Jeffrey Kipnis and Thomas Leeser. New York: Monacelli Press, 1997.

And Maurizio Ferraris. *A Taste for the Secret*. Ed. Giacomo Donis and David Webb. Trans. Giacomo Donis. Oxford: Blackwell, 2001 [*Il gusto del segreto*. Rome: Laterza, 1997].

And Jürgen Habermas. *Philosophy in a Time of Terror: Dialogues with Jürgen Habermas and Jacques Derrida*. Interviews with Giovanna Borradori. Chicago: University of Chicago Press, 2003 [*Le «concept» du 11 septembre: Dialogues à New York (octobre–décembre 2001) avec Giovanna Borradori*. Paris: Galilée, 2001]

And Catherine Malabou. *Counterpath: Traveling with Jacques Derrida*. Trans. David Wills. Stanford, CA: Stanford University Press, 2004 [*Voyager avec Jacques Derrida–La Contre-allée*. Paris: Quinzaine littéraire, 1999].

And others. *Questioning Judaism*. Interviews by Elisabeth Weber. Trans. Rachel Bowlby. Stanford, CA: Stanford University Press, 2004 [*Jüdisches Denken in*

Frankreich. Gespräche mit Pierre Vidal-Naquet, Jacques Derrida, Rita Thalmann, Emmanuel Lévinas, Léon Poliakov, Jean-François Lyotard, Luc Rosenzweig. Französischen übersetzt von Elisabeth Weber. Frankfurt am Main: Jüdischer Verlag, 1994].

And Elisabeth Roudinesco *For What Tomorrow: A Dialogue.* Trans. Jeff Fort. Stanford, CA: Stanford University Press, 2004 [*De quoi demain.* Paris: Flammarion, 2003].

And Bernard Stiegler. *Echographies of Television: Filmed Interviews.* Trans. Jennifer Bajorek. Oxford: Blackwell, 2002 [*Échographies de la télévision: Entretiens filmés.* Paris: Galilée, 1996].

And Paule Thévenin. *The Secret Art of Antonin Artaud.* Trans. Mary Ann Caws. Cambridge, MA: MIT Press, 1998 [*Antonin Artaud, dessins et portraits.* Paris: Éditions Gallimard, 1986].

And Gianni Vattimo. *Religion.* Stanford, CA: Stanford University Press, 1998 [*La Religion: Séminaire de Capri.* Paris: Éditions du Seuil, 1996].

Vincent Descombes

The Barometer of Modern Reason: On the Philosophies of Current Events. Trans. Stephen Adam Schwartz. New York: Oxford University Press, 1993 [*Philosophie par gros temps.* Paris: Éditions de Minuit, 1989].

The Mind's Provisions: A Critique of Cognitivism. Trans. Stephen Adam Schwartz. Princeton, NJ: Princeton University Press, 2001 [*Les Disputes de l'esprit.* Paris: Éditions de Minuit, 1995].

Modern French Philosophy. Trans. L. Scott-Fox and J. M. Harding. New York: Cambridge University Press, 1980 [*Le Même et l'autre: Quarante-cinq ans de philosophie française.* Paris: Éditions de Minuit, 1979].

Objects of All Sorts: A Philosophical Grammar. Trans. Lorna Scott-Fox and Jeremy Harding. Baltimore, MD: Johns Hopkins University Press, 1986 [*Grammaire d'objets en tous genres.* Paris: Éditions de Minuit, 1983].

Proust: Philosophy of the Novel. Trans. Catherine Chance Macksey. Stanford, CA: Stanford University Press, 1992 [*Proust: Philosophie du roman.* Paris: Éditions de Minuit, 1987].

Frantz Fanon

Black Skin, White Masks. Trans. Charles Lam Markmann. New York: Grove Press, 1967 [*Peau noire, masques blancs.* Paris: Éditions du Seuil, 1952].

The Fanon Reader. Ed. Azzedine Haddour. London: Pluto Press, 2002.

Studies in a Dying Colonialism. Trans. Haakon Chevalier. New York: Monthly Review Press, 1965 [*L'An V de la révolution algérienne.* Paris: F. Maspero, 1959].

Toward the African Revolution: Political Essays. Trans. Haakon Chevalier. New York: Monthly Review Press, 1967 [*Pour la révolution africaine: Écrits politiques.* Paris: F. Maspero, 1964].

The Wretched of the Earth. Trans. Constance Farrington. Preface by John-Paul Sartre. New York: Grove Press, 1963 [*Les Damnés de la terre.* Paris: F. Maspero, 1961].

The Wretched of the Earth. Trans. Richard Philcox. Introductions by Jean-Paul Sartre and Homi K. Bhabha. New York: Grove Press, 2004 [*Les Damnés de la terre.* Paris: F. Maspero, 1961].

Michel Foucault

Abnormal: Lectures at the Collège de France, 1974–1975. Ed. Valerio Marchetti and Antonella Salomoni with general editors François Ewald and Alessandro Fontana. Trans. Graham Burchell. New York: Picador, 2003 [*Les Anormaux: Cours au Collège de France, 1974–1975.* Édition établie sous la direction de François Ewald et Alessandro Fontana, par Valerio Marchetti et Antonella Salomoni. Paris: Éditions Gallimard/Seuil, 1999].

The Archeaology of Knowledge. Trans. A. M. Sheridan Smith. New York: Pantheon Books, 1972 [*L'Archéologie du savoir.* Paris: Éditions Gallimard, 1969].

The Birth of the Clinic: An Archeology of Medical Perception. Trans. A. M. Sheridan Smith. New York: Vintage Books, 1973 [*Naissance de la clinique: Une archéologie du regard médical.* Paris: Presses universitaires de France, 1963].

Death and the Labyrinth: The World of Raymond Roussel. Trans. Charles Ruas. Garden City, NY: Doubleday, 1986 [*Raymond Roussel.* Paris: Éditions Gallimard, 1963].

Discipline and Punish: The Birth of the Prison. Trans. Alan Sheridan. New York: Vintage Books, 1977 [*Surveiller et punir: Naissance de la prison.* Paris: Éditions Gallimard, 1975].

The Essential Works of Michel Foucault, 1954–1988. 3 Vols. Ed. Paul Rabinow. *Vol. 1: Ethics: Subjectivity and Truth.* Ed. Paul Rabinow. Trans. Robert Hurley. New York: New Press, 1997. *Vol. 2: Aesthetics, Method, and Epistemology.* Ed. James D. Faubion. Trans. Robert Hurley. New York: New Press, 1998. *Vol. 3: Power.* Ed. James D. Faubion. Trans. Robert Hurley. New York: New Press, 2000.

Fearless Speech. Ed. Joseph Pearson. Los Angeles: Semiotext(e), 2001.

The Foucault Effect: Studies in Governmentality: With Two Lectures by and an Interview with Michel Foucault. Ed. Graham Burchell, Colin Gordon, and Peter Miller. Chicago: University of Chicago Press, 1991.

Foucault Live: Interviews, 1966–1984. Ed. Sylvère Lotringer. Trans. John Johnston. New York: Semiotext(e), 1989.

The Foucault Reader. Ed. Paul Rabinow. New York: Pantheon Books, 1984.

The Hermeneutics of the Subject: Lectures at the Collège de France, 1981–1982. Ed. Frédéric Gros with general editors François Ewald and Alessandro Fontana. Trans. Graham Burchell. New York: Palgrave-Macmillan, 2005. [*L'Herméneutique du sujet: Cours au Collège de France, 1981–1982.* Édition établie sous la direction de François Ewald et Alessandro Fontana, par Frédéric Gros. Paris: Éditions Gallimard/Seuil, 2001].

History of Madness. Trans. Jonathan Murphy. New York: Routledge, 2005 [*Histoire de la folie à l'âge classique.* Paris: Plon, 1961].

The History of Sexuality. Vol. 1: An Introduction. Trans. Robert Hurley. New York: Vintage Books, 1980 [*Histoire de la sexualité. 1. La Volonté de savoir.* Paris: Éditions Gallimard, 1976].

The History of Sexuality. Vol. 2: The Use of Pleasure. Trans. Robert Hurley. New York: Pantheon Books, 1985 [*Histoire de la sexualité. 2. L'Usage des plaisirs.* Paris: Éditions Gallimard, 1984].

The History of Sexuality. Vol. 3: Care of the Self. Trans. Robert Hurley. New York: Pantheon Books, 1986 [*Histoire de la sexualité. 3. Le Souci de soi.* Paris: Éditions Gallimard, 1984].

*I, Pierre Riviere, Having Slaughtered My Mother, My Sister, and My Brother –
A Case of Parricide in the 19th Century.* Ed. Michel Foucault. Trans. Frank
Jellinek. New York: Pantheon Books, 1975 [*Moi, Pierre Rivière, ayant égorgé ma
mère, ma soeur et mon frère . . . Un cas de parricide au XIXe siècle.* Paris: Éditions
Gallimard, 1973].

Language, Counter-Memory, Practice: Selected Essays and Interviews. Ed. and
intro. Donald F. Bouchard. Trans. Donald F. Bouchard and Sherry Simon.
Ithaca, NY: Cornell University Press, 1977.

Madness and Civilization: A History of Insanity in the Age of Reason. Trans.
Richard Howard. New York: Pantheon Books, 1965 [Abridged English translation of *Histoire de la folie à l'âge classique.* Paris: Plon, 1961].

Maurice Blanchot: The Thought From Outside. Trans. Brian Massumi. New
York: Zone Books, 1987 [*La Pensée du dehors.* Saint-Clément: Fata Morgana,
1986].

Mental Illness and Psychology. Trans. Alan Sheridan. New York: Harper and
Row, 1976 [*Maladie mentale et psychologie.* Paris: Presses universitaires de
France, 1962. Significant revision of *Maladie mentale et personnalité.* Paris:
Presses universitaires de France, 1954].

The Order of Things: An Archeology of the Human Sciences. New York: Vintage
Books, 1970 [*Les Mots et les choses: Une archéologie des sciences humaines.* Paris:
Éditions Gallimard, 1966].

The Politics of Truth. Ed. Sylvère Lotringer and Lysa Hochroth. New York:
Semiotext(e), 1997.

Politics, Philosophy, Culture: Interviews and Other Writings, 1977–1984. Ed. and
intro. Lawrence D. Kritzman. Trans. Alan Sheridan and others. New York:
Routledge, 1988.

Power/Knowledge: Selected Interviews and Other Writings, 1972–1977. Ed.
Colin Gordon. Trans. Colin Gordon, et al. New York: Pantheon Books,
1980.

Religion and Culture. Ed. Jeremy R. Carrette. New York: Routledge, 1999.

Society Must Be Defended: Lectures at the Collège de France, 1975–76. Ed. Mauro
Bertani and Alessandro Fontana with general editors François Ewald and

Alessandro Fontana. Trans. David Macey. New York: Picador, 2003 [*Il faut défendre la société: Cours au Collège de France, 1975–1976*. Edition établie, dans le cadre de l'Association pour le Centre Michel Foucault, sous la direction de François Ewald et Alessandro Fontana, par Mauro Bertani et Alessandro Fontana. Paris: Éditions Gallimard/Seuil, 1997].

Technologies of the Self: A Seminar with Michel Foucault. Ed. Luther H. Martin, Huck Gutman, and Patrick H. Hutton. Amherst: University of Massachusetts Press, 1988.

This Is Not a Pipe. With illustrations and letters by René Magritte. Trans. and ed. James Harkness. Berkeley: University of California Press, 1983 [*Ceci n'est pas une pipe: Sur Magritte*. Montpellier: Fata Morgana, 1973].

And Ludwig Binswanger. *Dream and Existence*. Ed. Keith Hoeller. Trans. Forrest Williams and Jacob Needleman. Atlantic Highlands, NJ: Humanities Press, 1993 [*Le Rêve et l'existence*. Paris: Desclée de Brouwer, 1954].

And Duccio Trombadori. *Remarks on Marx*. Trans. R. James Goldstein and James Cascaito. New York: Semiotext(e), 1991 [*Colloqui con Foucault*. Salerno: Cooperativa Editrice, 1981].

Jean Hyppolite

Genesis and Structure of Hegel's Phenomenology of Spirit. Trans. Samuel Cherniak and John Heckman. Evanston, IL: Northwestern University Press, 1974 [*Genèse et structure de la "Phénoménologie de l'esprit" de Hegel*. Paris: Aubier, 1946].

Introduction to Hegel's Philosophy of History. Trans. Bond Harris and Jacqueline Bouchard Spurlock. Gainesville: University Press of Florida, 1996 [*Introduction à la philosophie de l'histoire de Hegel*. Paris: M. Rivière, 1948].

Logic and Existence. Trans. Leonard Lawlor and Amit Sen. Albany: State University of New York Press, 1997 [*Logique et existence: Essai sur la logique de Hegel*. Paris: Presses universitaires de France, 1953].

Studies on Marx and Hegel. Trans., intro., and biblio. John O'Neill. New York: Basic Books, 1969 [*Études sur Marx et Hegel*. Paris: M. Rivière, 1955].

Luce Irigaray

Between East and West: From Singularity to Community. Trans. Stephen Pluhácek. New York: Columbia University Press, 2002 [*Entre Orient et Occident: De la singularité à la communauté.* Paris: B. Grasset, 1999].

Democracy Begins Between Two. Trans. Kirsteen Anderson. New York: Routledge, 2001 [*La democrazia comincia a due.* Turin: Bollati Boringhieri, 1994].

Elemental Passions. Trans. Joanne Collie and Judith Still. New York: Routledge, 1992 [*Passions élémentaires.* Paris: Éditions de Minuit, 1982].

An Ethics of Sexual Difference. Trans. Carolyn Burke and Gillian C. Gill. Ithaca, NY: Cornell University Press, 1993 [*Éthique de la différence sexuelle.* Paris: Éditions de Minuit, 1984].

The Forgetting of Air in Martin Heidegger. Trans. Mary Beth Mader. Austin: University of Texas Press, 1999 [*L'Oubli de l'air chez Martin Heidegger.* Paris: Éditions de Minuit, 1982].

I Love to You: Sketch for a Felicity within History. Trans. Alison Martin. New York: Routledge, 1996 [*J'aime à toi: Esquisse d'une félicité dans l'histoire.* Paris: B. Grasset, 1992].

The Irigaray Reader. Ed. and intro. Margaret Whitford. Oxford: Blackwell, 1991.

Je, tu, nous: Toward a Culture of Difference. Trans. Alison Martin. New York: Routledge, 1993 [*Je, tu, nous: Pour une culture de la différence.* Paris: Éditions Grasset et Fasquelle, 1990].

Luce Irigaray: Key Writings. Ed. Luce Irigaray. London: Continuum, 2004.

Marine Lover: Of Friedrich Nietzsche. Trans. Gillian C. Gill. New York: Columbia University Press, 1991 [*Amante marine: De Friedrich Nietzsche.* Paris: Éditions de Minuit, 1980].

Sexes and Genealogies. Trans. Gillian C. Gill. New York: Columbia University Press, 1993 [*Sexes et parentés.* Paris: Éditions de Minuit, 1987].

Speculum of the Other Woman. Trans. Gillian C. Gill. Ithaca, NY: Cornell University Press, 1985 [*Speculum: De l'autre femme.* Paris: Éditions de Minuit, 1974].

Thinking the Difference: For a Peaceful Revolution. Trans. Karin Montin. New York: Routledge, 1994 [*Le Temps de la différence.* Paris: Librairie générale française, 1989].

This Sex Which Is Not One. Trans. Catherine Porter with Carolyn Burke. Ithaca, NY: Cornell University Press, 1985 [*Ce sexe qui n'en est pas un.* Paris: Éditions de Minuit, 1977].

To Be Two. Trans. Monique M. Rhodes and Marco F. Cocito-Monoc. New York: Routledge, 2001 [*Être deux.* Paris: B. Grasset, 1997].

To Speak Is Never Neutral. Trans. Gail Schwab. New York: Routledge, 2002 [*Parler n'est jamais neuter.* Paris: Éditions de Minuit, 1985].

The Way of Love. Trans. Heidi Bostic and Stephen Pluhácek. London. Continuum, 2002 [*La Voie de l'amour.* Forthcoming].

Why Different? A Culture of Two Subjects: Interviews with Luce Irigaray. Ed. Luce Irigaray and Sylvère Lotringer. Trans. Camille Collins. New York: Semiotext(e), 1999.

Sarah Kofman

Camera Obscura: Of Ideology. Trans. Will Straw. Ithaca, NY: Cornell University Press, 1999 [*Camera obscura: De l'idéologie.* Paris: Galilée, 1973].

The Childhood of Art: An Interpretation of Freud's Aesthetics. Trans. Winifred Woodhull. New York: Columbia University Press, 1988 [*L'Enfance de l'art: Une interprétation de l'esthétique freudienne.* Paris: Payot, 1970].

The Enigma of Woman: Woman in Freud's Writings. Trans. Catherine Porter. Ithaca, NY: Cornell University Press, 1985 [*L'Enigme de la femme: La Femme dans les textes de Freud.* Paris: Galilée, 1980].

Freud and Fiction. Trans. Sarah Wykes. Boston, MA: Northeastern University Press, 1991 [*Quatre romans analytiques.* Paris: Galilée, 1974]

Nietzsche and Metaphor. Trans. Duncan Large. Stanford, CA: Stanford University Press, 1993 [*Nietzsche et la métaphore.* Paris, Payot, 1972].

Rue Ordener, Rue Labat. Trans. Ann Smock. Lincoln: University of Nebraska Press, 1996 [*Rue Ordener, Rue Labat.* Paris: Galilée, 1993].

Smothered Words. Trans. Madeleine Dobie. Evanston, IL: Northwestern University Press, 1998 [*Paroles suffoquées.* Paris: Galilée, 1987].

Socrates: Fictions of a Philosopher. Trans. Catherine Porter. Ithaca, NY: Cornell University Press, 1998 [*Socrate(s).* Paris: Galilée, 1989].

Alexandre Kojève

Introduction to the Reading of Hegel: Lectures on the Phenomenology of Spirit. Assembled by Raymond Queneau. Ed. Allan Bloom. Trans. James H. Nichols, Jr. New York: Basic Books, 1969 [*Introduction à la lecture de Hegel: Leçons sur la "Phénoménologie de l'esprit" professées de 1933 à 1939, à l'École des Hautes Études.* Réunies et publiées par Raymond Queneau. Paris: Éditions Gallimard, 1947].

Outline of a Phenomenology of Right. Ed. Bryan-Paul Frost. Trans. and intro. Bryan-Paul Frost and Robert Howse. Lanham, MD: Rowman and Littlefield, 2000 [*Esquisse d'une phénoménologie du droit.* Paris: Éditions Gallimard, 1981].

Alexandre Koyré

The Astronomical Revolution: Copernicus, Kepler, Borelli. Trans. R. E. W. Maddison. Ithaca, NY: Cornell University Press, 1973 [*La Révolution astronomique: Copernic, Kepler, Borelli.* Paris: Hermann, 1961].

Descartes After Three Hundred Years. Buffalo, NY: University of Buffalo Roswell Park Publication Fund, 1951.

Discovering Plato. Trans. Leonora Cohen Rosenfield. New York: Columbia University Press, 1945 [*Introduction à la lecture de Platon.* New York: Brentano's, 1945].

A Documentary History of the Problem of Fall from Kepler to Newton. Philadelphia, PA: American Philosophical Society, 1955.

From the Closed World to the Infinite Universe. Baltimore, MD: Johns Hopkins University Press, 1957 [*Du monde clos à l'univers infini.* Traduit de l'anglais par Raïssa Tarr. Paris: Presses universitaires de France, 1962].

Galileo Studies. Trans. John Mepham. Atlantic Highlands, NJ: Humanities Press, 1978 [*Études galiléennes.* 3 Vols. Paris: Hermann, 1939].

Metaphysics and Measurement: Essays in Scientific Revolution. Essays III, V and VI. Trans. R. E. W. Maddison. Cambridge, MA: Harvard University Press, 1968.

Newtonian Studies. Cambridge, MA: Harvard University Press, 1965.

Julia Kristeva

About Chinese Women. Trans. Anita Barrows. New York: Urizen Books, 1977 [*Des Chinoises.* Paris: Éditions des Femmes, 1974].

Black Sun: Depression and Melancholia. Trans. Leon S. Roudiez. New York: Columbia University Press, 1989 [*Soleil noir: Dépression et mélancolie.* Paris: Éditions Gallimard, 1987].

Colette. Trans. Jane Marie Todd. New York: Columbia University Press, 2004 [*Le Génie féminin. Tome III. Colette.* Paris: Fayard, 2002].

Crisis of the European Subject. Trans. Susan Fairfield. New York: Other Press, 2000 [Essays published in *L'Infini.* 1995–9].

Desire in Language: A Semiotic Approach to Literature and Art. Ed. Leon S. Roudiez. Trans. Thomas Gora, Alice Jardine, and Leon S. Roudiez. New York: Columbia University Press, 1980.

Hannah Arendt. Trans. Ross Guberman. New York: Columbia University Press, 2001 [*Le Génie féminin. Tome I. Hannah Arendt.* Paris: Fayard, 1999].

In the Beginning Was Love: Psychoanalysis and Faith. Trans. Arthur Goldhammer. New York: Columbia University Press, 1987 [*Au commencement était l'amour: Psychanalyse et foi.* Paris: Hachette, 1985].

Intimate Revolt: The Powers and Limits of Psychoanalysis. Trans. Jeanine Herman. New York: Columbia University Press, 2002 [*Pouvoirs et limites de la psychanalyse. Tome 2. La Révolte intime.* Paris: Fayard, 1997].

Julia Kristeva, Interviews. Ed. Ross Mitchell Guberman. New York: Columbia University Press, 1996.

The Kristeva Reader. Ed. Toril Moi. New York: Columbia University Press, 1986.

Language–The Unknown: An Initiation Into Linguistics. Trans. Anne M. Menke. New York: Columbia University Press, 1989 [*Le Langage, cet inconnu: Une initiation à la linguistique.* Paris: Éditions du Seuil, 1981].

Melanie Klein. Trans. Ross Guberman. New York: Columbia University Press, 2002 [*Le Génie féminin. Tome II. Melanie Klein.* Paris: Fayard, 2000].

Nations Without Nationalism. Trans. Leon S. Roudiez. New York: Columbia University Press, 1993 [*Lettre ouverte à Harlem Désir.* Paris: Rivages, 1990].

New Maladies of the Soul. Trans. Ross Guberman. New York: Columbia University Press, 1995 [*Les Nouvelles maladies de l'âme.* Paris: Fayard, 1993].

The Portable Kristeva. Ed. Kelly Oliver. New York: Columbia University Press, 1997.

Powers of Horror: An Essay on Abjection. Trans. Leon S. Roudiez. New York: Columbia University Press, 1982 [*Pouvoirs de l'horreur: Essai sur l'abjection.* Paris: Éditions du Seuil, 1980].

Proust and the Sense of Time. Trans. and intro. Stephen Bann. New York: Columbia University Press, 1993 [University of Canterbury T. S. Eliot Lectures, 1992].

Revolt, She Said. An Interview by Philippe Petit. Trans. Brian O'Keeffe. Ed. Sylvère Lotringer. Los Angeles: Semiotext(e), 2002 [*Contre la dépression nationale: Entretien avec Philippe Petit.* Paris: Textuel, 1998].

Revolution in Poetic Language. Trans. Margaret Waller. New York: Columbia University Press, 1984 [*La Révolution du langage poétique: L'Avant-garde à la fin du XIXe siècle, Lautréamont et Mallarmé.* Paris: Éditions du Seuil, 1974].

The Sense and Non-Sense of Revolt. Trans. Jeanine Herman. New York: Columbia University Press, 2000 [*Pouvoirs et limites de la psychanalyse. Tome 1: Sens et non-sens de la révolte.* Paris: Fayard, 1996].

Strangers to Ourselves. Trans. Leon S. Roudiez. New York: Columbia University Press, 1991 [*Étrangers à nous-mêmes.* Paris: Fayard, 1988].

Tales of Love. Trans. Leon S. Roudiez. New York: Columbia University Press, 1987 [*Histoires d'amour.* Paris: Denoël, 1983].

Time and Sense: Proust and the Experience of Literature. Trans. Ross Guberman. New York: Columbia University Press, 1996 [*Le Temps sensible: Proust et l'expérience littéraire.* Paris: Éditions Gallimard, 1994].

And Catherine Clément. *The Feminine and the Sacred.* Trans. Jane Marie Todd. New York: Columbia University Press, 2001 [*Le Féminin et le sacré.* Paris: Stock, 1998].

Jacques Lacan

Ecrits: A Selection. Trans. Alan Sheridan. New York: W. W. Norton, 1977 [*Écrits.* Paris: Éditions du Seuil, 1966].

Ecrits: A Selection. Trans. Bruce Fink in collaboration with Héloïse Fink and Russell Grigg. New York: W. W. Norton, 2002 [*Écrits.* Paris: Éditions du Seuil, 1966].

Feminine Sexuality: Jacques Lacan and the Ecole Freudeinne. Ed. Juliet Mitchell and Jacqueline Rose. Trans. Jacqueline Rose. New York: W. W. Norton, 1982.

The Four Fundamental Concepts of Psycho-analysis. Ed. Jacques-Alain Miller. Trans. Alan Sheridan. New York: W. W. Norton, 1978 [*Le Séminaire. 11: Les Quatre concepts fondamentaux de la psychanalyse, 1964.* Paris: Éditions du Seuil, 1973].

The Language of the Self: The Function of Language in Psychoanalysis. Trans. and commentary Anthony Wilden. Baltimore, MD: Johns Hopkins University Press, 1968 ["Fonction et champ de la parole et du langage en psychanalyse." In *La Psychanalyse, Vol. I.* Paris: Presses universitaires de France, 1956].

On Feminine Sexuality: The Limits of Love and Knowledge. Trans. Bruce Fink. New York: W. W. Norton, 1998.

The Seminar of Jacques Lacan. Ed. Jacques-Alain Miller. New York: W. W. Norton, 1988– [*Le Séminaire.* Texte établi par Jacques-Alain Miller. Paris: Éditions du Seuil, 1973–]:

> Book 1: *Freud's Papers on Technique, 1953–1954.* Trans. John Forrester. New York: W. W. Norton, 1988 [*Le Séminaire. 1: Les Écrits techniques de Freud, 1953–1954.* Paris: Éditions du Seuil, 1975].

> Book 2: *The Ego in Freud's Theory and in the Technique of Psychoanalysis, 1954–1955.* Trans. Sylvana Tomaselli. Notes by John Forrester. New York:

W. W. Norton, 1988 [*Le Séminaire. 2: Le Moi dans la théorie de Freud et dans la technique de la psychanalyse, 1954–1955*. Paris: Éditions du Seuil, 1973].

Book 3: *The Psychoses*. Trans. Russell Grigg. New York: W. W. Norton, 1993 [*Le Séminaire. 3: Les Psychoses, 1955–1956*. Paris: Éditions du Seuil, 1981].

Book 7: *The Ethics of Psychoanalysis, 1959–1960*. Trans. Dennis Porter. New York: W. W. Norton, 1992 [*Le Séminaire. 7: L'Éthique de la psychanalyse, 1959–1960*. Paris: Éditions du Seuil, 1986].

Book 20: *Encore, 1972–1973*. Trans. Bruce Fink. New York: W. W. Norton, 1998 [*Le Séminaire. 20: Encore, 1972–1973*. Paris: Éditions du Seuil, 1975].

Television. Trans. Denis Hollier, Rosalind Krauss, and Annette Michelson; and *A Challenge to the Psychoanalytic Establishment*. Trans. Jeffrey Mehlman. Ed. Joan Copjec. New York: W. W. Norton, 1990 [*Télévision*. Paris: Éditions du Seuil, 1974].

Claude Lefort

Democracy and Political Theory. Trans. David Macey. Minneapolis: University of Minnesota Press, 1988 [*Essais sur le politique: XIXe–XXe siècles*. Paris: Éditions du Seuil, 1986].

The Political Forms of Modern Society: Bureaucracy, Democracy, Totalitarianism. Ed. and intro. John B. Thompson. Cambridge, MA: MIT Press, 1986.

Writing, the Political Test. Trans. David Ames Curtis. Durham, NC: Duke University Press, 2000 [*Écrire: À l'épreuve du politique*. Paris: Calmann-Lévy, 1992].

Claude Lévi-Strauss

Anthropology and Myth: Lectures, 1951–1982. Trans. Roy G. Willis. Oxford: Blackwell, 1987 [*Paroles données*. Paris: Plon, 1984].

Conversations with Claude Lévi-Strauss. Trans. Paula Wissing. Chicago: University of Chicago Press, 1991 [*De près et de loin. Entretien avec Didier Eribon*. Paris: Éditions Odile Jacob, 1988].

The Elementary Structures of Kinship. Ed. Rodney Needham. Trans. James Harle Bell and John Richard von Sturmer. Boston, MA: Beacon Press, 1969 [*Les Structures élémentaires de la parenté*. Paris: Presses universitaires de France, 1949].

From Honey to Ashes. Trans. John and Doreen Weightman. New York: Harper and Row, 1973 [*Mythologiques. 2. Du miel aux cendres*. Paris: Plon, 1949].

Introduction to the Work of Marcel Mauss. Trans. Felicity Baker. London: Routledge and Kegan Paul, 1987 [*Introduction à l'oeuvre de Marcel Mauss*. Paris: Presses universitaires de France, 1950].

The Jealous Potter. Trans. Benedicte Chorier. Chicago: University of Chicago Press, 1988 [*La Potière jalouse*. Paris: Plon, 1985].

Look, Listen, Read. Trans. Brian C. J. Singer. New York: Basic Books, 1997 [*Regarder écouter lire*. Paris: Le Grand livre du mois, 1993].

Myth and Meaning: Five Talks for Radio. Toronto: University of Toronto Press, 1978 [Talks broadcast on the CBC Radio series *Ideas*, December, 1977].

The Naked Man. Trans. John and Doreen Weightman. New York: Harper and Row, 1981 [*L'Homme nu*. Paris: Plon, 1971].

The Origin of Table Manners. Trans. John and Doreen Weightman. New York: Harper and Row, 1978 [*L'Origine des manières de table*. Paris: Plon, 1968].

The Raw and the Cooked. Trans. John and Doreen Weightman. New York: Harper and Row, 1969 [*Mythologiques. 1. Le Cru et le cuit*. Paris: Plon, 1964].

Results of the Conference of Anthropologists and Linguists. Baltimore, MD: Waverly Press, 1953.

Saudades do Brasil: A Photographic Memoir. Trans. Sylvia Modelski. Seattle: University of Washington Press, 1995 [*Saudades do Brasil*. Paris: Plon, 1994].

The Savage Mind. Chicago: University of Chicago Press, 1966 [*La Pensée sauvage*. Paris: Plon, 1962].

The Scope of Anthropology. Trans. Sherry Ortner Paul and Robert A. Paul. London: Cape, 1967 [*Collège de France. Chaire d'anthropologie sociale. Leçon inaugurale*. Nogent-le-Rotrou: Daupeley-Gouverneur, 1966].

The Story of Lynx. Trans. Catherine Tihanyi. Chicago: University of Chicago Press, 1995 [*Histoire de Lynx*. Paris: Le Grand livre du mois, 1991].

Structural Anthropology. Trans. Claire Jacobson and Brooke Grundfest Schoepf. New York: Basic Books, 1963 [*Anthropologie structurale*. Paris: Plon, 1958].

Totemism. Trans. Rodney Needham. Boston, MA: Beacon Press, 1963 [*Le Totémisme aujourd'hui*. Paris: Presses universitaires de France, 1962].

Tristes Tropiques. Trans. John Russell. New York: Criterion Books, 1961 [*Tristes tropiques*. Paris: Plon, 1955].

Tristes Tropiques. Trans. John and Doreen Weightman. New York: Atheneum, 1973 [*Tristes tropiques*. Paris: Plon, 1955].

The View from Afar. Trans. Joachim Neugroschel and Phoebe Hoss. New York: Basic Books, 1985 [*Le Regard éloigné*. Paris: Plon, 1983].

The Way of the Masks. Trans. Sylvia Modelski. Seattle: University of Washington Press, 1982 [*La Voie des masques*. Geneva: Skira, 1975].

Emmanuel Levinas

Alterity and Transcendence. Trans. Michael B. Smith. New York: Columbia University Press, 1999 [*Altérité et transcendance*. Saint-Clément: Fata Morgana, 1995].

Beyond the Verse: Talmudic Reading and Lectures. Trans. Gary D. Mole. Bloomington: Indiana University Press, 1994 [*L'Au-delà du verset: Lectures et discours talmudiques*. Paris: Éditions de Minuit, 1981].

Collected Philosophical Papers. Trans. Alphonso Lingis. The Hague: Martinus Nijhoff, 1987.

Difficult Freedom: Essays on Judaism. Trans. Seán Hand. Baltimore, MD: Johns Hopkins University Press, 1990 [*Difficile liberté: Essais sur le judaïsme*. Paris: A. Michel, 1976].

Discovering Existence with Husserl. Ed. and trans. Richard A. Cohen and Michael B. Smith. Evanston, IL: Northwestern University Press, 1998.

Emmanuel Levinas: Basic Philosophical Writings. Ed. Adriaan T. Peperzak, Simon Critchley, and Robert Bernasconi. Bloomington: Indiana University Press, 1996.

Entre Nous: On Thinking-of-the-Other. Trans. Michael B. Smith and Barbara Harshav. New York: Columbia University Press, 1998 [*Entre nous: Essais sur le penser-à-l'autre.* Paris: B. Grasset, 1991].

Ethics and Infinity. Trans. Richard A. Cohen. Pittsburgh, PA: Duquesne University Press, 1985 [*Éthique et infini: Dialogues, avec Philippe Nemo.* Paris: Fayard, 1982].

Existence and Existents. Trans. Alphonso Lingis. The Hague: Martinus Nijhoff, 1978 [*De l'existence à l'existant.* Paris: J. Vrin, 1947].

God, Death, and Time. Trans. Bettina Bergo. Stanford, CA: Stanford University Press, 2000 [*Dieu, la mort et le temps.* Paris: B. Grasset, 1993].

Humanism of the Other. Trans. Nidra Poller. Urbana: University of Illinois Press, 2003 [*Humanisme de l'autre homme.* Montpellier: Fata Morgana, 1972].

In the Time of the Nations. Trans. Michael B. Smith. Bloomington: Indiana University Press, 1994 [*A l'heure des nations.* Paris: Éditions de Minuit, 1988].

Is It Righteous To Be? Interviews with Emmanuel Levinas. Ed. Jill Robbins. Stanford, CA: Stanford University Press, 2001.

The Levinas Reader. Ed. Seán Hand. Oxford: Blackwell, 1989.

Nine Talmudic Readings. Trans. and intro. Annette Aronowicz. Bloomington: Indiana University Press, 1990 [*Quatre lectures talmudiques, précédées d'extraits traduits du Talmud.* Paris: Éditions de Minuit, 1968].

Of God Who Comes to Mind. Trans. Bettina Bergo. Stanford, CA: Stanford University Press, 1998 [*De Dieu qui vient à l'idée.* Paris: J. Vrin, 1982].

On Escape. Trans. Bettina Bergo. Stanford, CA: Stanford University Press, 2003 [*De l'évasion.* Paris: Livre de Poche, 1998].

Otherwise Than Being, or, Beyond Essence. Trans. Alphonso Lingis. The Hague: Martinus Nijhoff, 1981 [*Autrement qu'être ou au-delà de l'essence.* The Hague: Martinus Nijhoff, 1974].

Outside the Subject. Trans. Michael B. Smith. Stanford, CA: Stanford University Press, 1994 [*Hors sujet*. Fontfroide-le-Haut: Fata Morgana, 1987].

Proper Names. Trans. Michael B. Smith. Stanford, CA: Stanford University Press, 1996 [*Noms propres: Agnon, Buber, Celan, Delhomme, Derrida, Jabès, Kierkegaard, Lacroix, Laporte, Picard, Proust, Van Breda, Wahl*. Saint-Clément-la-Rivière: Fata Morgana, 1976. *Sur Maurice Blanchot*. Montpellier: Fata Morgana, 1975].

The Theory of Intuition in Husserl's Phenomenology. Trans. André Orianne. Evanston, IL: Northwestern University Press, 1973 [*La Théorie de l'intuition dans la phénoménologie de Husserl*. Paris: Félix Alcan, 1930].

Time and the Other and Additional Essays. Trans. Richard A. Cohen. Pittsburgh, PA: Duquesne University Press, 1987.

Totality and Infinity: An Essay on Exteriority. Trans. Alphonso Lingis. Pittsburgh, PA: Duquesne University Press, 1969 [*Totalité et infini: Essai sur l'extériorité*. The Hague: Martinus Nijhoff, 1961].

Unforeseen History. Trans. Nidra Poller. Urbana: University of Illinois Press, 2003 [*Les Imprévus de l'histoire*. Fontfroide-le-Haut: Fata Morgana, 1994].

Jean-François Lyotard

The Assassination of Experience by Painting – Monory. Trans. Rachel Bowlby. London: Black Dog, 1998 [*L'Assassinat de l'expérience par la peinture, Monory*. Bègles: Castor Astral, 1984].

The Confession of Augustine. Trans. Richard Beardsworth. Stanford, CA: Stanford University Press, 2000 [*La Confession d'Augustin*. Paris: Galilée, 1998].

The Differend: Phrases in Dispute. Trans. Georges Van Den Abbeele. Minneapolis: University of Minnesota Press, 1988 [*Le Différend*. Paris: Éditions de Minuit, 1983].

Driftworks. Ed. Roger McKeon. New York: Semiotext(e), 1984.

Heidegger and "the jews." Trans. Andreas Michael and Mark S. Roberts. Minneapolis: University of Minnesota Press, 1990 [*Heidegger et "les juifs."* Paris: Galilée, 1988].

The Inhuman: Reflections on Time. Trans. Geoffrey Bennington and Rachel Bowlby. Stanford, CA: Stanford University Press, 1991 [*L'Inhumain: Causeries sur le temps.* Paris: Galilée, 1988].

Jean-François Lyotard: Collected Writings on Art. London: Academy Editions, 1997.

Lessons on the Analytic of the Sublime: Kant's Critique of Judgment, §§ 23–29. Trans. Elizabeth Rottenberg. Stanford, CA: Stanford University Press, 1994 [*Leçons sur l'"Analytique du sublime": Kant, "Critique de la faculté de juger," paragraphes 23–29.* Paris: Galilée, 1991].

Libidinal Economy. Trans. Iain Hamilton Grant. Bloomington: Indiana University Press, 1993 [*Économie libidinale.* Paris: Éditions de Minuit, 1974].

The Lyotard Reader. Ed. Andrew Benjamin. Oxford: Blackwell, 1989.

Peregrinations: Law, Form, Event. New York: Columbia University Press, 1988 [*Pérégrinations: Loi, forme, événement.* Paris: Galilée, 1990].

Phenomenology. Trans. Brian Beakley. Albany: State University of New York Press, 1991 [*La Phénoménologie.* Paris: Presses universitaires de France, 1954].

Political Writings. Trans. Bill Readings and Kevin Paul Geiman. Minneapolis: University of Minnesota Press, 1993.

The Politics of Jean-François Lyotard. Ed. Chris Rojek and Bryan S. Turner. New York: Routledge, 1998.

The Postmodern Condition: A Report on Knowledge. Trans. Geoff Bennington and Brian Massumi. Minneapolis: University of Minnesota Press, 1984 [*La Condition postmoderne: Rapport sur le savoir.* Paris: Éditions de Minuit, 1979].

The Postmodern Explained: Correspondence, 1982–1985. Ed. Julian Pefanis and Morgan Thomas. Trans. Don Barry. Minneapolis: University of Minnesota Press, 1993 [*Le Postmoderne expliqué aux enfants: Correspondance, 1982–1985.* Paris: Galilée, 1986].

Postmodern Fables. Trans. Georges Van Den Abbeele. Minneapolis: University of Minnesota Press, 1997 [*Moralités postmodernes.* Paris: Galilée, 1993].

Signed, Malraux. Trans. Robert Harvey. Minneapolis: University of Minnesota Press, 1999 [*Signé Malraux.* Paris: B. Grasset, 1996].

Soundproof Room: Malraux's Anti-Aesthetics. Trans. Robert Harvey. Stanford, CA: Stanford University Press, 2001 [*Chambre sourde: L'Antiesthétique de Malraux.* Paris: Galilée, 1998].

Toward the Postmodern. Ed. Robert Harvey and Mark S. Roberts. Atlantic Highlands, NJ: Humanities Press, 1993.

And Eberhard Gruber. *The Hyphen: Between Judaism and Christianity.* Trans. Pascale-Anne Brault and Michael Naas. Amherst, NY: Humanity Books, 1999 [*Un trait d'union.* Sainte-Foy, Quebec: Le Griffon d'argile, 1993].

And Jean-Loup Thébaud. *Just Gaming.* Trans. Wlad Godzich. Minneapolis: University of Minnesota Press, 1985 [*Au juste: Conversations.* Paris: Christian Bourgois, 1979].

Gabriel Marcel

Awakenings: A Translation of Gabriel Marcel's Autobiography. Trans. Peter S. Rogers. Milwaukee, WI: Marquette University Press, 2002 [*En chemin, vers quel éveil?* Paris: Éditions Gallimard, 1971].

Being and Having. Trans. Katharine Farrer. Westminster: Dacre Press, 1949 [*Être et avoir.* Paris: Fernand Aubier, 1935].

Contributions of Gabriel Marcel to Philosophy: A Collection of Essays. Ed. William Cooney. Lewiston, NY: Mellen Press, 1989.

Creative Fidelity. Trans. Robert Rosthal. New York: Farrar, Straus, 1964 [*Du refus à l'invocation.* Paris: Éditions Gallimard, 1940].

The Decline of Wisdom. Trans. Manya Harari. London: Harvill Press, 1954 [*Le Déclin de la sagesse.* Paris: Plon, 1954].

The Existential Background of Human Dignity. Cambridge, MA: Harvard University Press, 1963.

Fresh Hope for the World: Moral Re-armament in Action. Trans. Helen Hardinge. London: Longmans, 1960 [*Un changement d'espérance à la rencontre du réarmement moral: Des témoignages, des faits.* Paris: Plon, 1958].

Homo Viator: Introduction to a Metaphysic of Hope. Trans. Emma Craufurd. Chicago: Henry Regnery, 1951 [*Homo viator: Prolégomènes à une métaphysique de l'espérance.* Paris: Plon, 1944].

The Influence of Psychic Phenomena on My Philosophy. London: Society for Psychical Research, 1956 [Frederic W. H. Myers memorial lecture, 1955].

Man Against Mass Society. Trans. G. S. Fraser. Chicago: Henry Regnery, 1952 [*Les Hommes contre l'humain*. Paris: La Colombe, 1951].

Metaphysical Journal. Trans. Bernard Wall. Chicago: Henry Regnery, 1952 [*Journal métaphysique*. Paris: Éditions Gallimard, 1927].

The Mystery of Being. Vol. 1: Reflection and Mystery. Trans. G. S. Fraser. *Vol. 2: Faith and Reality*. Trans. René Hague. Chicago: Henry Regnery, 1949, 1950 [*Le Mystère de l'être. Vol. 1: Réflexion et mystère. Vol. 2: Foi et réalité*. Paris: Aubier, 1949, 1950].

The Participant Perspective: A Gabriel Marcel Reader. Ed. Thomas W. Busch. Lanham, MD: University Press of America, 1987.

Philosophical Fragments, 1904 [i.e. 1909]–1914 and The Philosopher and Peace. Trans. Lionel A. Blain. Notre Dame, IN: University of Notre Dame Press, 1965 [*Fragments philosophiques: 1909–1914*. Louvain: Nauwelaerts, 1961].

The Philosophy of Existentialism. Trans. Manya Harari. New York: Philosophical Library, 1949 [1933, 1946, 1947].

Presence and Immortality. Trans. Michael A. Machado. Pittsburgh, PA: Duquesne University Press, 1967 [*Présence et immortalité*. Paris: Flammarion, 1959].

Problematic Man. Trans. Brian Thompson. New York: Herder and Herder, 1967 [*L'Homme problématique: Position et approches concrètes du mystère ontologique*. Paris: Plon, 1955].

Royce's Metaphysics. Trans. Virginia and Gordon Ringer. Chicago: Henry Regnery, 1956 [*La Métaphysique de Royce*. Paris: Aubier-Montaigne, 1945].

Searchings. New York: Paulist-Newman Press, 1967 [*Auf der Suche nach Wahrheit und Gerechtigkeit*. Frankfurt am Main: J. Knecht, 1964].

And Paul Ricoeur. *Tragic Wisdom and Beyond: Including Conversations Between Paul Ricoeur and Gabriel Marcel*. Trans. Stephen Jolin and Peter McCormick. Evanston, IL: Northwestern University Press, 1973 [*Paul Ricoeur, Gabriel Marcel: Entretiens*. Paris: Aubier-Montaigne, 1968].

Jean-Luc Marion

Being Given: Toward a Phenomenology of Givenness. Trans. Jeffrey L. Kosky. Stanford, CA: Stanford University Press, 2002 [*Etant donné: Essai d'une phénoménologie de la donation*, 1997].

Cartesian Questions. Trans. Jeffery L. Kosky, John Cottingham, and Stephan Voss. Chicago: University of Chicago Press, 1999 [*Questions cartésiennes: Méthode et métaphysique*. Paris: Presses universitaires de France, 1991].

The Crossing of the Visible. Trans. James K. A. Smith. Stanford, CA: Stanford University Press, 2004 [*La Croisée du visible*. Paris: La Différence, 1991].

Descartes's Grey Ontology: Cartesian Science and Aristotelian Thought in the Regulae. Trans. Sarah E. Donahue. South Bend, IN: St. Augustine's Press, 2004 [*Sur l'ontologie grise de Descartes*. Paris: Vrin, 1993].

God Without Being: Hors-Texte. Trans. Thomas A. Carlson. Chicago: University of Chicago Press, 1991 [*Dieu sans l'être: Hors-texte*. Paris: Librairie Arthème Fayard, 1982].

The Idol and Distance: Five Studies. Trans. Thomas A. Carlson. New York: Fordham University Press, 2001 [*L'Idole et la distance: Cinq études*. Paris: Grasset, 1977]

In Excess: Studies of Saturated Phenomena. Trans. Robyn Horner and Vincent Berraud. New York: Fordham University Press, 2002 [*De surcroît: Études sur les phénomènes saturés*. Paris: Presses universitaires de France, 2001].

On Descartes's Metaphysical Prism: The Constitution and the Limits of Onto-theo-logy in Cartesian Thought. Trans. Jeffery L. Kosky. Chicago: University of Chicago Press, 1999 [*Sur le prisme métaphysique de Descartes*. Paris: Presses universitaires de France, 1986].

Prolegomena to Charity. Trans. Stephen Lewis and Jeffery L. Kosky. New York: Fordham University Press, 2002 [*Prolégomènes à la charité*. Paris: La Différence, 1986].

Reduction and Givenness: Investigations of Husserl, Heidegger, and Phenomenology. Trans. Thomas A. Carlson. Evanston, IL: Northwestern University Press, 1998 [*Réduction et donation: Recherches sur Husserl, Heidegger et la phénoménologie*. Paris: Presses universitaires de France, 1989].

Maurice Merleau-Ponty

Adventures of the Dialectic. Trans. Joseph Bien. Evanston, IL: Northwestern University Press, 1973 [*Les Aventures de la dialectique.* Paris: Éditions Gallimard, 1955].

Consciousness and the Acquisition of Language. Trans. Hugh J. Silverman. Evanston, IL: Northwestern University Press, 1973 [*La Conscience et l'acquisition du langage.* Paris: Éditions Gallimard, 1964].

The Essential Writings of Merleau-Ponty. Ed. Alden L. Fisher. New York: Harcourt, Brace, and World, 1969.

Humanism and Terror: An Essay on the Communist Problem. Trans. John O'Neill. Boston, MA: Beacon Press, 1969 [*Humanisme et terreur: Essai sur le problème communiste.* Paris: Éditions Gallimard, 1947].

Husserl at the Limits of Phenomenology. Including Texts by Edmund Husserl. Ed. Leonard Lawlor with Bettina Bergo. Evanston, IL: Northwestern University Press, 2002 [*Notes de cours sur l'origine de la géométrie de Husserl. Suivi de Recherches sur la phénoménologie de Merleau-Ponty.* Sous la direction de Renaud Barbaras. Paris: Presses universitaires de France, 1998].

In Praise of Philosophy. Trans. John Wild and James M. Edie. Evanston, IL: Northwestern University Press, 1963 [*Éloge de la philosophie. Leçon inaugurale faite au Collège de France.* Paris: Éditions Gallimard, 1953].

The Incarnate Subject: Malebranche, Biran, and Bergson on the Union of Body and Soul. Ed. Andrew G. Bjelland, Jr. and Patrick Burke. Trans. Paul B. Milan. Amherst, NY: Humanity Books, 2001 [*L'Union de l'âme et du corps chez Malebranche, Biran et Bergson: Notes prises au cours de Maurice Merleau-Ponty.* Recueillies et rédigées par Jean Deprun. Paris: J. Vrin, 1978].

Maurice Merleau-Ponty: Basic Writings. Ed. Thomas Baldwin. New York: Routledge, 2003.

The Merleau-Ponty Aesthetics Reader: Philosophy and Painting. Ed. and intro. Galen A. Johnson. Translation editing by Michael B. Smith. Evanston, IL: Northwestern University Press, 1993.

Nature. Ed. Dominique Séglard. Trans. Robert Vallier. Evanston, IL: Northwestern University Press, 2003 [*La Nature: Notes, cours du Collège de France, suivi des Résumés de cours correspondants.* Etabli et annoté par Dominique Séglard. Paris: Éditions du Seuil, 1995].

Phenomenology, Language and Sociology: Selected Essays of Maurice Merleau-Ponty. Ed. John O'Neill. London: Heinemann Educational, 1974.

Phenomenology of Perception. Trans. Colin Smith. New York: Routledge, 1962 [*Phénoménologie de la perception.* Paris: Éditions Gallimard, 1945].

The Primacy of Perception, and Other Essays on Phenomenological Psychology, the Philosophy of Art, History, and Politics. Ed. and intro. James M. Edie. Evanston, IL: Northwestern University Press, 1964.

The Prose of the World. Ed. Claude Lefort. Trans. John O'Neill. Evanston, IL: Northwestern University Press, 1973 [*La Prose du monde.* Paris: Éditions Gallimard, 1969].

Sense and Non-Sense. Trans. Hubert L. Dreyfus and Patricia Allen Dreyfus. Evanston, IL: Northwestern University Press, 1964 [*Sens et non-sens.* Paris: Nagel, 1948].

Signs. Trans. and intro. Richard C. McCleary. Evanston, IL: Northwestern University Press, 1964 [*Signes.* Paris: Éditions Gallimard, 1960].

The Structure of Behavior. Trans. Alden L. Fisher. Boston, MA: Beacon Press, 1963 [*La Structure du comportement.* Paris: Presses universitaires de France, 1942].

Texts and Dialogues. Ed. and intro. Hugh J. Silverman and James Barry, Jr. Trans. Michael B. Smith, et al. Atlantic Highlands, NJ: Humanities Press, 1992.

Themes from the Lectures at the College de France, 1952–1960. Trans. John O'Neill. Evanston, IL: Northwestern University Press, 1970 [*Résumés de cours, Collège de France, 1952–1960.* Paris: Éditions Gallimard, 1968].

The Visible and the Invisible. Ed. Claude Lefort. Trans. Alphonso Lingis. Evanston, IL: Northwestern University Press, 1968 [*Le Visible et l'invisible.* Paris: Éditions Gallimard, 1964].

The World of Perception. Trans. Oliver Davis. Seven 1948 radio lectures on the theme of perception. New York: Routledge, 2004 [*Causeries, 1948.* Établies et annotées par Stéphanie Ménasé. Paris: Éditions du Seuil, 2002].

Emmanuel Mounier

Be Not Afraid: Studies in Personalist Sociology. Trans. Cynthia Rowland. New York: Harper and Row, 1954 [*La Petite peur du XXe siècle.* Paris: Éditions du Seuil, 1948; and *Quest-ce que le personnalisme?* Paris: Éditions du Seuil, 1947].

The Character of Man. Trans. Cynthia Rowland. New York: Harper and Row, 1956 [*Traité du caractère.* Paris: Éditions du Seuil 1946].

Existentialist Philosophies: An Introduction. Trans. Eric Blow. New York: Macmillan, 1949 [*Introduction aux existentialismes.* Paris: Denoël, 1947].

Personalism. Trans. Philip Mairet. Notre Dame, IN: University of Notre Dame Press, 1970 [*Le Personnalisme.* Paris: Presses universitaires de France, 1950].

A Personalist Manifesto. Trans. the monks of St. John's Abbey. New York: Longmans, Green, 1938 [*Manifeste au service du personnalisme.* Paris: Fernand Aubier, 1936].

Jean-Luc Nancy

Being Singular Plural. Trans. Robert D. Richardson and Anne E. O'Byrne. Stanford, CA: Stanford University Press, 2000 [*Être singulier pluriel.* Paris: Galilée, 1996].

The Birth to Presence. Trans. Brian Holmes and others. Stanford, CA: Stanford University Press, 1993.

The Experience of Freedom. Trans. Bridget McDonald. Stanford, CA: Stanford University Press, 1993 [*L'Expérience de la liberté.* Paris: Galilée, 1988].

A Finite Thinking. Ed. Simon Sparks. Stanford, CA: Stanford University Press, 2003 [*Une pensée finie.* Paris: Galilée, 1990].

The Gravity of Thought. Trans. François Raffoul and Gregory Recco. Atlantic Highlands, NJ: Humanities Press, 1997 [*L'Oubli de la philosophie.* Paris: Galilée, 1986].

Hegel: The Restlessness of the Negative. Trans. Jason Smith and Steven Miller. Minneapolis: University of Minnesota Press, 2002 [*Hegel: L'Inquiétude du négatif.* Paris: Hachette, 1997].

The Inoperative Community. Ed. Peter Connor. Trans. Peter Connor, Lisa Garbus, Michael Holland, and Simona Sawhney. Minneapolis: University of Minnesota Press, 1991 [*La Communauté désœuvrée.* Paris: C. Bourgois, 1986].

Multiple Arts: The Muses II. Ed. Simon Sparks. Stanford, CA: Stanford University Press, 2004

The Muses. Trans. Peggy Kamuf. Stanford, CA: Stanford University Press, 1996 [*Les Muses.* Paris: Galilée, 1994].

The Sense of the World. Trans. Jeffrey S. Librett. Minneapolis: University of Minnesota Press, 1997 [*Le Sens du monde.* Paris: Galilée, 1993].

The Speculative Remark: One of Hegel's bons mots. Trans. Céline Surprenant. Stanford, CA: Stanford University Press, 2001 [*La Remarque spéculative: Un bon mot de Hegel.* Paris: Galilée, 1973].

And Philippe Lacoue-Labarthe. *The Literary Absolute: The Theory of Literature in German Romanticism.* Trans. and intro. Philip Barnard and Cheryl Lester. Albany: State University of New York Press, 1988 [*L'Absolu littéraire: Théorie de la littérature du romantisme allemand.* Paris: Éditions du Seuil, 1978].

And Philippe Lacoue-Labarthe. *Retreating the Political.* Ed. and trans. Simon Sparks. New York: Routledge, 1997.

And Philippe Lacoue-Labarthe. *The Title of the Letter: A Reading of Lacan.* Trans. François Raffoul and David Pettigrew. Albany: State University of New York Press, 1992 [*Le Titre de la lettre: Une lecture de Lacan.* Paris: Galilée, 1973].

Jacques Rancière

Disagreement: Politics and Philosophy. Trans. Julie Rose. Minneapolis: University of Minnesota Press, 1999 [*La Mésentente: Politique et philosophie.* Paris: Galilée, 1995].

The Flesh of Words: The Politics of Writing. Trans. Charlotte Mandell. Stanford, CA: Stanford University Press, 2004 [*La Chair des mots: Politiques de l'écriture.* Paris: Galilée, 1998].

Ignorant Schoolmaster: Five Lessons in Intellectual Emancipation. Trans. Kristin Ross. Stanford, CA: Stanford University Press, 1991 [*Le Maître ignorant: Cinq leçons sur l'émancipation intellectuelle.* Paris: Fayard, 1987].

The Names of History: On the Poetics of Knowledge. Trans. Hassan Melehy. Minneapolis: University of Minnesota Press, 1994 [*Les Noms de l'histoire: Essai de poétique du savoir.* Paris: Éditions du Seuil, 1992].

The Nights of Labor: The Workers' Dream in Nineteenth-Century France. Trans. John Drury. Philadelphia, PA: Temple University Press, 1989 [*La Nuit des prolétaires.* Paris: Fayard, 1981].

On the Shores of Politics. Trans. Liz Heron. London: Verso, 1995 [*Aux bords du politique.* Paris: Éditions Osiris, 1990].

The Philosopher and His Poor. Trans. John Drury, Corinne Oster, and Andrew Parker. Durham, NC: Duke University Press, 2004 [*Le Philosophe et ses pauvres.* Paris: Fayard, 1983].

The Politics of Aesthetics: The Distribution of the Sensible. Trans. Gabriel Rockhill. London: Continuum, 2004 [*Le Partage du Sensible. Esthétique et politique* Paris: Éditions La Fabrique, 2000].

Short Voyages to the Land of the People. Trans. James B. Swenson. Stanford, CA: Stanford University Press, 2003 [*Courts voyages au pays du peuple.* Paris: Éditions du Seuil, 1990].

Paul Ricoeur

The Conflict of Interpretations: Essays in Hermeneutics. Ed. Don Ihde. Evanston, IL: Northwestern University Press, 1974 [*Le Conflit des interpretations. Essais d'herméneutique.* Paris: Éditions du Seuil, 1969].

The Contribution of French Historiography to the Theory of History. New York: Oxford University Press, 1980.

The Course of Recognition. Trans. David Pellauer. Cambridge, MA: Harvard University Press, 2005 [*Parcours de la reconnaissance: Trois études.* Paris: Stock, 2004].

Critique and Conviction: Conversations with François Azouvi and Marc de Launay. Trans. Kathleen Blamey. New York: Columbia University Press, 1998 [*La Critique et la conviction: Entretien avec François Azouvi et Marc de Launay.* Paris: Calmann-Lévy, 1995].

Essays on Biblical Interpretation. Ed. and intro. Lewis S. Mudge. Philadelphia, PA: Fortress Press, 1980.

Fallible Man. Trans. Charles Kelbley. Chicago: Regnery, 1965. Revd. trans. Charles A. Kelbley. New York: Fordham University Press, 1986 [*Philosophie de la volonté. II. Finitude et culpabilité. I. L'Homme faillible.* Paris: Éditions Montaigne, 1960].

Figuring the Sacred: Religion, Narrative, and Imagination. Ed. Mark I. Wallace. Trans. David Pellauer. Minneapolis, MN: Fortress Press, 1995.

Freedom and Nature: The Voluntary and the Involuntary. Trans. and intro. Erazim V. Kohák. Evanston, IL: Northwestern University Press, 1966 [*Philosophie de la volonté. I. Le volontaire et l'involontaire.* Paris: Éditions Montaigne, 1950].

Freud and Philosophy: An Essay on Interpretation. Trans. Denis Savage. New Haven, CT: Yale University Press, 1970 [*De l'interprétation: Essai sur Freud.* Paris: Éditions du Seuil, 1965].

From Text to Action. Trans. Kathleen Blamey and John B. Thompson. Evanston, IL: Northwestern University Press, 1991 [*Du texte à l'action.* Paris: Éditions du Seuil, 1986].

Hermeneutics and the Human Sciences: Essays on Language, Action, and Interpretation. Ed., trans., and intro. John B. Thompson. New York: Cambridge University Press, 1981.

History and Truth. Trans. and intro. Charles A. Kelbley. Evanston, IL: Northwestern University Press, 1965 [*Histoire et vérité.* Paris: Éditions du Seuil, 1955].

Husserl: An Analysis of his Phenomenology. Trans. Edward G. Ballard and Lester E. Embree. Evanston, IL: Northwestern University Press, 1967.

Interpretation Theory: Discourse and the Surplus of Meaning. Fort Worth: Texas Christian University Press, 1976.

The Just. Trans. David Pellauer. Chicago: University of Chicago Press, 2000 [*Le Juste.* Paris: Éditions Esprit, 1995].

A Key to Husserl's Ideas I. Trans. Bond Harris and Jacqueline Bouchard Spurlock. Ed., trans., revd., and intro. Pol Vandevelde. New York: Fordham

University Press, 1996 [*Edmund Husserl. Idées directrices pour une phénoménologie. 1. Introduction générale à la phénoménologie pure*. Paris: Éditions Gallimard, 1950].

Lectures on Ideology and Utopia. Ed. George H. Taylor. New York: Columbia University Press, 1986.

Main Trends in Philosophy. New York: Holmes and Meier, 1978.

Memory, History, Forgetting. Trans. Kathleen Blamey and David Pellauer. Chicago: University of Chicago Press, 2004 [*La Mémoire, l'histoire, l'oubli*. Paris: Éditions du Seuil, 2000].

Oneself as Another. Trans. Kathleen Blamey. Chicago: University of Chicago Press, 1992 [*Soi-même comme un autre*. Paris: Éditions du Seuil, 1990].

Paul Ricoeur on Biblical Hermeneutics. Ed. John Dominic Crossan. Missoula, MT: Society of Biblical Literature, 1975.

The Philosophy of Paul Ricoeur: An Anthology of His Work. Ed. Charles E. Reagan and David Stewart. Boston, MA: Beacon Press, 1978.

Political and Social Essays. Ed. David Stewart and Joseph Bien. Athens: Ohio University Press, 1975.

The Reality of the Historical Past. Milwaukee, WI: Marquette University Press, 1984.

A Ricoeur Reader: Reflection and Imagination. Ed. Mario J. Valdés. Toronto: University of Toronto Press, 1991.

The Rule of Metaphor: Multi-Disciplinary Studies of the Creation of Meaning in Language. Trans. Robert Czerny, Kathleen McLaughlin, and John Costello. Toronto: University of Toronto Press, 1977 [*La Métaphore vive*. Paris: Éditions du Seuil, 1975].

The State and Coercion. Geneva: John Knox House, 1957.

The Symbolism of Evil. Trans. Emerson Buchanan. Boston, MA: Beacon Press, 1967 [*Philosophie de la volonté. II. Finitude et culpabilité. II. La Symbolique du mal*. Paris: Éditions Montaigne, 1960].

Time and Narrative. 3 Vols. Trans. Kathleen McLaughlin and David Pellauer. Chicago: University of Chicago Press, 1984–8 [*Temps et récit. Tome 2. La Configuration dans le récit de fiction. Tome 3. Le Temps raconté*. Paris: Éditions du Seuil, 1983–5].

And Jean-Pierre Changeux. *What Makes Us Think? A Neuroscientist and a Philosopher Argue about Ethics, Human Nature, and the Brain*. Trans. M. B. DeBevoise. Princeton, NJ: Princeton University Press, 2000 [*La Nature et la règle: Ce qui nous fait penser*. Paris: Odile Jacob, 1998].

And André LaCocque. *Thinking Biblically: Exegetical and Hermeneutical Studies*. Trans. David Pellauer. Chicago: University of Chicago Press, 1998.

And Alasdair C. MacIntyre. *The Religious Significance of Atheism*. New York: Columbia University Press, 1969.

And Gabriel Marcel. *Tragic Wisdom and Beyond: Including Conversations Between Paul Ricoeur and Gabriel Marcel*. Trans. Stephen Jolin and Peter McCormick. Evanston, IL: Northwestern University Press, 1973 [*Paul Ricoeur, Gabriel Marcel: Entretiens*. Paris: Aubier-Montaigne, 1968].

Jean-Paul Sartre

Anti-Semite and Jew. Trans. George J. Becker. New York: Schocken Books, 1948 [*Réflexions sur la question juive*. Paris: Paul Morihien, 1946].

Baudelaire. Trans. Martin Turnell. Norfolk, CT: New Directions, 1950 [*Baudelaire*. Paris: Éditions Gallimard, 1947].

Being and Nothingness: An Essay in Phenomenological Ontology. Trans. and intro. Hazel E. Barnes. New York: Philosophical Library, 1956 [*L'Être et le néant: Essai d'ontologie phénoménologique*. Paris: Éditions Gallimard, 1943].

Between Existentialism and Marxism: Sartre on Philosophy, Politics, Psychology, and the Arts. Trans. John Mathews. New York: Pantheon Books, 1974 [*Situations VIII: Autour de 1968*; and *IX: Mélanges*. Paris: Éditions Gallimard, 1972].

Colonialism and Neo-Colonialism. Trans. Azzedine Haddour, Steve Brewer, and Terrence McWilliams. New York: Routledge, 2001 [*Situations V: Colonialisme et néo-colonialisme*. Paris: Éditions Gallimard, 1964].

The Communists and Peace, with a Reply to Claude Lefort. New York: G. Braziller, 1968 ["Les communistes et la paix." In *Situations. VI: Problèmes du marxisme. 1.* Paris: Éditions Gallimard, 1964; and "Réponse à Claude Lefort." In *Situations. VII: Problèmes du marxisme. 2.* Paris: Éditions Gallimard, 1965].

Critique of Dialectical Reason: Theory of Practical Ensembles. Ed. Jonathan Rée. Trans. Alan Sheridan-Smith. Atlantic Highlands, NJ: Humanities Press, 1976 [*Critique de la raison dialectique.* Paris: Éditions Gallimard, 1960].

The Emotions: Outline of a Theory. Trans. Bernard Frechtman. New York: Philosophical Library, 1948 [*Esquisse d'une théorie des emotions.* Paris: Hermann, 1939].

Essays in Aesthetics. Ed. and trans. Wade Baskin. New York: Philosophical Library, 1963.

Essays in Existentialism. (Original title: *The Philosophy of Existentialism.*) Ed. Wade Baskin. New York: Philosophical Library, 1965.

Existentialism. Trans. Bernard Frechtman. New York: Philosophical Library, 1947 [*L'Existentialisme est un humanisme.* Paris: Nagel, 1946].

The Family Idiot: Gustave Flaubert, 1821–1857. 5 Vols. Trans. Carol Cosman. Chicago: University of Chicago Press, 1981–93 [*L'Idiot de la famille. 3 Vols. Gustave Flaubert de 1821 à 1857.* Paris: Éditions Gallimard, 1971–2].

The Freud Scenario. Ed. J.-B. Pontalis. Trans. Quintin Hoare. Chicago: University of Chicago Press, 1985 [*Le Scénario Freud.* Paris: Éditions Gallimard, 1984].

The Ghost of Stalin. Trans. Martha H. Fletcher with the assistance of John R. Kleinschmidt. New York: G. Braziller, 1968 ["Le fantome de Staline." In *Situations. VII: Problèmes du marxisme. 2.* Paris: Éditions Gallimard, 1965].

The Imaginary: A Phenomenological Psychology of the Imagination. Revd. Arlette Elkaïm Sartre. Trans. and intro. Jonathan Webber. New York: Routledge, 2003 [*L'Imaginaire: Psychologie-phénoménologique de l'imagination.* Paris: Éditions Gallimard, 1940].

Imagination: A Psychological Critique. Trans. and intro. Forrest Williams. Ann Arbor: University of Michigan Press, 1962 [*L'Imagination.* Paris: Félix Alcan, 1936].

Jean-Paul Sartre: Basic Writings. Ed. Stephen Priest. New York: Routledge, 2001.

Life/Situations: Essays Written and Spoken. Trans. Paul Auster and Lydia Davis. New York: Pantheon Books, 1977 [*Situations X: Politique et autobiographie*. Paris: Éditions Gallimard, 1976].

Literary and Philosophical Essays. Trans. Annette Michelson. New York: Criterion Books, 1955 [*Situations I* and *III*. Paris: Éditions Gallimard, 1947, 1949].

Mallarmé, or, The Poet of Nothingness. Original text established and annotated by Arlette Elkaïm-Sartre. Trans. and intro. Ernest Sturm. University Park: Pennsylvania State University Press, 1988 [*Mallarmé: La Lucidité et sa face d'ombre*. Texte établi et annoté par Arlette Elkaïm-Sartre. Paris: Éditions Gallimard, 1986].

Notebooks for an Ethics. Trans. David Pellauer. Chicago: University of Chicago Press, 1992 [*Cahiers pour une morale*. Paris: Éditions Gallimard, 1983].

On Genocide. With a summary of the evidence and the judgments of the International War Crimes Tribunal by Arlette Elkaïm-Sartre. Boston, MA: Beacon Press, 1968 [1967].

The Psychology of Imagination. New York: Philosophical Library, 1948 [*L'Imaginaire: Psychologie phénoménologique de l'imagination*. Paris: Éditions Gallimard, 1940].

Quiet Moments in a War: The Letters of Jean-Paul Sartre to Simone de Beauvoir, 1940–1963. Ed. Simone de Beauvoir. Trans. and intro. Lee Fahnestock and Norman MacAfee. New York: Scribner's, 1993 [*Lettres au Castor: Et à quelques autres*. Paris: Éditions Gallimard, 1983].

Saint Genet, Actor and Martyr. Trans. Bernard Frechtman. New York: G. Braziller, 1963 [*Saint-Genet: Comédien et martyr*. Paris: Éditions Gallimard, 1952].

Sartre by Himself. Trans. Richard Seaver. New York: Urizen Books, 1978 [*Sartre par lui-même*. Paris: Éditions Gallimard, 1977].

Sartre on Cuba. New York: Ballantine Books, 1961 [*Sartre visita a Cuba, ideologia y revolución, une entrevista con los escritores cubanos, huracán sobre el azúcar*. Havana: Ediciones R, 1960].

Sartre on Theater. Ed. and intro. Michel Contat and Michel Rybalka. Trans. Frank Jellinek. New York: Pantheon Books, 1976.

Search for a Method. Trans. and intro. Hazel E. Barnes. New York: Knopf, 1963 [*Questions de méthode.* Published as preface to *Critique de la raison dialectique.* Paris: Éditions Gallimard, 1960].

Situations. Trans. Benita Eisler. New York: G. Braziller, 1965 [*Situations IV.* Paris: Éditions Gallimard, 1964].

The Spectre of Stalin. Trans. Irene Clephane. London: Hamilton, 1969 ["Le Fantome de Staline." In *Situations. VII: Problèmes du marxisme. 2.* Paris: Éditions Gallimard, 1965].

The Transcendence of the Ego: An Existentialist Theory of Consciousness. Trans. and intro. Forrest Williams and Robert Kirkpatrick. New York: Noonday Press, 1957 ["La Transcendance de l'ego." *Recherches philosophiques* 6 (1936–7)].

Truth and Existence. Original text established and annotated by Arlette Elkaïm-Sartre. Ed. and intro. Ronald Aronson. Trans. Adrian van den Hoven. Chicago: University of Chicago Press, 1992 [*Vérité et existence.* Texte établi et annoté par Arlette Elkaïm-Sartre. Paris: Éditions Gallimard, 1989].

War Diaries of Jean-Paul Sartre: November 1939–March 1940. Trans. Quintin Hoare. New York: Pantheon Books, 1984 [*Les Carnets de la drôle de guerre: novembre 1939–mars 1940.* Paris: Éditions Gallimard, 1983].

War Diaries: Notebooks from a Phony War, 1939–40. Trans. Quintin Hoare. Original text established and annotated by Arlette Elkaïm-Sartre. London: Verso Books, 1999 [*Carnets de la drôle de guerre: septembre 1939–mars 1940.* Texte établi et annoté par Arlette Elkaïm-Sartre. Nouvelle édition augmentée d'un cahier inédit de 170 pages. Paris: Gallimard, 1995].

What is Literature? Trans. Bernard Frechtman. New York: Philosophical Library, 1949 [*Situations II: Qu'est-ce que la littérature?* Paris: Éditions Gallimard, 1948].

"What is Literature?" and Other Essays. Trans. Jeffrey Mehlman. Intro. Steven Ungar. Cambridge, MA: Harvard University Press, 1988 [*Situations II: Qu'est-ce que la littérature?* Paris: Éditions Gallimard, 1948].

Witness to My Life: The Letters of Jean-Paul Sartre to Simone de Beauvoir, 1926–1939. Ed. Simone de Beauvoir. Trans. Lee Fahnestock and Norman

MacAfee. New York: Scribner's, 1993 [*Lettres au Castor: Et à quelques autres.* Paris: Éditions Gallimard, 1983].

The Words. Trans. Bernard Frechtman. New York: G. Braziller, 1964 [*Les Mots.* Paris: Éditions Gallimard, 1964].

The Writings of Jean-Paul Sartre. Ed. Michel Contat and Michel Rybalka. Trans. Richard C. McCleary. Evanston, IL: Northwestern University Press, 1974 [*Les Écrits de Sartre.* Paris: Éditions Gallimard, 1970].

And Albert Camus. *Sartre and Camus: A Historic Confrontation.* Ed. and trans. David A. Sprintzen and Adrian van den Hoven. Amherst, NY: Humanity Books, 2004.

And Vladimir Dedijer. *War Crimes in Vietnam.* Nottingham: Bertrand Russell Peace Foundation, 1971.

And Benny Levy. *Hope Now: The 1980 Interviews.* Trans. Adrian van den Hoven. Chicago: University of Chicago Press, 1996 [*L'Espoir maintenant: Les Entretiens de 1980.* Paris: Verdier, 1991].

Michel Serres

Angels, a Modern Myth. Ed. Philippa Hurd. Trans. Francis Cowper. Paris: Flammarion, 1995 [*La Légende des anges.* Paris: Flammarion, 1993].

The Birth of Physics. Ed. and intro. David Webb. Trans. Jack Hawkes. Manchester: Clinamen Press, 2000 [*La Naissance de la physique dans le texte de Lucrèce.* Paris: Éditions de Minuit, 1977].

Detachment. Trans. Genevieve James and Raymond Federman. Athens: Ohio University Press, 1989 [*Détachement: Apologue.* Paris: Flammarion, 1983].

Genesis. Trans. Genevieve James and James Nielson. Ann Arbor: University of Michigan Press, 1995 [*Genèse.* Paris: B. Grasset, 1981].

Hermes: Literature, Science, Philosophy. Ed. Josué V. Harari and David F. Bell. Baltimore, MD: Johns Hopkins University Press, 1982 [*Hermes, Vols. 1–5.* Paris: Éditions de Minuit, 1968–80].

The Natural Contract. Trans. Elizabeth MacArthur and William Paulson. Ann Arbor: University of Michigan Press, 1995 [*Le Contrat naturel.* Paris: Le Grand livre du mois, 1990].

The Parasite. Trans. Lawrence R. Schehr. Baltimore, MD: Johns Hopkins University Press, 1982 [*Le Parasite*. Paris: B. Grasset, 1980].

Rome: The Book of Foundations. Trans. Felicia McCarren. Stanford, CA: Stanford University Press, 1991 [*Rome: Le Livre des foundations*. Paris: B. Grasset, 1983].

The Troubadour of Knowledge. Trans. Sheila Faria Glaser, with William Paulson. Ann Arbor: University of Michigan Press, 1997 [*Le Tiers-instruit*. Paris: F. Bourin, 1991].

And Bruno Latour. *Conversations on Science, Culture, and Time*. Trans. Roxanne Lapidus. Ann Arbor: University of Michigan Press, 1995 [*Éclaircissements: Cinq entretiens avec Bruno Latour*. Paris: Le Grand livre du mois, 1992].

Jean Wahl

The Philosopher's Way. New York: Oxford University Press, 1948.

Philosophies of Existence: An Introduction to the Basic Thought of Kierkegaard, Heidegger, Jaspers, Marcel, Sartre. Trans. F. M. Lory. New York: Schocken Books, 1968 [*Les Philosophies de l'existence*. Paris: Armand Colin, 1954].

The Pluralist Philosophies of England and America. Trans. Fred Rothwell. London: Open Court, 1925 [*Les Philosophies pluralistes d'Angleterre et d'Amérique*. Paris: Félix Alcan, 1920].

A Short History of Existentialism. Trans. Forrest Williams and Stanley Maron. New York: Philosophical Library, 1949 [*Petite histoire de "l'existentialisme"; suivie de Kafka et Kierkegaard*. Paris: Club Maintenant, 1947].

And Marc Chagall. *Illustrations for the Bible*. Text by Jean Wahl, with an appreciation by Meyer Schapiro. New York: Harcourt, Brace, 1956.

Simone Weil

First and Last Notebooks. Trans. Richard Rees. New York: Oxford University Press, 1970 [*La Connaissance surnaturelle*. Paris: Éditions Gallimard, 1950; and *Cahiers. Nouvelle édition revue et augmentée*. Paris: Plon, 1970].

Gateway to God. Ed. David Raper, with the collaboration of Malcolm Muggeridge and Vernon Sproxton. New York: Crossroad, 1974.

Gravity and Grace. Trans. Arthur F. Wills. New York: Octagon Books, 1979 [*La Pesanteur et la grâce.* Paris: Plon, 1948].

The Iliad, or, The Poem of Force. Trans. Mary McCarthy. Iowa City, IA: Stone Wall Press, 1973.

Intimations of Christianity among the Ancient Greeks. Ed. and trans. Elisabeth Chase Geissbuhler. Boston, MA: Beacon Press, 1958 [*Intuitions pré-chrétiennes.* Paris: La Colombe, 1951; and *La Source grecque.* Paris: Éditions Gallimard, 1953].

Lectures on Philosophy. Presented by Anne Reynaud. Trans. Hugh Price. Cambridge: Cambridge University Press, 1978 [*Leçons de philosophie.* Paris: Plon, 1959].

Letter to a Priest. Trans. Arthur F. Wills. New York: Putnam, 1954 [*Lettre à un religieux.* Paris: Éditions Gallimard, 1951].

The Need for Roots: Prelude to a Declaration of Duties Toward Mankind. Trans. Arthur F. Wills. New York: Octagon Books, 1979 [*L'Enracinement: Prélude à une déclaration des devoirs envers l'être humain.* Paris: Éditions Gallimard, 1949].

The Notebooks of Simone Weil. Trans. Arthur F. Wills. London: Routledge and Kegan Paul, 1956.

On Science, Necessity, and the Love of God. Trans. and ed. Richard Rees. Oxford: Oxford University Press, 1968 [*Pensées sans ordre concernant l'amour de Dieu.* Paris: Éditions Gallimard, 1962].

Oppression and Liberty. Trans. Arthur F. Wills and John Petrie. Amherst: University of Massachusetts Press, 1973 [*Oppression et liberté.* Paris: Éditions Gallimard, 1955].

Selected Essays: 1934–1943. Ed. and trans. Richard Rees. Oxford: Oxford University Press, 1962.

Simone Weil. Ed. Eric O. Springsted. Maryknoll, NY: Orbis Books, 1998.

Simone Weil: An Anthology. Ed. and intro. Siân Miles. London: Virago, 1986.

Simone Weil: Formative Writings 1929–1941. Ed. and trans. Dorothy Tuck McFarland and Wilhelmina Van Ness. Amherst: University of Massachusetts Press, 1987.

Simone Weil on Colonialism: An Ethic of the Other. Ed. and trans. J. P. Little. Lanham, MD: Rowman and Littlefield, 2003.

The Simone Weil Reader. Ed. George A. Panichas. New York: McKay, 1977.

Simone Weil's The Iliad, or, The Poem of Force: A Critical Edition. Ed. and trans. James P. Holoka. New York: P. Lang, 2003.

Two Moral Essays: Draft for a Statement of Human Obligations and Human Personality. Ed. Ronald Hathaway. Wallingford, PA: Pendle Hill Publications, 1981.

Waiting for God. Trans. Emma Craufurd. New York: G. P. Putnam's Sons, 1951 [*Attente de Dieu.* Paris: La Colombe, 1950].

Works Cited and Consulted

"L'Agrégation de philosophie." *Bulletin de la Société Française de Philosophie*, vol. 38 (1938): 117–58.

Alain. *Les Philosophes*. Paris: P. Delaplane, 1901.

Alquié, Ferdinand. *Nature et vérité dans la philosophie de Spinoza*. Paris: Centre de documentation universitaire, 1965.

—— *Le Rationalisme de Spinoza*. Paris: Presses universitaires de France, 1981.

Althusser, Louis. *Éléments d'autocritique*. Paris: Hachette, 1974.

—— *Essays in Self-Criticism*. Trans. Grahame Lock. London: New Left Books, 1976.

—— *For Marx*. Trans. Ben Brewster. London: Verso, 1990.

—— "Ideology and Ideological State Apparatuses." In *Lenin and Philosophy and Other Essays*. Trans. Ben Brewster. London: New Left Books, 1971. Pp. 127–86.

—— *Lire "Le Capital."* 2 Vols. Paris: F. Maspero, 1965.

—— *Pour Marx*. Paris: F. Maspero, 1965.

Althusser, Louis, and Étienne Balibar. *Reading Capital*. Trans. Ben Brewster. London: New Left Books, 1970.

Annuaire de l'Association Amicale de Secours des Anciens Élèves de l'École Normale Supérieure. Paris: Bureau de l'Association, 1846–.

Annuaire du Collège de France. Paris: Imprimerie nationale, 1901–.

Annuaire Général de l'Université et de l'Enseignement Français 1942–43. Paris: L'Information Universitaire, 1943.

Aron, Raymond. *Memoirs: Fifty Years of Political Reflection*. Trans. George Holoch. New York: Holmes and Meier, 1990.

Bair, Deidre. *Simone de Beauvoir: A Biography*. New York: Summit Books, 1990.

Balibar, Étienne. *Spinoza et la politique*. Paris: Presses universitaires de France, 1985.

Balibar, Étienne. "Spinoza, the Anti-Orwell." In *Masses, Classes, Ideas: Studies on Politics and Philosophy Before and After Marx*. Trans. James Swenson. New York: Routledge, 1994. Pp. 3–37.

Bataille, Georges. *On Nietzsche*. Trans. Bruce Boone. New York: Paragon House, 1992.

Beauvoir, Simone de. *Le Deuxième sexe*. Paris: Éditions Gallimard, 1949.

—— *The Prime of Life*. Trans. Peter Green. New York: World Publishing, 1962.

—— *The Second Sex*. Ed. and trans. Howard Madison Parshley. New York: Alfred A. Knopf, 1952.

—— "*Les Structures élémentaires de la parenté* par Claude Lévi-Strauss." *Les Temps modernes* (November 1949): 943–9.

Bennington, Geoffrey, and Jacques Derrida. *Jacques Derrida*. Chicago: University of Chicago Press, 1993.

Bergson, Henri. *L'Evolution créatrice*. Paris: Félix Alcan, 1914.

Boirel, René. *Brunschvicg, sa vie, son oeuvre*. Paris: Presses universitaires de France, 1964.

Bouglé, Célestin. *The French Conception of "Culture Générale" and its Influence upon Instruction*. New York: Columbia University Press, 1938.

—— ed. *L'École normale supérieure. D'où elle vient, où elle va*. Paris: Hachette, 1934.

Bouillon, Jacques, Isabelle Brian, Ghislain Brune, and Bernard Roussel. *Le Lycée Henri-IV, Paris*. Thionville: G. Klopp, 1996.

Bourdieu, Pierre. "Fieldwork in Philosophy." In *In Other Words: Essays Towards a Reflexive Sociology*. Trans. Matthew Adamson. Stanford, CA: Stanford University Press, 1990. Pp. 3–33.

—— *Homo Academicus*. Trans. Peter Collier. Stanford, CA: Stanford University Press, 1988.

Bourdieu, Pierre, and Jean-Claude Passeron. "Sociology and Philosophy in France since 1945: Death and Resurrection of a Philosophy without a Subject." *Social Research* 34, No. 1 (Spring 1967): 162–212.

Bouveresse, Jacques. "Why I am so very unFrench." In *Philosophy in France Today*. Ed. Alan Montefiore. Trans. Kathleen McLaughlin. Cambridge: Cambridge University Press, 1983. Pp. 9–33.

Brunschvicg, Léon. "La Philosophie dans l'Enseignement supérieur à Paris." *Annales de l'Université de Paris* V, No. 3 (May-June 1930): 215–23.

—— *Spinoza*. Paris: Félix Alcan, 1894.

—— *Spinoza et ses contemporains*. Paris: Félix Alcan, 1923.

Bulletin administratif du Ministère de l'instruction publique. Paris: Imprimerie Nationale, 1882–1925.

Bulletin officiel du Ministère de l'éducation nationale. Paris: Ministère de l'Education nationale 1944– .

Canguilhem, Georges. "Hegel en France." *Revue d'histoire et de philosophie religieuses*, Vols. 28–9 (1948–9): 282–97. Reprinted in *Magazine littéraire*, No. 293 (November 1991): 26–9.

—— "Mort de l'homme ou épuisement du cogito." *Critique* 242 (July 1967): 599–618.

Cantin, Eileen. *Mounier: A Personalist View of History*. New York: Paulist Press, 1973.

Catalogue des thèses de doctorat soutenues devant les universités françaises. Paris: Cercle de la Librairie, 1959–85.

Catalogue des thèses et écrits académiques. Paris: Cercle de la Librairie, 1884–1959.

Cavaillès, Jean. "On Logic and the Theory of Science." In *Phenomenology and the Natural Sciences*. Trans. Theodore J. Kisiel. Evanston, IL: Northwestern University Press, 1970. Pp. 353–409.

Caws, Peter. *Sartre*. London: Routledge and Kegan Paul, 1979.

Cazenave, Annie, and Jean-François Lyotard, eds. *L'Art des confins: Mélanges offerts à Maurice de Gandillac*. Paris: Presses universitaires de France, 1985.

Centre Culturel International de Cerisy-la-Salle. *Cerisy: 30 ans de colloques et de rencontres*. Caen: Bibliothèque municipale, 1983.

Chalumeau, Jean-Luc. *Introduction aux idées contemporaines en France: La pensée en France de 1945 à nos jours*. Paris: Vuibert, 1998.

Chervel, André. *Histoire de l'agrégation: Contribution à l'histoire de la culture scolaire*. Paris: Éditions Kimé, 1993.

—— *Les Lauréats des concours d'agrégation de l'enseignement secondaire 1821–1950*. Paris: Institut National de Recherche Pédagogique, 1993.

Cixous, Hélène and Catherine Clément. *La Jeune née*. Paris: Union générale d'Éditions, 1975.

—— *The Newly Born Woman*. Trans. Betsy Wing. Minneapolis: University of Minnesota Press, 1986.

Clark, Terry Nichols. *Prophets and Patrons: The French University and the Emergence of the Social Sciences*. Cambridge, MA: Harvard University Press, 1973.

Cohn-Bendit, Daniel, and Gabriel Cohn-Bendit. *Obsolete Communism: The Left-Wing Alternative*. Trans. Arnold Pomerans. New York: McGraw Hill, 1968.

Collins, James. *The Existentialists*. Chicago: Henry Regnery, 1952.

Comte, Auguste. *The Positive Philosophy of Auguste Comte, Vol. 1*. Trans. Harriet Martineau. London: George Bell and Sons, 1896.

Comte-Sponville, André. *Petit Traité des grandes vertus*. Paris: Presses universitaires de France, 1995.

—— *A Small Treatise on Great Virtues: The Uses of Philosophy in Everyday Life*. Trans. Catherine Temerson. New York: Henry Holt, 2001.

Cuvillier, Armand. *Anthologie des philosophes français contemporains*, 2nd edn. Paris: Presses universitaires de France, 1965.

Debeauvais, Michel. *L'Université ouverte. Les dossiers de Vincennes*. Grenoble: Presses universitaires de Grenoble, 1974.

Delacampagne, Christian. *A History of Philosophy in the Twentieth Century*. Trans. M. B. DeBevoise. Baltimore, MD: Johns Hopkins University Press, 1999.

Delbos, Victor. "Husserl: Sa critique du psychologisme et sa conception d'une Logique pure." *Revue de métaphysique et de morale*, XIXe année, No. 5 (Sept.-Oct. 1911): 685–98.

——— *La Philosophie française*. Paris: Librairie Plon, 1919.

——— *Le Problème moral dans la philosophie de Spinoza et dans l'histoire du spinozisme*. Paris: Félix Alcan, 1893.

Deledalle, Gérard, and Denis Huisman. *Les Philosophes français d'aujourd'hui par eux-mêmes: Autobiographie de la philosophie française contemporaine*. Paris: CDU, 1963.

Deleuze, Gilles. *Dialogues*. Trans. Hugh Tomlinson and Barbara Habberjam. New York: Columbia University Press, 1987.

——— *Difference and Repetition*. Trans. Paul Patton. New York: Columbia University Press, 1994.

——— *Différence et répétition*. Paris: Presses universitaires de France, 1968.

——— " 'Il a été mon maître.' " In *L'Île déserte et autres textes: Textes et entretiens 1953–1974*. Ed. David Lapoujade. Paris: Éditions de Minuit, 2002. Pp. 109–13.

——— *Nietzsche and Philosophy*. Trans. Hugh Tomlinson. New York: Columbia University Press, 1983.

——— *Nietzsche et la philosophie*. Paris: Presses universitaires de France, 1962.

Derrida, Jacques. *Donner le temps. 1. La Fausse monnaie*. Paris: Galilée, 1991.

——— *Du droit à la philosophie*. Paris: Galilée, 1990.

——— *Eyes of the University: Right to Philosophy 2*. Trans. Jan Plug. Stanford, CA: Stanford University Press.

——— *Given Time: I. Counterfeit Money*. Trans. Peggy Kamuf. Chicago: University of Chicago Press, 1992.

——— *Qui a peur de la philosophie?* Paris: Flammarion, 1977.

——— "Structure, Sign, and Play in the Discourse of the Human Sciences." In *Writing and Difference*. Trans. Alan Bass. Chicago: University of Chicago Press, 1978.

——— "Structure, Sign, and Play in the Discourse of the Human Sciences." In *The Structuralist Controversy*. Ed. Richard Macksey and Eugenio Donato. Trans. Richard Macksey. Baltimore, MD: Johns Hopkins University Press, 1970. Pp. 247–72.

—— "The Time of a Thesis: Punctuations." In *Philosophy in France Today*. Ed. Alan Montefiore. Trans. Kathleen McLaughlin. Cambridge: Cambridge University Press, 1983. Pp. 34–50.

—— *Who's Afraid of Philosophy? Right to Philosophy I*. Trans. Jan Plug. Stanford, CA: Stanford University Press, 2002.

—— *The Work of Mourning*. Ed. Pascale-Anne Brault and Michael Naas. Chicago: University of Chicago Press, 2001.

Desanti, Jean-Toussaint. "A Path in Philosophy." In *Philosophy in France Today*. Ed. Alan Montefiore. Trans. Kathleen McLaughlin. Cambridge: Cambridge University Press, 1983. Pp. 51–66.

Descamps, Christian. *Interrogations philosophiques contemporaines en France*. Paris: Rendezvous en France, 1989.

Descamps, Christian, Jocelyn Benoist, and Eric Alliez, eds. *Philosophie contemporaine en France*. Paris: Ministère des affaires étrangères: ADPF, 1994.

Descombes, Vincent. *Modern French Philosophy*. Trans. L. Scott-Fox and J. M. Harding. New York: Cambridge University Press, 1980.

Dosse, Francois. *History of Structuralism. Vol. 1: The Rising Sign, 1945–1966; Vol. 2: The Sign Sets, 1967–present*. Trans. Deborah Glassman. Minneapolis: University of Minnesota Press, 1997.

Drouard, Alain. "A propos du statut de la sociologie et du sociologue en France." In *Le Personnel de l'enseignement supérieur en France aux XIXe et XXe siècles*. Paris: Editions du CNRS, 1985. Pp. 167–75.

Engel, Pascal. "Continental Insularity: Contemporary French Analytical Philosophy." *Contemporary French Philosophy*. Ed. A. Phillips Griffiths. Cambridge: Cambridge University Press, 1987. Pp. 1–19.

Eribon, Didier. *Michel Foucault*. Trans. Betsy Wing. Cambridge, MA: Harvard University Press, 1991.

Fabiani, Jean-Louis. *Les Philosophes de la république*. Paris: Éditions de Minuit, 1988.

Fanon, Frantz. *The Wretched of the Earth*. Trans. Constance Farrington. New York: Grove Press, 1968.

Ferry, Luc, and Alain Renaut. *French Philosophy of the Sixties: An Essay on Antihumanism*. Trans. Mary Schnackenberg Cattani. Amherst: University of Massachusetts Press, 1990.

Flood, Christopher, and Nick Hewlett. *Currents in Contemporary French Intellectual Life*. New York: St. Martin's Press, 2000.

Foucault, Michel. "Critical Theory/Intellectual History." In *Politics, Philosophy, Culture: Interviews and Other Writings, 1977–1984*. Ed. Lawrence D. Kritzman. Trans. Jeremy Harding. New York: Routledge, 1988. Pp. 17–46.

—— "The Discourse on Language." In *The Archeaology of Knowledge*. Trans. Rupert Swyer. New York: Pantheon Books, 1972. Pp. 215–37.

—— *Dits et écrits*. Paris: Éditions Gallimard, 1994.

Foucault, Michel. "The Ethics of Concern for the Self as a Practice of Freedom." In *The Essential Works of Michel Foucault, 1954–1988, Vol. 1: Ethics: Subjectivity and Truth*. Ed. Paul Rabinow. Trans. P. Aranov and D. McGrawth. New York: New Press, 1997. Pp. 281–301.

—— "Introduction" to Georges Canguilhem, *The Normal and the Pathological*. Trans. Carolyn R. Fawcett in collaboration with Robert S. Cohen. New York: Zone Books, 1989. Pp. 7–24.

—— *Les Mots et les choses: Une archéologie des sciences humaines*. Paris: Éditions Gallimard, 1966.

—— "Nietzsche, Freud, Marx." In *Transforming the Hermeneutic Context: From Nietzsche to Nancy*. Ed. Alan D. Schrift and Gayle L. Ormiston. Trans. Alan D. Schrift. Albany: State University of New York Press, 1990. Pp. 59–67.

—— "On the Genealogy of Ethics: An Overview of Work in Progress." In *The Foucault Reader*. Ed. Paul Rabinow. New York: Pantheon Books, 1984. Pp. 340–72.

—— *The Order of Things: An Archeology of the Human Sciences*. New York: Vintage Books, 1970.

—— "Polemics, Politics, and Problematizations: An Interview." In *The Foucault Reader*. Ed. Paul Rabinow. Trans. Lydia Davis. New York: Pantheon Books, 1984. Pp. 381–90.

—— "Theatrum Philosophicum." In *Language, Counter-Memory, Practice: Selected Essays and Interviews*. Ed. Donald F. Bouchard. Trans. Donald F. Bouchard and Sherry Simon. Ithaca, NY: Cornell University Press, 1977. Pp. 165–96.

—— *The Use of Pleasure*. Trans. Robert Hurley. New York: Random House, 1985.

—— "What is an Author?" In *The Foucault Reader*. Ed. Paul Rabinow. Trans. Josué V. Harari. New York: Pantheon Books, 1984. Pp. 101–20.

—— "What is Critique?" In *What is Enlightenment? Eighteenth-Century Answers and Twentieth-Century Questions*. Ed. James Schmidt. Trans. Kevin Paul Geiman. Berkeley: University of California Press, 1996. Pp. 382–98.

—— "What is Enlightenment." In *The Foucault Reader*. Ed. Paul Rabinow. Trans. Catherine Porter. New York: Pantheon Books, 1984. Pp. 32–50.

—— "Why Study Power: The Question of the Subject." In *Michel Foucault: Beyond Structuralism and Hermeneutics*. Ed. Hubert L. Dreyfus and Paul Rabinow. Chicago: University of Chicago Press, 1982. Pp. 208–16.

Francis, Claude, and Fernande Gontier. *Simone de Beauvoir: A Life... A Love Story*. Trans. Lisa Nesselson. New York: St. Martin's Press, 1987.

Frank, Manfred. *What is Neo-Structuralism?* Trans. Sabine Wilke and Richard Gray. Minneapolis: University of Minnesota Press, 1989.

Frickey, Gene H. "The Origins of Phenomenology in France, 1920–1940." Ph.D. Dissertation, Indiana University, 1979.

Fullbrook, Edward, and Kate Fullbrook. *Simone de Beauvoir and Jean-Paul Sartre: The Remaking of a Twentieth-Century Legend.* New York: Basic Books, 1994.

Galster, Ingrid, and Maurice de Gandillac. " «Ils auraient pu les mettre *ex aequo*»: Entretien avec le philosophe Maurice de Gandillac sur l'agrégation de Beauvoir et d'autres sujets." *Lendemains* 94 (1999): 19–36.

Gendzier, Irene L. *Frantz Fanon: A Critical Study.* New York: Random House, 1973.

Glucksmann, André. *The Master Thinkers.* Trans. Brian Pearce. New York: Harper and Row, 1980.

Gorman, Robert A. ed. *Biographical Dictionary of Neo-Marxism.* Westport, CT: Greenwood Press, 1985.

Guéroult, Martial. *Spinoza 1. Dieu (Éthique, I).* Paris: Aubier-Montaigne, 1968.

—— *Spinoza II. L'Âme (Éthique, II).* Paris: Aubier-Montaigne, 1974.

Guigue, Albert. *La Faculté des lettres de l'Université de Paris: Depuis sa fondation (17 mars 1808) jusqu'au 1er janvier 1935.* Paris: Félix Alcan, 1935.

Guitton, Jean. *Regards sur la pensée française, 1870–1940: Leçons de captivité.* Paris: Beauchesne, 1968.

Gunter, Pete A. Y. "Bergson." In *A Companion to Continental Philosophy.* Ed. Simon Critchley and William R. Schroeder. Oxford: Blackwell, 1998. Pp. 173–82.

Gurvitch, Georges. *Les Tendances actuelles de la philosophie allemande.* Paris: Librairie Vrin, 1930.

Gutting, Gary. *French Philosophy in the Twentieth Century.* Cambridge: Cambridge University Press, 2001.

Hansen, Emmanuel. *Frantz Fanon: Social and Political Thought.* Columbus: Ohio State University Press, 1977.

Hardt, Michael, and Antonio Negri. *Empire.* Cambridge, MA: Harvard University Press, 2000.

Heidegger, Martin. *Qu'est-ce que la métaphysique?* Paris: Éditions Gallimard, 1938.

Hellman, John. *Emmanuel Mounier and the New Catholic Left 1930–1950.* Toronto: University of Toronto Press, 1981.

Hering, Jean. *Phénoménologie et philosophie religieuse.* Paris: Félix Alcan, 1925.

Hourmant, François. *Le Désenchantement des clercs: Figures de l'intellectuel dans l'après-mai 68.* Rennes: Presses universitaires de Rennes, 1997.

Huisman, Denis, ed. *Dictionnaire des philosophes.* 2 vols., 2nd edn. Paris: Presses universitaires de France, 1993.

Hulin, Nicole. "La Section des sciences de l'ENS." In *École normale supérieure: Le Livre du bicentenaire.* Ed. Jean-François Sirinelli. Paris: Presses universitaires de France, 1994. Pp. 321–49.

Husserl, Edmund. *Cartesian Meditations: An Introduction to Phenomenology.* Trans. Dorion Cairns. The Hague: Martinus Nijhoff, 1960.

—— *Husserliana 1. Cartesianische Meditationen und Pariser Vorträge.* Ed. Stephen Strasser. The Hague: Martinus Nijhoff, 1950/1973.

—— *Logical Investigations, Vol. 1.* Trans. J. N. Findlay. New York: Humanities Press, 1970.

—— *Méditations cartésiennes et les conférences de Paris.* In *Oeuvres complètes (Husserliana).* Trans. Marc de Launey. Dordrecht: Kluwer, 1991; Paris: Presses universitaires de France, 1994.

—— *Méditations cartésiennes. Introduction à la phénoménologie.* Trans. Gabrielle Peiffer and Emmanuel Levinas. Paris: Armand Colin, 1931.

—— *The Paris Lectures.* Trans. Peter Koestenbaum. The Hague: Martinus Nijhoff, 1964.

Index Generalis: France 1958: Enseignement supérieure. Recherche scientifique. Paris: C. Klincksieck, 1959.

Irigaray, Luce. *Ce sexe qui n'en est pas un.* Paris: Éditions de Minuit, 1977.

—— *An Ethics of Sexual Difference.* Trans. Carolyn Burke and Gillian C. Gill. Ithaca, NY: Cornell University Press, 1993.

—— *Éthique de la différence sexuelle.* Paris: Éditions de Minuit, 1984.

—— " 'Je–Luce Irigaray': A Meeting with Luce Irigaray." An interview conducted by Elizabeth Hirsh and Gary A. Olson. Trans. Elizabeth Hirsh and Gaëtan Brulotte. *Hypatia: A Journal of Feminist Philosophy* 10, No. 2 (Spring 1995): 93–114.

—— *This Sex Which Is Not One.* Trans. Catherine Porter with Carolyn Burke. Ithaca, NY: Cornell University Press, 1985.

Jakobson, Roman. "Retrospect." In *Selected Writings, Vol. 2.* The Hague: Mouton, 1971.

Jamet, Michel. "La Classe de philosophie hier et aujourd'hui et l'enseignement de la philosophie." *Revue de l'Enseignement Philosophique*, 35ème Année, No. 2 (1984): 73–87, and No. 3 (1984): 81–90.

Janicaud, Dominique. *Heidegger en France. Tome 2: Entretiens.* Paris: Albin Michel, 2001.

—— *The Theological Turn of French Phenomenology.* Trans. Bernard G. Prusack. In Janicaud, et al. *Phenomenology and the "Theological Turn": The French Debate.* New York: Fordham University Press, 2000. Pp. 3–103.

Jankélévitch, Vladimir. "Léon Brunschvicg." *Sources.* Paris: Éditions du Seuil, 1984. Pp. 133–41.

—— *Traité des vertus.* Paris: Éditions Bordas, 1949.

Jardine, Alice, and Anne M. Mencke. *Shifting Scenes: Interviews on Women, Writing, and Politics in Post-68 France.* New York: Columbia University Press, 1991.

Julliard, Jacques, and Michel Winock. *Dictionnaire des intellectuels français: Les personnes, les lieux, les moments.* Paris: Éditions du Seuil, 1996.

Kojève, Alexandre. *Introduction à la lecture de Hegel: Leçons sur la "Phénoménologie de l'Esprit" professées de 1933 à 1939 à l'École des Hautes Études*. Ed. Raymond Queneau. Paris: Éditions Gallimard, 1947.

—— *Introduction to the Reading of Hegel: Lectures on the Phenomenology of Spirit*. Assembled by Raymond Queneau. Ed. Allan Bloom. Trans. James H. Nichols, Jr. New York: Basic Books, 1969.

Koyré, Alexandre. "Rapport sur l'état des études hégéliennes en France." In *Études d'histoire de la pensée philosophique*. Paris: Éditions Gallimard, 1971. Pp. 225–49.

Kristeva, Julia. *Desire in Language: A Semiotic Approach to Literature and Art*. Ed. Leon S. Roudiez. Trans. Thomas Gora, Alice Jardine, and Leon S. Roudiez. New York: Columbia University Press, 1980.

Lacan, Jacques. *Écrits*. Paris: Éditions du Seuil, 1966.

—— *Ecrits: A Selection*. Trans. Alan Sheridan. New York: W. W. Norton, 1977.

—— *The Four Fundamental Concepts of Psycho-Analysis*. Ed. Jacques-Alain Miller. Trans. Alan Sheridan. New York: W. W. Norton, 1978.

Lachelier, Jules. *The Philosophy of Jules Lachelier*. Ed. and trans. Edward G. Ballard. The Hague: Martinus Nijhoff, 1960.

Lacroix, Jean. *Panorama de la philosophie française contemporaine*. Paris: Presses universitaires de France, 1966.

Lalande, André. "Philosophy in France." *Philosophical Review* 14, No. 4 (1905): 429–55.

—— *Vocabulaire technique et critique de la philosophie*. Paris: Presses universitaires de France, 1928.

Lamont, Michèle. "How to Become a Dominant French Philosopher: The Case of Jacques Derrida." *American Journal of Sociology* Vol. 93, No. 3 (November 1987): 584–622.

Lecourt, Dominique. *The Mediacracy: French Philosophy since the mid-1970s*. Trans. Gregory Elliot. London: Verso, 2001.

Léna, Marguerite. *Honneur aux Maîtres*. Paris: Criterion, 1991.

Lévi-Strauss, Claude. *Anthropologie structurale*. Paris: Plon, 1958.

—— *De près et de loin. Entretien avec Didier Eribon*. Paris: Éditions Odile Jacob, 1988.

—— *Introduction à l'oeuvre de Marcel Mauss*. Paris: Presses universitaires de France, 1950.

—— *Introduction to the Work of Marcel Mauss*. Trans. Felicity Baker. London: Routledge and Kegan Paul, 1987.

—— *Mythologiques. 1. Le Cru et le cuit*. Paris: Plon, 1964.

—— *La Pensée sauvage*. Paris: Plon, 1962.

—— *The Raw and the Cooked*. Trans. John and Doreen Weightman. New York: Harper and Row, 1969.

—— *The Savage Mind*. Chicago: University of Chicago Press, 1966.

Lévi-Strauss, Claude. *Structural Anthropology*. Trans. Claire Jacobson and Brooke Grundfest Schoepf. New York: Basic Books, 1963.

Levinas, Emmanuel. *Ethics and Infinity*. Trans. Richard A. Cohen. Pittsburgh, PA: Duquesne University Press, 1985.

—— "Martin Heidegger and Ontology." Trans. Committee of Public Safety. *Diacritics* 26, No. 1 (Spring 1996): 11–32.

—— "Martin Heidegger et l'ontologie." *Revue philosophique de la France et de l'étranger* 63, No. 5/6 (1932): 395–431.

—— *Théorie de l'intuition dans la phénoménologie de Husserl*. Paris: Félix Alcan, 1930.

—— *The Theory of Intuition in Husserl's Phenomenology*. Trans. André Orianne. Evanston, IL: Northwestern University Press, 1973.

—— *Time and the Other*. Trans. Richard A. Cohen. Pittsburgh, PA: Duquesne University Press, 1987.

Lévy, Bernard-Henri. *Barbarism with a Human Face*. Trans. George Holoch. New York: Harper and Row, 1979.

Lukes, Steven. *Émile Durkheim: His Life and Works*. London: Penguin, 1973.

Lyotard, Jean-François. *Le Différend*. Paris: Éditions de Minuit, 1983.

—— *The Differend: Phrases in Dispute*. Trans. Georges Van Den Abbeele. Minneapolis: University of Minnesota Press, 1988.

—— *Phenomenology*. Trans. Brian Beakley. Albany: State University of New York Press, 1991.

—— *Political Writings*. Trans. Bill Readings and Kevin Paul Geiman. Minneapolis: University of Minnesota Press, 1993.

—— *The Postmodern Condition: A Report on Knowledge*. Trans. Geoff Bennington and Brian Massumi. Minneapolis: University of Minnesota Press, 1984.

Lyotard, Jean-François, and Jean-Loup Thébaud. *Au juste: Conversations*. Paris: Christian Bourgois, 1979.

—— *Just Gaming*. Trans. Wlad Godzich. Minneapolis: University of Minnesota Press, 1985.

McAllester Jones, Mary. *Gaston Bachelard, Subversive Humanist*. Madison: University of Wisconsin Press, 1991.

Macey, David. *The Lives of Michel Foucault: A Biography*. New York: Pantheon Books, 1993.

Macherey, Pierre. *Avec Spinoza: Études sur la doctrine et l'histoire du spinozisme*. Paris: Presses universitaires de France, 1992.

—— *Hegel ou Spinoza*. Paris: F. Maspero, 1979.

—— *Introduction à l'"Éthique" de Spinoza*. 5 Vols.: 1. ptie. *La Nature des choses*; 2. ptie. *La Réalité mentale*; 3. ptie. *La Vie affective*; 4. ptie. *La Condition humaine*; 5. ptie. *Les Voies de la libération*. Paris: Presses universitaires de France, 1994–8.

—— "Y a-t-il une philosophie française?" In *Histoires de dinosaure: Faire de la philosophie 1965–1997*. Paris: Presses universitaires de France, 1999. Pp. 313–22.

Macpherson, C. B. *The Political Theory of Possessive Individualism: Hobbes to Locke*. Oxford: Clarendon Press, 1962.

Maggiori, Robert. "Michel Henry ravi à la Vie." *Liberation*, July 8, 2002: 34.

Malmberg, Bertil. "Linguistique européene et linguistique américaine à la lumière du débat actuel." *Moderna språk* 67 (1973).

Marcel, Gabriel. *Journal métaphysique*. Paris: Éditions Gallimard, 1927.

—— *Metaphysical Journal*. Trans. Bernard Wall. Chicago: Henry Regnery, 1952.

Maritain, Jacques. *Existence and the Existent*. Trans. Lewis Galantiere and Gerald B. Phelan. New York: Pantheon Books, 1948.

Matheron, Alexandre. *Anthropologie et politique au XVIIe siècle: Études sur Spinoza*. Paris: Vrin, 1986.

—— *Le Christ et le salut des ignorants chez Spinoza*. Paris: Aubier-Montaigne, 1971.

—— *Individu et communauté chez Spinoza*. Paris: Éditions de Minuit, 1969.

—— *Individualité et relations interhumaines chez Spinoza*. Paris: Éditions de Minuit, 1969.

Matthews, Eric. *Twentieth-Century French Philosophy*. New York: Oxford University Press, 1996.

Memmi, Albert. *The Colonizer and the Colonized*. Trans. Howard Greenfeld. New York: Orion Press, 1965.

Merleau-Ponty, Maurice. *Éloge de la philosophie. Leçon inaugurale faite au Collège de France*. Paris: Éditions Gallimard, 1953.

—— "From Mauss to Claude Lévi-Strauss." In *Signs*. Trans. Richard C. McCleary. Evanston, IL: Northwestern University Press, 1964. Pp. 114–25.

—— *In Praise of Philosophy*. Trans. John Wild and James M. Edie. Evanston, IL: Northwestern University Press, 1963.

—— "On the Phenomenology of Language." In *Signs*. Trans. Richard C. McCleary. Evanston, IL: Northwestern University Press, 1964. Pp. 84–97.

—— *Phénoménologie de la perception*. Paris: Éditions Gallimard, 1945.

—— *Phenomenology of Perception*. Trans. Colin Smith. New York: Routledge, 1962.

Montefiore, Alan, ed. *Philosophy in France Today*. New York: Cambridge University Press, 1983.

Monzie, Anatole de. "Instructions du 2 septembre 1925." www2.ac-lyon.fr/enseigne/philosophie/txteoff/monzie.html.

Moran, Dermot. *Introduction to Phenomenology*. New York: Routledge, 2000.

Moreau, Pierre-François. *Spinoza*. Paris: Éditions du Seuil, 1975.

—— *Spinoza: L'Expérience et l'éternité*. Paris: Presses universitaires de France, 1994.

Mortley, Raoul. *French Philosophers in Conversation*. New York: Routledge, 1991.

Negri, Antonio. *The Savage Anomaly: The Power of Spinoza's Metaphysics and Politics*. Trans. Michael Hardt. Minneapolis: University of Minnesota Press, 1991.

Nietzsche aujourd'hui, 2 vols. Paris: Union générale d'Éditions, 1973.

Nizan, Paul. *The Watchdogs: Philosophers and the Established Order*. Trans. Paul Fittingoff. New York: Monthly Review Press, 1971.

Penrod, Lynn Kettler. *Hélène Cixous*. New York: Twayne Publishers, 1996.

Perrin, André, ed. *Philosophie: L'Histoire de la philosophie dans l'enseignement philosophique*. Montpellier: Académie de Montpellier, MAFPEN: CRDP, 1997.

Pétrement, Simone. *La Vie de Simone Weil*. Paris: Fayard, 1973.

Peyrefitte, Alain. *Rue d'Ulm: Chroniques de la vie normalienne*. 4th edn. Paris: Fayard, 1994.

Pinto, Louis. *Les Philosophes entre le lycée et l'avant-garde: Les Métamorphoses de la philosophie dans la France d'aujourd'hui*. Paris: L'Harmattan, 1986.

Poster, Mark. *Existential Marxism in Postwar France: From Sartre to Althusser*. Princeton, NJ: Princeton University Press, 1975.

Prost, Antoine. *L'École et la Famille dans une société en mutation*. Vol. 4 of *Histoire générale de l'enseignement et de l'éducation en France*. Ed. Louis-Henri Parais. Paris: Nouvelle Librairie de France, 1981.

Quillien, Jean, ed. *La Réception de la philosophie allemande en France aux XIXe et XXe siècles*. Villeneuve-d'Ascq: Presses universitaires de Lille, 1994.

Reagen, Charles E. *Paul Ricoeur: His Life and His Work*. Chicago: University of Chicago Press, 1996.

Revel, Jacques, and Nathan Wachtel, eds. *Une école pour les sciences social: De la VIe section à l'École des Hautes Études en Sciences Sociales*. Paris: Cerf, 1996.

Revue Universitaire. Paris: Armand Colin, 1892–1957.

Richman, Michele H. *Reading Georges Bataille: Beyond the Gift*. Baltimore, MD: Johns Hopkins University Press, 1982.

Ricoeur, Paul. *De l'interprétation: Essai sur Freud*. Paris: Éditions du Seuil, 1965.

—— "Emmanuel Mounier: A Personalist Philosopher." In *History and Truth*. Trans. Charles A. Kelbley. Evanston, IL: Northwestern University Press, 1965. Pp. 133–61.

—— *Freedom and Nature: The Voluntary and the Involuntary*. Trans. Erazim V. Kohák. Evanston, IL: Northwestern University Press, 1966.

—— *Freud and Philosophy: An Essay on Interpretation*. Trans. Denis Savage. New Haven, CT: Yale University Press, 1970.

—— "Phenomenology." Trans. Daniel J. Herman and Donald V. Morano. *Southwestern Journal of Philosophy* 5:3 (1975): 149–68.

—— "Structure and Hermeneutics." In *The Conflict of Interpretations: Essays in Hermeneutics*. Ed. Don Ihde. Trans. Kathleen McLaughlin. Evanston, IL: Northwestern University Press, 1974. Pp. 27–61.

Rieffel, Rémy. "Les Normaliens dans la société intellectuelle." In *École normale supérieure: Le Livre du bicentaire*. Ed. Jean-François Sirinelli. Paris: Presses universitaires de France, 1994. Pp. 215–39.

Ross, Kristin. *Fast Cars, Clean Bodies: Decolonization and the Reordering of French Culture*. Cambridge, MA: MIT Press, 1995.

—— *May '68 and its Afterlives*. Chicago: University of Chicago Press, 2002.

Roth, Michael S. *Knowing and History: Appropriations of Hegel in Twentieth-Century France*. Ithaca, NY: Cornell University Press, 1988.

Rouet, Gilles, and Stanislave Savontchik. *Dictionnaire pratique de l'enseignement en France*. Paris: Ellipses, 1996.

Rubenstein, Diane. *What's Left? The Ecole Normale Supérieure and the Right*. Madison: University of Wisconsin Press, 1990.

Sartre, Jean-Paul. *Being and Nothingness*. Trans. Hazel E. Barnes. New York: Philosophical Library, 1956.

—— "Black Orpheus." Trans. John MacCombie. Trans. revd. Robert Bernasconi. In *Race*. Ed. Robert Bernasconi. Oxford: Blackwell, 2001. Pp. 115–42.

—— *L'Être et le néant*. Paris: Éditions Gallimard, 1943.

—— *Existentialism and Human Emotions*. Trans. Bernard Frechtman. New York: Philosophical Library, 1957.

—— *L'Existentialisme est un humanisme*. Paris: Nagel, 1946.

—— "Merleau-Ponty." In *Situations*. Trans. Benita Eisler. New York: G. Braziller, 1965. Pp.156–226.

—— "Orphée noir." In *Situations III*. Paris: Éditions Gallimard, 1949. Pp. 229–86.

—— *Sartre by Himself*. Trans. Richard Seaver. New York: Urizen Books, 1978.

—— *Sartre par lui-même*. Paris: Éditions Gallimard, 1977.

—— *Search for a Method*. Trans. and intro. Hazel E. Barnes. New York: Knopf, 1963.

—— *The Transcendence of the Ego: An Existentialist Theory of Consciousness*. Trans. and intro. Forrest Williams and Robert Kirkpatrick. New York: Noonday Press, 1957.

Saussure, Ferdinand de. *Cours de linguistique générale*. Lausanne: Payot, 1916.

—— *Course in General Linguistics*. Ed. Charles Bally and Albert Sechehaye with the collaboration of Albert Riedlinger. Trans. Wade Baskin. New York: Philosophical Library, 1959.

Scheler, Max. *Nature et formes de la sympathie. Contribution à l'étude des lois de la vie émotionnelle*. Trans. M. Lefebvre. Paris: Payot, 1928.

Schrift, Alan D. "Judith Butler: Une nouvelle existentialiste?" *Philosophy Today* (Spring 2001): 12–23.

Schrift, Alan D. "Spinoza, Nietzsche, Deleuze: An Other Discourse of Desire." In *Philosophy and Desire*. Ed. Hugh A. Silverman. New York: Routledge, 2000. Pp. 173–85.

Senghor, Léopold Sédar, ed. *Anthologie de la nouvelle poésie nègre et malgache de langue française*. Paris: Presses universitaires de France, 1948.

Serres, Michel, and Bruno Latour. *Conversations on Science, Culture, and Time*. Trans. Roxanne Lapidus. Ann Arbor: University of Michigan Press, 1995.

—— *Éclaircissements: Cinq entretiens avec Bruno Latour*. Paris: Le Grand livre du mois, 1992.

Sirinelli, Jean-François, ed. *École Normale Supérieure: Le Livre du bicentenaire*. Paris: Presses universitaires de France, 1994.

Sirinelli, Jean-François. *Génération intellectuelle: Khâgneux et normaliens dans l'entre-deux-guerres*. Paris: Presses universitaires de France, 1994.

Smith, Robert J. *The Ecole Normale Supérieure and the Third Republic*. Albany: State University of New York Press, 1982.

Sontag, Susan. "Preface." In *Writing Degree Zero*. Trans. Annette Lavers and Colin Smith. New York: Hill and Wang, 1968.

Soulié, Charles. "Anatomie du goût philosophique." *Actes de la recherche en sciences sociales*, No. 109 (October 1995): 3–28.

Spiegelberg, Herbert. *The Phenomenological Movement: A Historical Introduction*, 3rd edn. The Hague: Martinus Nijhoff, 1960/1982.

Swartz, David. *Culture and Power: The Sociology of Pierre Bourdieu*. Chicago: University of Chicago Press, 1997.

"Témoignage de Jean Hyppolite." *Bulletin de l'Association des Amis d'Alain*, No. 27 (December 1968).

Thuillier, Pierre. *Socrate fonctionnaire: Essai sur (et contre) l'enseignement de la philosophie à l'université*. Paris: R. Laffont, 1970.

Trotignon, Pierre. *Les Philosophes français d'aujourd'hui*. Paris: Presses universitaires de France, 1967.

—— *Les Philosophes français de 1945 à 1965*. 5th edn. Paris: Presses universitaires de France, 1994.

Tuillier, André. *Histoire de l'Université de Paris et de la Sorbonne. Vol. 2: De Louis XIV à la crise de 1968*. Paris: Nouvelle Librarie de France, 1994.

Vieillard-Baron, Jean-Louis. *La Philosophie française*. Paris: Armand Colin, 2000.

Wahl, Jean. *Tableau de la philosophie française*. Paris: Fontaine, 1946.

—— *Vers le concret*. Paris: Vrin, 1932.

Wilke, Joachim, Jean-Marc Gabaude, and Michel Vadée, eds. *Les Chemins de la raison: XXe siècle: La France à la recherche de sa pensée*. Paris: L'Harmattan, 1997.

Index

Page numbers for biographical and bibliographical entries are noted in bold.

CPSIA information can be obtained at www.ICGtesting.com
Printed in the USA
BVOW11s0614190814

363338BV00005B/9/P